Factors and Actors

A Global Perspective on the Present, Past and Future of Factoring

P.I.E. Peter Lang

Bruxelles · Bern · Berlin · New York · Oxford · Wien

Patrick DE VILLEPIN (ed.)

Factors and Actors
A Global Perspective on the Present, Past and Future of Factoring

With the financial support of FCI.

This publication has been peer reviewed.

No part of this book may be reproduced in any form, by print, photocopy, microfilm or any other means, without prior written permission from the publisher. All rights reserved.

© P.I.E. PETER LANG s.a.
Éditions scientifiques internationales
Brussels, 2018
1 avenue Maurice, B-1050 Brussels, Belgique
www.peterlang.com; brussels@peterlang.com

Printed in Germany

ISBN 978-2-8076-0683-8
ePDF 978-2-8076-0684-5
ePub 978-2-8076-0685-2
Mobi 978-2-8076-0686-9
DOI 10.3726/b14098
D/2018/5678/39

CIP available at the Library of Congress and the British Library.

Bibliographic information published by "Die Deutsche Nationalbibliothek"

"Die Deutsche National Bibliothek" lists this publication in the "Deutsche Nationalbibliografie"; detailed bibliographic data is available on the Internet at <http://dnb.de>.

Table of Contents

Table of Abbreviations 11

Introduction: Factoring at a Crossroads 15
  Patrick de Villepin

Prologue: Strength of a Multilateral Organisation 27
  Patrick de Villepin

  1. FCI, a New Chain for Tomorrow 31
     Peter Mulroy

  2. IFG, Developing the Factoring Industry Worldwide 43
     Erik Timmermans

  3. EU Federation, Defending Factoring
     and Commercial Finance in Europe 51
     John Gielen & Erik Timmermans

  4. New Trends in Worldwide Factoring 57
     Daniela Bonzanini

PART I:
PAST – FACTORING ROOTS AND EVOLUTION
(3ʳᵈ CENTURY BC TO 20ᵀᴴ CENTURY AD)

Introduction 67
  Patrick de Villepin

A – Roots 71

  5. Factoring: Origins Rooted in Ancient Times 71
     *Damien Agut, Véronique Chankowski &
     Laetitia Graslin-Thomé*

  6. Getting Cash from Receivables in Ancient Rome 85
     Gérard Minaud

7. Factors in the Middle Ages, Credit and Society at the Dawn of a New Profession..99
   Armand Jamme & Enza Russo

B – Evolution 115

8. Blackwell Hall Factors in England, the Beginning of the Story 115
   Michael Bickers

9. Early Growth of Factoring in America from 1628 to 1960 123
   David B. Tatge & Jeremy B. Tatge

Part II:
Present – Emerging of Modern Factoring (1960s to Present)

Introduction 143
   Patrick de Villepin

A – Anglo-Saxon Base 147

10. Factoring in the UK, the Rise of Invoice Finance and ABL in Europe's Most Mature Market 147
    Jeff Longhurst

11. Factoring in the United States since 1960 161
    Stuart Brister & Brian Martin

B – Enlarging to Continental Europe 173

12. Secured and Highly Regulated, the French Factoring Model 173
    Patrick de Villepin

13. Prussian Thinking as the Basis of Made in Germany 185
    Joachim Secker

14. The Italian Way, a Creative Business under Legal and Regulatory Constraints 197
    Mario Petroni & Liliana Innocenti

PART III:
FUTURE – FACTORING TOMORROW (THE 21ST CENTURY)

Introduction 213
    Patrick de Villepin

A – Globalisation 217

    15. Factoring in Asia, a Promising Future 217
        Ilyas Khan

    16. Factoring in China, an Ambitious Tiger 229
        Jiang Xu

    17. Future Trends for Factoring and Commercial
        Finance in America 235
        Andrew Tananbaum

    18. Factoring in Latin America and the Caribbean,
        a Sleeping Region 245
        Alberto Wyderka

    19. Factoring in Russia, a Self-Sufficient Market 253
        Mikhail Treyvish

B – Emerging Countries 263

    20. Factoring in Emerging Countries 263
        Margrith Lütschg-Emmenegger

    21. Turkey, Bridging the Continents via Factoring 269
        Çağatay Baydar

    22. Factoring in Maghreb and the Middle East,
        Still a Limited Market 281
        Fatma Bouraoui, Alexandre de Fournoux &
        Haitham Al Refaie

    23. Factoring in Africa, an Emerging Continent 291
        Benedict Oramah

**Epilogue: Disruption and New Environments
in a Dangerous World** 305
    Patrick de Villepin

A – Disruption 309

24. Factoring vs. Invoice Discounting 309
Adrian Rigby

25. Reverse Factoring and Confirming 319
Josep Sellés

26. Asset Based Lending (ABL) 327
John Brehcist

27. Fintech, Between Innovation and Regulation 335
John Brehcist

B – New Environment 347

28. From National Laws to European Supervision, Factors in a Varied and Changing Regulatory Landscape.............347
Diego Tavecchia & Magdalena Wessel

29. Compliance, a Necessary Constraint 361
Peter Ball

30. Risk Awareness to Tackle Fraud 371
Patrick de Villepin & Peter Mulroy

Conclusion: Ten Proposals to Promote Factoring 381
Patrick de Villepin

Appendices 385

Factoring History at a Glance 385

FCI at a Glance 386
1. FCI Annual Meetings 386
2. FCI Chairpersons 387
3. FCI Secretary General 387

Glossary 389

Bibliography 403

Authors' Biographies 417

Photo Credits 431

Acknowledgments 433

Table of Abbreviations

A

ABFA	Asset Based Finance Association
ABL	Asset Based Lending
ABN	Algemene Bank Nederland
ACPR	Autorité de Contrôle Prudentiel et de Résolution (French Financial Supervisory Body)
ABS	Asset Backed Securities
AEF	Asociación Española de Factoring (Spanish Factoring Association)
AFC	Association of Factoring Companies
AFI	Association of Financial Institutions
AML	Anti-Money Laundering
API	Application Programming Interface
A/R	Accounts receivable
ASF	Association française des Sociétés Financières (French Factoring Association)

B

B2B	Business to Business
B2C	Business to Customer
BaFin	Bundesanstalt für Finanzdienstleitungsaufsicht (German Federal Financial Supervisory Authority)
BAFT	Bankers Association for Finance and Trade
BCBS	Basel Committee on Banking Supervision
BRIC	BRIC Countries: Brazil, Russia, India and China
BRSA	Banking Regulation and Supervision Agency

C

CAGR	Compound Annual Growth Rate
C2B	Consumer to Business
CBRC	China Banking Regulatory Commission
CBRT	Central Bank of the Republic of Turkey
CFA	Commercial Finance Association

CFEC	Commercial Factoring Expertise Committee
CGA	Compagnie Générale d'Affacturage
CIT	Commercial Investment Trust
COC	Code of Obligations and Contracts
COFIT	Certificate of Finance in International Trade
CRR	Capital Requirement Regulation

D

DFV	Deutscher Factoring-Verband e.V. (German Factoring Association)
DRA	Department of Revenue Administration
DRC	Data Risk Centre

E

EBA	European Banking Authority
EBRD	European Bank for Reconstruction and Development
EC	European Commission
ECAI	External Credit Assessment Institution
ECB	European Central Bank
ECJ	European Court of Justice
ECS	Specialist Credit Institution
ERP	Enterprise Resource Planning
ESAs	European Supervisory Authorities
EU	European Union
EUF	European Federation for Factoring and Commercial Finance

F

FAC	Factors Association of China
FATF	Financial Action Task Force
FCF	Fortis Commercial Finance
FCI	Factors Chain International
FDA	Factors and Discounters Association
FFH	Factofrance Heller
FNBB	First National Bank of Boston
FNCB	First National City Bank of New York (now Citibank)
FSB	Financial Stability Board

G
GAAP	Generally Accepted Accounting Principles
GCC	Gulf Cooperation Council
GDP	Gross Domestic Product
GDPR	General Data Protection Regulation
GİB	Gelir İdaresi Başkanlığı (the Turkish Revenue Commission)
GRIF	General Rules of International Factoring

I
IAS	International Accounting Standards
IATA	International Air Transport Association
ICC	International Chamber of Commerce
IF	International Factors
IFG	International Factors Group
IFRS	International Financial Reporting Standards
IRB	Internal Rating Based Approach

L
LA	Latin America
LA & C	Latin America and the Caribbean
LC	Letter of Credit
LCR	Liquidity Coverage Ratio
LGD	Loss Given Default

M
M&A	Mergers and Acquisitions
MBI	Management Buy In
MBO	Management Buy Out
MENA	Middle East and North Africa
ML	Money Laundering
MOOC	Massive Open Online Course

N
NBFI	Non-Bank Financial Institutions
NEXIM	Nigerian Export Import Bank
NFC	National Factoring Company
NSFR	Net Stable Funding Ratio
NYSE	New York Stock Exchange

O
O/A	Open Account
OBOR	One Belt, One Road
OFAC	Office of Foreign Assets Control
OHADA	Organisation pour l'Harmonisation en Afrique du Droit des Affaires

P
P2P	Peer to Peer
PD	Probability of Default
PPP	Purchasing Power Parity
PR	Public Relations
PZF	Polish Factoring Association

R
ROE	Return On Equity
RRC	Receivables Recording Center
RWA	Risk Weighted Asset

S
SA	Standardised Approach
SCF	Supply Chain Finance
SFF	Société Française de Factoring
SME	Small and Medium Sized Enterprise

T
TBML	Trade Based Money Laundering
TF	Terrorist Financing

U
UCC	Uniform Commercial Code
USGAAP	US Generally Accepted Accounting Principles

V
VAT	Value Added Tax
VSE	Very Small Enterprise

W
WTO	World Trade Organization

Introduction

Factoring at a Crossroads

Patrick DE VILLEPIN

Global Head of Factoring, BNP Paribas

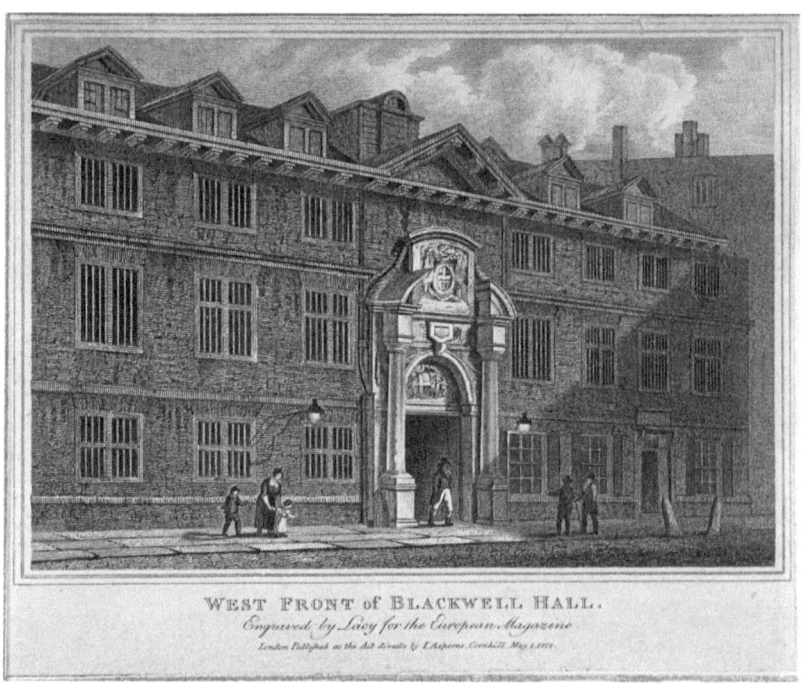

This book is meant to fill a significant gap: there are no works that are both historical and global in nature, across all continents, covering the profession of factoring, neither old nor recent. My book in French, *La Success Story du Factoring* (2015), acted as a first milestone and gave me the idea of an ambitious project. I suggested to the directors of Factors Chain

International* (FCI, the global association of the 400 factors active in 90 countries) that the 50th anniversary of FCI might be commemorated in an original manner:
- by bringing together excellent historians with the top experts in the field;
- by unifying these specialists around a common purpose – both academic and professional – reaching out over space and time;
- by producing a single vision of past legacies, current developments and future possibilities.

As a result, the *Factors and Actors* project was born. From the very outset, it has been collaborative, and the plan has been developed and fleshed out step by step. It has never been restricted to any particular region of the world, nor any particular context or product. It took shape, continued to develop and finally exploded into a professional production of reflection and progress.

The collective work offered to the reader now includes 30 contributions from 37 contributors who, each in their own way, cast a different eye over the genesis of the origin of a different type of financing, its last 50 years of evolution and future development.

The objective of this project is to increase awareness about a very special financing activity and its numerous virtues supporting the real economy, via both history and geography. 50 years after its inception, today factoring stands at a crossroads. Ten years after the start of an unprecedented financial crisis, the time is ripe to promote this sound form of secure and innovative financing.

Above and beyond the history of words and semantics, factoring deserves to be looked at from all of its product and trade components. In matters of finance, guarantees, or management of invoices, the client experience requires a genuine "factoring factory". From old-line factoring (or full notification factoring) to multiple types of short-term financing (with or without recourse, credit insurance and collection), from a domestic base to cross-border transactions, the technical sophistication and complexity of the methods involved highlight the

---

* Since the FCI Annual Meeting in October 2016, the legal name of Factors Chain International was formally changed to its initials, FCI. The new mission statement also approved at this same meeting mentions the words "factoring" but also supply chain finance (SCF) and invoice finance.

many developmental issues of a not-very-well-understood financing solution. Initiation into the arcane mysteries of factoring therefore requires a few definitions.

Origins of the Words "Facteur", "Factor" or "Factoring"

Derived from the substantive form "factum" of the Latin verb "facere", "factor" denotes a doer, and, by extension, "someone who does something on behalf of someone else".

Initially recorded in 1326, the French word "facteur" is a phonetical mutation from Latin. It denotes an intermediary who trades for the benefit of a third party. The term flourished during the time of Jacques Cœur, King Charles VII's Finance Minister (1430-1450): his 300 "facteurs", who had to travel to far-off lands to sell all sorts of merchandise, were correspondents of the various trading posts, or "factoreries".

During the Hundred Years' War (1337-1453), the word "factor" appeared in England, subsequently finding a home in France by means of personal contact. It was not just on the battlefield that words in English and French confronted one another. In Aquitaine, Burgundy and right across the kingdom, the Plantagenets set their distinguishing mark on the language. Such a long period of time encouraged a specific lexical transmigration. Porosity between languages spread at the same time as trade and its vocabulary. Even today, it makes its presence felt in business language, in particular, with the words budget and asset;

– budget: a small leather pouch used for carrying coins, the "bougette" (in French) became "bowzette" in England in 1432, then "boget" a century later and eventually "budget" from 1611 onwards. In return, the French borrowed the word "budget" no later than 1764;

– asset: from the Latin "satis" (sufficiently), colloquial Latin created "adsatis", which gave rise to the old French "asez" and the modern French "assez".[1] It is from this mutation that the English "assets" derives. Before referring to the shareholders of a company, since

---

[1] *Dictionnaire historique de la langue française*, *Dictionnaire le Robert*, Paris, 1998 (Ed. consulted, 2006), p. 233, col. 1, v° assez. Special thanks to Gérard Minaud for his help on this semantic analysis.

1531 the term "assets" denotes the ability of an individual to fulfil his obligations, in other words, to have sufficient resources ("assets") to pay his debts.

Less well-known, the word "factor" developed along similar lines. Emerging in the middle of the 15th century, it was mentioned in the English (1563)[2] and Scottish (1565)[3] dictionary in the form of "factour", which was obviously derived from the French "facteur". "Factor" belongs to that group of words which circulate, transmigrate and adapt themselves, in times of both war and peace, contingent upon the needs of the moment, be they military or economic. The English "factor" is an agent, a doer, a designation which can be traced back to its ancient roots in the Latin "factor": "facere" in Latin, and "to do" in English. In England, therefore, a factor is "a doer or transactor of business for another; one who buys and sells goods for others on commission".[4] In this respect, it is very close to the French "facteur".

The "factor" carries out a "factorage" as part of his "factorship". In Diderot & D'Alembert's *Encyclopédie*, "factorage" corresponds to the factor's or the commissioner's salary.[5] In English, a commercial factor is given an invoice, which is seen as "a particular account" or "a list of the particular items of goods shipped or sent to a factor, consignee, or purchaser, with their value or prices, and charges".[6]

During the 16th century, this "invoice" crossed over from France to England via the word "envoy", an old practice of sending a shipment letter to accompany the merchandise. Ironically, the French "facture" (invoice) maintained a semantic link with the Latin "factor", via the

---

[2] *The Oxford English Dictionary,* Clarendon Press, Oxford, 1933, Ed. consulted 1989 (second edition), Vol. V, p. 654, c. 1, v° factor. *An Etymological Dictionary of Modern English,* John Murray, London, 1921, col. 542, v° factor.
[3] *Supplement to the Etymological Dictionary of Scottish Language,* John Jamiesson, Edinburgh, 1825, Vol. I, p. 380, v° factor.
[4] *Chambers' Etymological Dictionary of English Language,* W&R Chambers, London – Edinburgh, 1874, p. 172, col. 1, v° factor.
[5] *Encyclopédie ou dictionnaire raisonné des sciences, des arts, et des métiers,* Briasson, David, Le Breton, Durand, Paris, 1756, Vol. 6, p. 620, v° factorage.
[6] *An Etymological Dictionary of English Language (John Oswald),* Philadelphia, 1840, p. 506, v° invoice. *An Etymological Dictionary of the English Language (Walter Skeat),* Oxford, The Clarendon Press, 1888, Ed. consulted, Dover Publications, Mineola, 2103, p. 308, col. 1, v° invoice. *The Oxford English Dictionary,* Clarendon Press, Oxford, 1933, Ed. consulted 1989 (second edition), Vol. VIII, p. 55, c. 1, v° invoice.

"facteur", a commercial agent.[7] Following a number of lexical journeys back and forth, English language gained the words "factor" and "invoice". Imported from England at the beginning of the 17th century, "factor" had established itself in the United States by the middle of the 19th century. True to Latin etymology, the Americans simply anglicised it in the second half of the 20th century. Adding the suffix *-ing* onto the end of the past participle of a verb, or, by implication, of a common noun, expresses an action that is currently being carried out. In this particular case, the words "action" and "doing" constitute a redundancy. The word "factoring" emits such power that it is difficult to imagine that, decades ago, it could have had negative connotations!

The Full Factoring Triangle

At the heart of inter-company relationships and the real economy, modern day factoring is based on a triangular relationship between three economic players, brought about in order to work together within the context of financing the operating cycle:
- the factor;
- the seller, the factor's client;
- the buyer, the seller's debtor.

The factor can, to a greater or lesser extent, be partly or totally involved in the three main services likely to be incorporated into the contract signed between the factor and its client:
- the purchasing and financing of invoices;
- guarantees against bad debts;
- collection of receivables and the handling of receipts.

---

[7] *Dictionnaire historique de la langue française*, *Dictionnaire le Robert*, Paris, 1998, Ed. consulted, 2006, Vol. 2, p. 1386, col. 1, v° facture.

Table 1: The factoring triangle

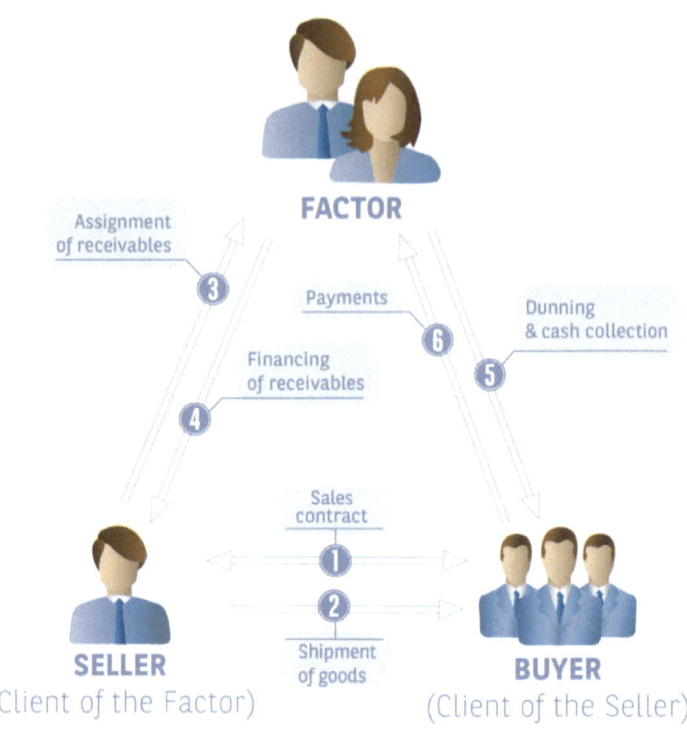

The factor's services are played out mainly in two stages:
- initially, the seller (or client) delivers its goods to a buyer (or debtor), which results in an invoice being issued (step 2 on the diagram above). This invoice is then transferred to the factor, who finances its client in the amount of the debt, less commission (steps 3 and 4) and possible deductions related to the risk of dilution vis-à-vis the client;
- then, as a second stage, if the client accepts that its contract will be notified (i.e. made known to its buyers) and managed, then the factoring company handles collection as well as receiving buyer payments (steps 5 and 6). Should this not be the case, steps 5 and 6 are not carried out by the factor but "delegated" to the client itself. Thus, one says that the contract is notified/managed or not notified/not managed. Not notified/not managed means "confidential" or silent, in other words known only to the seller and not to its buyers. In addition to the issue of management or notification, the factoring contract is with or without recourse to the seller:

- with recourse: in the event of non-payment by the buyer, the factor has the right to claim the financing back from the seller;
- without recourse: the financing made available to the seller is reimbursed to the factor by the buyer, if there is only one (mono-debtor contract), or by a portfolio of several buyers. Where there are several buyers the factor is able to spread its risk in the event of non-payment by a buyer.

The invoice is always at the centre of this three-way relationship: the factor finances the invoices that are raised by the seller, that are certain and payable by the buyer. Even if factoring is well and truly a purchasing of receivables, it is, however, not limited to simple financing but rather encompasses a whole gamut of services.

From Full Factoring to Other Short-term Financing Products

The most secure form of financing, full factoring today is, more often than not, provided to clients in the traditional markets (apparel, textiles, footwear, etc.), and outside of that, only of interest to average sized clients or ones that are difficult in terms of risk. There is no doubt that it is bound to develop from strength to strength once again, to make it possible for a large client base, retail or mid-cap, to take advantage of this cash accelerator, of this oxygen that is so necessary for the survival and for the advancement of companies.

Nonetheless, in the last twenty years, factoring has undergone exponential growth, concentrated on corporates and large corporates, with solutions that are, more often than not, off-balance sheet in IAS or USGAAP terms, tending to transfer the total and absolute ownership of the invoices to the factor.

Alternatives to classical full factoring, these programmes mark out a global map of evolving products according to geography. From one country to the next, the range of products can vary, especially with regard to regulations, local cultures, or the needs of the client: the balance top-up is a French innovation, whilst data factoring is Belgian or Dutch-inspired, confirming sounds Spanish (Santander), Asset Based Lending (ABL) was born in the

United States, invoice discounting on a full recourse basis is specific to the United Kingdom[8], and maturity factoring is an Italian innovation.

In English-speaking countries, ABL is gradually replacing old-line factoring which had not progressed at all in the United States in the last fifteen years (in terms of volume, however, old-line factoring is still more than 70% of American volume) and, at the same time, decreased to 10% of the working capital market in the United Kingdom. Offering wider and more flexible financing, ABL is not only based on an invoice but also other collateral (for example, stocks).

Table 2: Factoring and commercial finance products

---

[8] Mills, Ruddy & Davidson, *Salinger on Factoring*, 5th Ed. (Thomson Reuters (Professional) UK Limited, t/a Sweet & Maxwell, 2017) reports, at Sections 1-22 thru 1-26, pp. 8-9, that many small and several larger finance houses in London and some of the larger provincial cities, who the text does not identify, began invoice discounting on a full recourse basis in the early 1950s, the text stating that "the trader guaranteed payment by the customers by a specific number of days after invoice date."

Meanwhile, in Western Europe and the rest of the world, what is being offered is mainly concentrated on two types of products:
- receivables finance, with or without recourse to the client, notified or not, managed or not, i.e. with or without collection of payment of the client's invoices;
- payables finance, i.e. confirming (Spain, Portugal) or reverse factoring (Northern Europe, Germany, France, Italy), enabling numerous suppliers to benefit from financing at advantageous rates.

In addition to domestic factoring, which still represented almost 78% of the world market in 2016 (85% in 2010), the growth of international factoring (22% in 2016) remains quite modest. Import or export factoring may be carried out through one of two mechanisms. The factor can act directly; doing so will require sufficient knowledge of the foreign country's rules and protocols, as well as the need to have a local collection capability. Alternatively, it can use the resources of a local partner via the FCI two-factor system. This latter approach is based on an Inter-Factor Agreement (IFA) between an import factor and an export factor, each sharing a role in financing the supplier, guaranteeing against the debtor default or bankruptcy, and the management (collection and handling of receipts), as per the following model:

Table 3: Import and export factoring flows

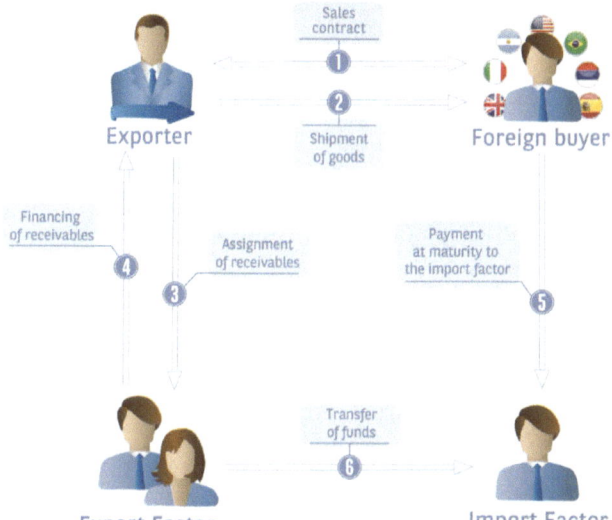

Whether importing or exporting, the factor acts as the client's active partner supporting its international trading activities globally. The differences between national jurisdictions are, nevertheless, a major obstacle to overseas development. Once a client has researched the local environment and established that a market exists for his products or services, there is the challenge of:

- trading with buyers in a different language, and
- overcoming cultural differences that can increase misunderstandings in communication.

To be able to develop international business, one needs time, maturity and the willingness to face a steep learning curve.

Secured Credit, a European Innovation

Factoring has its roots in the English-speaking world. However, within the space of half a century, it has established itself in every continent, building on a solid European foothold.

Born in Great Britain in the 15th century and reshaped in America in the 20th century, today's model has to prove its legitimacy and facilitate "secured credit" as the solution to the financial crisis and the answer to ever-increasing legal requirements.

Mature in terms of product range, the European market is number one in the world. At the end of 2016, it represented nearly 68% of the total factoring turnover, well ahead of Asia (20%), America (9%), Oceania and Africa (3%).

On the eve of the financial crisis in 2007, European business still represented 72% of the global market. Following the 2008 crisis (67%), the decline of market share accelerated (61% in 2014), before stabilising at its current level. The dominance of commercial bank factors (92%), as compared to independents (8%), and that of factoring with recourse (60%) as compared to non-recourse (40%), has no doubt contributed to this resilience.

Since World War Two, the United Kingdom has been the leader in factoring on the European market (20.5% in 2016), well ahead of other countries: France (17%), Germany (14%), Italy (13%), Spain (8%), The Netherlands (5%) and Belgium (4%). Poland, Turkey and Russia trail considerably behind.

In Europe, in 2016, the potential for recovery in factoring remains significant: at 10.1%, the average ratio of factored turnover to Gross Domestic Product (GDP) leaves a considerable margin for improvement. Germany (6.9%) lies well behind Belgium (14.9%), Great Britain (13.8%), Portugal (13.2%), Italy (12.5%), France (12.1%) and even Spain (11.7%).

The number of factored clients in Europe in 2017 was estimated at 180,000 (compared to 160,000 in 2012). With its 43,000 clients, France's contribution appears to be the most important, far ahead Germany, Italy, and even the UK. The 2015 European Banking Authority (EBA) report confirms the under-representation of Very Small Enterprises (VSEs) and professionals in European factoring, compared to larger companies. An increase in the number of clients therefore constitutes a major developmental challenge in order to ensure a good balance between the small and large segments of the clientele.

Having gone through the emerging countries' crisis and the ups and downs of the Chinese economy, Europe's relative weight has continued to increase since the beginning of the millennium. Whilst the USA has remained frozen around the EUR 100 billion turnover mark ever since, China, which was the world number three in 2010, slightly behind France, made a spectacular leap ahead the following year. Propelled to the top of the world between 2011 and 2014 (from 13.6% to 17.0% market share respectively), it lost its crown to Great Britain in 2015 (a drop to 14.9% and even further in 2016 to 12.7% market share). The economic slow-down, numerous frauds and insufficient regulatory control have placed a strong brake on its development.

Today, China remains a leading player in Asia, far ahead of the others, followed by Japan, whose share was cut in half between 2010 and 2016, Taiwan, Hong Kong and Singapore. The Chinese crisis spread across the whole of the Asian continent (less turnover in 2016 than its level in 2011), put a brake on the development of the world factoring market, which declined during the 2014-2016 period, before recovering in 2017.

Even if, when compared to other continents, the European Union (EU) appears to be the most integrated market in the field of factoring, one has to acknowledge that a European style of factoring does not exist. Status, legislations, and even regulations differ greatly from one country to another. Players can be banks, specialised credit institutions, financial institutions, or commercial companies. It will be necessary to harmonise the rules and practices to enable European factoring companies to speak with one, comprehensible voice on the international stage.

Globally, the increased growth in Europe that has become apparent since 2017 should make it possible for factoring to bounce back, both in Europe itself and in the rest of the world, making it possible to contemplate its centenary with confidence. This book has therefore been structured around six steps along a single progression:

- a prologue focusing on European and international cooperation between factors;
- a first retrospective section covering the roots of secured financing;
- a second up-to-date section on the emergence of modern factoring;
- a third forward-looking section on the outlook for the profession;
- an epilogue dedicated to disruptive technologies and the new regulatory environment (regulation, compliance and risk management) in a world rife with threats and dangers;
- and a conclusion with ten proposals to promote factoring.

Over the centuries and throughout the decades of its modern renaissance, factoring has been able to prove its legitimacy and act as the lifeblood of the real economy. Discreetly and without overstepping the mark, it has become the driving force behind sound and responsible financing. FACTORS are indeed the ACTORS of change, supporting the multiple facets and opportunities presented by this mode of secured financing.

Prologue

Strength of a Multilateral Organisation

Patrick DE VILLEPIN

Global Head of Factoring, BNP Paribas

The modern form of factoring began to take shape in the early 1960s, although the profession had already existed in America for centuries. But it had always been a marginal activity restricted to a specific sector, the textile industry, limiting it to a somewhat archaic image of only serving troubled companies. In 1962, the total turnover achieved in the United States by the Industry was a modest three billion dollars. US banking finance was predicated on techniques of the "plain vanilla" variety or ABL, based on different types of collateral.

Via a boomerang effect, these short-term financing methods innervated the British model. In the rest of Europe, mainly Italy and France, old-line (or full service) factoring took root, evolved and developed under a multitude of local influences. Even before penetrating domestic markets, the establishment of global factoring associations imposed the technique in cross-border European and international trade.

Contrary to the path pursued in the 16th century, from the late 1950s US factors sought more appropriate solutions for exporting their know-how to the old continent, with Britain serving as a bridgehead. Soon, the new "common market" offered a fitting environment and interesting perspective. Just a few years apart, two global factoring chains were launched:

- 1963: International Factors Group (IFG) (see chapter 2). To develop their business on the other side of the Atlantic, US factors refined their strategy and established alliances. At the initiative of the First National Bank of Boston (FNBB), the company International Factors Ltd was founded in Britain (1961) and, two years later, the holding company International Factors AG was established in Switzerland (1963). Within a few months, it took stakes in existing companies, exploiting an extensive network of correspondents. In 1966, IFG had subsidiaries in 16 countries, mainly in Europe, but also in the USA, Canada, Australia, South Africa and Israel. Earlier, in November 1960, Meinhard & Co., a CIT subsidiary, aided by UK backers in the City of London known as the Alexandria Finance Company, formed a short-lived factoring affiliate;[1]

---

[1] See Tatge, Flaxman, Tatge & Franklin, *American Factoring Law* (Bloomberg/BNA 2009) ("AFL"), at p. 289-290 of the 2017 Cum. Supplement, discussing (1) the formation by Meinhard & Co., a factoring subsidiary of CIT, of a UK factoring affiliate in November, 1960, together with the Alexandria Finance Co. in London, and (2) two months later, early in 1961, the formation of International Factors Ltd in the UK, by, among others, the First National Bank of Boston. Melvin Westlake's book, *Factoring* (Pittman Publishing, 1975), referenced in AFL as one of two sources on the history of these companies, the first two UK factors old-line (full service) factors, describes the new Meinhard & Co. -Alexandria Finance Company UK factoring entity as having been "short-lived." In contrast, International Factors Ltd, initially formed as Towergate Securities, was, essentially, the first UK old-line (full service) factor of any significance. Westlake reports, at p. 82, that First Bank of Boston took a 25% initial equity stake in International Factors Ltd, with a 50% equity stake taken by Tozer, Kemsley & Millbourn, a confirming house, with the remaining 25% equity in International Factors Ltd held by M. Samuel & Co., a London merchant bank. Westlake says that despite some heavy early losses, before a 70% ownership stake in International Factors Ltd was later taken in 1968 by Lloyd's and Scottish Finance

- 1968: Factors Chain International (FCI) (see chapter 1). Under the influence of operators based in Northern Europe and United States, FCI was created five years after IFG. Starting in 1964, four Scandinavian Factors, one from the UK and one from the US together developed a two-factor system for import and export, under the name Factors Chain. In November 1968, they held a conference in Stockholm, to which most of their peers from the period were invited. From the very outset, FCI exploited a brand-new logo.

IFG and FCI were to play a major role in promoting the industry internationally, with their head offices in Brussels and Amsterdam respectively, proof of the firm European foundations of the profession and its sustainable influence on the other continents. This powerful base established the rise and success of domestic factoring, notably in the UK and in France.

A new era commenced following the arrival of Jeroen Kohnstamm, a brilliant Dutchman and powerful secretary general of FCI for over forty years (1972-2013), and the driving force behind the incredible growth of factoring in Asia. After setbacks in 2000 and 2009, the third attempt was to prove successful: the process of a merger between FCI and IFG took place in an inexorable manner. In June 2015, in Singapore, the annual meeting of FCI voted overwhelmingly (82%) in favour of the merger. The general meeting of IFG ratified the process in Vienna in November 2015. Since the 1st of January 2016, the Industry has spoken with a single voice on the international economic stage.

Successive chairmen and the two secretary generals must be congratulated on their commitment in support of the alliance. Following Jeroen, both Peter Mulroy, former chairman of FCI (2009-2010) and new secretary general (2013), and Erik Timmermans, secretary general of IFG since 2005, leave their mark on the history of factoring. They rapidly set to work in order to consolidate their hitherto separate objectives:

- The former strives to provide a vision of the new chain by adopting a strategic plan, based on the idea of ultimately doubling the number of members (from 250 in 2013 to 500) and of advocating, for those who so wish, an extension of the two-factor system to a dedicated reverse factoring platform;

---

group (owned by Lloyd's Bank and the Royal Bank of Scotland), International Factors Ltd was still the UK's largest commercial factor more than a dozen years later.

- The latter opens up the organisation to new categories of partners and affiliated members (notably IT providers), while bringing into the fold the European lobbying body, EU Federation, founded in 2009 (see chapter 3), to support and defend the profession in the face of the growing demands of regulators in terms of liquidity, solvency, compliance and anti-fraud measures.

Over the years, these initiatives reinforced the legitimacy and credibility of the organisation, enabling it to establish its position as the sole interlocutor for various international bodies, including the World Trade Organization (WTO) and the International Chamber of Commerce (ICC). To accommodate the new trends in factoring (see chapter 4) over the medium term, numerous challenges must be faced:

- The increasing role played by international factoring in trade finance, with Letters of Credit (LC) gradually being replaced by open account (O/A);
- The extension of the client base to all company segments, from Very Small Entreprises (VSEs) and SMEs to large corporates;
- The ever-increasing demands of regulatory constraints in order to attenuate and pool risks;
- Disruptive technologies in terms of product innovation and the rise of the fintechs;
- Finally, the increasingly decisive contribution of education and the promotion of good practices by all operators.

Faced with such developments and issues, the factoring community is now able to draw strength from a global, strong, united and determined organisation, promoting a method of secured financing as a powerful weapon to counter crises and speculative bubbles in the service of economic growth.

1. FCI, a New Chain for Tomorrow

Peter MULROY

Secretary General, FCI

FCI has evolved into one of the most unique associations in the field of O/A trade finance as it possesses a combination of special traits. FCI acts as a trade association supporting the growth of receivables finance around the world, offers a legal foundation and a communication platform to conduct cross-border transactions, provides advice, learning, and guidance through a robust education platform, and is led by an engaged and focused Secretariat. As a comparison, FCI is a combination of a rules making body like the ICC banking commission, offers a global O/A trade finance messaging system like SWIFT, is a best in class non-profit trade association like the Bankers Association for Finance and Trade (BAFT), and elicits a spirit of volunteerism like the Peace Corps. But this did not occur by chance. FCI has been blessed with a litany of great leaders, like our founding fathers, Claes-Olof Livijn, who in 1964 had the vision, together with Mr Ruve Bennum from Shield Factors, UK, and Öivind Gunnerud, AS Factoring, Norway, to band together to create Factors Chain, when receivables finance was just getting started in Europe. This chapter looks at the reasons why FCI has developed into a success story, but, equally important, focuses on the areas of opportunity for growth that remain untapped in order to maximise its potential and move the association into the next stage of its evolution.

I. The Beginning

The 1960s were a tumultuous period, but not for what you might think. The end of World War Two, the birth of the Marshall Plan, the rise of multi-nationals, and the beginning of a global trading society were all birthed during this era. It also witnessed the formation of numerous nation states, coming out of the old colonial past. But this decade is also known for the rise in social disintegration, the assassination of global leaders, and the evolutions of the civil rights movement. But during this period, the building blocks were laid for the creation of a global Factoring Industry.

When FCI started, domestic factoring was only available in North America and a few European countries. The concept of cross-border factoring was still new and restricted by its lack of geographic reach.

Recognising the potential for international factoring, the founding FCI members realised an umbrella organisation was needed, firstly to introduce factoring in countries where it was not yet available, and secondly to develop a framework for international factoring that would allow factoring companies in the country of the exporter and the importer to work closely together.

In 1964 world merchandise exports totalled only slightly less than USD 500 billion, of which only a small portion was conducted on open account terms. In 2016 it reached nearly USD 20 trillion. And of this amount, approximately 80% of global trade is contracted on O/A terms. In fact, a Bain report estimates that over 90% of world trade will be conducted on O/A terms by 2020.[1] How are such significant figures financed? This brings me to the start of the story of FCI and the factoring and receivables finance industry. As more and more suppliers entered the global trading community, they encountered the demand by buyers to ship to them on an O/A basis. This creates opportunities but also challenges. You can go back to this period in the 1960s to see this on a smaller micro level. Factoring had been a relatively accepted form of finance for domestic business in the US and this know-how was transferred to Europe in the 1950s. There were factoring companies first formed in Scandinavia and the UK, that were dealing with SMEs who required financing for their exports to one another such as textiles from England to Sweden and seafood from Norway to the US. These factoring companies needed a means to finance export invoices on O/A terms but also denominated in foreign currency. Hence, the basis of the concept of FCI was formed.

FCI's origins were initially developed in 1964 when Shield Factors Limited (chaired by Mr Ruve Bennum, London) in the United Kingdom (today HSBC) and Svenska Finans AB Sweden formed an alliance called the "Shield Agreement". The organisation got its initial start in 1964, thanks to the vision of Mr Claes-Olof Livijn, president of Svenska Factoring AB, a wholly owned subsidiary of Svenska Handlesbanken out of Stockholm. In 1965, four other primary companies joined the

---

[1] Bain Capital Group (BCG) Global Payments Study 2012.

chain, including William Iselin & Co. Inc., from USA (represented by Mr Henry Hubshman, New York today CIT Commercial Services); A.S. Factoring Finans from Norway (represented by Mr Öivind Gunnerud, Oslo); Factoring Rahoitus Oy from Finland (represented by Mr Aimo Salokoski, Helsinki); and Forenede Factors (represented by Mr Arne Buch-Nielsen, Copenhagen, today BNP Paribas Factor, Denmark) and they coined the name of this group "Factors Chain".

However, it was not until February 1968 when Factors Chain hosted a factoring conference in Baden-Baden, West Germany, that FCI was born. Only six companies were members of the network then, but many would follow. Their first task was to create a code of reciprocal factoring customs to do business with each other.

The first council meeting of FCI was held later that year in Stockholm (Sweden) on the 22nd November 1968. They chose to name the business Factors Chain International (FCI) and agreed in principal to form the legal entity in the Netherlands as a non-profit association, mainly due to the favourable tax benefits offered to non-profits but also thanks in part to an offer by FCI's first Dutch member, Algemene Bank Nederland (today ABN AMRO), to find a home. First elected chairman was Ruve Bennum (Shield Factors Ltd) and Claes-Olof Livijn vice-chairman. In the first executive committee we also find:

- Aimo Salokoski, Factoring Rahoitus Oy, Finland;
- Bent Frantzen, Forenede Factors A/S, Denmark;
- Henri Picq, Sofinter, France;
- Hans Göldenboog, Diskont und Kredit AG, West Germany;
- Charles Yates, William Iselin & Co., Inc., USA;
- Öivind Gunnerud, AS Factoring, Norway.

By the end of the year, FCI would be represented by fifteen member companies based in twelve countries, located in either the US, UK or eight different countries in continental Western Europe.

Three out of the six founders would become chairmen of FCI:

1969-1970: Ruve Bennun;

1971-1972: Claes-Olof Livijn;

1973: Öivind Gunnerud.

The first temporary office of the FCI Secretariat was housed inside one of the founding members, Factoring-Rahoitus Oy in Finland.

When FCI was founded, it was decided that its aims would be to 1) promote the growth of factoring between trading nations of the world 2) to develop the uniform factoring techniques and best practices for these international cross-border transactions and 3) to help in solving the legal and technical problems in international factoring and address other problems pertaining to factoring in general.

In those early days, there was no permanent Secretariat. In fact, the FCI Secretariat was initially planned to be headquartered in Switzerland. FCI ended up in Amsterdam because during the 1968 annual meeting in Stockholm an attending executive from Factormaatschaapij Nederland NV offered to let his department do some research on legislation, taxation, office rental price, etc. The other board members gladly accepted the offer. So, it was this offer that resulted in the Secretariat finding Amsterdam as its home. FCI opened its first office in a building in the Amsterdam city center in April 1969, and immediately hired its first administrator, Mrs Sandra Gerlach, who would go on to work in the Secretariat for nearly 40 years, who in 2006 would be replaced by Jacqueline Wolde Yohannes, who would earn the title of Director of Administration. Two years later, in 1971, FCI would post an ad in *the Economist* for a full-time secretary general position.

Ironically, the Canadian member of FCI at the time, Aetna Financial Services (a precursor to our member, Accord Factors today) was up for sale and Bank of Montreal had originally shown an interest in the service. There was a young Dutch executive by the name of Mr Jeroen Kohnstamm who was working for them in Montreal during his first year there, who responded to the ad. Knowing his employer was considering this acquisition of Aetna, he used the opportunity to study the due diligence paperwork from Bank of Montreal to prepare for the interview, learning as much as he could about factoring and FCI. The initial interview was conducted by Merrold Suhl, the then president of Aetna Factors Corporation Ltd and Ken Hitzig from Aetna (who would later go on to found Accord Financial, another long-term member of the chain).

Although Claes-Olof was somewhat sceptical, having never met Jeroen, he was hired nonetheless in 1972. There were only 26 members by the time Jeroen moved to Amsterdam to take up the position. The Secretariat was now complete with a functioning Administrator in Sandra and Secretary General in Jeroen, based in Amsterdam, a fitting city for a global trading network. FCI's belief in the future is symbolised by the Secretariat's decision to acquire a 400-year-old canal house, built along the Keizersgracht in Amsterdam, which would become its permanent home.

The 25 year period that followed added considerable strength to the Industry. Like any chain, it continues to add new links, and by the start of the new millennium, FCI sprouted into an organisation representing nearly 150 members and volume of EUR 750 billion globally. The growth continued in the developed markets but by the late 1990s we started to see some of the emerging markets begin to generate domestic and cross-border business, including in China, India, and Indonesia. However, the outbreak of the Asian financial crisis 1996-1997 severely impacted this initial growth, resulting in numerous factoring companies going out of business, especially in Indonesia. Still today, the effects of the crisis as it relates to the product can still be felt.

The start of the new millennium was also a significant turning point for FCI. The period of the late 1990s will be known as the true beginning of global O/A trade and the rise of the emerging markets, led by a dominant China. Three major changes brought this about: 1) a substantial shift of trade terms from traditional letters of credit to O/A, especially from suppliers in the developing world, pushed by the major retailers/importers in the developed world 2) the impact of the global recession and the shift from unsecured to secured asset backed lending/factoring; and 3) the rise of China as a factoring market.

During this time, FCI and the Industry grew, from little more than 150 members to over 400 members by the end of 2016. The true growth spurt was accelerated after the Millennium. In 2000, the Industry was generating approximately EUR 750 billion. By the end of 2016, FCI generated over EUR 2.35 trillion in volume, a nearly 8% Compound Annual Growth Rate (CAGR) during this 16-year period. This was due to three major reasons: 1) the rapid expansion of business in Asia, led by China; 2) the resurgence in cross-border factoring, both direct and indirect via correspondent factoring; and 3) the rapid expansion of factoring in Europe.

1. Regarding China, by the end of the century, FCI only had two members in China, with very little business. However, by 2014, China would surpass the UK to become the largest factoring market in the world. Today, FCI has nearly 50 members in China and accounts for 12.7% of the global factoring market. Asia, therefore, accounts for 23.2% of the world.
2. Cross-border factoring has led the charge. From 2000-2016, cross-border factoring has been growing at a 15% CAGR. This

has been led by China, which again accounts for more than one third of the total export factoring from the region. But Hong Kong, Taiwan, Singapore, Japan and others have contributed to this growth.
3. And lastly, Europe. Factoring in the EU countries has grown from less than EUR 300 billion in 2000 to over EUR 1.5 trillion today. Europe accounts for over 68% of the global factoring market. This was due to the massive acceptance of factoring as a safe and secure means of financing SMEs. But it has expanded into medium to large sized corporates, due to its attractive off-balance sheet benefit but also the lower capital allocation required under factoring transactions, again stemming from their lower risk profile.

Educating a Chain for Tomorrow

Education has also played a key role in the development of factoring during the last 50 years. In 1989, FCI developed its first education offering, the Correspondence Course on Factoring, which was made available to all members at the time. In 2006, the FCI executive committee approved the creation of an Education Director position, and chose Mrs. Aysen Cetintas, a factoring executive from Istanbul, Turkey to lead this effort. During the next ten years, FCI would go on to educate nearly 10,000 students in over 90 countries around the world. The Correspondence Course was converted into three successive courses including Foundation, Intermediate and Advanced. In fact, the Foundation Course would later be translated into four different foreign languages and offered to both existing and prospective members of FCI. The three principal courses would lead to the development of a "career path" for students of factoring around the world and prepare the Industry for tomorrow's factoring leaders.

General Rules of International Factoring (GRIF)

FCI has also experienced tremendous success as a result of the strong rules they have deployed. The GRIF has been the cornerstone of rules for all players involved in international factoring since its inception in 2001. Not only is most of the O/A cross-border factoring business conducted within the framework, but FCI also provides a legal foundation for it. The General Rules of International Factoring (GRIF) form the legal basis under which nearly all international factoring transactions are conducted, and this legal framework has been accepted by nearly every factoring company engaged in cross-border business around the world. The very first legal bilateral contract that was formed was called the Shield agreement, which was the initial forerunner to the GRIF, developed by Shield Factors in the UK (today HSBC). When FCI was formed in 1968, their first task was to create the Reciprocal Factoring Customs (RFC 68) to replace the Shield Agreement. In the late 1970s, FCI developed the Code of International Factoring Customs, which went through many iterations and lasted until it was replaced by the GRIF in July 2002.

Edifactoring Communication Platform

FCI members also use a proprietary communication system called edifactoring.com. Like the SWIFT messaging system, edifactoring.com provides a sound and secure means by which members can a) issue factor guarantees b) remit invoice data c) issue dispute notices and d) provide payment advice. The linchpin of FCI today is its communication system, and as Jeroen once quipped, "it is the glue that binds the members to work together". The first factoring system was developed in 1984 and in July 1985 the FACT system was created, at which time over USD 1 billion in volume was handled, of which only 23 members of FCI were using FACT. It was after the annual meeting in 1990 that FCI started to carry out the complex task of developing the edifactoring standards. A special workgroup was formed, led by Paolo Bolzoni, FCI Director of Planning and Development, with support from the communication committee. Edifactoring as we know it now was a project led by Dieter Engler and Harry Biletta, chairman of the FCI Communication Committee, who would later replace Paolo Bolzoni. Edifactoring.com was officially released to members on the 20th of September 2001, going live on the 8th of April 2002. Today edifactoring.com serves nearly 400 members worldwide, allowing them to facilitate nearly 100% of the world's two factor business in a safe and secure environment.

Rules of Arbitration

Disputes do occur, and when business is being conducted on a cross-border basis, especially when it involved transfer of ownership issues and global risk, resolving differences via arbitration is the best route to take. FCI established its own rules of arbitration in 1976, stemming from an arbitration case that was brought to the ICC in The Hague, since FCI at the time did not have a mechanism in place for resolving disputes. What was learned from this case was the challenge in finding arbitrators within the ICC, who generally lack the understanding and awareness of the unique aspects of factoring. Concepts such as transfer of ownership of intangible assets, trade credit, dilution risk, and adherence to the rules of the GRIF are obviously quite foreign to most. Hence, it was decided to create the FCI rules of arbitration and use actual practitioners and legal experts in the factoring space as potential arbitrators. Over the past 50 years, only six cases have gone before the FCI Arbitration process, and in every award that was rendered, the losing party fulfilled its obligation. FCI arbitration is binding and final. So, you can say that the GRIF works quite effectively, considering only approximately one case per decade has been brought before the FCI Arbitration Tribunal.

Global Statistics on Factoring, Annual Review and FCI Newsletter

FCI began publishing global statistics on the Factoring Industry in 1980 and began publishing an annual review that same year. The annual review has given its readers a preview into the previous year's performance as well as looking ahead to what members can anticipate. The data has been used by banks, factoring companies, governments, regulators, policy makers, and universities for nearly 40 years. Quality is the word that is used when people speak about the robust data that FCI has provided the Industry. Today, FCI has added much more analytics in its review, and attempts to make sense of the trends in the business. The very first FCI quarterly newsletter was released back in November 1989. Since then, the publication has grown, with nearly 10,000 recipients around the world each year. The newsletter started out as a blog about Jeroen's global travels, as readers followed the detailed diary of his business developments around the world, meeting and encouraging existing members, supporting and guiding new ones. The newsletter had had many names, from *FCI Matters, Horizons*, to today's *In-Sight*. The aim of the FCI newsletter is to create a branded, industry led trade publication covering everything of interest in the receivables finance space.

II. The Following

The Financial Crisis and What We Learned

During the financial crisis in 2008-2009, the factoring and receivables finance industry was tested like never before. It placed the stability of the financial system at risk, in part due to the significant leverage that was never adequately revealed. However, the factoring community had no direct correlation to the weak credit practices experienced during this period, such as the financing of sub-prime paper or other high-risk derivatives and, most importantly, did not contribute to the stress of the banking system. On the contrary, factoring helped alleviate the effects of the credit crunch when many banks withdrew from the market. Factors themselves are neither traditional deposit-taking institutions, nor are they in the business of taking on excessive leverage. In fact, factors only finance up to the value of the eligible receivable balance that has been assigned by their clients. What was learned during this heightened test is that factoring took over when commercial banks withdrew from the market, especially relating to the financing of SMEs. With few exceptions, many factors experienced a significant increase in the number of new clients during this period, as SMEs quickly learned the necessity of diversifying their source of funds instead of relying solely on traditional bank lending.

When assessing the global systemic risk of factoring companies, it has to be taken into account that factoring and commercial finance has proven to be a real and frequently used alternative to the classic bank loan and has helped to alleviate much of the burden caused by the recent credit crunch, especially for SMEs.

Factoring companies use strong credit metrics. They become secure not only from the assignment of the receivable but also from the intricate management system supporting the process: a robust technology platform that ledgers the receivable, supports the credit underwriting on both the seller and their buyer(s), and has the capacity to alert the factor in such areas as a rise in dilution or concentration risk, keeping credit losses to a minimum. Besides the fact that the receivables factored are usually under 180 day terms, client/debtor credit lines are normally considered uncommitted, meaning that the factor can pull the lines at any time, which allows the factor to exit a facility quickly. Also, the flow of funds to a factor does not come from the seller but rather from the clients' buyers, as they make payment directly to an account controlled by the factor, increasing the likelihood of repayment. All of these important aspects of factoring have been recognised by policy makers and regulators around the world, resulting in the knowledge that factoring is considered a safe and secure means of financing working capital. As such, most factors are able to capitalise on the lower regulatory capital requirements that the service affords. The financial crisis resulted in the formation of Basel III, which introduced stricter rules regarding capital requirements that made banks look for and turn to more "capital-efficient" businesses (i.e. low risk/low capital requirements). As factors can typically finance up to 6-8 times their capital, and due to the low risk nature of the service and the beneficial capital treatment factoring affords, many banks have turned to factoring and receivables finance as the primary driver of financing working capital.

All of this has led to a nearly doubling in the size of the factoring and receivables finance industry on a global scale, from EUR 1.28 trillion at the start of the financial crisis in 2008 to EUR 2.35 trillion in 2016. This growth story led to the necessity of bringing the two industry leaders, FCI and IFG, together. Over many years, both organisations made numerous attempts to join forces. This dream was finally realised in 2015 when both councils approved a union, bringing together the two associations and creating one voice under the banner of FCI to form the largest, non-profit association dedicated to the global O/A receivables finance industry.

2018 and Beyond

FCI will officially turn 50 years old in 2018. It will certainly be a cause for celebration of a financial service and an association that has ably led the Industry and has brought factoring to all corners of the world. This has resulted in an entirely new push by FCI to support the business and capitalise on a positive outcome from the financial crisis. The strong rebound in world trade after the global recession marked a significant milestone for trade in general and trade finance in particular. Throughout the past decade, there has been a gradual shift in the development of new, non-traditional forms of trade finance that have focused on capturing new trade flows in those transactions conducted on O/A. The evolution and importance in such services like credit insurance, payables finance, reverse factoring and other Supply Chain Finance (SCF) programs, including traditional factoring, all products with a focus on solving the dilemma posed by buyers globally who demand trade be conducted on O/A terms, have resulted in a dynamic shift in the financial services sector. But one product has been around for centuries, and it has captured the attention of banks and finance companies globally. In fact, the rise in international factoring has been the fastest growth product in the trade finance arena over the past two decades.

Opportunities for the Industry on the horizon include the rise in technological disruptions via the formation of fintechs, which have the ability to seamlessly cut through the red tape and provide funding in an electronic manner directly to SMEs. Blockchain and distributed ledger technology has the opportunity to help speed up the flow of capital and bank transfers, but also to connect all parties and to provide collection services, debtor credit underwriting and financing all in a highly secure way, using e-invoices and other e-documents to increase the efficiency of transferring the much-needed capital quicker to the SME. FCI will also make investments into building a new global payables finance/reverse factoring platform called FCIreverse. This will not only allow members to access an operating platform to on-board both anchor buyers and their domestic and international suppliers, but it would also allow the use of export factors around the world to support this effort, by educating the supplier on the benefits of reverse factoring, signing a local factoring contract with the supplier, proving Know Your Customer (KYC)/Anti-Money Laundering (AML) guidance, and potentially even funding the assigned receivables, if requested, by the anchor buyer's bank. And lastly, the trend of e-invoicing continues to gain steam. Today, approximately 10% of all invoicing is done on an electronic basis. However, with the evolution in e-commerce increasing, and the deployment of government initiatives requiring most businesses to operate in an e-commerce environment, especially for government procurement purposes, by issuing electronic invoices, we anticipate this will be a significant game changer for the Industry. And although more regulations will impact the factoring business, FCI will need to ensure that the interests of our stakeholders are protected, by lobbying to convince regulators and legislatures that factoring should be given the recognition it deserves as an asset class, with a proven and very low historical default rate, with the objective of ultimately lowering the capital required by factoring companies to set aside against their exposures. FCI has been the undisputed leader in providing factoring data for decades and has a strong reputation for the quality of its data. Obtaining loss data from factoring companies around the world will be quite challenging. However, we believe it is in the economic interest of our members to do so. Hence, and with the support of the ICC and WTO, we anticipate we will be able to achieve this objective in the near term.

III. Conclusion

Since the founding of this great association, FCI has achieved incredible success and has resulted in the expansion of receivables finance from just a handful of countries to supporting its growth in over 90 countries today. With the advent of globalisation starting in earnest in the late 1990s, the push to offer O/A terms on a global scale, the positive impact the financial crisis in 2008-09 had on the Industry, the lower capital reserve requirements that factoring affords, and coupled with the union between the two largest chains, FCI and IFG in 2016, FCI is the undisputed leader and voice for the receivables finance industry throughout the world today. The achievements of FCI are owed to so many, but it is this never-ending spirit of volunteerism and good will from the FCI members that has truly created this chain effect! As they say, the past is an indicator of the future. As such, FCI has many more strong years ahead of it, blending the many great achievements of the past, with all of the possibilities of the future.

2. IFG, Developing the Factoring Industry Worldwide

Erik T<small>IMMERMANS</small>

Past Secretary General, IFG

Writing the history of the International Factors Group is not an easy task. In the 1980s, the most important documents of the first twenty years of existence of IFG were destroyed in a flood at the IFG offices in Brussels. Most of the key actors who were involved in the start of IFG have passed away. Therefore, it is necessary to start this section with a disclaimer: this history of IFG does not have an ambition to be complete or entirely accurate, and some of the founding fathers may not receive sufficient credit. A large part of the information contained in this chapter has been collected by interviewing a number of people who have kindly contributed. John Gielen, former chairman of International Factors Belgium and long-time board member of IFG; Michèle Cardoens, who started work as secretary for IFG in 1977 and who is still one of the staff members of the FCI-IFG union in 2016; Francis Moock, former international manager of International Factors Belgium; Liliana Innocenti, former international manager of International Factors Italia (IFITALIA); Jean-Pierre Gaertner, former international manager of SFF-International Factors France and Leif Palmblad, the first secretary general of IFG. Without their enthusiastic support, it would not have been possible to write this History.

I. Born in the USA: The Creation of the First Global Factors Network (1961-1975)

In the years 1950-1960, FNBB was a prospering bank with more than USD 1.5 billion of assets. Factoring – the practice of buying accounts receivables from merchants and assuming responsibility for their collection – became a substantial part of its business during this time. In 1959, the bank posted record revenues of USD 20.4 million.

The USA wanted to promote its exports to reduce their trade deficit, and factoring was one of the techniques to support exports. In the early 1960s, FNBB rolled out an ambitious plan to internationalise its factoring operations.

It created a new subsidiary, Boston Overseas Financial Corporation, that became the key driver for the start of factoring activities in Europe and other parts of the world. Mr Arthur Fraser and Mr Peter Fischoeder, from Boston Overseas Financial Corporation, identified local partners in different European countries to set up joint ventures specialised in factoring activities. The idea was to combine the factoring knowledge and experience at FNBB with the knowledge and experience in different markets from local market players. The first factoring company thus founded in Europe was International Factors Ltd in London in 1961, a joint venture between Boston Overseas Financial and British Merchant Bankers M. Samuel & Company and Tozer, Kemsley and Millbourn. In 1962, FNBB set up additional joint ventures in the Netherlands (IF-Netherlands), Switzerland (Factors AG), Australia, South Africa and France (Société Française de Factoring or IF-France). From 1963 onwards, other countries followed: Italy (IF-Italy), Belgium (IF-Belgium), Austria (Factorbank), Spain (IF-Spain), Portugal (IF-Portugal), Germany (IF-Germany) and Sweden (IF-Sweden).

The creation of the first international network of factoring companies was a fact. In the early years however, the main focus was on developing factoring activities in the different countries, adapting the tools to sometimes very different legal environments. FNBB's know-how was of tremendous importance for these young factoring companies. Since all "members" of the International Factors environment were linked by the same shareholder (Boston Overseas Financial Corporation), there was no need to create a separate "group vehicle" and the different International Factors companies worked together as members of the same family for their export-import transactions through guidelines from FNBB in the USA. The two-factor system was born.

In the mid-1970s, the need was felt to create an international structure that would deal with the export-import cooperation between the International Factors companies. This was for two reasons: firstly, because the volumes traded between correspondents were steadily growing and secondly, because FNBB started to sell its stake in some of its joint ventures. Without a common shareholder, the "group" needed to create a professional structure to manage the two-factor system, allowing it to expand into new markets and develop a communication system between correspondents. Under the leadership of Dr Paltzer from Factors AG and Paul Vergote from IF-Belgium, the foundations were laid for the creation and expansion of the IFG.

II. Growing up: The Years of Expansion (1975-1990)

IFG effectively started as an operational entity in 1975 with the hiring of its first secretary general, Mr Leif Palmblad from Sweden. Together with the founding chairman, Paul Vergote from IF-Belgium, Kurt Schaer from Factors AG Switzerland, Renaud de Moustier and Yves Delarue from International Factors France-Société Française de Factoring (SFF), Mr Palmblad developed IFG into a world-class network of correspondent factors. IFG was hosted in the offices of International Factors Belgium in Brussels. In 1977, Michèle Cardoens joined IFG as secretary to Leif Palmblad and she has remained active in the organisation until now. On the 6th of July 1977, IFG Holding SA was founded in Luxemburg. The founding shareholders were IF-Belgium, IF-Netherlands, Inter-Factor Bank Germany, IF Ltd UK, Factors AG Switzerland, Factor Bank International Factors Austria and International Factoring and Leasing AG in Switzerland. The three board members were Paul Vergote (IF-Belgium), Heinz Herreiner (Inter-Factor Bank Germany) and Kurt Schaer (Factors AG Switzerland). A few years later, on the 27th of March 1980, the holding company created IFG SA in Belgium. Apart from the shareholders of the holding company and the holding company itself, the following companies were founding shareholders in IFG SA: Commerce Factors Ltd Canada, SFF and International Factors Española. After almost twenty years of cooperation between factoring companies, mostly through their common shareholder FNBB, the creation of a special purpose "association" was a fact. The mission of IFG SA according to its by-laws was the following:

"The company's goal is to deliver services to the companies belonging to the International Factors Group in the area of coordination, control and assistance of the international factoring activities of these companies".

The three board members of IFG SA were Kurt Schaer (MD of Factors AG), Dr Edgar Paltzer (Chairman of Factors AG) and Oscar De Bouvere (MD of IF-Belgium).

The International Factors Group was, during this period, based on principles of exclusivity (as a result of the common shareholder of FNBB in many members) and strong rules for cooperation. The group expanded into twenty countries: Australia, Austria, Belgium, Canada, Denmark, Finland, France, Germany, Ireland, Israel, Italy, Japan, Korea, Netherlands, Norway, Portugal, Spain, Switzerland, UK and USA. In many of these countries, the member was still called "International Factors" as a heritage of the launch of factoring activities with the support from FNBB.

But the shareholding link disappeared with the withdrawal of FNBB from overseas factoring activities. The cooperation between the different IF companies remained and was strengthened through the IFG structure.

IFG created the Uniform Communication System (UCS), the rules for cooperation, which later evolved into the GRIF and established arbitration provisions. Its members signed Inter Factor Agreements (IFA) with each other to provide a legal framework for their cooperation. The one member–one country principle offered the advantage of a very tight cooperation between the correspondent factors. Its disadvantage was, of course, that with only one member, there was no alternative solution in that country. For this reason, at the end of the 1970s, IFG decided to allow a second member in each country who was given the status of associate member. In 1985, the principle of exclusivity was entirely abandoned and more than two full members from each country could join IFG.

Another important characteristic in the operational structure of IFG was the "standardised commission scheme". The remuneration for an import factor's services in terms of collection and credit protection was decided annually by the members at the annual meeting and was the same for all countries. This fixed commission scheme offered a commercial advantage because export factoring contracts could be negotiated with exporters, without having to wait for a price quotation from different import factors. The disadvantage was, of course, the fact that the factoring environments were far from the same all over the world, which made the fixed commission scheme unprofitable for some import factors, which could lead to a reduction in service quality. Many exceptions started to be agreed on a bilateral basis and the standard commission scheme was transformed into the worldwide commission scheme in which members posted their own standard fees.

Equally important in IFG was the fact that the entire export factoring turnover from a member to a particular country had to go through the two-factor system. Members were not allowed to work on a direct basis. This rule was certainly one of the key reasons of the successful development of the two-factor turnover in IFG during the 1970s and 1980s. But the rule was not sustainable in the long run as we will see further.

One of the big advantages of being a closed group was the possibility for the IFG to be at the forefront of investing in the automation of data exchange between members. As early as 1975, the first IFDEX system was launched. IFDEX stood for International Factors Data Exchange and was a messaging system developed and hosted by GEISCO (GE Group).

In those days, when IT systems were still heavy, expensive and slow, it was an important commercial advantage for the members of the IFG to be able to send information by satellite to correspondents all over the world.

Over the years, the cooperation between the members of IFG became less exclusive and members needed more flexibility to enter or leave the group. On the 21st of March 1991, the shareholders of IFG SA decided to transform the company into a cooperative company "International Factors SCRL", to allow for this flexibility. Some people of the founding board of the SCRL would play an important role in the coming years: Yves Delarue (SFF-IF France) who was also chairman of the group, Paul Vergote (IF-Belgium), Klaus Herbert (DG Diskontbank Germany) and Thomas Hutson (IF Ltd UK). At the end of the 1980s, a new secretary general (Bert Meerman) took over from Leif Palmblad who had steered the organisation to a professional and well respected two-factor network.

III. Thunder Road: a Changing Environment (1990-2002)

The 1990s were turbulent times for the IFG. The biggest part of two-factor turnover was realised between European members. With the Maastricht treaty of 1992 (foundations for a true EU) and the creation of the Eurozone in 1999, it became easier for European factoring companies to treat the export receivables from their clients within the EU on a direct basis, without using the two-factor system. Already in 1989, IFG had to allow its members to work on a direct basis (until then the only allowed form of international factoring business for its members was based on the two-factor system). And then there was also the dangerous shadow of "Y2K" (year 2000) lurking over IFDEX: would the system be capable of handling the effects of a two-position year "00"? An ambitious project to update IFDEX and transform it into a modern, intuitive, user-friendly, "intelligent gateway" was undertaken and IFDEX 2000 was launched.

Unfortunately, the project failed, and a new IT-project had to be launched which resulted in the XML, internet-based IFexchange system. In the meantime, the competitor group FCI had outgrown IFG in number of members and in two-factor volumes, not in the least because of their growing volumes coming from Asia.

The IFG struggled to find answers to these new challenges. Both its management time and its financials were under pressure as a result of the high investments in IFDEX 2000. In 1996, a first attempt was made to come together with FCI, to merge into one global, two-factor platform based on FCI's edifactoring system.

In 1996, IFG had 57 members in 32 countries, whereas FCI had 120 members in 44 countries.

In 1999, Jan Becher took over from Bert Meerman as secretary general of IFG. In 2000, a new project for a merger with FCI was launched, which was approved by the majority of members of both organisations during a joint annual meeting in Paris. This led to the creation of a joint legal committee that developed the GRIF, which would become the standard rules for conducting international two-factor operation for the following years, regardless of the group a member belonged to. But the merger between FCI and IFG did not take place after FCI pulled out of the negotiations and invited IFG members to join FCI.

The board of IFG had to reconsider its options and did so under the leadership of some visionary members: Tony Cox of Venture Finance UK, Dominique Charpentier of Eurofactor France, John Gielen of IF-Belgium and Ted Ettershank of Lloyds Commercial Finance UK. A new strategic repositioning plan for IFG was developed and put into place.

IV. The Rising: a New Mission (2002-2016)

A memo for the repositioning of IFG was presented by the board to the members at the 2002 annual meeting in Cyprus. The new direction for IFG was described as follows:
- Maintaining and enhancing the infrastructure for two-factor business;
- Adding a wider range of services to members allowing them to expand their cross-border activities on secure ground by allying with related industries in the supply chain, i.e. credit insurers, collection companies, lawyers and accountants;

- Building alliances with other powerful national and/or global associations for the purpose of monitoring and influencing vital decisions of a legal nature in international trade (WTO, EU etc.).

It is remarkable to notice that it took the global Factoring Industry 40 years to start thinking about its "advocacy" function. Compared to similar specialist finance industries such as leasing, it was probably too focused on the immediate benefit of cross-border business and did not invest resources in creating and supporting a general positive environment for factoring. In the next ten years, this shift of focus would, however, become extremely important, and would also be the foundation for the success of the "new IFG".

When Erik Timmermans became secretary general of IFG in 2005, he found an association in survival mode. Many members had switched their two-factor business to FCI, fearing the IFDEX 2000 problems in IFG. Almost 90% of the two-factor turnover was realised between a handful of group members who also contributed for the biggest part of the IFG budget through the IFexchange transaction fees. But what he also found was a strong culture of cooperation and belief in the importance of the Industry.

The new strategy was clearly spelled out and approved. What was needed was someone who would take the ball and start running with it. In the next decade, the IFG would expand its membership from around 50 members in 35 countries to more than 150 members in over 60 countries. Membership was opened to service providers from IT, legal and risk who interacted with factoring members and added value to IFG's knowledge hub. The financials of IFG rapidly became sound again and were less dependent on a few big group members. In 2007, at the Istanbul annual meeting, the transaction fees for IFexchange, which still counted for 20% of IFG's income budget, were abolished. Two years later, the budget was again in balance, through the growth of membership and income from networking and educational activities.

In a few years, IFG transformed itself from a two-factor network into the association representing and defending factoring and invoice finance worldwide. From 2006, a yearly Global Industry Activity Report was published with information about facts and figures, going beyond the two-factor statistics. The IFG annual meeting was transformed from an inward-looking, full week meeting of international managers into a yearly three-day convention of the thought leaders in the Industry. A broad range of new educational initiatives were launched, starting with new e-learning in five different languages, to the IFG Academy: a residential course in best practices in factoring. The cherry on the education cake was the Certificate of Finance in International Trade (COFIT), a cooperation between IFG and the University of Malta that led, for the first time ever, to a university certificate in finance of international trade and factoring. Strategic cooperation with other associations was actively pursued and led to some important successes. The most important being the creation of the EU Federation for Factoring and Commercial Finance in 2008, a project that started between IFG and the UK association ABFA.

IFG started a successful cooperation with Afreximbank, the supra-national trade finance bank for Africa, based in Egypt. Together, new markets were explored, and important initiatives for creating awareness and understanding of factoring in these emerging markets were launched.

IFG's legal committee created a factoring model law to support emerging markets, with a blueprint for a legal environment that was in line with best practices in the world as well as with the principles of the UNCITRAL convention on the international assignment of receivables. IFG successfully re-invented itself and became the relevant body for factoring worldwide.

But one important realisation was still missing: the creation of one voice for the Industry. After the failed merger discussions with FCI in 1996 and in 2000, and another quickly aborted attempt in 2009, it seemed impossible to bring the two arch-rival associations together, notwithstanding the clear support from many of the big and small industry players. In 2014, the leadership of IFG (Margrith Lütschg-Emmenegger and Erik Timmermans) and FCI (Daniela Bonzanini and Peter Mulroy) decided to give it another shot. And this time things fell quickly into place. The new positioning of IFG created more synergies and less overlap with the FCI strategy that was still primarily focused on the support of two-factor activities. The rapidly changing regulatory environment for finance worldwide created additional pressure to give one strong global voice for factoring. On the 1st of January 2016, the assets and activities of IFG were transferred to FCI. The Industry finally had its unique voice to speak with all stakeholders. The story of IFG came to an end but a new, exciting story for the global receivables finance industry has been written since 2016.

3. EU Federation, Defending Factoring and Commercial Finance in Europe

John Gielen
Past Chairman, EU Federation

Erik Timmermans
Past Secretary General, IFG
Past Chairman, EU Federation

Since the start of modern factoring in the early 1960s, Europe has always been on the forefront of market development. The whole continent represents more than two thirds of the world factoring turnover and has shown impressive and often double-digit growth figures. In itself, the total amount of factoring in EU countries in 2016 reached EUR 1.5 trillion. Notwithstanding the fact that Europe can be considered to be the epicentre of the factoring world, it took the Industry almost 50 years before it successfully organised a joint advocacy function at a European level. In the years 1980-1990, there was an initiative called "EuropaFactoring" through which some of the European national associations tried to organise themselves on an EU level. Under the leadership of Dr Ulrich Brink, who was, in those years, managing the German Factoring Association, EuropaFactoring played a role in the development of the UNCITRAL convention on assignment of receivables in international trade. Not many European countries had an organised national factoring association and EuropaFactoring therefore only represented some EU countries (the main members were Germany, France, Italy, Spain, Portugal and Belgium).

The federation was part of the successful European leasing association (Leaseurope) but did not have sufficient traction or drive to become a true voice for European factoring. From the mid-1990s, EuropaFactoring became dormant and was finally closed down. Only in 2008 a new EU initiative saw the light: the EUF – EU Forum for factoring and commercial finance. Almost 50 years after the first factoring activities were launched in Europe, the Industry would finally have a representative body on an EU level.

I. The Start of a New European Initiative for Factoring (2008-2009)

Since the European Economic and Monetary Union became a reality in 1988, the influence of the EU commission and parliament and the European central bank on legal and regulatory matters was becoming increasingly important, not in the least for the financial world. The Factoring Industry was, for a long time, hesitant in getting organised sufficiently to have its voice heard in Brussels. One person in particular was trying to change this.

The MD of Lloyds Commercial Finance in the UK, Ted Ettershank, was one of the important thought leaders of the business in the early years of the new millennium. As chairman of the British Asset Based Finance Association (ABFA) and as a board member of IFG, Ted Ettershank understood that factoring, and invoice finance generally, needed to be represented "in Brussels" to raise awareness about its role and to defend it against EU regulatory initiatives that could harm the development of the Industry. Already in 2006, ABFA and IFG started to work together in a number of areas, such as the development of a first EU study on the various legal environments for factoring in Europe. Kate Sharp, the CEO of ABFA, and Erik Timmermans, secretary general of IFG, attended as observers at each other's executive committee meeting.

On the 15th of February 2008, a meeting was organised at the offices of GE Capital in the centre of London. This meeting set the wheels in motion for what would become the EUF. Present at the meeting were (amongst others): John Jenkins (MD of GE Capital UK), Ted Ettershank (MD of Lloyds Commercial Finance UK) and his Strategy Director John Brehcist, as well as Kate Sharp and Erik Timmermans. The purpose of the meeting was to brainstorm ideas on the creation by ABFA and IFG of a joint lobby vehicle at a European level. Erik Timmermans suggested opening this initiative up to other interested national factoring associations in Europe, in order to increase the relevance and representation of the Industry.

It was agreed at this meeting that it was an interesting idea but, based on past experience of initiatives such as EuropaFactoring, there was not much confidence in the likelihood of bringing the sometimes very different factoring environments in Europe together under one initiative. But everyone agreed that it was worth a try.

Kate Sharp and Erik Timmermans started to work on a draft document that would create a division in IFG, called "EU Chapter" with following mission:

Both ABFA and IFG feel that there is a need for a reinforced Trade Association activity on EU level in terms of:
- Educating the market and the policy makers;
- Promoting the benefits of factoring, receivables financing and ABL as a flexible form of growth finance;
- Gathering information and publishing papers, articles, news, books on industry-related subjects;
- Observing law and EU Policy initiatives affecting the Industry and lobby in favour of policy decisions that can increase its growth and effectiveness or lobby against policy initiatives that would put barriers on the business.

A final document called "EU Industry Association Forum" was approved by the executive committees of both IFG and ABFA in early May 2008. Meetings took place in Brussels with representatives from IFG, ABFA, DFV (Germany), ASF (France), Assifact (Italy) and AEF (Spain) on the 2nd of June and 29th of July 2008. Very quickly there was a consensus on the necessity of together creating this EU lobby vehicle as a division of IFG. The division would operate under its own name (EU Forum for Factoring and Commercial Finance), have its own budget, a separate bank account, its own rules between members, a separate executive committee and separate technical committees. During a meeting on the 3rd of September 2008, and another one on the 5th of November 2008, the foundations for the EUF were approved. A Memorandum of understanding and rules between members were signed by five of the inaugural members: IFG, ABFA, ASSIFACT, AEF, as well as the Polish Factoring Association, PZF. In early 2009, DFV and ASF joined as two more inaugural members and finally FCI was accepted as the 8th inaugural member in March 2009. John Gielen, board member and then chairman of IFG was nominated as the inaugural chairman of the EUF. Being retired from the banking industry and not linked to a "big" country or company, John Gielen's independent chairmanship was a key factor in the success of the early years of the EUF. Kate Sharp (ABFA) became vice-chairperson and other members of the first executive committee were: Erik Timmermans for IFG, Rony Hamaui for Assifact, Josep Sellés for AEF, Andrzej Zbikowski for PZF, Magdalena Wessel for

DFV, Françoise Palle-Guillabert for ASF and Jeroen Kohnstamm for FCI.

The first official executive committee meeting of the EUF was held in Brussels on the 7th of May 2009. By then, a EUF website and a brochure were developed, and a contract for advocacy outsourcing activities was operational. Fifteen months after the brainstorming meeting in London, the EU Forum for Factoring and Commercial Finance was a reality and could start its activities.

II. The Development of the EUF (2009-2016)

With a press release on the 1st of July 2009 and a first position paper on the EU late payments directive on the 29th of July 2009, the EUF started its real work of informing EU stakeholders about the importance of the Factoring Industry for SME financing, support for employment and economic growth at low risk for financial institutions. These key messages remained the backbone for EUF communication and position papers during the next seven years. From the start, two committees (and in particular their chairpersons) took a leading role in the development of EUF activities: the legal committee, chaired by Magdalena Wessel from the German DFV, and the economics and statistics committee, chaired by Diego Tavecchia from Assifact, the Italian association.

A few years after the start, a new committee was launched: the prudential risk committee that focused on aspects of regulation and capital requirements, while the legal committee continued to focus on legal aspects. The EUF has an extremely light structure and low-cost base but can count on the cooperation of volunteer committee members from the different national association members.

The European Factoring Industry is very enthusiastic about the EUF initiative that very quickly gained visibility and recognition with many European stakeholders. In 2010, six new member associations joined the EUF:

- The Portuguese Factoring and Leasing Association (ALF);
- Association Professionnelle Belge des sociétés de Factoring (APBF) – Belgium;
- Österreichischer Factoring Verband (OFV) – Austria;
- The Hellenic Factors Association (HFA) – Greece;

- Factoring and Asset based financing Association Netherlands (FAAN) – Netherlands;
- Czech Leasing and Finance Association (CLFA) – Czech Republic.

Later, the Danish and Swedish Association made the member picture complete.

EUF had, from that time, sixteen members (fourteen national and two international associations) that between them cover more than 97% of the market share in the EU.

At the end of 2009, the EUF changed its name from "EU Forum" to "EU Federation for Factoring and Commercial Finance" to better reflect its scope of activities.

In the following years, the EUF has been permanently monitoring EU legal or prudential initiatives that could influence the Factoring Industry. With the help of Brussels based Euralia, a European public affairs company, and the EUF coordinator John Brehcist, many position papers were published on a multitude of topics such as capital requirements, Liquidity Coverage Ratio (LCR), Net Stable Funding Ratio (NSFR), targeted longer-term refinancing operations, shadow banking or AnaCredit. On many of these issues, the voice of the Industry was heard by policy makers.

Here are just two examples: in the specific case of the LCR, the EUF obtained an adaptation for factoring. Without this adjustment, factoring activities would have been severely damaged. The same can be said when in Italy the regulator wanted to impose full KYC-AML procedures on all debtors: the EUF successfully supported its Italian member Assifact and convinced the Italian regulator that this obligation would have an extremely negative impact on the business and therefore also on availability of SME financing.

The EUF does not limit its activities to monitoring and reacting. It also has an important proactive role in raising awareness and understanding about factoring and invoice finance generally. The comparative legal study of factoring environments in Europe which was first launched by ABFA and IFG in 2006, was now taken over by the EUF who updated the study in 2011, 2013 and 2016. A glossary in eight languages about terminology related to factoring is published and updated regularly. The EUF plays an active role in the development of the harmonisation of e-invoicing in Europe and has ensured that the assignment of an invoice is included as part of the core information of a standard e-invoice. Connections are made with like-minded organisations such as Leaseurope. The statistics for factoring in Europe are published annually and commented on by the EUF. Meetings are organised with policy makers in the EU parliament, the EU Commission, the European Banking Authority and European Central Bank. In 2015, a first EU Summit for factoring was organised in Brussels, which has quickly evolved into the annual convention for the European business. In 2016, the EUF published a "white paper" demonstrating that factoring in Europe supports SME lending in the real economy and therefore also employment. For the first time, the Paper gathered objective cross-border evidence to demonstrate its low risk for the financial system, i.e. expected losses are four times lower than in the case of traditional non-secured bank lending. When founding chairman John Gielen in 2016 handed over the chair of the EUF to Erik Timmermans, the EUF had grown into a relevant platform and voice for the Factoring Industry in Europe.

III. The Future for EU Representation for the Factoring Industry

With a growing stream of new regulations in the financial world, the need for a strong representation on an EU level will continue to increase. Many new challenges in terms of European capital requirements, Basel rules, AnaCredit, etc. are on the table. The success of the EUF is a direct result of the efforts and the work behind the scenes from the technical committees and their respective chairpersons. If the EUF wants to become stronger and more proactive, publish studies, interact with policy makers in Brussels, raise awareness about the necessity to treat specialised non-bank financial services in a different way to banking, it will be necessary in the future to add more resources and create a stronger permanent structure for the EUF. It takes visionary industry leaders to make this happen. Time for a "new Ted Ettershank" for factoring in Europe?

4. New Trends in Worldwide Factoring

Daniela Bonzanini

Head of International Business, Banca IFIS
Past Chairperson, FCI

In recent decades, factoring has established itself as an important form of financing, particularly for SMEs and increasingly for corporates. The unique structure and risk attributes of factoring make it possible for it to be offered where other more traditional forms of finance are either inappropriate or not available. Combined with the dynamic nature of factoring, which is directly linked to the performance of the funded company, factoring solutions are increasingly important within the current economic climate. Its importance has continued to grow over the years and in 2016 it represented around 3.5% of total global GDP. Increasingly, the continuous launch of new financial products and the development of new technological solutions in the market are driving change and adaptation in factoring, which due to its nature and flexibility continues to support a range of different industries and their diversified needs.

Five new trends of worldwide factoring can be considered:
- The increasing role of factoring solutions in funding trade;
- The evolution of factoring from being SME focused to being an all business solution;
- The central position of factoring as risk mitigation in an increasingly regulatory constrained environment;
- The new challenge of technology and innovation from fintech competition;
- The decisive importance of education and promotion of best practice.

I. The Increasing Role of Factoring Solutions in Funding Trade

Recent global events have placed trade markets in an environment of uncertainty. General low growth, the low price of commodities – especially the price of oil – and low interest rates, complicated by the impact of events such as the Brexit decision and the instability of some banks, have resulted in the World Bank forecasting a general weakness in prospects, with slow growth predicted in advanced economies and a slightly firmer position in emerging markets. The forecast is further impacted by geopolitical environments such as the global risk of terrorism, the refugee emergency and the rise of protectionism in some countries.

How has this general situation impacted on factoring? Factoring has often been considered a countercyclical product which performs well when the general economy is less strong. In the last twenty years a 9% compound annual growth rate has been recorded. However, this perception is not fully confirmed by the latest statistics. The reality is that, in 2016, expansion was seen in some regions and countries and contraction in others, each area presenting different performance and growth rates, which were influenced by the local economic environment and the level of knowledge and market penetration of the product.

Globally, factoring is currently offered in around 90 countries and new markets continue to develop within the Industry; a vision of universal near-future coverage is reasonable.

The trajectory of the Industry as a source of funding for international trade also compares increasingly well with its direct competitors. In 2016, the estimate for cross-border factoring was USD 550 billion (USD 355 billion in 2011) with 9.2% CAGR, short-term credit insurance volume was USD 1.634 billion with 1.7% CAGR, and Letters of Credit (LC) USD 3.040 billion with 1.6% CAGR.[1] This comparative growth pattern presages a medium-term transition where O/A methods gradually substitute documentary approaches such as LCs.

---

[1] The LC figures from ICC/SWIFT study. Swift does not release LC issuance data, but in December 2010 its board agreed to carry out a 'trade snapshot', releasing the number of MT700 commercial standby and guarantee messages, including average invoice size. All figures are estimates based on actual data (2016 estimated). Short-term credit insurance figures reported by the Berne Union (2016).

The growth of cross-border factoring is based on two main components:

- The growth of O/A trade at the expense of letters of credit;
- The continuous success of import-export factoring worldwide.

The advantages of international factoring have proven to be very attractive to cross-border traders. With 82% of global trade on O/A terms and forecasted growth of over 90%, there is great potential for international factoring.

This potential for growth remains even though challenges faced by the international economy in 2016 continue to weigh on international trade flows, and bodies such as the WTO have lowered their forecasted growth rates for world trade in 2017. The solution is considered favourably by governments and central banks in many countries, not only those that are highly industrialised but also those that are still developing.

WTO studies have evidenced that a 10% increase in factoring (availability) granted globally, and to a country in the case of country pair analysis, leads to a 1% increase in real trade flows.[2]

II. The Use of Factoring from a SME Prospective to Being an all Encompassing Business Solution

By number, SMEs are the largest users of factoring. Since the economic crisis that started in 2008, many companies, particularly SMEs, have experienced greater difficulties in gaining access to bank financing. Notwithstanding the increased liquidity and the reduced cost of borrowing, this trend has not significantly improved in recent years. There are many reasons for this, the most significant being insufficient capitalisation, which is a characteristic of this sector, along with the strict liquidity requirements and risk ratios introduced by Central Banks and Basel III that limit the amount of financing that can be allocated to SMEs.

Factoring is a stable financing alternative for many companies. Its main benefit to SMEs is that it is:

- Accessible: the first consideration is the quality of the sales ledger, not balance sheet strength and a positive track record. Thus, if the receivables are of good quality, the SME can access more funding and the level of funding can increase with its sales growth;

---

[2] European Union Federation (EUF), *White Paper on the Default rate for the Receivables Finance Industry in the European Union*, 2015.

- Flexible: funds can be drawn in line with actual needs and take into account factors such as the seasonality of the business, increasing financing volumes during peak periods;
- Efficient: streamlining payment collection activities and the control of the accounts receivables status, taking advantage of factoring companies' high-level technology;
- Useful complementary services are available, especially the assessment of the buyers' credit standing, and protection from their financial inability to pay. This is a critical issue for SMEs because non-payment from their buyers considerably increases the risk of bankruptcy;
- Competitive: funds released against accounts receivables allows payment terms towards buyers to be extended.

According to research by the EUF, in Europe the main client industrial sectors are, by user numbers: manufacturing (27%), services (23%) and distribution (17%).

Over 70% of the estimated 180,000 users in Europe are in the SME category; it is clear that through these businesses, factoring plays a critical role in funding the real economy, creating wealth and supporting employment.

Although by number large corporates only represent around 10% of the number of users in Europe, they account for around 60% of the EUR 200 billion of funds advanced. This proportion is likely to increase as users and their advisers become better acquainted with the opportunities and support that factoring type solutions can give large corporates.

Advantages for such large-scale users include:

- The same finance and outsourcing benefits as for SMEs;
- The finance is generally offered with fewer operating and performance conditions (covenants) compared to other forms of funding;
- The opportunity to link to more extensive ABL, where other assets of the business are included and contribute to the finance package;
- Not based on balance sheet strength, but on current performance;
- It can raise more working capital than traditional lending approaches;
- In some environments, it can be used to improve the Return on Asset/ Equity Ratios of the user's business (ROA/E);

- The opportunity to protect against bad debt;
- It can help support merger and acquisition activity.

Being more and more an all business solution, factoring has increasingly become a non-recourse product where the factor assumes the risk of the debtor's default. In 2016, non-recourse factoring reached a share exceeding 44% of the total volume realised by FCI members, which represents over 60% of worldwide factoring.

III. Factoring as Risk Mitigation: Increasing Regulatory Constraints to Mitigate and Pool Risk

Factoring has full control over the buyers and the entire credit process and this reduces the risk of lending. In fact, loss rates in the Industry are very low even when financing SMEs, which are generally relatively weak prospects from a financial/credit-based point of view. In the EUF white paper, a pan-European survey demonstrated that Loss Given Default (LGD) in the case of factoring was around four times lower than that experienced in the case of traditional non-secured bank lending, strongly confirming the long-held belief that it is a highly secure form of funding.

Factoring is, however, largely delivered through banking corporations, either as departments or through wholly owned subsidiaries (in Europe, this represents around 95% of the market volume) and over recent years, globally, there has been a rapid increase in the amount and intensity of prudential supervision and regulation affecting the delivery and governance of banking solutions.

The impact of Basel III and CRD IV (the EU implementation mechanism) has been significant on the capital provision and governance approach for those entities based in or operating in Europe. Whilst the Factoring Industry recognises the real and appropriate need for a prudent regulatory environment, it also seeks to ensure that where regulation affects the business, it does so in a manner that is proportional to the (lower) risks, and adapted to the specific nature, of the solution (short-term self-liquidating assets). The nature of some of the regulation does not map easily to factoring operations or indeed its risks. As a result, it is important that the Industry has a voice to lobby and ensure that such regulation is adapted and proportionate to our environment.

This has been the basis of the activity of the EUF for Factoring and Commercial Finance, an FCI facilitated body which includes the national associations of the EU 28 and represents 97% of the turnover in the region. Successes in adapting the regime include in the application of the LCR, AnaCredit and, it is hoped in the near term, the NSFR.

In emerging markets, the sharing of best practice through, for example, the delivery of a model law and providing assistance to local bodies that are involved in the development of the Industry, creates a role for FCI in supporting the creation and implementation of legal and regulatory environments that are consistent on a global basis.

As markets continue to develop and evolve, a consistent level playing field becomes an ever more important goal to create a stable international platform for operations.

IV. The New Challenge of Technology and Innovation Development in a Fintech Competition

Over recent years, the rapid development both in the scale of the Industry and the capability of the IT that supports it have transformed what used to be a highly labour-intensive, paper-based industry.

The widespread availability of low cost financial accounting packages has removed one of the original benefits of factoring (the ledger administration service) but has facilitated the implementation of data extraction, transfer and instant processing, providing faster funding opportunities:

- Mobile apps now allow instantaneous remote review of accounts and the opportunity to manage advance payments without intervention;
- Multi-ledger, multi-currency capability is now the standard, allowing both provider and user to focus on service and risk management; in-depth, sophisticated analysis of ledger performance is now available and integration with other banking and financial services, such as credit information, is also widespread;
- The rapid rise and standardisation of e-invoicing and, in some countries, the launch of centralised registers is also offering opportunities to improve overall security and control.

Yet the development of technology is also creating new methods of interaction which can both enhance and challenge traditional factoring methods; for example, the rise of trading platforms and other fintech can create new markets and opportunities for collaboration as well as engender direct competition.

Technological developments are facilitating speed, control, quality, reliability and cost; they will continue to be the source of key competitive advantages within the Industry.

V. The Decisive Importance of Education and Promotion of Best Practice

Education is universally recognised as one of the most fundamental building blocks for human development and it can be a powerful driver of development for the Factoring Industry as well.

In its general sense, education is a form of learning in which knowledge, skills and habits of a group of people are transferred from one generation to the other through teaching, training and research. In factoring, this is not always possible; particularly in emerging countries where the Industry is still young and specialised, factoring know-how is not yet generally available at universities and other higher learning institutes.

Recognising the critical importance of education, demand in educational programs at different levels is increasing. In order to support the spreading of factoring knowledge and the sharing of best practice all over the world, FCI has developed online courses and seminars on a range of topics which are offered both to members and non-members. So far, thousands of students have benefited from the FCI educational platform and more and more financial institutions, associations and universities are approaching the organisation looking for cooperation agreements aiming to offer educational support to their members.

IV. Conclusion

Our factoring environment is constantly developing and changing. Some of the main trends evident in the Industry include:
- Market development: while mature countries continue to represent the largest part, many important emerging nations are entering the business and in the medium term their weight will be increased; the role of international factoring in facilitating trade finance will continue to develop;

- User types: by number, SMEs remain the largest beneficiary of factoring facilities but at the same time large corporates are increasingly using factoring type services and this will bring higher global turnover;
- Regulation and legal environments: factoring awareness is progressing, and actors need to work with regulatory bodies and central banks to develop appropriate rules and frameworks to support growth within a secure environment;
- Technology: IT is supporting the development of the Industry and while it is simultaneously creating new opportunities it is also facilitating alternative competitive approaches;
- Education: creating knowledge and capability is key. An understanding of its importance is becoming more widespread.

PART I

PAST – FACTORING ROOTS AND EVOLUTION (3rd CENTURY BC to 20th CENTURY AD)

Introduction

Patrick DE VILLEPIN

Global Head of Factoring, BNP Paribas

During times when the concepts of "invoice" or "currency" did not yet exist, the development of trade transactions went hand-in-hand with the urgent necessity of guaranteeing performance. Payment security laid at the heart of this development.

Although only some of the solutions later covered by factoring existed during antiquity, those early attempts constituted the very roots from which it sprouted some millennia afterwards, in a different context (see chapter 5). According to some authors, the first blueprints of factoring are the fruit of the ancient Mesopotamian civilisation, born in the extreme south of modern-day Iraq, between the Tigris and Euphrates. The Hammurabi code is sometimes mentioned as the first evidence of an early form of finance. Displayed in the Louvre museum in Paris, this code (c. 1750 BC) is a set of economic and financial rules engraved on a large stele of black basalt. It reflects the King of Babylon's will to protect financial operations and to secure intermediate activities in a legislative framework. As such, it can be considered as a first attempt of factoring law even if it does not establish any business practice. A full package of formal and informal measures taken by ancient civilisations to efficiently structure economic and financial life, the Hammurabi code is a testimony of permanent needs, even if answers and remedies have undoubtedly evolved from the past to the present.

It is obviously needless and anachronistic to use artificially modern words on old drafts and schemes. Yet the essential issues, the main concerns do date from this era. Written documents in Egypt and Mesopotamia reveal complex connections very near to modern factoring. In parallel to ever more complex trade transactions, they are not yet to lead to the invention of factoring as such. But they do incorporate certain needs that would lead to the emergence of this financial technique: the requirement for trade financing, security and fluidity. The concept of a trade intermediary emerges, the interface between seller and buyer and the beginning of a three-party relationship.

Dating back to the end of the 18th century BC, letters from Larsa in southern Iraq illustrate a system introduced by the palace to sell the wool produced by its flocks. Delegations of the sale of wool to third parties were responsible for providing the corresponding funds at a date set out in the contract.

In the Greek world, credit only rarely concerned commercial enterprises. Frequently high risk, such financing most frequently fell within the category of "bottomry" loans. This method of maritime trade financing places the risk (shipwreck, damage, loss of cargo, etc.) on the financial backer. The capital is only repaid if the ship reaches port. Such loans were provided by rich merchants (such as the father of Demosthenes) who played the role of intermediary, as demonstrated by the *Versus Lakritos* loan (c. 340 BC), a commercial contract based on a financing agreement and related guarantee to secure supplies on the major maritime routes. The appearance from the Roman Era (see chapter 6) of specialists in debt collection (the "coactores") confirms the existence of the three elements in the factoring jigsaw puzzle, although they remained disassociated and somewhat dispersed. Like the father of Horatius who practiced the profession, the "coactores" received a commission of up to 1% of the money collected from the debtor.

These ancient techniques merely represent a crude outline for the modern factor's methods of operation. Scattered and fleeting in nature, only very infrequently did they contribute to support trade. No economic operator had the idea of incorporating financing, guarantees and receivables management within a single product. In spite of their origins in Greek and Roman antiquity, such methods would not survive the fall of Rome (476) and the subsequent collapse of the Western Roman Empire.

In the Middle Ages (see chapter 7), the appearance of the first "factors" bore no relation to previous practices. With the Renaissance, the term acquires a more economic function in England and in France. Jacques Cœur is reputed to have had some 300 "factors", trade correspondents at the various trading posts (or "factoreries") established between around 1430-1440 in France and all along the Mediterranean rim. During this period, the "factor" has nothing to do with factoring and securing trade, even if bankers from Lombardy launched a partial and primitive version of factoring via the *Star del Credere* (from the old Italian for "have trust"), a sort of commission paid to those agents who guarantee against payment default and collect from buyers in distant towns, whose profiles were difficult for the seller to assess.

Introduction

But the profession was yet to evolve, mature and be structured in a meaningful manner. In England, during the 15th century followed by America in the 17th century, factoring gradually took on its current form:

- 15th century in England (see chapter 8): Blackwell Hall, the centre of English factors for the textile trade, was established in 1450. These factors progressively expanded the scope of their activities. Initially, the agents charged a fee to handle, store and sell the products entrusted to them by wool producers and drapers. But their good contacts with clients and the lengthy payment periods for the export trade subsequently led them to grant advances and to guarantee the creditworthiness of certain clients. From the first half of the 17th century, the most enterprising among them played a role in the development of European ports and the further expansion overseas. From one Atlantic coast to the other, close relations were established in America. The overseas factors are at the root of this migratory trend. In the American ports, factors and agents spring up as a kind of custodian-reseller to channel goods from or to England;

- 17th century in America (see chapter 9): in 1620, William Bradford and the first English colonists from the Mayflower land at Plymouth Rock, Massachusetts, and found the Plymouth Colony. A few years later, a first contract between the immigrants and three London factors authorised the financing of imports and exports. In the USA, the cotton production sector played a significant role in the emergence of factoring. Between the production phases (cotton harvest) and marketing (ultimate sale on the other side of the Atlantic), the factors financed the cash interval.

The involvement of American factors would progressively be limited to the financial sphere. In the 19th and 20th centuries, the growing sophistication of old-line factoring turned the American factors into the pioneers and founders of a profession which initially operated on an international basis before branching out into the domestic sphere: before anything else, factoring emerged on a cross-border basis between the Atlantic coasts. In broad terms, this Anglo-American saga of secured financing warrants more in-depth and step-by-step analysis.

A – Roots

5. Factoring: Origins Rooted in Ancient Times

Damien Agut
Permanent Researcher, CNRS

Véronique Chankowski
Professor of Aegean history, Lyon II University

Laetitia Graslin-Thomé
Assistant Professor, University of Lorraine

In the middle of the 7th century BC, Hesiod gave his brother the following advice: "Measure with care what you lend to your neighbour and give all he asks for and more if you can; one day, you may have to call on him to render you the same service". In ancient writings, credit and, in general, any deferred payment, is often said to be a necessary practice to ensure all of a family's needs are met, but also warn how it can lead to poverty. It is therefore important to borrow as little as possible, only when really needed, and to reimburse the lender as quickly as possible. In reality, ancient economies were essentially smallholding economies. Lending was mainly between neighbours involving foodstuffs and seed for the next harvest, to ensure families had enough to eat. However, the development of financial practices, together with, in certain periods, the monetisation of societies, led to the spread of new practices involving reserves, financiers' and bankers' capital. In some circles and circumstances, lending drove economic growth. In varying degrees, it appears that, throughout antiquity, lending and the use of money in general gave rise to numerous economic activities that would not otherwise have been possible.

Historians have often been interested in such lending, which has the characteristics of a double-edged sword: a sign of tensions in farming societies when subsistence loans are involved, but also a sign of the vitality and inventiveness of antique societies to overcome such tensions and to invent new economic activities, such as long-distance trading and large-scale farming. Historians have been all the more interested in such lending since, in the often-unknown world of ancient economic history, lending is one practice for which written traces have survived; rare and valuable sources on which ancient history has been written. To finalise a loan, a debt must be enshrined in a written document, which, sometimes, despite the amount of time elapsed, survives as ancient documents. It is the case of Mesopotamia, a rich alluvial plain located in present-day Iraq where one of the first complex human civilisations developed.[1] Acknowledgement of debt, which was kept by the creditor and broken when the debt was repaid, existed, dating from at least the third millennium BC. Depending on the region and historical period, the name of the two interested parties, the reason for the loan, repayment date and interest rate, if any, are recorded. But the text never differs too much from the following text, which dates from the beginning of the second millennium BC: "Ea-iddinam, son of Ea-turam, has lent a hundredweight of barley with interest to Digir-manšum, son of Iluni. He will measure the barley and interest when the barley is harvested."[2]

In Egypt and Greece, debts were acknowledged in writing as often as in Mesopotamia, using a similar standard text. But, in Egypt, such acknowledgements were recorded on papyrus, which is more fragile than the clay tablets of Mesopotamia. Consequently, barely 170 examples of debt acknowledgements in Egyptian writing, mainly in demotic cursive text, have survived. In Greece, debt acknowledgements were written on material of such fragility that none survive. But other documents that have survived teach us about the workings of business and credit in ancient times. Stone inscriptions, recording the honours granted by cities to benefactors and listing their donations, are highly valuable in helping to understand day-to-day practices, in particular financial, of such notables. Furthermore, pleadings, kept for their literary value, teach us about how business was conducted in ancient Athens. The *Versus Lakritos* of the Athenian orator Demosthenes cites verbatim, for the purpose

---

[1] For an introduction to ancient mesopotamian history and economy, see N. Postgate, *Early Mesopotamia: Society and Economy at the Dawn of History*, London, 1992, F. Joannès (*et al.*), *Mésopotamie – De Gilgamesh à Artaban (3000 av. J.-C. à 224 apr. J.-C.)*, Paris, 2017. For Egypt, see Muhs Brian, *The Ancient Egyptian Economy (3000-30 BCE)*, Cambridge, 2016; Moreno Garcia Juan Carlos (dir.), *Économie de l'Égypte ancienne* (Annales. Histoire, Sciences Sociales, 69), 2014, Paris. For Greece, see Bresson Alain, *L'économie de la Grèce des cités (fin VIe-I^e siècle A. C.)*, Paris, 2008-2009.

[2] Hudson Michael, Van de Mieroop Marc (eds.), *Debt and economic renewal in the ancient Near East: colloquium, held at Columbia University, November 1998*, Bethesda 2002.

Factoring: Origins Rooted in Ancient Times 73

of the proceedings, a maritime loan agreement that sheds light on the complexity of financial relationships forged in ancient Athens and the leverage afforded by the system of loans with interest.

Such varied and heterogeneous documentation has given rise to numerous studies on credit and its function in ancient societies. Was it a simple spiral towards indebtedness as those with primitive views of ancient economies have wanted to believe or, was it more a factor facilitating exchange and economic growth as believed by historians sometimes qualified as modernists. Thinking of factoring gives another way of looking at this documentation and to view some ancient practices in a new light.

In the modern world, those who say factoring are thinking of bills. However, it does not seem that ancient societies used bills in the modern sense of the word of documents of a commercial and accounting nature that specify *a posteriori* the terms and conditions of the purchase and sale of products. Accounting documents did indeed exist. They were even numerous in temples, which kept detailed records of assets held in the temple's reserves and the sums paid in exchange. But they were documents for internal use. They did not, like today's bills, have a value of a debt owed to a supplier by its buyer. Likewise, in ancient Greece and Mesopotamia, there were service contracts concluded by craftsmen. They provided for the performance of a task in consideration of a paid salary. We also have documents attesting the transfer of title to land. To know whether these documents are or are not bills, it is necessary to know when the transfer of title occurred, which is difficult to ascertain from the documents that have survived. In ancient Greece, it is commonly believed that the transfer of title occurred when payment was made. In the 6th century BC, in a treaty, *On contracts*, of which only fragments survive, Theophrastus explicitly states: "As regards the acquisition of property, the sale is irrefutable once the price has been paid and once (the parties) have done what is required by law, such as the registration, swearing of an oath or rendering of a service or services to neighbours."

The documents that have survived are therefore not bills in the sense of payment demands, but rather documents produced *a posteriori* to confirm that the transaction has been properly undertaken. However, in the details, the Mesopotamian texts and ancient Greek inscriptions are testament to a broad range of practices that are similar to today's bills: payment of deposits or collection of guarantees for hidden defects were frequent. Some Mesopotamian and Egyptian debt acknowledgements might, in fact, have the same value as a bill that is payable by a specified due date: the beneficiary of the loan acknowledges that he will have to have paid back the loan and interest by a given date. Maybe certain Egyptian documents that establish the existence of a debt so as to trigger the debt's payment should be considered as bills. But such documents are rare, and bills, as we understand them, at the heart of factoring as practiced today, do not seem to have been common practice in ancient societies. The reason for the absence of bills lies in the profound differences between how our contemporary society operates and how ancient societies operated.

I. Differences Between Ancient and Modern Societies

A Non-monetised Economy

We might first think that ancient economies are too different from modern economies to have processes similar to factoring. One of the most obvious differences is the absence of coins for part of the period. Coins appear only at the end of the 7th century BC, subsequently spreading to Greece in the middle of the 6th century BC. Coins were not used in Egypt before the end of the 5th century BC and in Mesopotamia not before the 4th century BC.[3] Ancient economies were therefore essentially economies operating without money. Instead, they use what historians call quasi-money: weighed silver, barley or other products used as units of account, safe havens or means of exchange. However, debts involving such products cannot function in the same way as money loans as practiced in modern societies. These quasi-money products are perishable products whose value is subject to the year's price fluctuations and that lose all value by the end of a relatively short period of time. Any delay in paying off a debt therefore changes its very nature. The separation in time between a debt being issued and its recovery at a date provided for, which is fundamental to factoring, is particularly important in such ancient economies. In ancient Greece, a monetary economy began to be introduced from the middle of the 6th century BC, even if other forms of exchange continued to be practised throughout antiquity. With money, banking activities and the development of a broad range of financial instruments (such as payment orders) developed, accelerating the pace of transactions and facilitating long-distance exchanges. Egyptian papyri of the Hellenistic period show for instance the complexity of certain

---

[3] Agut Damien, « "L'orge et l'argent" Les usages monétaires à 'Ayn Manâwir à l'époque perse » *Annales. Histoire, Sciences Sociales*, 2014/1, 69e année, p. 75-90.

exchange networks, which used eastern Mediterranean warehouses and locally placed intermediaries to undertake transactions and payments.

Legal Framework

Another significant difference, in a world where the State in the modern sense did not exist, is an unstable economic environment. In such a situation, the simplest and most certain solution is for the goods to be transferred at the exact time of payment. However, the complexity of economic life sometimes requires that there is a separation in time between when an object is delivered, or service rendered, and its payment. In ancient Sumer, from the third millennium BC, contracts known as "šu ba-an-ti" provided for work to be undertaken, and a salary to be paid at a later date.[4] The ancients endeavoured to adopt a legal framework that secured this type of transaction with deferred payment.[5] In the second millennium BC, the famous Hammurabi code[6] brought together more than 200 legal rules, some of which concerned credit and have sometimes been considered as the first forms of factoring. Alongside these formal rules, other informal but just as stringent rules applied. The importance for people to maintain their reputation and personal ties was a greater incentive to respecting contracts than a central, sometimes distant, power. In Mesopotamia, from the beginning of the second millennium, merchants' letters attest to this: contracts had to be respected, debts honoured, and one had to prove to be a good trading partner or run the risk of being excluded from the community or losing both social status and income sources. The Athenians formalised this institutional framework, which helped to secure transactions. In the 4th century BC, they introduced *dikai emporikai*, that is to say, courts specifically for merchants who came to Piraeus to trade. These courts gave merchants the assurance of a quick judgement concerning trade affairs. In such a system, several accounts from claimants testify to the prime importance of the trust in which the institutions that enforced the law and contracts were held.

---

[4] Steinkeller Piotr, "Money-Lending Practices in Ur III Babylonia: The Issue of Economic Motivation", Hudson Michael, Van de Mieroop Marc (eds.), *Debt and economic renewal in the ancient Near East*, Bethesda, 2002, p. 109-137.

[5] On mesopotamian ancient law, see Westbrook Raymond (ed.), *A History of ancient Near Eastern Law*, Leiden, 2003.

[6] Roth Martha, *Law collections from Mesopotamia and Asia Minor*, Atlanta, 1995, p. 71-143.

Material Constraints

Material constraints that made debt recovery particularly complex were another feature of antique economies. Once transactions were undertaken outside the familiar local environment, such as the village economy, the distance between trading partners became a material constraint. In a world where all travel was expensive, both in time and money, the interested parties could not always physically be in the same place. It was then difficult to have contracts or debts honoured, that were concluded with partners separated by great distance. To offset these difficulties, antique societies heavily relied on personal ties, which served the purpose that modern contracts would later serve. From the beginning of the second millennium BC, merchants conducting long-distance trade relied on ties of confidence and even friendship.[7] Contracts were honoured, and goods paid for, in the name of such personal ties, without having to use the formal document of a bill. Again, in ancient Greece, pleadings presented to Athenian courts confirm the importance of such mechanisms based on reputation: debts or goods could be granted to such and such individual because he was of honourable standing. Lenders were often not professional bankers, but individuals belonging to the social or family circle. This is of great importance because it is possible that a part of the functions undertaken anonymously by today's factors were undertaken within a more personal framework in ancient times. From the historian's point of view, such functions are more difficult to understand since this type of personal relationship was not the subject of a written contract likely to survive the ravages of time.

Moral Constraints

In antique societies, loans had great moral and symbolic significance. The first loans were no doubt solidarity loans. For some loans, the appearance of interest rates changed the relationship with credit because one man's debt became another's enrichment. Loans with interest were

---

[7] At the beginning of second millennium BC, a trading network has been established in central Anatolia by merchants coming from Assur, in northern Mesopotamia. Many letters have been found in one of their trading settlements, Kanesh, modern Kültepe. They give very valuable evidence on communication of merchants across long distances. They gave a rare first-hand testimony of the personnal relations linking those merchants. On this archive, see Larsen Mogens Trolle, *Ancient kanesh, a Merchant Colony in bronze Age Anatolia*, Cambridge, 2015. For an example in first millennium Mesopotamia, Graslin Laetitia, *Les échanges à longue distance en Mésopotamie au premier millénaire av. J.-C.*, Paris, 2009.

therefore morally discredited, so that creditors were not given too much power in order to maintain social stability. In such conditions, debt recovery was not taken for granted when the debt was a subsistence debt. Mesopotamian kings of the second millennium often promulgated *mišarum*, general remission of non-commercial debts.[8] In ancient Greece, in Hellenistic times, several major decrees are a testament to social developments, including the remission of debts in periods of political crises. Debt recovery therefore did not have absolute legitimacy. The ancients were well aware that lending was crucial to the economy: subsistence loans were essential in lean times. Commercial loans contributed to economic development to such a degree that *mišarum* did not apply to them. The ancients therefore sought to ensure loans were possible without making them socially unacceptable.

Different Perception of Time

The importance of material constraints in economies based mainly on farming perhaps explains the fact that time was perceived differently in antique economies compared with the modern world. In ancient times, time was principally perceived as cyclical, with the return of the seasons, the harvest or navigation periods being important reference points. Such cyclical rhythms attached themselves to certain economic transactions: numerous Mesopotamian contracts involved agricultural products being delivered at harvest time. Connected to such cyclical time, a second perception of time, of much greater length, allowed debts to be repaid or contracts to be performed in periods of time that seem excessively long for the modern observer: profit expected by Greek notables was realised only over the very long-term, assets were seized only after many years after a contract had been breached or a debt had not been repaid, and, in Mesopotamia and ancient Greece, many examples are testament to the frequency at which debts were not repaid. This difference in the perception of time impacted the practices of lending and all economic activities. In antiquity, the absence of bills in the modern sense is perhaps explained by the fact that in antiquity the same associations were not made as in modern societies between establishing a contract, rendering a service or supplying goods, and paying the price. Furthermore, very often, the benefits expected by notables from their investments were not

---

[8] On *Mišarum* dating from Hammurabi's time, see Charpin D., *Hammurabi of Babylon*, Cambridge, 2012.

expressed in economic terms, but in terms of prestige and recognition from the community.

II. Answers in Antiquity to Needs Met by Today's Factoring

Antique economies therefore seem to have been very constrained by what historians, after economists, call transaction costs: the uncertainty of any activity outside simple neighbour relations, constraints of distance, lack of assurance in general regarding the respect of contracts and debt repayment, and the lack of liquidity all hamper economic activity. On close examination, these difficulties to which antique societies seemed particularly exposed are not that different from those to which factoring provides a solution. Some antique practices are a testament to preoccupations common to both modern factors and antique economic agents. Factoring is a tripartite relationship between a buyer, a seller and a factor. The factor's function is to provide his client with security by shielding him from non-payments, allowing the client to delegate debt recovery, and innovate by distinguishing between when the financing is provided and when the debt is collected. Such needs were particularly relevant in antiquity for reasons specific to antique economies mentioned above. What solutions did antique societies develop to offset the absence of factoring?

Protection against Non-payments

Protection against non-payments through the use of sureties and mortgages has been known and practised since the third millennium BC.[9] In Egypt, most deeds that related to sales, leases or inheritance were secured by a penalty clause. In the event that a party to an agreement did not keep his word as transcribed in the document, he had to pay a penalty in kind (most often wheat) or in silver (weighed or counted). In documents related to the acknowledgement of debt, the penalty could accrue as and when the debt became overdue. The deadly nature of the process of cumulative indebtedness is underlined by an Egyptian proverb: "[He] who spends without having an income adds interest to interest, (as sure as with an incurable disease), death results."[10]

---

[9] Westbrook Raymond, Jasnow Richard (ed.), *Security for debt in ancient Near Eastern law*, Leiden, 2001.
[10] Frankišek Lexa, *Papyrus Insinger*, Paris, 1926.

The penalty could involve material objects, but also human beings, even the borrower himself in the case of slavery for debt, a practice much feared and denounced in antiquity. It could then give rise to considerable social tensions, which could only be resolved by violent or radical means: the revolt of the masses in ancient Rome, stasis, and social unrest that marked Greece at the end of antiquity. In a group of merchants, bankruptcy was a bad outcome for all concerned, both for the creditor and debtor. At the beginning of the second millennium BC, Mesopotamian merchants did not make their debtors pay back the debt at all costs. Instead, they preferred to have the debtor undertake trade expeditions for them. It was then said that the debtors were "held by money" for a given period of time. In some way, the legal process of factoring, which ensures debt recovery, is a response to what had been a cause of great instability in antiquity.

Factoring is also more effective than the use of pledges, whose seizure is never easy. Debt recovery can also be complicated by the debtor's personality. In a letter from the beginning of the first millennium BC, a rich financier requests the Mesopotamian King Sargon II the money he had lent that was used in building the king's capital city. We do not know the outcome of the financier's request, but the debtor's social status casts doubt on the financier's chances of recovering the money.

Securing the Debt Relationship

Factoring, moreover, introduces a third party, a provider of security, in the debt relationship. Again, the process is commonplace in antique societies. Personal relationships were at the heart of all economic activity. They ensured debts were repaid, either formally through the practice of surety, or informally through mechanisms based on reputation. Numerous merchants' letters dating from the beginning of the second millennium BC have been found in the ancient town of Kanesh, in Anatolia. They provide an invaluable window into merchants' practices at that time. They show the importance of personal relationships. A little later, the code of Hammurabi devotes several articles to trade partnerships and the solidarity arising therefrom. A little later again, pleadings presented to Athenian courts confirm the importance of relations based on personal trust for businessmen involved in maritime trade. Loans were granted to those known by the lender, or who had been recommended by a partner held in high regard. Very often, partners invested all their capital in the same ship, thereby pooling the risk, so that it was in all their interests for the operation to succeed.

In Egypt, there were various forms of complex sureties, created because of the requirements of Egyptian tax authorities during the Hellenistic period (from the 4th century BC to the 1st century BC). Every year, the State auctioned tax farms.[11] The bidders had to prove to the tax authorities that they were financially sound. To that end, the bidders produced a surety document, a long list of individuals that stood surety for the farmer in the event that he defaulted.[12] This primary guarantee was sometimes backed by a second, which was more social in nature than strictly financial: the farmer's financial partners guaranteed to the State that the farmer would not abandon his post and disappear to escape any debts. This was social control at the strictest level possible in a society where everyone knew one another: sociology, mainly rural in nature, ensured a very effective form of social control. At the heart of the community, this practice of surety contributed to a system of mutual financial assistance, gathering around the farmer a network of notables and allies. To secure their bids, those wishing to buy one of these tax farms from the State could call upon the support of numerous persons practising various professions, such as priests, soldiers, as well as craftsmen and smallholders.

In societies where it was difficult to establish contracts directly between the involved parties, personal relationships were often the only means to ensure debt was collected. Proxies therefore played a role, often neglected, in the functioning of antique economies. They were especially prevalent in Roman times, when rich Roman senators entrusted the management of their properties to their agents, who were interestingly called "grain factors". For earlier periods, there are few examples since the practice of a trustworthy man enabled the interested parties to remain within the scope of personal relationships and dispense with having to write a text, which could have survived. We are, however, led to believe that in Egypt such proxies existed at all levels of society. The most famous case is that of the vast estate owned by the finance minister of the King Ptolemy II, in Fayoum, Egypt. The estate was administered by a certain Zenon, who left us numerous archives.[13] From a financial point of view,

---

[11] Manning Joseph, "The Auction of Pharaoh," in *Gold of praise. Studies in Honor of Edward F. Wente*. Larsen John A., Teeter Emily (eds.), Chicago, 1999, p. 277-84.

[12] De Cenival Françoise, *Cautionnements démotiques du début de l'époque ptolémaïque*, Le Caire, 1973.

[13] Orrieux Claude, *Les papyrus de Zénon, l'horizon d'un Grec en Égypte au IIIe siècle avant J.-C.*, Paris, 1983.

the proxy behaved as if he were the master of the property of the person he represented: he managed the profits, paid the costs and tax. This practice ensured the flow of revenue generated by the farming estates; the fact that the master was not present did not lead to an accumulation of outstanding payments. Bills had no role within this system.

In ancient Greece, the role of third parties that stood surety for loans contracted by others is well documented by epigraphy. Several inscriptions thank notables who had accepted to act as intermediaries for their city when the city had to take out loans or incur expenses. It is, for example, the case of a certain Boulagoras, who was honoured by a long inscription found in Samos, in which the city thanks him for having advanced the money to buy wheat, by assuming liability for the debt in place of the city. The exact role played by these notables is a subject of much historiographical debate: were they just guarantors, or did they take on the debt incurred by the city, meaning that they assumed the risk? In any case, cities preferred to use intermediaries that were recognised as trustworthy, members of the local nobility and keen to maintain a positive image in the eyes of the other citizens. Those powerful individuals practised *evergetism*[14], which placed them under the social control of the whole city. In Roman times, such individuals were often close to those with political power, which further increased their own power. The city, thereby, avoided dependence on the first grain merchant that happened to come along. In today's factoring, the relationship is secured by the factor's standing. In ancient times, the relationship was secured by the personal standing of the guarantors or intermediaries that were called upon.

Fluidity and Security of Transactions

Finally, the last function of factoring is to promote innovation, by securing transactions and ensuring their fluidity. It places an intermediary company, although not state-owned, between the two parties to a contract. Factoring, thereby, ensures that economic relations are fluid, thus promoting innovation. In economic language, we could say that factoring enables companies that use it to limit and maintain transaction costs at a predictable level. It therefore promotes innovation by transferring the transaction costs

---

[14] Evergetism is an important social practice of greek and roman world. It consisted in using the wealth, network and relations of the richest citizen for the benefit of the city: it was expected from them that they voluntarily performed public office or duty at their own expenses. In return, they got honours awarded by the city.

to a third party. The question of the ability of antique economies to innovate is hotly debated. Yet there is no doubt that the securing of transactions, or more precisely the feeling of security by interested parties, is an important factor of economic growth. In antiquity, the solutions found in the search for security are varied. During the Ptolemaic dynasty in Egypt, binding sales with the additional security of surety, which was examined above, helped to attract investors, who, until then, preferred agricultural investment. The use of surety, involving several tens of interested parties, helped to attract local notables to certain types of industrial productions, including brewing, food oil or lighting oil, and even the activity of washing household linen. These processing activities thereby passed from the hands of craftsmen and small local establishments to groups of notables, who agreed to share the risk by jointly standing surety.

In the 4th century BC, Athens developed another solution known as "*dikai emporikai*". Proof that the process of "*dikai emporikai*" promoted economic growth is provided when "*dikai emporikai*" were suspended when the Athenian empire collapsed. Aegean trade also stalled until another confederation known as the Nesiotic League allowed for common rules to be applied again. This example shows the crucial importance of rendering transactions sure in promoting economic growth. The crucial factor here is the important role played by the institutional framework and, more precisely, how such a framework is viewed by the interested parties. Confidence in transactions is a crucial factor, underpinning economic vibrancy and innovation. In modern times, factoring is a testament to this within the framework of our contemporary, standardised and legal world. It enables anyone to undertake a transaction, safe in the knowledge that a good outcome is assured, without any unexpected additional cost. Ancient societies sought other solutions to the same problem and found them in the form of personal relationships or specific legal structures, such as "*dikai emporikai*".

Distant Precursors of Today's Factors

Today's factoring is based on a certain number of principles and practices: protection against non-payment, introduction of a third party standing surety and fluid transactions. Ancient societies did not conceptualise these principles; but their pragmatism sometimes led them to adopt similar practices. The emergence of a few great families, known as entrepreneurs, constituted a new development in Babylonia, in the second half of the first millennium BC. The region was then under

Persian rule, which demanded, contrary to common practice, that a portion of taxes be paid in silver. However, local producers did not have a ready supply of silver. Businessmen, known as *Murašu*, made fortunes by exchanging agricultural produce for silver, thus enabling rural producers to pay their taxes.[15] The *Murašu's* economic activity was not enshrined by bills of modern times, but was solely based on agricultural produce. Yet, like today's factors, they were involved in a tripartite relationship: the creditor (the Persian governor wishing to collect tax), the debtor (the rural producer who was liable for the tax) and the businessman, who enabled the debtor to meet the demands of the creditor. Can we not see in these Babylonian businessmen of the first millennium BC the distant precursors of today's factors? Later, the storage networks of the Greek world played a similar role. We now know that their activities were not limited to simple storage but extended to banking activities, to such an extent that, in the Roman world, storage could be used for guarantees for loans. Numerous Roman sources of the imperial period are a testament to the versatility of warehouse keepers, who, without being bankers themselves, were at the head of a network whose economic functions were not that dissimilar to those of today's factors.

III. Conclusion: Why Did the Ancients not Invent Factoring?

From the time when human economies first evolved, the ancients had many preoccupations: the attention given to the social regulation of lending and to the need of ensuring that debts were collected without the economy creating unacceptable tensions, as well as the attention given to providing creditors with the relative certitude that their debts would be paid. All of which made lending possible and helped create an economy that functioned properly, while avoiding making such lending socially unbearable. Preoccupations that also exist in connection with today's factoring, which, as in ancient times, contributed to social regulation. We are left with the question of why ancient societies never developed the practice of factoring as such. Indeed, the material possibility of transferring one's debts rarely appears in the documentation even if it is not entirely absent. From the second millennium BC, in connection with Assyrian merchants, there are references to acknowledgements of debt

---

[15] On this family, see Stolper Matthew W., *Entrepreneurs and Empire: the Murašû archive, the Murašû firm, and Persian rule in Babylonia*, Istanbul, 1885.

that do not mention any named creditor, but only the *tamkaru*, a kind of chief merchant. This clause suggests that debts could be transferred, made necessary by the fact that the creditor and debtor were not in the same place. Merchants involved in long-distance trade could, therefore, have transferred debts. Yet the existence of a credit superstructure, which is the mark of today's factoring, was never common practice.

It is difficult to say what the technical stumbling blocks were that hampered such practices in antiquity. The personal ties between businessmen and their proxies must have played an important role since they helped to otherwise resolve the problems to which factoring provides a solution. The fact that there were no bills, which are at the heart of modern activity, was also a technical stumbling block, the causes and consequences of which should be the subject of further study. But more crucially, the key problem, and a recurring problem in antique societies, is perhaps that of access to liquidity. Liquidity was concentrated in the hands of a few notables. Yet the great mass of the rural population had very little access to liquidity. These two groups were very disconnected in antique economies whereas, in a certain way, today's factoring contributes to linking economic groups that do not necessarily have easy interactions. This lack of access to liquidity has often been identified as the main stumbling block for ancient societies. To study it through the prism of today's factoring reveals new aspects, on which little light has been shed by modern research. Conversely, we hope that these reflections on ancient practices have helped to understand the nature and originality of today's factoring.

6. Getting Cash from Receivables in Ancient Rome

Gérard MINAUD

Associate Member, Centre Camille Jullian

"Slow receivables, but not bad ones": these words express the uncertainty felt by any manager facing long unpredictable delays occurring in debt collection. There is nothing modern in the financial difficulty pointed to by this expression, for its author, the famous Seneca the Stoic (c. 4 BC and AD 1-65), penned it between AD 61 and 63![1] This tutor and later advisor to Nero was not only a remarkable philosopher and talented dramatist, but also a very rich man, one of the wealthiest in his days. Seneca had a fortune worth 300 million sesterces, this amount represented between 1.8% and 2.2% of the Empire's GDP when Augustus died in AD 14.[2] It seems legitimate, therefore, to lend some credence to the Roman philosopher's remarks on financial and accounting matters even if he did not personally manage his affairs: like all aristocrats of his time, he just regularly oversaw the conduct of his business. When Seneca refers to receivables in his writings, he only uses a metaphor to illustrate his philosophical statements. His readers understood the analogy because it referred to a very current practice in their days.

In the Roman Empire, borrowing money to finance a business transaction and purchasing goods on credit was commonplace, if not customary. Two situations, one literary and the other legal, clearly illustrate this phenomenon. In one of his letters to Lucilius, Seneca reminded:

---

[1] Seneca, *De beneficiis* 5.22.1. All translations from Latin are my own. Unless otherwise indicated, all dates in this article refer to years of the Christian era.

[2] Tacitus, *Annals* 13.42.4; 14.52-56. Cassius Dio, *Roman History* 61.10.3. Hopkins Keith, "Rome, Taxes, Rents and Trade", in *Journal of Ancient History*, 6/7, 1995, p. 41-7; "Taxes and Trade in the Roman Empire (200 B.C.-A.D. 400)", *The Journal of Roman Studies*, 70, 1980, p. 101-125. Maddison Angus, *Contours of the World Economy, 1-2030 AD. Essays in Macro-Economic History*, University Press, Oxford, 2007, p. 43-47; p. 50, table 1.10; p. 54, table 1. 12.

"In order to be able to do business, you have to find a loan".[3] Moreover, thanks to the consensual purchase and sale contract (*emptio-uenditio*), classical Roman law recognised the faculty of separating in time the delivery of the item purchased and its payment. The two operations did not need to be simultaneous as in earlier sales processes.[4] In this context, two categories of creditors can be distinguished in particular: moneylenders and the vendors of a good or service.

Having receivables were a common feature in the Roman business world, to the point of potentially revealing a structural fragility of the economy, so great was the burden of debt. In another letter, written shortly before AD 65, Seneca confirmed this paradox.[5]

Despite his receivables, a Roman citizen could, himself, be deeply in debt. Because of this arithmetical phenomenon, in AD 33 the economic situation in the Roman Empire was so precarious that emperor Tiberius imposed on individuals a maximum debt to credit ratio that could not exceed 50%.[6]

Since Roman bankers did not practice investment lending, notwithstanding the needs of numerous economic players[7], rich individuals with excess liquidity engaged in this activity. According to Cicero, a half-century before Seneca, bankers sometimes matched lenders with borrowers. For his own era, Seneca referred to such intermediaries or other brokers in general terms as *proxeneta*. Almost a century later, the jurist Ulpian (c. 170-223) would use the same word to specify the function and responsibilities of the same group of people.[8] For at least three centuries of Roman history, agents brought together persons needing capital for their business affairs with others willing to lend it to

---

[3] Seneca, *Epistulae* 20.119.1.
[4] Gaius, *Institutes* 3.141. Accarias Calixte, *Précis de droit romain*, Paris, Cotillon, 1871; edition consulted, Paris, Cotillon et Cie, 1874, Vol. 2, p. 430, § 601. Girard Paul-Frédéric, *Manuel élémentaire de droit romain*, Paris, Arthur Rousseau, 1896; edition consulted, Paris, Arthur Rousseau, 1898, p. 523. Zimmermann Reinhard, *The Law of Obligation, Roman Foundations of the Civilian Tradition*, Oxford, Oxford University Press, 1996, p. 230-270. Birks Peter, *The Roman Law of Obligations*, Oxford, Oxford University Press, 2014, p. 60-95.
[5] Seneca, *Epistulae, Epistulae* 87.7.
[6] Minaud Gérard, *La comptabilité à Rome*, Lausanne, Presses Polytechniques Universitaires Romandes, 2005, p. 220-221, § 381-382.
[7] Andreau Jean, *La vie financière dans le monde romain. Les métiers de manieurs d'argent (IVᵉ siècle av. J.-C.-IIIᵉ siècle apr. J.-C.)*, Rome, École française de Rome, 1987, p. 667-668.
[8] Cicero, *De officiis* 3.14.59. Ulpian, *Digest* 50.14.

them. Thereafter, this process probably made its way to Constantinople, since the analyses of Ulpian regarding *proxeneta* are found in the *Digest*, the famous compilation of Roman law drawn up at the behest of the emperor Justinian in the 6th century for use in his empire.

Historical indicators to reconstruct an image of the economy in the Roman world suggest that the material environment of this time was fully compatible with the modern notions of factoring and factor. Unfortunately, no immediate conclusion is possible about their existences in imperial Rome. Ancient sources actually paint an intense and dynamic picture of financial exchanges and flows occurring throughout Roman antiquity, but for this entire period there is no direct information about the treatment of receivables held until maturity in spite of their sizeable volume.

What was going on? Were the Romans forced to wait patiently for the dates recorded on their payment schedule to recover their liquidities? This question is not a convoluted theoretical view; more recent European historical contexts justify it, for example, in France.

Since 1804, a conventional transfer of receivables is absolutely lawful in France on the basis of Article 1689 and the twelve following ones of the Civil Code. Previously, it was impossible: one must nevertheless remember that prior to that time, ancient law had not envisaged this procedure. In the 17th century, the great French jurist Pothier affirmed this unambiguously:

> A debt claim being a personal right of the creditor, right inherent in his person, it cannot, as per the subtlety of the law, be transferred to another person, nor consequently can it be sold. It may, however, be passed on to the creditor's heir because the heir is the successor to the person and to all the personal obligations of the deceased, but according to the subtlety of the law, it cannot be passed on to a third party because the debtor is obligated to a certain person and cannot, by a transfer of a debt not of his making, become the debtor of another.[9]

The absolute rule upheld by Pothier is in fact an echo of earlier provisions of Roman law.[10] This detail is important in a diachronic analysis of factoring and its actors because it highlights a gap between the law of the Romans and the financing of their economy.

---

[9] Pothier Robert-Joseph, *Traité du contrat de vente selon les règles tant du for de la conscience que du for extérieur*, Paris, Debure, Paris – Orléans, Veuve Rozeau-Montaut, 1773, tome 2, p. 68, § 550.

[10] Doneau Hugues, *Commentaria juris civilis*, Frankfurt, 1589-1596, lib. 15, c. 44, No. 5. Savigny Friedrich Carl von, *System des heutigen römischen Rechts*, Berlin, Veit, 1840-1849, III, §105, No. 5.

Roman businessmen obviously faced a paradox. The requirements of ancient law made it impossible for them to convert the financial belongings at their disposal in the form of receivables into liquidity at any time; yet these were nevertheless considered to be intangible assets according to the classification of Gaius, the eminent law professor of the second half of the 2nd century.[11] This ancient situation was so singular that it drew the attention of several French and German jurists throughout the second half of the 19th century[12], even inspiring several theses. What emerged is that nothing was set in stone. Well before the establishment of the Empire, in the late centuries of the Republic, innovations were introduced to refinance receivables.[13] Later, imperial chanceries would perfect these legal institutions and go almost so far as to create financial instruments, while the tragic political crisis of the 3rd century spread.

I. The Refinancing of Receivables

For Roman jurists, receivables were obligations created between two parties; that is to say, a temporary right intended to expire upon the performance of an agreed service. This temporary quality does not hold true of property, which, on the contrary, is a perpetual right. Another

---

[11] Gaius, *Institutes* 2.14.

[12] Bigot Julien-Armand, *De la cession de créance en droit romain et en droit français*, Paris, J.-B. Gros, 1854. Cambon-Lavalette Jules, *De la cession de créance en droit romain et en droit français*, Toulouse, Bayret, Pradel & Cie, 1858. Malecot Louis-Aristide, *De la cession de créance en droit romain et en droit civil*, Paris, Paris, 1868. Berland Claude, *De la cession de créance en droit romain*, Aix, Makaire, 1870. Pignerol Adrien, *De la cession de créance en droit romain et en droit français*, Paris, Pichon-Lamy, 1870. Gérard Paul, *De la cession de créance en droit romain et en droit français (procuratio in rem suam)*, Paris, N. Blanpain, 1873. Garraud René, *De la nature juridique de la cession de créance en droit romain et du paiement des dettes héréditaires*, Paris, Pichon, 1873. Gide Paul, "Du transport des créances en droit romain", in *Revue de législation française et étrangère, ancienne et moderne*, 1874, p. 33-71. Beauregard Paul-Victor, *Du paiement avec subrogation, ses origines en droit romain*, Paris, A. Parent, 1876. Gide Paul, *Études sur la novation et le transport de créances en droit romain*, Paris, Larose, 1879. Sureau Gustave, *De la cession de créance en droit romain et en droit civil français*, Paris, N. Blanpain, 1878. Charoy Albert, *De la cession de créance en droit romain. De la Transmission des titres en droit français*, Poitiers, Oudin Frères, 1880. Crevoisier Rémi-Jules-Henri de, *De la cession de créance en droit romain : de la subrogation légale en droit français*, Paris, G. Crépin-Leblond, 1882. Paulmier Edgard, *De la subrogation réelle en droit romain et en droit français*, Orléans, G. Jacob, 1882. Eisele Fridolin, *Die actio utilis des Cessionars: Festschrift für J. W. von Planck d. Juristenfacultät zu Freiburg*, Freiburg, Mohr i.Br, 1887. Demangeat Adolphe, *De la cession de créance : droit romain. De la juridiction en matière de prises maritimes : droit des gens*, Paris, Giard, 1890.

[13] Girard Paul-Frédéric, *op. cit.*, p. 714.

distinction reinforces this difference between property and receivables: property can be transferred from one person to another, whereas receivables form an obligation between two specific persons. As a consequence, the creditor cannot, on his sole initiative, transfer this obligation to a third party: in other words, he cannot assign receivables.[14] At this stage of legal development, the concept of factoring is not possible in the Roman uses. Gaius did not allow for any exemption to this principle except in the form of a legal fiction through the heir, who inherits a debt from a deceased creditor.[15] In his *Institutes*, after having presented the different modes for transferring property, Gaius specified clearly this point:

> However they were contracted, obligations cannot be transferred in these ways. If I really wish that what a third party owes me should be owing to you, we cannot achieve this by any of the modes whereby tangible assets are transferred.[16]

The analysis Gaius provided in these few words was probably already several hundred years old at the time he wrote it. For a very long time, the principle invoked fulfilled the needs of the inhabitants of Rome, who were initially focused on Latium and Italy, but it ultimately posed an obstacle to the economic expansion around the Mediterranean and even beyond. It became imperative to find a legal solution enabling the refinancing of receivables. In order to do so, new appropriate and licit procedures were required. Such novelties appeared, but it is impossible to say whether they arose out of practice or from a theoretical reflection.

The general development of Roman law would have an impact on the management of receivables by introducing a written procedure alongside the traditional solemn, formalistic and oral procedure. While the simple substitution of persons on a private basis would come to be accepted and widely practised, it nevertheless also gave rise to the contracts of mandate.

The Change of Creditor

In the early Roman tradition, receivables were personal obligations between the parties. In fact, the Latin word *nomen* ultimately would come

---

[14] Girard Paul-Frédéric, *op. cit.*, p. 711. Accarias Calixte, *op. cit.*, tome 2, p. 537.
[15] Maynz Charles-Gustave, *Cours de droit romain*, Brussels, Librairie polytechnique d'A. Decq – Paris, A. Durand, 1859; edition consulted (3rd), 1870, Vol. 1, p. 283, § 95. Petit Eugène, *Traité élémentaire de droit romain*, Paris, A. Rousseau, 1892; edition consulted (5th) 1906, p. 568.
[16] Gaius, *Institutes* 2, 38.

to mean both "name" and "entry in a debt ledger". How, then, should a creditor be enabled to use his receivables as soon as possible without changing their maturity dates or their objects as regard the debtors? The interest was not only to get cash from receivables, but also to use them to make donations or attach them to dowries.

It was impossible to create at one and the same time a debt based on an existing debt without retiring it, and to create a new contract identical in every way to the one already in existence.[17] To clear a contract, a new, different one was needed. In such a case, one had to retire an earlier debt by creating a new one. To create such a novation, several conditions were required: the existence of a former obligation, a new obligation based on a formal contract, the intention to retire the old obligation, an unchanged amount of debt, and above all, a new element. Failing that, there would only have been the addition of a new obligation to the first one.[18]

In order to assign receivables, the procedure first conceived was to bring in a new creditor to replace the initial one, without passing on the original credit to the assignee in question. The initial creditor, as the assignor, procured a new debt for the assignee with the same purpose as his own. He would delegate his debtor to the assignee, making the former promise henceforth to fulfil his undertakings exclusively to the assignee. The debtor was not, however, required to accept this. In that case, the novation was impossible; in order to create one, the consent of the assignor who thereby lost his debt claim was required, as well as the consent of both the debtor and the assignee. This was a verbal procedure, and Ulpian in fact mentions recourse to an oral contract, or stipulation, for creating a novation.

By changing creditors, there was a novation of the debt, or, in Latin, *nouatio*. Only the new debt would exist, the former one being retired, removing any future legal demand of payment. Ulpian confirmed this quite clearly.[19]

Novation provided the initial creditor the same financial advantage as an assignment, but the two operations were not entirely equivalent. First, the novation could not take place without the consent of the debtor. Furthermore, the sureties (mortgages, pledges, securities) and the

---

[17] Pomponius, *Digest* 45.1.18. Ulpian, *Digest* 45.1. 58. Gide Paul, *op. cit.*, p. 85-97.
[18] Fresquet Raymond-Frédéric de, *Traité élémentaire de droit romain*, Paris, Maresq et Dujardin, 1852, tome 2, p. 316. Girard Paul-Frédéric, *op. cit.*, p. 678-679. Accarias Calixte, *op. cit.*, Vol. 2, p. 684-685. Ulpian, *Digest*, 46, 2, 6. Florentinus, *Digest* 46. 2.16. Florentinus, *Digest*, 46.2.28.
[19] Ulpian, *Digest*, 46.2.1. pr; 46.2.8.5. Girard Paul-Frédéric, *op. cit.*, p. 684.

Getting Cash from Receivables in Ancient Rome 91

exceptions borne by the original obligation were not taken up in the new one, since the parties were different.[20]

The sources remain silent as to the consideration that the assignee paid to the assignor, any funds advanced and the risks taken, since the sureties attached to the initial debt had disappeared.

Novation was intended not only to change creditor, but it could also introduce a new debtor. In both cases, this was a matter of *novatio inter nouas personas* as opposed to a *nouatio inter easdem personas*, whereby the parties remained the same but only the terms of the obligation were changed.[21] This new legal framework is far from factoring, but it begins to admit the possibility by modifying the links between a creditor and a debtor.

The Contract of Mandate

The evolution of Roman law would offer a second solution for transferring receivables to a third party. A profound change came about between the years 150 and 120 BC, with the *lex Æbutia*. This law allowed for the introduction of written formulas in legal proceedings while at the same time avoiding a strict oral and gestural formalism where the least error could lead to the loss of a case. Whereas for centuries taking legal action on behalf of another person had been impossible except in limited cases such as freedom, guardianship or on behalf of the people, thanks to the new formal procedure, a contract of mandate was finally allowed.[22]

Thanks to this procedural innovation, the creditor could henceforth appoint a person acting in his name, a *cognitor in rem suam*. This authorised representative became an assignee by paying the creditor an advance on the sums he would himself recover at a later time. Fortunately, a text drawn up in AD 242 sets out the details of this mechanism.[23]

The *cognitor* and the *procurator* were designated by separate procedures. The *cognitor*, whether present or not, was designated orally before a magistrate by the two parties in person. Gaius' presentation of the terms used at the time shows that they were solemn and well established. If necessary, it was even possible to use Greek. The *procurator*,

---

[20] Papinian, *Digest* 13.1.17. Ulpian, *Digest* 13.7.4.
[21] Girard Paul-Frédéric, *op. cit.*, p. 680-682.
[22] Gaius, *Institutes*, 4.30; *Institutiones* 2.10.
[23] Gaius, *Institutes* 2.39. Ulpian, *Digest* 3.3.25; 3.3.55. *The Code of Justinian* 4.10.1. Eisele Fridolin, *Cognitur and procuratur. Untersuchungen zur Geschichte der processualen Stellvertretung*, Freiburg and Tübingen, C. B. Mohr, 1881.

by contrast, was designated without any formalities. Before becoming an authorised representative, he was probably an administrator with general competence.[24]

Certain persons could not be designated as *cognitor* or *procurator*. The Praetor, the magistrate responsible for rendering justice, decided which persons could not plead on their own behalf or on behalf of anyone else. In the first category, there were young people under seventeen years of age, as well as deaf-mutes, who could not take part in an oral procedure. In the second category were women, the blind, persons exposed to infamy, and later on, soldiers. Logically, criminals could not serve as *cognitor* or as *procurator*: no one could represent them in their infamy.[25]

In a contract of mandate, the assignee retained all sureties linked to the debt, unlike in a *nouatio*. Nevertheless, the contract of mandate was highly useful in launching legal proceedings before a magistrate. The *cognitor* or *procurator* was designated with full legal effect to sue the debtor on behalf of his principal, the assignor, but only for his own advantage.[26] To do so, it was necessary to wait for the debt maturity date.

Once the debt came due, a procedure was launched before a magistrate that unfolded in several phases. With the formulary procedure, the magistrate designated to hear the case issued a formula providing all the details of the future court case. The document began with the *intentio litis*, summing up the claimants' demands. Next, in the *litis contestatio*, he enjoined the judge expressly named to preside at the trial to condemn the debtor. In the case of a contract of mandate, the *intentio litis* was made in the name of the initial creditor, whereas later, the condemnation would be drawn up to the benefit of the person acting for him, that is, in the name of the assignee. To prevent the case from expiring, the judge designated in the formula to hear the dispute, had ten months to render a decision according to Gaius. At the end of the procedure, the *cognitor* or the *procurator in rem suam* could be dispensed from having to render accounts to the assignor, and as soon as the formula was drawn up, he became the *dominus litis*, the master of the proceedings, that is, the

---

[24] *Theodosian Code* 7.2.12. Gaius, *Institutes* 4.83. *Vatican Fragments* 317-318. Girard Paul-Frédéric, *op. cit.*, p. 995. Gaius, *Institutes*, 4, 84.

[25] *Digest* 3. 1. 1. 5; 3.1.1.6; 3.1.1.11; 3.1.1.3; 3.1.3.3; 3.3.43 pr. *The Code of Justinian* 2.12.7. Accarias Calixte, *op. cit.*, Vol. 2, p. 1287, § 932.

[26] Cantin-Cumyn Madeleine, Cumyn Michelle, "La notion de biens", in Silvio Normand (ed.), *Mélanges offerts au professeur François Frenette. Études portant sur le droit patrimonial*, Québec, Presses de l'université de Laval, 2006, p. 127-150, esp. p. 131.

applicant. From that time on, the principal could no longer revoke the *cognitor* or the *procurator*.[27]

The contract of mandate seems more sophisticated than novation, but it nevertheless had its limitations, one voluntary, and the other natural. The assignor could revoke the contract of mandate, and his death cancelled it. In both cases, the assignee had no more rights to the debt claim.

This process of substitution to assign receivables appears to have had a major disadvantage – it was very slow. The longer a case took to reach a conclusion, the greater the risk of seeing its outcome change. To improve monetary circulation, and consequently encourage economic exchanges, more guarantees had to be given to those who bought receivables. The imperial authority seemed to be moving in this direction, willing to go so far as to create reliable financial tools. Henceforth, the modern historian can find some aspects of factoring in the Roman law.

II. Financial Instruments

Transfers of receivables probably played an important economic role, for several imperial constitutions of the 2nd and 3rd centuries completed the legal rules governing them. Indirectly, this development revealed all the legal difficulties encountered over the centuries in using this act, both ordinary and frequent. If this financial process had in fact been exceptional, it probably would not have attracted the attention of the chancellery in order to perfect it. Progressive improvements were made to try to provide more security to the assignees and limit potential abuses. This evolution of monetary and financial uses is not a specific feature of the Roman world; during the 20th century, a similar legal concern guided the growth of factoring. In the Roman world, law changed to incorporate financial uses obtained from practical experiences favouring the movement of claims. In the modern world, states adapt their national laws to admit factoring, for it is already a widespread technique in countries who have become indispensable business partners.

The Security of the Assignee

The authorised representative or assignee had to wait for the *litis contestatio* to inform the debtor of his right to the receivables he held.

---

[27] Gaius, *Institutes* 4.104. Accarias Calixte, *op. cit.*, Vol. 2, p. 1287-1288, § 933. Fresquet Raymond-Frédéric de, *op. cit.*, tome 2, p. 206.

His ability to act was reduced solely to the actions of the assignor in accordance with the contract of mandate entrusted to him. Several situations increasingly caused concern on the part of the imperial authorities.

The assignee was not protected from dishonest acts, since his rights were fixed definitively only after the *intentio litis* had been drafted, once the maturity date was reached. The assignor still held the debt claim and a direct action against its debtor. The creditor could always receive the payment of the sum due, remit it or assign it once again. A constitution of the emperor Gordian III, with an uncertain chronology dated to June 239, would offer guarantees to the assignee while also defining the rights of the assignor. This text is clear and unambiguous:

> The emperor Augustus Gordian to Marcianus. If the delegation was not declared to your debtor, and given that action remains within your power despite your demands made to your creditor to act against him in payment, there is nothing to prevent you from demanding your due from your debtor and thus from prohibiting your creditor to recover from him as long as no proceedings have been initiated, he has not accepted any of the debt and has not notified your debtor to pay into his hands […] Given on the 5th of the ides of June, under the Consulship of Gordian and Aviola.[28]

In practice, this notification, a *denuntiatio*, was issued by questioning the interested person and setting out the facts before witnesses.[29] Private testimonies were then inscribed on wax tablets, sealed, and stored away.

In case of the death of the assignor or of his decision to revoke the contract of mandate, the situation was a delicate one for the assignee as well since he would lose all his interest in the matter. Imperial law would modify, in several stages, the provisions in force in order to limit such effects.

Another constitution of the emperor Gordian III, a bit later than the one previously mentioned, given in April 242, would strengthen the assignee's rights. If the latter could not benefit from the actions of the mandate, or *actiones mandatae*, he would preserve them in terms of "useful actions", that is to say, actions granted because of their usefulness and not under the strict application of the rule governing them. This development was slow because before it was allowed for credits, *actio utilis* had first of all been useful for transmissions globally and for sales of

---

[28] *The Code of Justinian* 8. 41(42).3.
[29] Boyé André-Jean, *La denuntiatio introductive d'instance sous le Principat*, Bordeaux, Y. Caderet, 1922, p. 122-154, esp. p. 128 and p. 126 (note 15).

inheritances under Antoninus Pius, emperor from 138 to 161, some 80 years earlier.[30] Without being its principal object, the text clearly reveals the details of an assignment of receivables.

> August Gordian to Valeria. You state that in exchange for a certain sum of money given to the person you mention, the latter transferred to you the rights to the mandate against a debtor, and that before launching judicial proceedings to recover the debt, the said creditor who fulfilled his task died without heir. If that is the case, you are entitled to invoke useful action. Given on the 5th of the calends of May, during the Consulship of Atticus and of Praetextatus.[31]

According to Ulpian and a constitution of the emperors Diocletian and Maximian dating from 294, the assignee, having recourse to *actio utilis*, acted apparently in his own name as he did in *nouatio*, and no longer in the name of the assignor by virtue of *actiones mandatae*.[32]

Just before the middle of the 3rd century, a Roman assignee who held a contract of mandate could, by diligent effort, have a guarantee of holding in his own hands the debt claim that had been assigned to him. All he had to do was inform the debtor of his rights. Moreover, he no longer lost his entitlement in case of the death or bad faith of his assignor, who could discreetly revoke the contract of mandate or collect the debt. As regards the assignee, the contract of mandate became as certain as novation.

Despite all these precautions, other abuses could sometimes arise in respect of outstanding receivables.

Prohibiting Abuses

With the experience of centuries and the needs of the day, formal rules were increasingly adopted in Ancient Rome to regulate the assignment of receivables. These constraints were even further reinforced in the 3rd century, despite the military anarchy in progress. Since law is intended for humankind, human turpitude would ultimately come to trouble the carefully elaborated legal framework.

As it became easier to get cash from receivables, abuses soon made an appearance. However, the necessary substantive rules were gradually introduced, aimed at both the quality of the parties involved and that of the assigned receivables, without forgetting the speculators.

---

[30] *Digest* 2.14.16.
[31] *The Code of Justinian* 4.10.1.
[32] *Digest* 3.3.55. *The Code of Justinian* 4.15.5.

The Powerful

The first legal obstacles put in place to prevent excesses appeared a few years after the constitution of the emperor Gordian III given in 242. Between 268 and 270, the emperor Claudius Gothicus banned persons of influence from holding the function of *procurator*, in order to protect the humbler free men. This provision is known only indirectly through a constitution of the emperors Diocletian and Maximian that reinforced it in 293.[33]

The effect of this ban probably faded away over time, since in 422, the emperors Honorius and Theodosius II prohibited, on pain of nullity, the assignment of receivables to a more powerful person. The terms chosen in their constitution are rather virulent:

> The emperors Honorius and Theodosius to John, Praetorian Prefect. If rights of this type are transferred to influential persons, the creditors shall be condemned to lose their receivables. The voracity of creditors is clear and manifest, by entrusting the subsequent stages of their rights to cash collectors. Given on the 5th of the ides of July in Ravenna, during the 13th Consulship of Augustus Honorius and the 10th of Augustus Theodosius.[34]

In 538, Justinian would extend this ban and its consequences to all guardians and trustees. He prohibited them from serving as assignees for persons whose property they had previously administered.[35]

The spirit of each of these two prohibitions would not remain exclusive to Roman and later Byzantine law but would be found clearly expressed in France in the Civil Code of 1804, in Articles 1597 and 450 respectively. Moreover, one of the Code's draftsmen, Maleville, noted this fact.[36]

Contested Debts

From the year 380, not all receivables could be assigned. A constitution of the emperors Gratian, Valentinian, and Theodosius I prohibited assignments of receivables in the event of dispute. A constitution of the emperor Justinian would reinforce this prohibition in 532.[37]

---

[33] *The Code of Justinian* 2.13(14).1.
[34] *The Code of Justinian* 2.13(14).2.
[35] *Novellae* 72 c. 5.
[36] Maleville Jacques de, *Analyse raisonnée de la discussion du Code civil au Conseil d'État*, Paris, Vve Nyon- Lenormant-Vve Dufresne, 1805, tome 1, p. 453-454.
[37] *The Code of Justinian* 8.36(37).3. *The Code of Justinian* 8.36(37).5(4).

The Speculators

In the early 6th century, the market for the assignment of receivables had apparently attracted speculators. Some of them had made a business out of buying up receivables at a price lower than their nominal value, while entertaining the hope of recovering the full amount at a later date. A constitution of the emperor Anastasius dated 506 gives a glimpse of this situation. The text sought to put an end to the practice and to discourage those who were profiting from the financial needs of the assignors. Based on Anastasius' decision, the debtor was allowed to repay solely the amount actually paid for the purchase of his debt, potentially increased by the interest due:

> The emperor Anastasius to Eustachius, Praetorian Prefect. There is no doubt that by "buyers of others' receivables" is meant those who wish such assignments to end up in their favour. For this reason, we order by this law that in the future, such a practice may no longer take place. That is to say, if anyone has made such an assignment for a given price, he shall be allowed to carry out the rights purchased solely for the amount of the sum paid plus interest, even if the name of the sale has been registered as an assignment […] Given on the 10th of the kalends of August, during the Consulship of Arovindus and of Messalus.[38]

A few decades later, Justinian would recall this text to extend it to donations. The spirit of Anastasius' constitution is found today in Articles 1536 and 1537 of the Spanish Civil Code.[39]

III. Conclusion

While over the centuries the Romans perfected the circulation of receivables, this movement did not concern the professional money handlers at all. However, there were probably no large financial institutions in Ancient Rome. Bankers carried out their trade in a stall where passers-by could see piles of registers and tablets. Some more modest ones only had a table set up in the street. Thus, while the circulation and trade in receivables eluded these professionals, individuals by contrast found solutions for trading and financing these instruments among themselves.

---

[38] *The Code of Justinian* 4.35.22.1.
[39] Cuadrado Perez Carlos, *La cesión de créditos*, Madrid, Editorial Dykinson, 2014, p. 17.

Incidents and court proceedings in respect of such practices must have been numerous since the imperial authorities constantly sought to improve the legal framework for assignments of receivables. Their attention was such that they came close to professionalising the procedure, while the professionals of the financial world had overlooked it.

In the more advanced stages of Roman law, the assignee of receivables had the capacity to substitute himself immediately for the assignor and could use all legal means to recover the debt at its maturity without it becoming litigious. For his part, the debtor was protected from arbitrary recovery actions.

Most of the necessary legal bases for factoring existed at that time; however, the lack of real financial institutions in the Roman Empire, and the political collapse of this age-old world postponed the emergence of this practice for several centuries.

7. Factors in the Middle Ages, Credit and Society at the Dawn of a New Profession

Armand JAMME
Research Director, CNRS[1]

Enza Russo
Professor of Literature, Higher Institute Turin

"I know your concerns very well: you like selling a lot of wheat at a high price, protecting yourself by a letter, a pledge, or a security; buying low and selling high, going on usury and deceiving people, then making of one, two devils… because Hell is too deserted"! Three centuries before Shakespeare, who, as Shylock in the *Merchant of Venice*, draws a portrait of a usurer so acquisitive and merciless in justice, Rutebeuf criticised, in similar terms, the greed and amorality of the middle-class in the capital of the French kingdom.[2] For someone who does not know the doctrinal thoroughness of society at this time, Rutebeuf's verses could lead one to think that anything was allowed, and to imagine that morality was reduced to nothing, in other words, that here was the real ground of the most absolute liberalism. It is therefore important to point out that the author was a strong protester, one of the more critical lay writers of this society that the 13th century has revealed.

In the course of the century before, when Europe entered a long phase of economic growth, significantly marked by the revival of international trade, a great part of the activities that are now the ones found in current factoring could obviously do nothing but develop themselves. If we define factoring as a credit function based on the transfer of debts, involving services of a banking nature (finance, insurance against outstanding payments, recovery of debts, etc.), it is clear that it did not exist in the Middle Ages as a constituted job or business. However, its origins are obviously there, as all over Europe there were numerous individuals

---

[1] Pages 99-108 have been written above all by Armand Jamme, pages 108-113 above all by Enza Russo.
[2] *Nouvelle complainte d'Outremer*, in *Œuvres complètes*, Paris, (ed.) Zink Michel, 2 vol., 1989-90.

called factors from the 13th century onwards. This process of conjunction between practice and terminology is, nonetheless, not clear.

What we are going to try here, is to delineate the development of factoring, coming first to the context in which the term appears, then presenting the socioeconomic structures of the expansion of factoring and debates it generated in the last centuries of what we call by convention the Middle Ages. If, in these times, a factor could fulfill various missions, more and more in business, and above all in companies considered as multinationals exercising real professionalised functions, the origins of factoring are unmistakeable, although different from those carried out today by factors.

I. Economic Growth and Christian Society

The relationship between economic theory and economic practice is one of the questions most discussed by medieval historiography, especially when related to credit. The traditional position tends to be that the ecclesiastical conception of credit was totally unsuitable for economic development and constantly behind the times. Another position supports that the ecclesiastical production of norms had an influence on economic practice, as they were promoting those considered as licit and limiting those that were morally suspicious. The clerks' theoretical reflections nevertheless supplied a series of abstract categories, contributing to an understanding of economic phenomena and directing their development.[3]

The techniques of partnership, were based as much on international maritime trade as on local production and commerce, and presented, in medieval times, strong similarities to that of the Roman *societates*. It has long been known that medieval civil lawyers barely consulted the *Corpus Iuris civilis* of Justinian in the discussion they had about partnership in their time. But the origins of what was called the *commenda* contract, used both in land and maritime trade, does not seem to be solely found in the Roman *nauticum fenus* et *societas*, but also in Jewish, Byzantine and Muslim experiences of partnership.[4]

---

[3] Todeschini Giacomo, *I mercanti e il tempio. La società cristiana e il circolo virtuoso della ricchezza fra Medioevo ed Età Moderna*, Bologna, 2002; Id., *Ricchezza francescana: dalla povertà volontaria alla società di mercato*, Bologna, 2004; Id., *Come Giuda. La gente comune e i giochi dell'economia all'inizio dell'epoca moderna*, Bologna, 2011.

[4] Pryor John H., *The origins of the Commenda contract*, in *Speculum* 52 (1977), p. 5-37; Ceccarelli Giorgio, *Denaro e profitto a confronto: le tradizioni cristiana e islamica nel Medioevo*, Milano, 2008.

Two main forms of contracts were in use in the Mediterranean medieval world. In the *commenda* contract, the investor provided capital and bore all financial risks for one limited operation; he was then rewarded with ¾ of the profits, while the travelling partner, who furnished labour and of course marketing expertise, received around ¼ of the profits. In the *societas* contract or *compagnia*, there was a joint, unlimited liability of a longer duration: partners shared profits and losses. But there was great flexibility between both types of contract: in the naming (in Genoa a *commenda* contract was called *societas maris*, in Venezia *colleganza*), in the profit share (the dividing line between the two not always having been sharply drawn), and in the way of writing them (a *commenda* contract could be considered a loan and then treated as usury).

The commonly recorded practice for credit was the recognisance, which entailed a purchase agreement and established the formal recognition of debt. In trade, various forms were used to avoid speaking of a credit contract promising, for example, future delivery of goods. It is generally considered that a great variety of merchandise was bought and sold on full credit: luxury items, raw materials and food. In a basic recognition of debt, the contractant confessed owing to the creditor a specific sum of money quoted in real coins or in money of account for particular goods, briefly described in qualitative but rarely in quantitative terms. This debt was often guaranteed with the obligation of one or several persons (*fidejussores*) and goods, and submitted to one or several jurisdictions, to give the creditor a legal recourse in case of default. The interest rate could be huge (it could be more than 30%) and depended on two components: first the incurred risk, very strong for maritime trade; secondly, the level of supply and demand of money in the place the loan was subscribed. If supply was high, the cost of money was less.[5] Other matters could be included in a loan agreement, particularly when dealing with powerful individuals who would require particular clauses.

As early as the 12th century, the practice of exchange permitted a borrower to obtain credit in the form of local coinage, allowed repayment in a different coinage, and at a different geographic location, developed to meet the needs of economic growth and evidently had an impressive effect on the European network of changers. Notarial contracts of exchange gave emphasis to the credit aspect of the operation, less on the real exchange, as the sum quoted was often expressed in the currency in which it had to be reimbursed. The guarantees were similar to those of

---

[5] Palermo Luciano, *La banca e il credito nel Medioevo*, Milano, 2008.

loans and recognitions of debt. The famous bill of exchange was, in fact, a holograph letter and for that reason, in contrast to the formal notarial instrument, its development was really slow: it can only be found, outside of Italy and Flanders maybe, at the end of the 14th century.[6] It is therefore very clear that if the bill of exchange accelerated financial exchanges, it played only a secondary role as a facilitating instrument, rather than a booster, in the expansion of exchange.

The last form of contracting to consider is insurance: it appears from the 11th century among the clauses of *commenda* contracts related to the *rischio di mare e di gente*, i.e. storms and pirates. But it could be older, as it seems the first type of insurance was a deposit by the carrier in the hands of the merchant, who gave it back after the goods arrival at its destination (a system found in 13th century Sicily). This means that the first insurers were, in reality, the ship's captains. The origins of insurance are not clear, partly due to the fact that Tuscan traders rarely used the skills of notaries for it. Historians therefore have to deduce the subscriptions of insurance from the account books, which nevertheless provides an image from the first decades of the 14th century of a high level of economic integration in some parts of Europe. In 1348, for example, the representative of the Alberti company in Napoli sent, towards Florence, some bottles of wine; but near Porto Pisano, the ship was attacked, and corsairs seized the cargo, which was partly insured. Two Genoese, who had settled in Naples, paid a modest sum to a Neapolitan banker to whom the Alberti had an account – revealing that the service was not very expensive and possibly common.[7] Such a case shows, of course, the high level of integration of the Italian financial mechanisms in the 13th-14th centuries.

Nevertheless, Medieval Europe developed in a complex economic environment, in which polymetallism and double monetary systems – the one fictitious, for accounts, the other real, a system due to the extreme diversity of cash – governed trade opportunities. On the other hand, as shown in the development of various forms of partnership and insurance, for a long time, Europe did not know the shackles of the Church dogma on which the historiography dwelt. Certainly, for the clerks, money should not produce money and, according to Aristotle's writings, earnings should only be the result of the man's work. Certainly, the canons of the councils repeatedly restated the necessary ban of interest-bearing

---

[6] De Roover Raymond, *L'évolution de la lettre de Change XIVe-XVIIIe s.*, Paris, 1953.
[7] *Due libri mastri degli Alberti. Una grande compagnia di Calimala 1348-1358*, Florence, (ed.) Goldthwaite Richard A., Settesoldi Enzo, Spallanzani Marco, 2 vol., 1995, p. XCV-CII.

loans on the grounds that giving free credit terms was a moral duty and that payment of interest was impoverishing the debtor. But historians inferred, a bit too hastily from all this, that credit in the Middle Ages had been given up to the Jews, and that the Christians who were involved in were putting themselves outside the community.

Research in social history has shown that medieval societies widely lived on credit. Lending, free or not, first of all had an inclusive function, whatever the social stratum considered. Etienne de Montdidier, son of a merchant of Orléans and councillor of the Parliament, had 117 acts of credit when he died in the middle of the 15th century, secured and not, with members of his family, craftsmen, traders, clients, etc.[8] Loan was an inherent part of professional activity. It was included in the relationships of the craftsman or the storekeeper with his customer, of the tenant with his owner, etc. Even in a small Provencal village like Trets, it has been proven that each of the 380 homes of the community had, between 1297 and 1348, seen a notary to borrow some money at least once.[9]

Secondly, the position of the Church on credit was significantly relaxed, proof of the development of a new economic thinking, integrating positive and negative aspects of the expansion of credit. The clerks understood the necessities of growth. They tried to moralise the practice of giving credit, initiating, for example, fruitful discussions on a fair price, but getting tough on the excesses of the credit market. They admitted that the capital advanced by way of a loan was by definition lacking to its holder (*lucrum cessans*), that it was sometimes at risk, and that the sum could be paid off at a distant place, all conditions which called for some compensation.[10] The elliptic statement of the loan contracts (the increase of the real sum initially advanced) was less the result of an ecclesiastical censorship than the desire to clearly express the true and definite terms of a contract.

Therefore, ecclesiastical legislation against interest-bearing loans became blurred after the middle of the 13th century. It concentrated on usury, particularly in the 14th century, which was affected by serious

---

[8] Claustre Julie, *Vivre à crédit dans une ville sans banque (Paris, XIV-XVe s.)*, in *Le Moyen Âge*, 119 (2013), p. 567-596.
[9] Drendel John, *Le crédit dans les archives notariales de Basse-Provence au début du XIVe s.*, in *Notaires et crédit dans l'Occident méditerranéen médiéval*, 2004, p. 279-304.
[10] Ceccarelli Giorgio, *Risky Business: Theological and Canonical Thought on Insurance from the Thirteenth to the Seventeenth Century*, in *Journal of Medieval and Early Modern Studies*, 31/3 (2001), p. 607-658; Kaye Joel, *Economy and Nature in the Fourteenth Century. Money Market Exchange and the Emergence of Scientific Thought*, Cambridge, 1998.

crises that stopped and reversed economic growth. But in this fight, the Church and political powers (i.e. cities and princes) came into conflict with public opinion, which sometimes ended up in violent riots. They did not provide a strong or united defence and did not clearly define what usury was (in Italy, the normative texts of the communes fixed the average around 15%, in France Philip the Fair declared in 1311 interest would be reprehensible after 20%), nor did they remove it. The fight against usury became less important in the 15th century, while in the 16th century legislation dealt accurately with the matter again.[11] In other words, sanctions against usury may seem merciless, but they have always been closely related to precise economic and social situations: their efficiency remained very low; it was both financial markets and more or less scrupulous borrowers, who governed credit.

II. Collecting Debts: Legal Problems, Social Issues

Indebtedness was a massive phenomenon in medieval times. Far from consolidating the monopoly of a more or less marginalised profession, it concerned all the economic actors and all levels of society. As a loan was generally made for a very short time, the debtors could easily fall into insolvency and over-indebtedness. But on the question of the collection of debts, medieval powers and societies introduced various judicial remedies, marks of the jurisdictional particularities of these times.

It is clear that the generalisation of credit urged public authorities to develop appropriate institutions to assure the confidence of creditors. They might resort to the appointment of a *procurator* to act on their behalf, with mandates directed at the recovery of all credit or for specific outstanding ones. Disputes over debts would lead to settlements *ex causa amicabilis compositionis*, eventually in front of a notary or a judge. But they could also set up various forms of constraint to prompt the cancellation of the debt: municipal authorities insisted on banishment in the North of France, in the south on the custom of the *ostagium* (consignment in the residence of the creditor), ecclesiastical courts on excommunication.

In 13th century Bologna, public denunciation of the insolvent debtor was preferred. This injurious treatment resulted from the complaint of a creditor against a debtor who had not repaid him in the planned term and had not answered to the convocation presented to its residence by the

---

[11] Baldwin John, *Masters, Princes and Merchants. The social views of Peter the Chanter and his circle*, Princeton, 1970.

judge. His name was then shouted in streets and on fairs and registered in a particular book, from which it could only be removed if he paid off the creditor and a fine to the judge. For a single half-year in 1250, 1041 inhabitants of the city and 558 countrymen were banished for debt in this way. The Bolognese documentation of the 13th century reveals loans going from 14 deniers up to 375 pounds, but almost ¾ of debts did not exceed 10 pounds, the price of an ox. In 10% of the cases, the accusatory creditor was not the one with whom the debt had been contracted, proof that a real market of claims' transfer existed, which could be considered as a form of legal currency, a market for which the most recurring actors were notaries.[12]

From the end of the 13th century, another tool for social constraint was developed against defaulters: excommunication, which is exclusion from Christian community and ecclesiastical communion. Only a cleric could impose such a sentence, not conceived as a pain or a punishment, but as a remedy and a penance. Yet, more and more creditors in the last two centuries of the Middle Ages turned to ecclesiastical courts, which threatened and then condemned failing debtors, a reality that contributed in the 16th century to Martin Luther's criticisms. There again, the lever of strain was honour, as the priests had to denounce the names of the excommunicated every Sunday, so that other members of the parish could avoid meeting them. Registers of absolution show the importance for the excommunicated to be freed from this sentence, especially before Easter, a symbolic feast of inclusion in the Christian community, both from a spiritual and social perspective, from which nobody wanted to be left behind.[13]

The moral doctrine excluded confinement for debt, which was considered initially as an abuse, but with the increase in cases of insolvency in the last decades of the 13th century, a reforming ordinance in France made jail the main instrument against debtors. The simultaneity between legal reversal (in 1303) and the beginnings of the long economic depression of the 14th century is striking. Montpellier's statutes give detailed explanations of the ways a creditor could act against defaulting debtors. In case of non-payment, a request for reimbursement had to be made before the local jurisdiction. Then, to avoid the debtor attempting to flee, the

---

[12] Gaulin Jean-Louis, *Les registres de bannis pour dettes à Bologne au XIIIe s.*, in *Mélanges de l'Ecole française de Rome-Moyen Âge* 109 (1977), p. 479-499.

[13] Beaulande Véronique, *Le malheur d'être exclu ? Excommunication, réconciliation et société à la fin du Moyen Âge*, Paris, 2006.

creditor could ask for the seizure of the person and his confinement until satisfaction or promise of satisfaction had been obtained.[14]

The jurisdiction of the Châtelet of Paris seems to have played a pioneer role in this matter, but the documentation we have reveals this only for the 15th century. Even here the victims were essentially ploughmen of the countryside, craftsmen and workers; it means that jail essentially affected the least solvent social categories. If we follow the register of 1488-89, three individuals were put into the jails of the Châtelet each day, which permanently had about twenty prisoners for debt, as much as in the 18th century when the Parisian population was three or four times higher. The turnover was important. To prove jail was really Hell, it should be remembered that half of the liberations occurred in less than two days and three quarters before a week. Confinement was to force the debtor to honour its commitments. A prisoner for debt could recover his freedom by obtaining cancelling royal letters (letters of respite), assigning goods or property to the creditor or to a third party for a new loan, concluding an agreement with the creditor for a deferred repayment, etc. For the prisoner, the discharge did not involve the extinction of the debt but generally transferred it to a new obligation. The creditor, in most cases, obtained repayment or promise of later satisfaction. The number of debtors freed on the same day of their arrest is a proof of the efficiency of the Châtelet de Paris, as an accelerator to getting debt relief. And just as in 13th century Bologna, notaries played a major role in the cession of claims. Since the royal decree of 1355 forbade any transfer of a debt to a powerful person or king's officer, claims passed through the writing of a "transport", sealed in the Châtelet (an act simply given to a third party was not enforceable anymore), a decision that increased the influence of notaries on transferring debts: they were the most capable for playing the role of brokers.[15]

Acts of cession of rights against debtors were numerous from the 13th century onwards. It means the act of credit had become a negotiable instrument. Cession of credit was a common practice among foreign merchants as it was a convenient means of clearing obligations. The creditor might have been willing to take a loss on the original debt and in this sense to discount the credit in favour of the new purchaser. That is what occurred in the case of the Metz bishop's debts. In 1237, they

---

[14] Reyerson Kathryn, *Business, Banking and Finance in Medieval Montpellier*, Toronto, 1985.

[15] Claustre Julie, *Dans les geôles du roi : l'emprisonnement pour dette à Paris à la fin du Moyen Âge*, Paris, 2007.

already amounted to the colossal sum of 9,200 marks (2,000 to citizens of Metz, 1,000 to Sienese merchants, 6,191 to Roman merchants, of whom one had to receive 2,300 marks). To get back these sums, Giovenale Manetti and his partners brought in the Apostolic See. But the bishop had numerous creditors, and some had very high social ranks (the King of Navarre, Count of Bar, Count of Juliers, etc.). The popes sent various negotiators to plan agreements for rescheduling of the debt, transferred from generation to generation until the end of the century.[16]

Methods to recover debts and repay obligations were obviously also tied to the financial system. The degree of negotiability of obligations, and the transferability of assets and credits, affected the means through which debts were repaid. Liquidating them with clearinghouse techniques based on deposit banking in Tuscany, and in the Champagne fairs in Bruges, permitted the cancelling of debts between clients of the same banker, or between clients of changers who carried mutual accounts. Changers were, among the specialists of medieval finance, the most closely linked with deposit banking because of their involvement in international trade. Around 1400 in Bruges, R. de Roover found that bank transfers outnumbered cash transactions in the changer's accounts.[17] This was already the case a century earlier in the main cities of Tuscany. The diffusion in the main financial places of these *scritti di banchi*, based on mutual accounts among the art of changers, facilitated transfer banking on behalf of their clients.

Many loans made to the princes were granted for free, a fact that led historians to consider that lenders received a counterpart in the form of privileges or concessions of taxes and pensions. But it is certain that from the 13th century the generalised indebtedness of cities and princes encouraged the development of more or less speculative markets of public debts. The general treasurer of King Alfonso the Magnanimous, Mateu Pujades, came, for example, to buy back their claims on third parties from traders who agreed to lend money to the monarchy; but he also requested the same creditors lend more, granting them new securities for their old loans with later terms, therefore being negotiable during a

---

[16] Jamme Armand, *De Rome à Florence, la curie et ses banquiers (XIIᵉ-XIIIᵉ s.)*, in *Die römische Kurie und das Geld*, (dir.) Maleczek Werner, Ostfildern, to be published in 2018.

[17] De Roover Raymond, *Money, Banking and Credit in Medieval Bruges: Italian merchants-bankers, Lombards and Money-Changers*, Cambridge Mass., 1948.

longer time.[18] It is highly probable that they asked for a percentage on the credit, as remuneration for service, quite similar to factoring nowadays.

III. Mediterranean Polysemy of a Word

In old French, a *faitor*, a *faitres* was above all a creator. The term was used in this sense from the middle of the 12th century at least, appearing repeatedly in the *Roman of Alexander*, the most widely distributed book in Europe after the Holy Bible. In texts of daily life, we find it appearing later, but this could be a consequence of the bad preservation of these documents before the 14th century. A factor was a person "in charge of a trade for another one".[19] Even if it is said to be stemming from the classical Latin *factor*, derived from the verb *facere*, it is more likely in this case a Frenchifying of the Italian term *fattore* that we must apply. Why?

In Italy as well the term *factore*, *facturi*, *fattor* denoted primarily as a maker, starting of course with the great architect, God himself, creator of all things, *fattore del cielo e della terra*. By extension, it referred to city founders, craftsmen, authors etc. even those who could commit a crime: *sarai tu lo fattore della mia morte*? But a factor was, moreover, at least from beginnings of the 13th century, a person who attends and substitutes an authority in the exercise of its duties: it appears in this sense in a treaty between Venice and the Aleppo's sultan in 1207-8. But the term also referred to the activities linked to various forms of management. Factors appear as administrators of domains, performing the function of butler for great lords, and as representatives abroad for merchants.

It is therefore possible to consider that this term, because it has been so polysemous, could not be used to designate a precise office: the word would have been too common to indicate an official function, inevitably defined on the basis of its typicality. Actually, *factor* did not appear in the legal lexicon, civil or canonical, of the delegation of authority, which preferred prosecutor, vicar, lieutenant, vice-gerens, etc. Italian literature from the 14th century highlights the intimate, domestic, and thus hierarchical relation between the factor and his superior, who entirely

---

[18] Russo Enza, *La tesoreria generale della Corona d'Aragona ed i bilanci del Regno di Napoli al tempo di Alfonso il Magnanimo (1416-1458)*, thesis València University, 2016.

[19] *Trésor de la langue française* : http://stella.atilf.fr/Dendien/scripts/tlfiv5/advanced.exe?8;s=1587662385.

dominated him.[20] To a certain extent the factor appears here as the "creator" of the one who appointed him to this function. Great lords always had their factors in big cities, that is merchants who took care to supply them with commodities to fulfil their redundancies; traders and companies sometimes appointed impressive numbers of representatives and employees, who were not all given this title. But in the 14th century, maybe because it had become current and particularly significant for the administrative functions carried out in the name of a third person, the term began to appear in the organisation of princely States.

Pandolfo III Malatesta, a condottiere who governed several towns between Brescia and Ascoli Piceno, appointed, in 1408-09, a factor to manage its court's expenses. Some decades later, the first duke of Este created a *Fattoria*, with responsibilities across Chancery and Treasury to improve government efficiency, two *fattori generali* in charge of the execution of payment orders. Even in the papal administration of the Patrimony of Saint-Peter, we meet, in 1466, factors of the Apostolic Chamber.[21] It is therefore not surprising to also find this title in other States, outside Italy, up to the frame of expeditions sent to New Spain! On the 17th of June 1527, five ships left Sanlúcar of Barrameda for Florida and among the officers who commanded that fleet was a *factor y veedor*, who had responsibility for attending to the cast iron metal and all the exchanges, collections, purchases, sales and payments related to the rights of the King of Castile.[22] However, it seems that the State dimension of the factor never left Mediterranean space.

In the British islands, the use of the term appeared quite late. Old English *factour* could be derived from the French of course, if we think about the great and perilous embrace which bound France and England during the Hundred Year's war. English documentation testifies to the liveliness of French language in the English aristocracy and the institutions they governed: did the King of England still not consider himself as King of France? But in England, *factour* appears only in use with an economic

---

[20] Dates of quotations are respectively 1292, 1333, around 1350 and 1342 (*Tesoro della Lingua Italiana delle Origini* (http://tlio.ovi.cnr.it/TLIO).

[21] Falcioni Anna, Ciambotti Massimo, *Il sistema contabile di Pandolfo III Malatesti e il Liber rationum curie del 1409*, in *Le pouvoir de compter et décompter. Genèses, formes et logiques des pratiques médiévales (XIII*e*-XV*e *siècle)*, (dir.) Jamme Armand, to be published in the Collection de l'EfR; Folin Marco, *Note sugli officiali negli Stati Estensi (sec. XV-XVI)*, in *Gli Officiali negli Stati Italiani del Quattrocento*, ed. Covini Nadia Maria, 1999, p. 99-154, p. 136; Archivio di Stato di Roma, Tesoreria del Patrimonio, No. 45.

[22] Cabeza de Vaca Alvar Nuñez, *Relation et commentaires*, Paris, Mercure de France, 1980, p. 39.

dimension: it was solely a person who bought and sold for others. The term therefore entered the English language directly in competition with an older one with Germanic ascendancy: a broker was the one who dealt with others' affairs for them: financial, commercial, marital, and even in certain cases dirtier transactions.[23] It is then possible to consider that *factour*, as other terms of the economic and financial English lexicon – let us think about the manager for example! – diverted directly from the organisational models of the great Italian companies.

IV. Factors in Medieval Companies

Italian companies, born on the basis of a *societas* contract, were undivided corporations including partners of the same status, almost always members of the same family. Already in the 13th century, they could develop several branches of the parent company in the main commercial places of France, Germany and England, the last submitted to a quasi-seizure of its economic resources by Italian traders after John Lackland's reign. But to limit the risks after a long series of more or less resounding bankruptcies in the decades 1290-1340, the structure of these companies started to change. Capital holders created new companies abroad, autonomous from the parent company, but participating in the overall activity: this structure called "holding company" (Roover), "system of companies" (Melis) or "partnership agglomerate" (Goldthwaite)[24], remained based on the activity of a man or a family, who also valued forms of association with limited liability, precise ends and determined times (*commenda*), to be present on various commercial areas.

All these employed different people: branch managers, accountants, notaries, errand boys, etc. But the documentation does not always make a clear distinction between these jobs, or even between partners and employees: the "Rothschild of the 13th century", the Bonsignori, had their *compagni fattori* at the Champagne fairs, such as another big boss had a *factore e discepulo*[25] 40 years later. This, evidences the extreme

---

[23] http://www.etymonline.com/index.php?allowed_in_frame=0&search=broker.
[24] De Roover Raymond, *Il Banco Medici dalle origini al declino (1397-1494)*, Firenze, 1970, p. 113; Melis Federico, *Aspetti della vita economica medievale. Studi nell'Archivio Datini di Prato*, Siena, 1962, p. 130-133; Goldthwaite, *The Economy of the Renaissance Florence*, 2009, p. 70.
[25] Respectively in 1279 and 1320: see *Tesoro della Lingua Italiana delle Origini* (http://tlio.ovi.cnr.it/TLIO) and Archivio di Stato di Firenze, Mercanzia 11299, fol. 86rv (thanks to C. Quertier).

diversity of statutes and partnerships within the company. When they had a management function abroad, factors had a general power of attorney delivered by one or several leaders of the company. They were salaried employees, i.e. paid independently from their financial results. The oath sworn on the Bible by a factor of the Salimbeni in 1282 retells their obligations: obviously he had to provide his accounting services, was not able to join or work for another company, another person or for himself or to receive presents on behalf of a third person; finally he promised to accede to a certain moral standard, forbidding cohabitation and gambling.[26]

The salary, which was variable, was fixed by the employer for indefinite duration and if he was dishonest his redundancy was easy. The most dynamic of them received premiums, and in times of crisis could keep their employment with reduced wages. Between 1310 and 1345, the Bardi used up to 346 factors, frequently for very short times. That of the Peruzzi employed 133 factors between 1331 and 1343 (88 for the one year in 1336), operating in Spain, England and the Maghreb.[27] In the second half of the century, with the crisis and the change of entrepreneurial structures, staff were less impressive: in 1348, the Alberti employed only 21 factors in Florence, Avignon, Naples and Bruges. It seems in 1371-72, the Lucchese companies would even had contented themselves with a pair of factors![28]

Nonetheless, factors remained the real backbone of the companies. Because of their intermediate position between the "maggiori", owners of the company, and the errand boys, they can be seen as middle managers.[29] During the first period, it was rare for factors to reach partner status: none among the employees of the Peruzzi; only five among the 346 employees of the Bardi! But after the trend reversal of the mid-14th century which

---

[26] Ed. by Sapori Armando, *Studi di storia economica (sec. XIII-XV)*, 2 vol., Firenze, 1955, Vol. 2, p. 762-3.

[27] Id., *Il personale delle compagnie mercantili nel medioevo, Ibid.*, p. 717-754.

[28] *Due libri mastri*, p. XLII and De Roover Raymond, *The Organisation of Trade*, in *The Cambridge Economic History of Europe, Volume 3: Economic Organisation and Policies in the Middle Ages*, Cambridge UP, 1963, p. 42-118, p. 106.

[29] Bullard Myriam M., *Middle managers and middlemen in renaissance banking*, in *Travail et travailleurs en Europe au Moyen Âge et au début des Temps Modernes*, Toronto, 1991, p. 273-275. In 1486, the *factor* in Lisbon of Bartolomeo Marchionni, linked to the Cambini family, had under his command two young florentine dealers and a dozen prosecutors (Igual Luis David, *Valencia e Italia en el siglo XV, Rutas, mercados y hombres de negocios en el espacio económico del Mediterráneo Occidental*, thesis València University, 1996, p. 348-9).

favoured the development of looser entrepreneurial structures, they began to be more and more numerous, as the Florentines Tommaso del Bene e Bernardo di Rabata, who worked first as factors and associated in the company of the Nero, which traded with Spain (1478-99).

The extension in Europe of big business dominated by Italians from the 12th-13th centuries tended to make their entrepreneurial model a reference point. Indeed, it had strong influences on the organisation of companies in the rest of Europe, through additional adaptations and reorganisations. In the 15th century Valencia, a factor working in a company, often of small size, was frequently a partner, even if he was operating in regions as distant as Brittany. In the company of the brothers Guerau and Joan Bou who traded with Flanders, the factor performed the functions of an accountant; elsewhere, he was called *negociador o administrador*, and sometimes he replaced the owner of a table of exchange or a shop, in the exercise of his daily duties.[30]

In 1415, the Florentine legislation on bankruptcy identified rather clearly the functions of factors, "prosecutors and business managers or disciples of companies and of their partners". Their powers could be proved by a public instrument appointing them to their function and by the account books of the company. The model then appeared unchanged from the 13th century, as shown in a sentence of the Court of the Mercanzia of Florence in 1426, which required the appearance in London in front of the commissioner, sent especially by the company of the Alberti of their factor here, to examine its accounts and administration.[31] It was then this model which was transmitted to the rest of Europe. To follow the Burgundian chronicler Georges Chastellain, the big trader Jacques Cœur, also *Grand Argentier* of King Charles VII, would have employed not less than 300 factors – a figure obviously exaggerated that must be divided by three at least! – who performed for him similar functions to those of Italian factors[32], just as the factors in London of the merchants of Burgos, whose networks were used by Spanish kings to communicate with their ambassadors in England.[33]

---

[30] Cruselles Gómez Enrique, *Hombres de negocios y mercaderes baomedievales valencianos*, thesis València University, 1996, p. 417, 419, 426-9.
[31] Archivio di Stato di Firenze, Mercanzia 11313, fol. 43 (Thanks to C. Quertier).
[32] Mollat du Jourdin Michel, *Jacques Cœur ou l'esprit d'entreprise au XVe siècle*, Paris, 1988, p. 53.
[33] Caunedo del Porto Betsabé, *Mercaderes castellanos en el Golfo de Vizcaya [1475-1492]*, Madrid 1983, p. 43-4.

V. Conclusion

If the Middle Ages are obviously a time of birth for modern factoring, it must be reminded that the job carried out by medieval factors were not systematically connected with credit functions. But at the end of this period the numerous reorganisation of capital facilitated by this entrepreneurial structure in holding companies opened the way to factors, who created their own company, sometimes in joint-ventures with local traders. It is without any doubt this new business start-up spirit of the second half of the 15th century, truly considered as a new moment of growth of the European economy, which can also explain the birth in London of a company of factors which received, stored and sold products required for the textile industry.[34]

---

[34] Villepin Patrick de, *La Success story du factoring*, Paris, Association pour l'histoire et la promotion du Factoring, 2015, p. 25.

B – Evolution

8. Blackwell Hall Factors in England, the Beginning of the Story

Michael Bickers

Managing Director, BCR Publishing

From the late 14th century until the early 19th century, Blackwell Hall in the City of London was the centre of the British textile trade. The factors of Blackwell Hall, who operated initially as agents for woollen cloth manufacturers (clothiers), over time extended their services to include the direct financing of the clothiers' sales and as such became the forerunners of modern factoring.

I. Blackwell Hall

During the early part of the 14th century under Edward III, the wool weaving industry in the northern counties of England grew rapidly. In those early days, merchants travelled to Yorkshire and bought relatively small amounts of cloth which were spun and woven at homes in the region. As the trade grew, particularly in export and itinerant merchants were gradually replaced by more London based operators with foreign "connections", the system became inadequate. Spot cash purchases became largely impracticable as export trade required a certain amount of time for overseas debt to be collected. As such, working capital became more important and a common and convenient meeting place for buyers and sellers was required.[1] A suitable premises, then known as Bakewell Hall, became such a place, operating as a market for country clothiers and drapers.

---

[1] Hillyer William Hurd, "Four Centuries of Factoring", *The Quarterly Journal of Economics*, Vol. 53, No. 2, Oxford University Press, February 1939, p. 305. See also, Maitland W., *History and Survey of London*, London, T. Osborne and J. Shipton, 1739, p. 464.

The building itself was first owned by Adam Basing who was the Sheriff of the City of London in 1243 and reputedly built the Hall as his substantial family home. It subsequently came into the possession of a Thomas Bakewell and became known as Bakewell Hall in 1397. In that same year, a license was granted by King Richard II, enabling the Hall to be converted into a market house for the sale of woollen cloth and owned by the mayor and commonality of London – the City of London's municipal governing body. Shortly after trading began the name of the property was corrupted to become Blackwell Hall. Trading there lasted for four centuries.

II. The Factors

The factors of Blackwell Hall were not originally established to provide business finance but were commissioned sales agents for clothiers based mainly in the west country who were selling wool and cloth – the word 'factor' meaning 'agent'. The term 'Blackwell Hall Factor' was used in the English commercial world for more than three hundred years.

The factors operated as cloth workers who folded, sorted and displayed the cloth for the clothier manufacturers, who were based mainly in the west country, until sold. The buyers were drapers and foreign merchants. The cloth workers, who were the initial receivers of the goods from the clothiers, naturally gravitated to become middlemen between buyers and sellers.

The factors would purchase fabric from the clothiers and would charge commission or mark up a percentage of the purchase price to buyers. The factors would sell to merchants engaged in the export trade or to wholesale drapers in London or the provinces.

The factors would undertake various other operations as agents for the clothiers, from finding purchasers to advising on which products to manufacture and how to market them. They also became skilful in the assessment and judgement of quality of the cloth they sold on behalf of the clothiers and could carefully match the requirements of the merchants they sold to. In fact, such was the level of expertise gained by the factors that the clothiers became very reliant on them.

After some time, the factors offered their clients credit facilities. Like much of the information surviving from the period, records are sparse as to the precise nature of the arrangements. However, "A piece of cloth worth 12 shillings a yard in ready money would cost 14 shillings if full credit, presumably for at least a year, were allowed". The additional charge was made up of one shilling for commission and another shilling for the credit given.[2]

III. Undertaking of Banking and Finance

The clients of the factors – the retailers, tailors and wholesale merchants – all expected to be allowed a long period for payment (and in fact, credit was required along every part of the supply chain). Some of these trade terms were for more than a year, particularly those demanded by British and foreign exporters.

The clothing manufacturers who had to purchase raw materials and pay wages were not in a position to allow much credit, but often needed it themselves from their suppliers in order to help manage their cash flow effectively. This, however, was often insufficient for their requirements.

The factors saw an opportunity to earn additional money and, with the support of bankers and financiers in London, were able to act as intermediaries in not only cloth but also money. They did this by allowing the clothier suppliers to draw bills on them according to the value of the goods supplied. As such, the factors became 'accepting houses' for the clothiers. Bills were still a common form of currency at that time and drafts accepted by a recognised firm with a good reputation could be used for making payments or discounted for cash.

The usual practice was that the bills could be drawn as soon as the cloth was sold by the factor. As such, when cloth was sent to London, the clothier was not allowed to draw a bill on the factor while they remained waiting for sale. Despite this restriction, some clothiers were drawing too

---

[2] See Gill Conrad, "Blackwell Hall Factors". *The Economic History Review*, Vol. 6, Issue 3, Wiley, 1954, p. 274. "A factor was primarily a commission agent, and a considerable part of the income of Hanson and Mills must have been made by their charge of a percentage on sales. But of this important side of their business we learn very little from existing records. In one letter it was said that a piece of cloth worth 12s. a yard in ready money would cost 14s. if 'full credit', presumably for at least a year, were allowed. The additional charge of 2s. was made up of 1s. for commission and 1s. for 'time' – the period allowed for credit. Another letter stated that 1s. was 'for cash', and the other for 'selling risk etc'. These payments, Hanson said, were 'the constant rule of the trade', but had 'been found by experience not enough'. From clothiers no commission was demanded: they paid only the cloth-workers' charges and 'cloth money', which may have been an allowance for warehousing and other overhead expenses. It was quite small: on one occasion, and probably as a regular practice, it amounted to 2s. for a whole piece."

soon and had to be warned that if they continued to do so, their drafts would not be accepted. The factors also learnt to be careful of advancing against goods that were old or damaged or likely to be rejected by the buyers (parallels can be made with modern factoring arrangements in this respect in terms of clients sometimes fraudulently attempting to factor invoices before goods have been sold or delivered). Sometimes advances were made to clothiers prior to sale – perhaps at 50% of the sale value, and possibly with an additional further advance of maybe 20%.

Factors also performed bookkeeping and collection functions for their clients in respect of the accounts receivable from credit sales. They forwarded the amounts collected to their clients less their fees, costs and advances made. Factors may have also provided for an additional *del credere* fee to guarantee a debtor's ability to pay. However, although the *del credere* factor might guarantee that the debtor was *able* to pay, if the debtor chose not to pay because the debtor disputed the quality, quantity or timing of the goods purchased from the *del credere* factor's consignor client, such a dispute would not be within the credit risk assumed by the *del credere* factor. In the event of such a "quality" dispute, the Blackwell Hall factor would, therefore, still have been able to recover its advances and fees from its consignor client, this "quality" dispute being the consignor client's responsibility.[3]

The system of the provision of finance became essential to the clothiers in helping with their cash flow and for the Blackwell Hall factors it became a considerable source of income.

In 1677, the London Directory reported by name 38 Blackwell Hall Factors and towards the end of the 17th century there were about 50 factors operating. The extent of their services had become quite broad by this stage. The factors at Blackwell Hall "(1) received, stored and sold the merchandise consigned to them by the clothiers; (2) made advances on the security of such merchandise; (3) advised the merchant of the

---

[3] Tatge David, *Legal Aspects of Factoring*, Washington (presentation), Epstein Becker Green, 2014. See also Tatge, Flaxman, Tatge & Franklin, *American Factoring Law* (Bloomberg/BNA 2009) (AFL), 2017, Cum. Supp. at Ch. 1.A, p. 139-146, and C. 1.B.2.3, p. 160-162 (both discussing the factors at Blackwell Hall); see also the 2017 Cum. Supp. at Ch. 1.B.14, p. 209-211, titled *Factors at English Common Law had "quality recourse," meaning ordinary and* del credere *factors both had recourse to their clients in respect of factored accounts that could not be collected because the account debtor disputed and refused to pay the same, due to issues with the quality of quantity of goods or services provided to it by the factor's client.*

clothier's financial responsibility and vice versa; and (4) warranted such financial responsibility for a stated consideration".[4]

By 1739, it was said that the provision of finance had become the most valuable part of the factor's business. It seems that the factors grew rapidly into wealth and power and it was reported as early as 1677 that some factors had risen from poor backgrounds to be worth from GBP 5,000 to 10,000 and, by 1685, some of them were worth GBP 40,000 or 50,000. These were huge sums at the time and the latter two figures are equivalent to several million pounds today. Approaching the end of the 18th century, they began to include woollen and worsted manufacturers in Yorkshire as their clients. However, instead of taking orders directly from the clothiers, they dealt with intermediaries in Yorkshire.[5] The financing business, like their traditional trade, was seasonal. In the winter there was little business, but activity increased through spring, reaching a peak in the summer which continued into early autumn.

IV. Dominance and Control

There were several circumstances that operated which made the services offered by Blackwell Hall Factors popular. The convenience to the clothier and to the merchant buyers was such that it enabled them to focus more on their core activities. However, the factor's separation of the clothier seller and the merchant buyer reduced the merchants' need to be an expert examiner of cloth – a skill that previously he would have spent some considerable time learning and training for and then practiced every day. As a result, the clothier became dependent on the factor to provide the key skills of examining and assessing the quality of the cloth.

The factors also began purchasing the materials and equipment needed and employing workers to manufacture, becoming clothiers themselves as well continuing to factor. This gave the factors a commercial advantage and they were able to undercut clothiers if they refused to use the factors' services.

The factor could also extend considerable control over the clothier's business in the time taken to forward the proceeds of the sale (or balance in the case of advances). The factors tended to favour the larger, wealthier clothiers and the less well-off became very dependent.

---

[4] Hatton Edward, *Gent, Merchant's Magazine*, London, 1726, p. 211-213.
[5] See Westerfield Ray, Bert, *Middlemen in English Business, Particularly Between 1660 and 1760*, New Haven, Yale University Press, 1915, p. 296.

The factors' extensive system of business credit developed further through foreign trade, where merchants were given six months to pay for cloth purchased at Blackwell Hall. However, the six-month terms were not kept, and the payment could take up to fifteen months to be made. This affected the clothiers' cash flow and forced them to purchase from their suppliers on credit.

In the situation that the clothier's cash flow was still hampered, they had no alternative but to use the factor for finance in advance of the sales' proceeds being received, or indeed the factor deciding to make payment. The holding back on such payments was very profitable for the factors and they charged very high rates for advances to the clothiers.

The factors increased their grip over the clothiers by investing in Spanish wool and gained a monopoly for the purchase of the wool. As such, if the clothier wished to purchase Spanish wool, they could only obtain it from the factors who then made significant sums from charging the purchase to the clothiers' factoring account.

The factors also had considerable control over the merchant buyers in terms of how much credit to allow. The longer the credit terms given to the merchants, the more the clothiers' cash flow suffered and the greater the need to use the factors' financing services.

A large number of the west country clothiers were dealing with Blackwell Hall and considerable concern and anger grew among them at the level of control of the factors. By 1660, Blackwell Hall Factors had developed such a monopoly and control over the clothiers that a protest against the extent of their influence was made leading to an act of common council in 1678 being passed for their regulation and, following this, an act of parliament in 1696.

Despite the act of parliament, designed to stop the monopoly and credit manipulations of the factors, the statute remained effective for only a few years. This was because the factors developed methods of circumventing the stipulations of the act and the previous abuses returned once again.[6]

---

[6] *Ibid.*, p. 300. The methods used by the factors to avoid the restriction of the Act are "so lucidly told by one of the abused" clothiers that Westerfield has included the full quotation as follows: "For a little while this Act had its desired effect; these notes were immediately returned to the clothier, who carried them to market for wool, etc., and by that means, made them answer in Trade almost as well as cash itself. The factors thus stripped of the most valuable part of their business, immediately concerted such measures as rendered the whole Act ineffectual – This was done, by tampering with those of the 'Trade' whose circumstances were most precarious who, induced by the

V. The Demise of Blackwell Hall Factors

In the last years of the 18th century, the business of the cloth halls began to decline. This was due to various reasons. Some clothier manufacturers accrued sufficient capital to trade directly with their clients without the need for middlemen factors and certain merchants began to manufacture cloth themselves dealing directly with tailors and retailers.

In 1795, there was still much activity at Blackwell Hall. At the end of the year there was a reduction in business that initially was thought to be just seasonal. However, in 1796, the expected recovery did not materialise.

Britain was at war with France and the cost of this had put the British economy under strain and businesses were hampered by the general shortage of cash. The discounting of bills reduced considerably and, as a result, trade suffered.

The cost of the war with France was also causing severe problems with trade and the British economy in general. From 1797 onwards, there was a shortage of raw material and especially Spanish wool – essential for fine garments. Stocks remained low for many years and the factors were suffering. As a result, the clothier manufacturers were being put under pressure to repay the money advanced to them by the factors.

For a while, in the early years of the 19th century, there was an improvement in business and supplies of wool increased once more. This lasted for some time and, when Blackwell Hall was closed in 1820 (to extend the Guildhall), there were still many factors working there.

However, from about 1830, a fundamental change took place and cloth manufacturing in the west country was in decline. Some merchants began to manufacture cloth themselves and some of the wealthier

---

Promise of speedy Sale for their Goods, prior to those of any other Maker, were easily prevailed upon to forego the Advantage of the Notes granted them by Parliament. This fatal Precedent being once set, the Factors instantly exacted a like Compromise from the rest; and if any refused not one Piece of their Cloth was sold. This important Point carried … . they again allowed the Drapers such unreasonable Credit, that it was impossible for the most substantial Clothier to carry on the Trade, while the Returns were so slow and precarious. On an universal Complaint therefore of this grievance, they graciously condescended to insure the Debt to be paid twelve Months after it was contracted; but in Return of so great a favor, insisted on two and a half per cent as a Reward; and if any was rash or stubborn enough to disrelish or oppose this new Imposition, he had the mortification to wait six months longer for his money, that is to say, a year and a half in all." See also; Defoe Daniel, *The Complete English Tradesman*, London, Charles Rivington, 1727, p. 337.

clothiers began to trade directly. Other clothiers, some long established, ceased to manufacture and closed.

At the same time, new ranges of diverse goods, especially fancy cloth and new varieties of fabric which undermined the traditional methods of production of broad cloth, became increasingly prominent.

VI. Conclusion: Legacy

Despite the criticisms of the Blackwell Hall factors, they acted as middlemen and financiers to the textile trade in England for nearly 200 years. It is hard to imagine that they would have lasted so long if there had not been an overall benefit in the services they provided. Indeed, one would have expected ordinary market forces to have had more of a hand in determining pricing and the quality and nature of the factors' business relationships than many of the few reports that exist from the period suggest.

The roots of modern factoring can readily be seen in the practices of Blackwell Hall Factors. The Factoring Industry that began in the USA at the end of the 19th century was clearly influenced by the factors at Blackwell Hall, as was the re-introduction of Factoring in the UK in the 1960s. In both the USA and the UK, the textile trade was still a major aspect of factoring business at the time and diversification into other sectors is now widespread.

9. Early Growth of Factoring in America from 1628 to 1960

David B. Tatge
Shareholder (member), Epstein Becker & Green, PC

Jeremy B. Tatge
*Manager, founder & member,
Capitol National Factors Company, LLC*

Factoring came to America in 1628, with the Pilgrims who settled in the Massachusetts Bay colony in Plymouth. At that time, common law factors served as commissioned sales agents and provided billing and collection services to their consignor clients. But, in 1628, they did not provide credit checking and approval of prospective client sales, credit protection, on approved accounts purchased at the factor's risk, nor client finance, in the form of factor advances. Over the next 400 years, factoring in America evolved into the modern *old-line* (aka "full service") non recourse factoring where, by 1920 or so, this new breed of "factors" arose, who no longer acted as commissioned sales agent for a consignor client, selling from a stock of consigned goods held by the factor, as at common law. These new factors provided all three of these additional services (credit checking, credit protection, on approved accounts, and client finance), and other ancillary services as well, such as lending (against client held and controlled inventory), over advances, letters of credit, purchase order finance, etc. Old-line factoring was the principal form of factoring in America, both in 1920, in 1960, and in all intervening years.

Even today, as this material is written, it remains the predominant form of factoring in America, being 72.5% of the USD 91.7 billion volume reported by a 2016 survey of America's largest factors, conducted by the Commercial Finance Association (CFA) in New York City.

I. Factoring Came to America With the Pilgrims in 1628, Shortly after They Landed

Under a letter of agreement dated the 18th of November 1628, five leading Pilgrims, William Bradford, governor of the Massachusetts colony, Isaak Allerton, Myles Standish, William Brewster and Ed Winslow, called "merchants", appointed two London merchants, James Sherley, a goldsmith and John Beuchamp, a salter, as their "true and lawful agents, factors, substitutes and assigns," to receive, store and sell the American merchant group's shipments to London of furs, fish, timber and other goods.[1] The London factors also bought goods in England on behalf of their American merchant clients, both for their use and for trade with the local Indians. The factors agreed to sell the consigned goods on credit, as agents of their Pilgrim merchant clients, and they surely accounted for and paid over the collected proceeds of sale, but nothing more. Thus, the Pilgrim's London factors did not investigate the credit of prospective buyers of the goods which the factors received from the Pilgrims and held in inventory for later sale, did not make advances to their Pilgrim clients, pre-sale or post-sale, against the security of the consigned inventory, nor investigate or guarantee the credit of the buyers to whom the Pilgrim's goods were sold. Let alone beyond that, guarantee that when goods were sold on credit by the factor, the bill of exchange, promissory note or the O/A taken in exchange would be collected when due, at maturity, irrespective of the buyer's credit.

II. Common Law Factoring in America Prior to 1889

Between 1628 and 1889, the best known factors worldwide were the textile factors located at Blackwell Hall in London, known commercially as "Blackwell Hall Factors." That said, English factors of the period were active not just in textiles, wool and cloth, but in all manner of commerce beyond that, involving goods such as boots, coal, cocoa, cotton, corn, fish, flour, grain, gum, hops, indigo, jute, malt, oats, rice, silk, skins, sugar, tallow, tar, timber, tobacco, wheat, and wine. In America, many of the leading factors in the early 1800s were European immigrants located in New York City, often representing and selling cloth and other goods produced by European textile mills owned by their relatives. Others

---

[1] See Tatge Jeremy B., *Pilgrim's Pride: America's Very First Factoring Agreement*, 19 Commercial Factor, N° 2, April 2017, p. 30-39.

represented unrelated European clients who shipped finished goods of various other types into America for sale here, and American clients selling various goods of other types. Moreover, factors in America, from colonial times onward to the 20th century, represented American clients who sold and shipped American cotton, fish, timber, tobacco and other products for sale abroad, not only to Europe but as far away as Australia and Asia.

As time went on, the business practices of factors worldwide and related English commercial law both continued to evolve. In 1720 or so, English factors started accepting supplemental *del credere* commissions whereby, depending on the view of the court, they either guaranteed (i) the sale itself, in the view of certain of the earlier English cases followed by many American states, including New York State, or (ii) the buyer's credit, in the view of later English cases.[2] This form of supplemental commission ultimately came to America around 1814, only after European exporters of goods to the American market had suffered significant credit losses. As would be expected, these *del credere* commissions, ranging from 2.5-5% or so, quickly produced "great integrity" in the American market.

By 1738, if not even earlier, English law had evolved to require ordinary factors, who did not accept a *del credere* commission, to at least investigate the credit of prospective buyers.[3] In 1755, English law

---

[2] See American Factoring Law (Bloomberg/BNA 2009) ("AFL") at Ch. 1.I.F, *Emerging American View of the Del Credere Factor as More Than A Mere Guarantor*, Main Vol. p. 13. See also AFL Ch. 1.II.B.4, *Early View of the Del Credere Factor as a Mere Guarantor of the Buyer's Credit*, Main Vol. p. 27-28, Ch. 1.II.B.6, *The Del Credere Factor as an Obligor for the Sales Price of the Goods (Net of the Del Credere Factor's Advances and Costs)*, Main Vol. p. 28-31, and D. Tatge and J. Tatge, *A Brief Look at Factors Under Early English Commercial Law*, 18 Commercial Factor N° 2, March/April 2016 (hereinafter *"Factors Under Early English Commercial Law"*) at 19-21, discussing *Scrimshire v. Alderton*, decided 1743, reported 1795, [1795] Eng. R. 3051, (1795) 2 Strange 1182, 93 EngR 1114(D). See also, in the 2017 Cum. Supp., AFL Ch. 1.B.5, *Del Credere Commissions*, p. 165-175, discussing the same case, which referred to *del credere* factoring as a "new method," in England. See also AFL's Main Vol., at Ch. 1.A – Ch. 1.II.B, pgs. 8-47, discussing early common law factoring in America between the time of the Pilgrims and 1900, and the roots thereof, and in the 2017 Cum. Supp. Ch. 1.A and Ch. 1.B.1-3, p. 136-161, discussing the early textile factors at Blackwell Hall in London, as well as Ch. 1.B.4-12, p. 162-268 of the supplement, covering the development of English factoring law between 1739 and 1900. AFL's 856-page main volume and its 1062-page 2017 Cum. Supplement served as the principal source for this chapter.

[3] See e.g., as to English law, *Froth's Case*, [1738] EngR 339, (1688-1710, 1738) Holt KB 675, 90 ER 1273 (A), and, as to American factoring law on this issue, AFL Ch. 1.II.A.3, *Responsibility of Ordinary Factor to Its Principal for Credit Losses if Factor sold*

recognised that factors held a lien on consigned goods, to secure the factor's open advances, as well as unpaid fees and commissions due, and this lien was later extended to the proceeds of sale in 1775[4], the year that the American Revolutionary War began.

English common law remained in America when it declared its independence in 1776 as well as after the Revolutionary War ended, in 1783. As more fully discussed in other sources[5], common law factors in America before 1889 acted as commissioned sales agents for their consignor clients, often European textile mills, selling goods sent to them by their clients to the local population, often on credit, and receiving a sales commission (aka a "factorage"), typically 5% or so, for doing so.

The factors, spurred on by the security of factor's liens on consigned goods and their proceeds in the possession of the factor, extended financing to their factoring clients by advancing funds against the estimated market value of the consigned goods held in inventory by the factor; 50% or so, pre-sale, and another 25-30%, post-sale, holding 20-25% as a "reserve" to cover buyer disputes and "quality" claims of defective merchandise. The majority rule of American courts at common law treated factor advances to the client as partial prepayments to the factor's principal of its own anticipated sales proceeds, on the consigned inventory which the client owned, but the factor held and sold. Therefore, client advances were not generally treated as loans by the factor to its client unless the parties' intent that the advance be deemed an interest bearing loan was

---

on *Unreasonable Credit Terms*, Main Vol. p. 19-21, discussing *Greely v. Bartlett*, 1 Me. 172, 178, 1821 Me. LEXIS 6 (1821).

[4] See *Factors Under Early English Commercial Law* at p. 18-24, discussing *Kruger v. Wilcox*, [1755] EngR 14, (1755) Amb. 253, 27 E.R. 168 (recognising factor liens on inventory in the possession of the factor) and *Drinkwater v. Goodwin*, [1775] EngR 35, (1775) (1 Cowp. 251, 98 E.R. 1070 (May 12, 1775) (extending the factor's lien to the proceeds of sale, as long as they were in the possession of the factor.) See also, the later published AFL 2017 Cum. Supp. Ch. 1.B.8, *English Common Law Gave Factors Acting As Commissioned Sales Agents A Lien On The Consigned Inventory Held by the Factor, And a "Property Interest," More Than A Lien, in Accounts Receivable Due the Factor's Client, Representing Uncollected Proceeds Arising From the Sale of Consigned Goods, to the Extent of the Factor's Open Advances and Unpaid Fees*, p. 177-186, discussing these two cases and others as well.

[5] Principally, AFL. See in particular Ch. 1.IV.A, *Birth of the Modern American Factor*, Main Vol. p. 50-96. See also *Connecting The Dots: The Evolution of Old-Line Factoring in America, 1628-1960: What It Is (And Is Not), How It Contributed to the U.C.C., And Why It Creates A "True Sale" Of Accounts* in the AFL 2017 Cumulative Supplement at p. 10-135, analysing both old-line factoring and bankruptcy "preference" litigation brought against two old-line factors, later settled, in *Dots, LLC v. Milberg Factors, Inc. (In re Dots, LLC)*, 562 B.R. 286 (Bankr. D. N.J. 2017).

expressly stated.[6] If, however, the sales proceeds ultimately received were inadequate to satisfy open advances and fees owing, the law implied an obligation on the factor's client to make its factor good for the shortfall.

For a supplemental *del credere* commission, typically 2.5-5%, factors warranted to their factoring clients either, in the view of the later English cases and that of the courts in some American states, the solvency of the client's buyer (account debtor) obligated for the purchase price when the goods were sold on credit; or in the view of earlier English cases, and in the majority view of most American courts, including in New York, something more: that the proceeds of client's goods sold on credit would "absolutely" be timely collected when due, and paid to the consignor client at maturity, irrespective of the solvency of the buyer. In effect, under this view, the *del credere* factor was treated as the buyer and guaranteed the sale itself, at least between the factor and his client, *inter-se*, for this purpose.[7]

These early American factors provided bookkeeping services and periodic accounting to their clients, often foreign concerns across the Atlantic, with respect to the factored accounts, and collected, for their clients, the proceeds of the consigned goods when they were sold, often by the factor on credit.

In addition, factors also gave marketing advice to their factoring clients, such as the latest styles and merchandise which might best find favor in the local market area with the client's buyers there; and provided, at the factor's discretion, seasonal over-advances and other financial accommodations to the client, such as unsecured or secured loans or, in some cases, term loans, as the particular circumstances warranted.

---

[6] See *American Factoring Law*, CH. 1.II.B.10, *Were Advances by the Del Credere Factor a Loan by the Factor to Its Client or a Partial Prepayment of the Purchase Price of the Underlying Goods?*, discussing relevant cases.

[7] See the sources cited in N° 3 and N° 5, *supra*. See also a brief summary of the applicable law in AFL Ch. I.I.D, *Factor's Assumption of Credit Risk in Consideration of a Supplemental Del Credere Commission on Credit Sales Only*, in Ch. 1.I.E, *The Scope of the Del Credere Factor's Duties at English Common Law*; in Ch. 1.I.F, *Emerging American View of the Del Credere Factor As More Than A Mere Guarantor*, and in Ch. 1.I.G. *Consequences of the Del Credere Factor's Absolute Liability to Its Principal*, p. 9-14 Main Vol., as well AFL Ch. 1.II.B, *The Role of the Del Credere Factor in Early American Factoring Law*, p. 24-47, Main Vol. If an account debtor on a covered sale went bankrupt *before* the account arising from the sale matured and became due, a *del credere* factor was obligated to pay its client only *at* the *later* maturity date. *Swan v. Nesmith*, 24 Mass. 220 (1828); *Leverick v. Meigs & Reed*, 1 Cow. 645, 664, 1824 N.Y. LEXIS 123 (Supr. Ct. Jud. 1824).

"Ordinary" factors who did not have open advances could not, in their own name, sue the buyers (account debtors) for the sales proceeds owed when the principal's goods were sold by the factor on trade credit. Where, however, an "ordinary factor" had open advances, or the factor was a *del credere* factor, it was treated as holding a "special property interest" and, therefore, it was entitled to sue the buyer (account debtor) to collect in the factor's own name.[8] Even when this form of supplemental commission was accepted on a particular consignment, the factor's consignor client, as the owner of both the consigned goods and their sales proceeds, had the ability to direct collect itself as well. Thus, *del credere* factors lost their right to collect when the principal appeared and took collection action directly against the account debtor provided, however, that in order to direct collect, the consignor principal was obligated to first satisfy the factor's lien for outstanding advances, fees and costs.

If the factor had accepted a *del credere* commission, the sale was made on credit, and the consignor client generally did *not* move to direct collect the sale proceeds (the buyer's note, a bill of exchange, or, less often, an account) at or after its maturity. Later, in common law, the *del credere* factor itself became the full legal owner of the uncollected sales proceeds, by subrogation, upon either: (1) the factor paying its consignor client in cash, at maturity, an amount equal to the uncollected sales proceeds or (2) by the consignor client taking judgment against the factor for the amount of the uncollected sales proceeds not yet received.[9]

We can conclude that a leading American born factor emerged in 1854. Specifically, as time went on, America began to produce its own native born factors who sold for American clients, often textile mills. The most well-known of these was unquestionably James Talcott, a Yankee who came to New York City around 1854 to represent and sell on commission the goods of his brother, an owner of a woolen mill in New Britain, Connecticut.

---

[8] See e.g. *White & Elder v. Chouteau*, 10 Barb. 202, 208, 1850 N.Y. App. Div. LEXIS 188 (1850) and *Gibson v. Stevens*, 49 U.S. 384 (1850).

[9] See e.g. AFL Ch. 1.II.B.14, *Subrogation Rights of the Del Credere Factor*, p. 44-47, Main Vol. and *In re Merrick's Estate*, 5 Watts & Serg. 9, 1842 Pa. LEXIS 232 (Pa. 1842).

III. Factors During the American Civil War (1861-1865) and Afterwards

The American Civil War of 1861-1865 (aka the War Between the States) and its aftermath transformed America from a largely agricultural to a largely industrial economy. During the war, credit terms were significantly shortened, to only 30 days or so, as creditors sought to avoid the vagaries of longer repayment terms and currency deflation during the war. Mr Talcott's business boomed during the Civil War years with the demand for goods by the Union Army.

Common law factoring in America continued after the Civil War into the 1930s and beyond, but on a much more limited scope as time went on. Indeed, common law factoring of cotton, tobacco and other agricultural products grown in the South, including on a *del credere* basis, resumed almost immediately. It continued into the 1920s and the early 1930s. Common law factors in America after the Civil War also factored clients who produced and sold goods in other areas of the country as well, such as, sellers of California raised fruits and vegetables. Thus, common law *del credere* factoring was still found, sporadically, into the 1950s and beyond that, in timber, produce and other transactions.

IV. Modern (Old-line) Factoring Arises in America (1889–1960)

The Rise of Modern Old-line Factoring in America

Several events led to the rise of modern old-line factoring in America, around the turn of the 20th century. After the American Civil War, the American economy grew rapidly. Transportation and communication links continued to improve. As a result, there was less need for the employment of factors who often represented several sellers. Now mills and factories employed their own in-house sales forces, and goods could be shipped to buyers nationwide from the company's own warehouses. Moreover, the shorter terms for repayment of accounts receivable, as a result of the Civil War, made trade accounts more attractive as collateral.

Modern old-line factoring started to emerge in America in 1889 and evolved thereafter for the next 70 years or so, until 1960. It began in 1889, when American factors in New York City who represented the wool and textile trade there began to drop their sales and marketing functions. The following year, the very steep McKinley tariffs of 1890, almost 50%

on European imports, forced American factors to look increasingly for domestic clients. Over the next 50 years or so, almost all factors in America likewise dropped the role of commissioned sales agent. As they did, factors stopped referring to themselves as "commission merchants" or, particularly for factors of the Southern staples of cotton and tobacco, as "factors and commission merchants."

During this evolution, the historic roles of, and the credit and business risks assumed by, *del credere* factors in common law were modified. This new type of American factor who arose, principally between 1895 and the 1930s, became known commercially in the 1930s as an "old–line" factor, which, as its principal client service, reviewed proposed purchase orders submitted by the factor's client and, where the credit of the buyer and the terms of sale were satisfactory, provided the factor's written credit approval to the client, either on an order-by-order basis or by the sale falling within a factor-approved credit line for the client's sales to the particular account debtor in question.

As the client thereafter accepts the order and delivers the goods or provides the services, these "old-line" factors purchase the accounts arising at a discount (i.e., net of [less] the factor's "commission," aka "discount fee"), with both parties, expressly, recognising that the subject accounts, both those bought at the factor's risk and those purchased at the client's risk, are sold and assigned to the factor in absolute ownership. The accounts purchased are either all accounts as they arise or, under some factoring agreements, only those accounts which are offered by the client for sale and thereafter are expressly accepted by the factor for purchase. Before 1960, an old-line factor almost always billed all the purchased accounts itself and stamped the invoices sent to the account debtors with a notice that their payment obligations had been sold to the factor and, going forward, they were to pay only to the factor. Before adoption by the various states of the Uniform Commercial Code (UCC), starting in the 1950s but largely in the 1960s, the factor "perfected" its ownership interest in purchased accounts by giving account debtors this "notice of assignment." With the adoption of the UCC, however, commercial factors now simply file a UCC-1 financing statement to "perfect" both their ownership interest, as buyer of the purchased accounts and their lien interest, as lender, in non-purchased accounts and other assets pledged to the factor by its client. The non-purchased accounts and other assets are provided as security for the client's duties, obligations and indebtedness owed to the factor under the factoring agreement. Today, in most cases, the factor's client is obligated by contract to stamp or electronically place such a "notice of assignment" on the invoices which the client sends to the account debtors, with the factor merely checking for compliance. Notification factoring today is much greater, 78% or so of volume in 2016, as compared to non-notification factoring, where the client collects as agent of the factor, without the account debtors, pre-default, being noticed of the assignment.

The only risk which an old-line American factor assumes contractually is credit risk, on approved accounts, to the extent of the credit limit set by the factor. All other risks are those of the factor's client. Therefore, old-line factors, consistent with factors at common law, do not accept "quality" risk, have full "quality recourse," and can charge their clients or chargeback to their clients the following:

(1) client risk accounts, never credit approved to start with, which do not collect;
(2) ineligible accounts sold to the factor in breach of seller representations and warranties, e.g., that the account is not disputed, not subject to set-off or recoupment claims, nor subject to liens, competing ownership and security interests, etc.;
(3) purchased accounts which the account debtor refuses to pay because it disputes the quality, quantity or timing of the goods and services received from the factor's client;
(4) allowances and credits taken by the account debtor;
(5) credits and short pays;
(6) bill and hold and consignment sales; and
(7) other offsets or failures of the factor to collect not rooted in the assumed credit risk.

In certain forms of factoring, the factors may have to provide client financing, by making, in the case of "advance factoring," cash "advances" to the client of 70-90% or so of the contractual purchase price of approved accounts. The advances are treated as either interest-bearing loans, at least in the "advance factoring" agreements to which the largest national old-line factors are parties, or as partial non-interest bearing prepayments of the factor's purchase price, by some smaller American factors. Old-line factors also make, in the case of "discount factoring" agreements, a (discounted) prepayment of the factor's full purchase price owed on the subject accounts, discounted back from the average maturity date to the purchase date at an agreed interest rate.

Old-line factors provide bookkeeping services as well for their clients, with the factor keeping and maintaining the sales ledger for all purchased accounts, booking them onto the factor's own balance sheet, and also periodic accounting to the client for related activity (advances, chargebacks, disputes, credits, fees, interest, trade allowances, etc.). Finally, factors generally provide collection services for the purchased accounts.

Beyond this, old-line factors in America also offer several ancillary client services (at least in the case of the larger national old-line factors), including cash loans against client owned inventory at, say, 50% loan to value; similar to how factors at common law loaned against consigned inventories held by the factor on site except that now, the inventory collateral is under the client's control, off-site.

Old-line factors also supply various other financial accommodations including, for example, seasonal over advances (loans, secured or not, above the factor's financing commitment, if any), letters of credit, asset-based loans, purchase order financing, etc., similar to how factors in common law provided supplemental services of this sort to their clients.

Finally, factors can give miscellaneous business advice (although rare, today), and in the past they also provided space for the factoring client to display, store, ship, and deliver merchandise, sometimes assisting a third party on-site agent with those functions, and arranging for insurance; all without any duty of the old-line factor to actually make the sale (unlike in common law, where all factors were sales agents who sold consigned goods on commission). These storage, delivery and shipping functions of the old-line factor all petered out by 1950 or so.

Old-line factors in America pay their clients the purchase price owed for purchased accounts at different times, depending on the type of factoring agreement that the parties use.

In a "maturity factoring" agreement, the old-line factor provides credit checking, credit protection, on factor-approved accounts, as well as bookkeeping and collection services, but provides *no* client financial services via cash advances or prepayments. Here, the factor pays its purchase price to the client on the weighted average maturity date of the accounts purchased by the factor during the particular month, *plus* an agreed number of days thereafter for collection.

In a "collection factoring" agreement, the old-line factor provides the same services and, again, does not provide client financing in the form of either purchase date advances or prepayments. Here, the factor pays its purchase price when the factor *collects* the purchased accounts (but not earlier than their maturities, unless expressly agreed) and, in this regard, confirms to treat accounts purchased at the factor's risk as "deemed collected" on the earlier of: (a) the account debtor's bankruptcy or (b) if no event as in (a) has happened by an agreed date, often 90-150 days post-maturity, at that time, provided, however, there is no evidence, in the case of (a) or (b), that the accounts were not collected because the account debtor disputed its payment obligations, such as by claiming deficiencies in the quality, quantity or timing of the goods and services delivered to it by the factor's client, or that the account debtor breached its representations and warranties, or that the failure to collect was otherwise outside the credit risk assumed by the factor.

An "advance factoring agreement," aka "conventional factoring," is either "collection factoring" or "maturity factoring" but where the factor also provides, at its sole discretion, financial services to its client in the form of cash "advances" to the client of 70-90% or so of the purchase price of approved accounts, most often as an interest-bearing loan but, in some cases, treated as a non-interest bearing partial prepayment of the contractual purchase price (which then reflects a relatively higher factoring commission). Here, the factor pays its purchase price to the client at the same time as in "maturity factoring" or "collection factoring", whichever is applicable.

Finally, in "discount factoring" agreements (relatively rare) the old-line factor makes a (discounted) prepayment to the client of the factor's full purchase price on the date of purchase itself, as discounted back from the average maturity date at an agreed rate. Factoring agreements are sometimes structured with discounted payments of the factor's full purchase price in this fashion to avoid loan covenants of senior lenders which prohibit new loans but, perhaps, may not bar a client from selling its accounts in consideration of a discounted payment of the factor's full purchase price.[10]

Old-line Factoring Distinguished from Both Common Law Factoring and Lending

In 1925, the New York Supreme Court ruled that a modern old-line factor was not a common law *del credere* factor on the basis that, among other things, the duty of "sales agent" of the common law factor had been

---

[10] See the further discussion of discount factoring in AFL Ch. 3.X.B, *Discounted or Non-Interest Bearing Advances*, p. 179-181.

abandoned by the factor who was before the court, who guaranteed only "credit risk," on approved accounts purchased at the factor's risk, rather than, as in common law in New York, the sale itself. The court noted also that the factor might not even be an "ordinary factor" if, on remand, expert testimony could show that the term "factor," as it was understood in common law, had been supplanted by a more modern commercial use of the term, in New York City, to now mean a modern factor who was more akin to a commercial banker and no longer a sales agent. The same year, a lower New York appellate court ruled that factors did not have to be regulated as bank lenders because they did more than lend money; they also stored and sold the goods, guaranteed the principal's credit, made advances to the principal, accounted for the disposition of merchandise and sometimes arranged to convert unfinished goods. Factor advances to the factoring client, the appellate court said, were "incidental" to the factor's services and necessary to keep its mill client producing fresh goods which could generate further commissions for the factor when sold.

Emergence of Competition from Asset Based Receivables Financiers (1904-1940)

Between 1904 and 1940, factors in America faced significant new competition from the many commercial finance companies, aka discount finance companies, formed in America during this time, who provided dealer financing (aka floor plan financing). Discount finance companies financed the dealer's retail sales of consumer goods on an installment plan, sometimes without recourse, sometimes with recourse, and sometimes with partial recourse. They provided commercial finance by "purchasing" accounts from persons other than dealers in a like fashion from mills, wholesalers, distributors and others, sometimes on a full recourse basis; made business and consumer loans of various types, and provided casualty insurance, credit insurance and other products. In the early years of this form of commercial finance some of these new financiers styled themselves as "factors" even when they "bought" all accounts, in form, with full recourse, i.e. taking no credit risk, and they also made immediate demand for direct collection, to the account debtors. When clients objected to this practice, perhaps under pressure from their buyers, the finance companies quickly developed non-notification financing – which is known today as ABL.

Another important moment in factoring history concerns a factor's lien on inventory collateral that is not in the factor's possession, and on the accounts arising from their sale, which lien was recognised by statute in New York State in 1911. Briefly, American factors, after the turn of the 20th century, were now being asked by clients to, among other things, lend against the value of off-site inventory held by the client at its own business premises, under the client's control. This, and several cases decided in New York State between 1904 and 1911, caused factors to worry that a court might find they did not have the requisite possession of off-site inventory which the common law, and later a New York statute enacted in 1830, required to create a "factor's lien." Prodded by both local factors and these concerns, in 1911 New York State enacted Section 45 of its Personal Property Law to facilitate inventory lending of a non-possessory nature, beyond the possessory lien on inventory earlier recognised by New York's factor's lien law of 1830 and, before, by common law. Section 45, as enacted, allowed factors to receive a lien on inventory beyond their possession, and on the accounts arising when it was sold, to secure factor advances made or to be made on the security of the merchandise, provided that, among other things, (1) a bill, invoice, statement or notice was mailed or delivered to the account debtor; (2) notice of the factor's lien was placed on the entrance of the building where the merchandise was kept giving the name of the factor and designating it as either a lienor, factor or consignee, with (3) notice of the lien to be filed "[i]n every town or city where the merchandise subject to the client or any part thereof is or at any time shall be located, kept or stored." By later amendments, in 1931, 1935 and 1941, the factor's lien in New York was extended further to, among other things, accounts pledged as loan collateral which did not arise from goods on which the factor held a lien; in other words, to cover "straight" accounts receivable financing.

Old-line Factors Defined Commercially in America in the 1930s

During the 1930s, modern American factors who bought credit-approved accounts without recourse, accepting the credit risk that these purchased accounts could not be collected at maturity by the factor due *solely* to the financial inability to pay of the client's various account debtors obligated thereon, became known in American commercial circles as "old-line" factors. This was to distinguish them from the newer commercial finance companies of the period who sometimes called themselves "factors" even when they "bought" all accounts with full recourse to the client, with a right to chargeback if the "purchased" accounts did not collect within an agreed period, for any reason whatsoever. Learned treaties soon stated that the primary distinguishing feature of an "old-line" factor was that it assumed credit risk, i.e., that factor-approved purchased accounts would not collect at maturity due *solely* to the account debtor's financial inability to pay thereon. Whereas, in sharp contrast, secured asset-based lenders providing receivables financing, by loaning on accounts collateral (and factors who "buy" accounts with full recourse), assume no credit risk at all.[11]

This period also marks a consolidation of the early Factoring Industry, at the time when old-line factors expanded their clientele in the 1930s and, in some cases, raised funds publicly. During the 1930s, American factors were forced, by the Great Depression, to diversify their clientele, expanding beyond their traditional base in textiles, apparel and woolens into many other areas. By World War Two, American factors had expanded out to serve clients in chemicals, cosmetics, electronics, furniture, glassware, hosiery, linen, home furnishings, shoes, toys and many other areas. Between 1924 and 1936, the American Factoring Industry experienced its first wave of consolidation as several of the larger commercial finance companies, recently formed as noted earlier, now bought established factoring companies to run as stand-alone subsidiaries, to expand their product lines. In 1936, James Talcott, Inc., incorporated in 1914, shortly before the death of its founder, made a public offer of equity in the stock market. In 1939 a Georgia bank became one of the first banks, if not *the* first bank, to begin to factor accounts in America.

Enactment of Factor Lien Laws in a Majority of States, Beyond New York and Impacts Thereof (1938-1959)

From 1938-1959, more than half of the states in America enacted "factor's lien" statutes modelled, more or less, on Section 45 of New York's Personal Property Law. These statutes hurt the recognition that factoring created a "true-sale" of accounts as they created the misleading impression that the principal role of a modern American old-line factor was to lend against inventory. In fact, while old-line factors provide

---

[11] See e.g. AFL Ch. 1.IV.A.10, Main Vol. p. 10, and Saulnier & Jacoby, *Accounts Receivable Financing* (Bureau of Economic Research, Inc., 1943) at 19, Chapin, *Credit And Collection Principles And Practice* (6th Ed. New York, McGraw-Hill, 1953), and Monroe Lazere, Ed., *Commercial Financing* (The Ronald Press Company, 1968), p. 73-74.

inventory loans, this is an ancillary, lesser role, as compared to their principal roles discussed above, which are to provide credit checking, credit protection, billing and collection services in respect of purchased accounts and, in some cases, to provide client financing as well.

Likewise, in the 1940s and 1950s, American courts continued to recast the "purchase" of accounts with full recourse to the "seller" as secured loan transactions. Since the 1940s, some factors started divisions which provided client finance by "buying" all accounts with full recourse. American courts, beginning with a ruling of the United States Supreme Court in 1916 and continuing into the 1940s and 1950s, and even today, often recast full recourse agreements of this nature as being secured loans, not respecting the "form" of a "sale" of accounts.[12]

During this same period, American factoring volume (speaking now solely in terms of old-line factoring) helped, surely, by the boom in America's economy during World War Two, continued to rise. For example, in 1948, domestic American factoring volume was USD 2.5 billion, a massive increase over the USD 542 million reported in 1935. However, ABL continued to make inroads. In 1955 the volume of ABL exceeded old-line factoring volume in America for the first time.

Starting in the 1950s, American courts began to recognise that old-line factors purchase accounts from their clients in an outright "true sale", consistent with both the "form" of old-line factoring agreements and with the underlying economics as well. These rulings are well grounded in that, among other things:

(1) the parties expressly intend the accounts to be purchased and sold in a "true sale";

(2) old-line factors assume credit risk on approved accounts purchased at the factor's risk which, as to any particular old-line factoring agreement, generally represent the majority, and often the vast majority, of the accounts purchased by the factor, by dollar amount over time, whereas neither secured lenders nor full recourse factors ever assume any credit risk;

---

[12] See e.g. *Home Bond Co. v. McChesney*, 239 U.S. 568, 36 S.Ct. 170, 60 L. Ed. 444 (1916); *Brieley v. Commercial Credit Co.*, 43 F.2d 730 (7th Cir. 1930), *In re Ace Fruit & Produce Co., Inc.*, 49 F. Supp. 986, 987 (S.D.N.Y. 1943) and *Brewster Shirt Corp. v. Commr.*, 159 F.2d 227, 229-230 (2d Cir. 1947): "It is clear that as soon as accounts were assigned and advances made thereon the agreement and assignments involved security transactions which in law constituted a mortgage. What legally is a mortgage is a matter of substance and not one of mere form…The fact that the security was given in the form of outright assignment is quite unimportant when the transaction was in effect a mortgage".

(3) old-line factors contract, *ab initio*, to pay their client the purchase price of accounts purchased at the factor's risk at an agreed date, whether they have yet been collected or not, net of fees and expenses owing and, in advance factoring, net of prior advances; whereas no ABL lender or commercial finance company lending on accounts collateral, or buying accounts with full recourse, would ever commit to make a "balance payment" of this sort once it knows that the uncollected accounts serving as loan collateral or "purchased" are not likely to collect in full;

(4) old-line factors oftentimes pay a purchase price that, as a percentage of invoice, that is far above the 80% or so which an asset based lender would normally advance against accounts in a borrowing base;

(5) in two forms of old-line factoring, "maturity factoring" and "collection factoring," factors make no client "advances" so there is nothing to impute as loan principal;

(6) old-line factors cannot charge their credit losses to factor reserves, which are held by old-line factors as security only for "quality" recourse items like disputes, etc.;

(7) the client has no "equity of redemption" so cannot, if the factor objects, repurchase accounts previously sold to the factor by merely paying off open advances and fees;

(8) old-line factors are entitled to any surplus in collections over their purchase price;

(9) old-line factors can resell or re-pledge their ownership interest in the purchased accounts as they see fit;

(10) account debtors are, most often, notified that their accounts have been sold and assigned to the factor and that they must only pay the factor, whereas lenders do not typically give such notices, pre-default, and

(11) the old-line factor cannot look to other client assets or those of affiliated third-party guarantors to cover the factor's credit losses if accounts purchased at the factor's risk do not collect due *solely* to the financial inability of the account debtors to pay, while, in comparison, secured lenders and full recourse factors have such recourse rights.

Thus, a sale of installment loan contracts, without recourse, was recognised as a "true sale" of the contracts to the factor in the late 1940s.[13]

In the late 1950s, in California state court litigation, an old-line factoring agreement was recognised as a "true sale" of all accounts purchased, both those bought at the factor's risk and those purchased at the client's risk as factor-risk accounts were the majority, in dollar

---

[13] *In re Nizolek Furniture & Carpet Co.*, 71 F. Supp. 1012 (D. N.J. 1947), *aff'd per curium*, 165 F.2d 788 (3d Cir. 1948) (where the entire purchase price of the installment contracts was paid up front).

amount, showing that the agreement was intended to be a purchase and sale of accounts transaction, not a loan.[14]

Finally, CIT, via its subsidiary Meinhard & Co., formed a short-lived old-line (full service) factoring company in London in November 1960, together with the Alexandria Finance Co. there, exporting American old-line factoring abroad. More significantly, two months later, early in 1961, the First National Bank of Boston took a 25% equity stake in another new UK old-line factor, International Factors Ltd, the remaining equity therein owned by M Samuel & Co., a London merchant bank, and Tozer, Kemsley & Millbourn of the UK. More than a dozen years later, International Factors Ltd was still the UK's largest factoring company.[15]

---

[14] *Refinance Corp. v. Northern Lumber Sales, Inc.*, 163 Cal. App. 2d 73, 329 P.2d 109 (Cal. Ct. App. 1958), discussed in AFL 2017 Cum. Supp. Ch. 1.F.15, *American Courts Begin To Recognize "True Sale" in the 1950s*, p. 110-114.

[15] See AFL 2017 Cum. Sup. Ch. 1.IV.A.13.a, p. 289-290, discussing the formation of both CIT's new UK factoring affiliate, late in 1960, and shortly thereafter, early in 1961, the formation of International Factors Ltd in England by the First National Bank of Boston together with two English companies as co-owners.

PART II

PRESENT – EMERGING OF MODERN FACTORING (1960s to PRESENT)

Introduction

Patrick de Villepin

Global Head of Factoring, BNP Paribas

In England as in the USA, factoring techniques were to prosper, initially in the textiles sector before subsequently spreading out to traditional industrial companies.

Clearly, the Anglo-Saxon base has determined the development and modes of factoring throughout the 20th century.

But in time, and notably following the rise of the services sector, being known for supporting companies in difficulty, the profession expanded to offer invoice discounting, a more flexible non-notified and non-administered solution, or "plain vanilla" short-term credit akin to the bank overdraft. Today, in these countries, factoring only accounts for a little less than 10% of receivables finance. In other words, the countries that constitute the cradle of factoring activity have not retained the traditional rules as the dominant model:

- In the UK (see chapter 10), the market leader in Europe (20.5%) and worldwide (13.75%), traditional factoring activity is concentrated within the banks and comes far behind invoice discounting or ABL;
- In the USA (see chapter 11), only the world's 7th largest player (with 3.8% of the global market) behind the UK, China, France, Germany, Italy and even Spain, ABL and "plain vanilla" have essentially remained banking products, whereas pure factoring (in the sense of full factoring) is the business of specialist companies which have frequently remained independent.

A conceptual and operational transformation currently explains how this dominant UK-US basis has been able to be exported and successfully transferred to other countries. In France, Italy, Germany and Spain the extension of the model to continental Europe has taken place by adapting to local realities. Of external and foreign origins, the financial technique has been incorporated within existing traditions, although not without difficulty. In just a few decades, it has become an integral part of the business world in these countries:

- In France (see chapter 12), the second largest player in Europe (16.8%) and the third worldwide (11.3%), the penetration of factoring was all the less obvious as it entered into direct competition with classical forms of short-term credits distributed by the commercial banks (promissory notes and mobilisation of receivables in the form of a discount or "Dailly" assignment). Today, the "French model" is well known although it is not actually codified in law. Among the top ten countries, it has seen the highest growth over the past ten years. The main actors have expanded the scope of their domestic market to the entire EU. Unfortunately, this fine success is subject to a constraint imposed by the French regulator ("Autorité de Contrôle Prudentiel et de Résolution" or ACPR) and as a result most French factors have had to opt for the status of ECS ("établissement de credit spécialisé" or specialist credit institution), akin to that of a bank, rather than that of SF ("société financière" or financial institution) in order to continue to freely benefit from the European passport, of which they are the main users within the EU;

- In Germany (see chapter 13), the 3rd largest in Europe (13.6%) and fourth worldwide (9.1%), the growth of factoring is a relatively recent phenomenon. For a long time, it stood shoulder to shoulder with Spain (which suffered greatly from the crisis and the disengagement of factors from the public sector), the country only overtook Italy in 2012. The German market is very much open to foreign entrants as four of the top five players are French: Targo Commercial Finance (ex GE Capital), Coface, BNP Paribas Factor and Eurofactor (Crédit Agricole Leasing and Factoring). Only PostBank is a pure local actor. This is a unique situation in Europe and worldwide. Still, German law sets out a clear separation between banking and factoring activities, essentially limited to non-recourse unlike in other countries. This specific status explains the conceptual divergence between German and French factors on the European AnaCredit reporting process, based on clients for the French and on a mix of client-with-recourse/buyer-non-recourse for the Germans. This pooling of buyers does not represent any lesser risk attenuation factor, all the more as the portfolio is usually reinsured at a level of more than 90% by credit insurers;

– In Italy (see chapter 14), the fourth largest in Europe (13.1%) and fifth worldwide (8.8%), as in Germany the practice of factoring is regulated by law. Very demanding for the factor operationally, it can also prove to be burdensome in terms of regulatory reporting (as with BaFin, the Federal Financial Supervisory Authority in Germany). But it also strives to protect the client's interests, notably during the "suspect period" before or after a bankruptcy petition. The "Revocatoria" is notably able to invoke the liability of the factor and increase its cost of risk.

Each of these countries contributes to the development of a legal and operational framework for factoring. In its own way, continental Europe promotes this Industry which could support the growth of factoring globally. However, Brexit or other national movements could jeopardize this opportunity. For a long time to come, the EU is likely to remain the main market for factoring if the ECB and national regulators decide to harmonise the rules, once and for all.

A – Anglo-Saxon Base

10. Factoring in the UK, the Rise of Invoice Finance and ABL in Europe's Most Mature Market

Jeff Longhurst

Managing Director, Membership Events & Training, UK Finance

After years of being regarded as a form of alternative finance, invoice finance (factoring and invoice discounting, accompanied by ABL) has, following the rise of the fintechs and development of new alternative finance providers, recently become seen as almost a mainstream product. Perhaps it is more surprising that it has taken so long, given that at time of writing the UK is the biggest user of invoice finance worldwide with sales assigned of EUR 350.8 billion in 2016.[1]

Yet, whilst sales to users of invoice finance account for 14.7% of UK GDP[2], growth of the market in the UK continues to be hampered by misconceptions about invoice finance, particularly about its cost, loss of control by a business over its sales ledger and most particularly by the image of factoring as lending of the last resort.

This explains why, of assigned sales in 2016, only 7% related to (full) factoring and the remaining 93% to invoice discounting, which has become the invoice finance product of choice for UK businesses. The figures are substantially affected by a relatively recent shift in invoice finance away from being merely a product for small businesses to one utilised by mid corporates and above. This has been fashioned to some extent by the rise of ABL but also by the recognition of sponsors that invoice finance is a product which fits very well with M&As, MBOs, MBIs, restructuring and growth generally. So, understandably, what

---

[1] Asset Based Finance Association Statistics. FCI 2016 statistics only mention EUR 327 billion.
[2] European Federation of Factoring and Commercial Finance (EUF) Statistics.

follows considers, and generally refers to, invoice finance and ABL in the UK rather than factoring.

I. Recent History

In the 16th and 17th centuries, as the methodology of trade across the UK and across countries became more and more complex, there developed a need for participants, which were neither involved in production of goods nor their distribution or, directly, in their sale. They did not add value to the goods or even transport them, but merely acted as a conduit for passing goods from one stage to the next – the creation of the "middleman" to work between supplier and buyer.

From Textile Industry to Factoring

Specifically, within the textile industry these middlemen became known as "factors" and, as previously seen, can be traced back to the Mid-15th century and businesses such as Blackwell Hall Factors in a market for woollen cloth. Initially the cloth manufacturers would bring their products to market, but as time progressed, they instead shipped their product and used factors to sell their cloth for commission.

Factoring was introduced to the UK in 1960s when International Factors Ltd was incorporated. That company was followed over the next few years by, amongst others, Portman Factors, Shield Factors, Mercantile Credit and Alex Lawrie. Some were dedicated to non-recourse factoring, others to recourse factoring.

These innovators took full advantage of the beneficial UK legislative framework which facilitated not just the purchase of invoices through factoring, but also the taking of charges against book debts which might fail to vest in them through assignment – a true belt and braces approach.[3]

From Factoring to Invoice Finance[4]

In the early 1970s, the UK clearing banks started to acquire factoring companies, recognising how close this business was to their own offerings and facilities. This gave impetus to the Industry by providing access

---

[3] Hawkins Richard, Wilde Edward, Peers Robin, *Asset Based Working Capital Finance*, Canterbury, Financial World Publishing, 2001.
[4] Davidson Nigel, Mills Simon, Salinger Freddie R., *Salinger on Factoring*, Sweet and Maxwell, London, 5th edition, December 2016.

to relatively unlimited funding and a steady source of new business introductions. In this decade, the Industry educated itself, initially by experience but later through training arranged by the Association of British Factors, later the Association of British Factors and Discounters (est. 1976). This association continued to develop and established its own charitable education foundation to provide training and education to the invoice finance industry.

Although the 1980s started and ended with recessions, the intervening years were very successful and generally profitable. Technology was introduced to provide electronic links with clients, which overcame the potential clients' fear of losing touch with their ledgers. It also enabled clients to send invoice details to the factor electronically, saving time and effort for the client, and for the factor the expensive and repetitive task of data punching.

In the 1990s, factors and discounters introduced flexible finance against other assets such as stock, plant and machinery, encouraged by new entrants from the USA and Europe. The Factors and Discounters Association took over from the Association of British Factors and Discounters in 1996 to protect and promote the Industry, provide education and training, publicity, legal and technical support, and ultimately set professional standards.

As the market has developed within the United Kingdom, many terms have been introduced to describe the products and services offered within the Industry in order to differentiate them from factoring. The term invoice finance is now seen as a collective term incorporating all types of factoring and invoice discounting. However, those financiers which have extended their product range to include funding other assets such as stock, plant and machinery etc. are more and more recognised under the term asset based lenders.

II. The Shape of the Current UK Market

The Industry is now represented in the UK by UK Finance which produces statistics annually on the market. These show continuous strong growth of invoice finance in the UK, from EUR 1 billion in 1978 to EUR 35 billion in 1995, EUR 202 billion in 2005 and EUR 350 billion in 2016.

Products

A full range of invoice products are available in the UK supported by ABL.

Full Factoring

A continuous arrangement between an invoice financier and a company, where the invoice financier will purchase from the company the invoices payable, for an immediate cash advance, with the balance being paid on receipt of funds from the debtor less the invoice financiers fees. The invoice financier will notify the debtors of the arrangement and will provide sales ledger maintenance, collection services and in some cases credit protection against bad debts. There are many variations of factoring, including CHOCC (Client Handles Own Credit Control), agency, maturity and confidential factoring.

Invoice Discounting

Similar to factoring but there is a very significant difference in that the invoice financier does not operate a detailed sales ledger showing each of the invoices outstanding, only a control account showing the total of the outstanding sales ledger. The client manages its own sales ledger and carries out its own credit control, collecting the proceeds of the debts as an agent and trustee for the financier.

Confidential and Disclosed Invoice Discounting

There are two main types of invoice discounting – confidential and disclosed. In the case of confidential invoice discounting, the agreement between the invoice discounter and the client is not disclosed. Assignment is not notified to the debtors and the invoices do not bear an assignment notice. So, debtors are unaware that the debt has been assigned to a third party to whom there is no obligation to pay. Disclosed discounting, as its name suggests, includes disclosure to debtors of assignment, but otherwise operates in the same way. Either form of discounting can be recourse or non-recourse as for factoring.

International Invoice Financing

International invoice financing encompasses the same principles as the core products listed above and has been developed to accommodate the increasing levels of international trade. Invoice discounting predominates in the UK. Some providers under a factoring arrangement will collect direct from the end buyer but many others use the benefits of membership of the international trade body and trading platform FCI. This two-factor system has the benefit of a factor in the country of the debtor using local knowledge to provide credit insurance and collection.

Selective Invoice Finance

Under all the arrangements we have looked at above, the agreement will, in nearly all circumstances, require the client to assign all invoices to the invoice financier, unless a specific agreement has been made. With selective factoring, the client and the invoice financier will agree which of the client's debtors will be factored rather than taking all of them. This product is seeing significant growth through the emergence of online auction platforms for invoice finance, although it is still less than 0.2% of the invoice finance market.

ABL

ABL is when a financier, in addition to invoice finance, advances money to an organisation against their invoices, stock, plant, machinery, property, or sometimes, even their brand name. It delivers sophisticated solutions for a variety of scenarios including growth, acquisitions, MBOs, MBIs, M&As, refinancing, turnarounds, and public to private transactions (across both a European and a global arena). It is not uncommon for several asset based lenders to work together in what is known as a 'syndication', to combine the lending power required.

Market

The UK market has developed differently from both the USA, and from the rest of Europe, which has continued to embrace factoring, and particularly non-recourse factoring. In the UK, invoice discounting dominates.

A breakdown of the market at the end of 2016 shows that invoice discounting remains the leading product with almost 93% of the EUR

350 billion market volume, far above factoring, domestic (6.5%) or international (0.6%). By number of clients using the different products however, the figures are more even at around 60/40 showing that smaller businesses are still offered factoring by providers as a less risky product for less credit worthy businesses. Non-recourse invoice finance, although small by comparison with recourse, is nevertheless a not insignificant EUR 46.3 billion. ABL continues to grow in the UK with additional facilities in stock finance, financing of plant and machinery, and property amounting to EUR 1.48 billion.[5]

III. Evolution of the Industry's Trade Association (Now UK Finance)

Until June 2017, the Asset Based Finance Association (ABFA) represented the interests of the invoice finance and ABL industry in the UK. The association was the most recent iteration of what started as a few leaders meeting regularly in the early 1970s. In 1976, the Association of British Factors (ABF) was formed by subsidiaries of the UK Banks and later the smaller, privately owned factors formed the Association of Invoice Factors (AIF) to represent their interests.

Then, as the Industry changed, and invoice discounting became the predominant product, the ABF changed its name to more properly represent the reality of the business, becoming the Association of British Factors and Discounters (ABFD). In September 1996, the ABFD merged with the AIF and the European Chapter of the Commercial Finance Association to become the Factors and Discounters Association (FDA). Then again, to reflect the change in emphasis towards ABL, in 2007, the association changed its name to the Asset Based Finance Association. On the 1st of July 2017, the members of the ABFA joined UK Finance which represents over 250 banks and finance providers in the UK.

The UK membership of the association reflects, too, the changing nature of the UK Industry as privately-owned businesses get bought and sold, banks change their names and foreign owned banks enter and leave the UK market, as shown in the table below:

---

[5] Asset Based Finance Association Statistics.

Factoring in the UK, the Rise of Invoice Finance and ABL 153

Table 4: Evolution of market players in the UK

Factors and Discounters Association December 2006	Asset Based Finance Association December 2016	Comments
	Amicus Commercial Finance Ltd	New
	Ashley Commercial Finance	New
Aston Rothbury Factor Ltd		Purchased by SME / Metrobank
Bank of America, NA		
Bank of Scotland Cashflow Finance		Part of Lloyds
Barclays Sales Financing	Barclays Trade & Working Capital UK and Ireland	
Bibby Financial Services Ltd	Bibby Financial Services Ltd	
Burdale Financial Ltd	Wells Fargo Capital Finance Ltd	Acquisition
Cashflow Partners Ltd		No longer trading
Cattles Invoice Finance Ltd	Aldermore Invoice Finance Ltd	
Charterhouse Commercial Finance Plc		No longer trading
City Invoice Finance Ltd		Acquired by ABN AMRO Commercial Finance
Close Invoice Finance Ltd	Close Invoice Finance Ltd	
Clydesdale Bank Plc	Clydesdale Bank Plc	
Coface Receivables Finance Ltd		No longer trading
Davenham Trade Finance Ltd		No longer trading
DCD Factor Plc		No longer trading
Enterprise Finance Europe		No longer trading
Eurofactor (UK) Ltd		Purchased by GE
Euro Sales Finance (UK)		No longer trading
	Factor 21 Ltd	New
	Firstsource Solutions Ltd	New
Five Arrows Commercial Finance Ltd	Paragon Bank Business Finance Plc	Acquisition
Fortis Commercial Finance Ltd	BNP Paribas Commercial Finance Ltd	Acquisition

Factors and Discounters Association December 2006	Asset Based Finance Association December 2016	Comments
GE Commercial Finance Ltd	GE Capital Bank Ltd	
	Gapcap Ltd	New
	Gener8 Finance Ltd	New
GMAC Commercial Finance Plc		No longer trading
	HH Cashflow Finance Ltd	
	Hitachi Capital (UK) Plc	
HSBC Invoice Finance (UK) Ltd	HSBC Invoice Finance (UK) Ltd	
Independent Growth Finance	IGF Invoice Finance Ltd	Acquisition
JP Morgan		
	Leumi ABL Ltd	New
Lloyds TSB Commercial Finance Ltd	Lloyds Bank Commercial Finance Ltd	
	Nucleus Commercial Finance Ltd	New
	Positive Cashflow Finance Ltd	New
	Pulse Cashflow Finance Ltd	New
RBS Invoice Finance Ltd	RBS Invoice Finance Ltd	
RDM Factors Ltd		Purchased by SME / Metrobank
Regency Factors Plc	Regency Factors Plc	
	Santander Invoice Finance	
	Secure Trust Bank Commercial Finance	New
	Shawbrook Business Credit	
	Siemens Financial Services Ltd	New
Skipton Business Finance Ltd	Skipton Business Finance Ltd	
SME Invoice Finance Ltd	Metro Bank Asset and Invoice Finance	Acquisition
	Team Factors Ltd	New
Ultimate Finance Group Plc	Ultimate Finance Group Plc	

Factors and Discounters Association December 2006	Asset Based Finance Association December 2016	Comments
	Working Capital Partners Ltd	New
Venture Finance Ltd	ABN AMRO Commercial Finance	Acquisition

As can be seen from the above, over the last ten years, there has been an average of more than one change of ownership per year. Similarly, there has been on average more than one new entrant a year. This reflects the continued and continuing changes in the UK market to meet the changing needs of UK businesses.

Polarisation of the Market

As the market in the UK has become more mature, and whilst the UK clearing bank subsidiaries maintain an 80-85% share of the market, then so have participants tended to concentrate on particular/niche areas of the market to compete.

The subsidiaries of the UK clearing banks are Barclays, HSBC, Lloyds and Royal Bank of Scotland (and latterly Santander). They have dominated the market since first entering it in the 1970s and are likely to continue to keep that control for the foreseeable future, despite the incursions of the challenger banks, foreign banks and independently owned invoice finance providers. They offer all forms of invoice finance and ABL to all sizes of businesses, from SMEs upwards.

Other players tend to specialise in chosen areas so that they can compete on their specialisms and on service. They are either providers of invoice finance specifically so that they can focus on service to SMEs, or the focus is on a full ABL facility where, in addition to invoice finance, stock, plant and machinery, and property may also be financed. This second area has particular requirements for skilled staffing expertise in understanding the cash requirements of sophisticated businesses along with associated risk management skills.

IV. Legal Environment and Regulation Relating to Invoice Finance

The relationship between an invoice financier and its client is governed by the debt purchase agreement between the two parties. Generally, these will be whole turnover agreements which provide that all debts are assigned to the invoice financier on creation, and set out the various terms of the relationship including the client's obligations and warranties.

Legal Environment[6]

Statutory law on assignment is based on s136 of the Law of Property Act 1925. This sets out the conditions which must pertain if the assignor is to obtain sole right to receive payment from the debtor. It provides that a legal assignment must be in writing under the hand of the assignor, must be assignment absolutely of the whole debt, and notice of the assignment must be given in writing to the debtor.

Without this, the assignor can obtain merely an equitable assignment. The risk therefore of operating a confidential invoice discounting facility without the giving of notice to the debtor is that, should the debtor pay the client, the assignor (discounter) has no rights against the debtor to receive payment or obtain redress.

So, to obtain additional collateral/security, the industry has tended to insist that the agreements are supported by fixed or floating charges on the client's book debts or, increasingly, a full debenture over all the assets of the business. These charges allow, should a client cease trading, for the appointment of an administrative receiver over these assets so that the administrator can realise the worth in the assets on behalf of the invoice financier, and even trade the business on until buyer contracts are completed to ensure that debts are paid. Unlike the law in many countries, the insolvency of a business does not diminish the security held by the invoice financier which retains title to the debts assigned.

For ABL, which in the UK is predominantly invoice finance with the addition of funding against other assets such as stock, plant and property, this ability to trade a business whilst in the course of administration has become an absolute necessity.

---

[6] Clarke Robin, Wilde Edward, *Cashflow Finance*, Factors and Discounters Association, 2005.

The situation for sole traders and partnerships is somewhat different as it requires that the agreements be registered as bills of sale under the Bills of Sale Act 1878. The Law Commission is currently reviewing this archaic legislation to improve the bureaucracy involved in operating invoice agreements under this provision.

Regulation

Invoice finance is regarded as an unregulated financial service in the UK. There is no specific legislation or regulation related specifically to invoice finance or its providers. However, as the majority of providers of invoice finance are banks or other regulated financial institutions, they are all governed by the regulations applicable to financial services generally. And of course, every provider is covered by regulations in respect of anti-money laundering and data protection provisions.

In July 2013, the members of the ABFA decided that it was incumbent upon themselves to create their own standards framework, including a code of conduct under which its members would operate, to offer protection for the smallest businesses (SMEs with turnover up to GBP 6.5 million). An independent professional standards council was set up to administer the framework, which each year is revised and updated to meet changing needs. The framework is supported by a complaints process which includes provision for submission of complaints to an independent Ombudsman. This alternative dispute resolution offering has been adopted by UK Finance for those of its members which offer invoice finance.

V. The Future

Asset Based Finance (ABF) is increasingly being used as a source of funding by high growth companies – from small businesses, to those owned by private equity, to innovative businesses and subsidiaries of some of the world's largest companies. A thorough and up-to-date understanding of this form of funding is therefore important for anyone involved with finance and company funding.[7]

---

[7] *GROWTH through Asset Based Finance – Best-Practice Guideline 65*, Institute of Chartered Accountants of England and Wales (ICAEW) Corporate Finance Faculty, ABFA.

Although the UK has seen growth in the ABL market in particular, that growth has slowed in recent years. So, during 2016, the ABFA conducted a survey amongst both clients and introducers of business to get their views on factoring, invoice discounting and ABL post-recession.[8]

Respondents were able to clearly identify invoice finance as an effective method of assisting cash flow/providing working capital. They were positive towards invoice discounting:

- "It is a straightforward and flexible way to fund working capital requirements";
- "Flexible option, cheaper financing and better supports working capital cycles";
- "Best way to provide working capital for the business".

But they remain negative towards factoring with 40% of clients responding that they would not choose factoring as an option:

- "It is like handing your business over to someone else";
- "Expensive and removes the relationship between buyer and supplier";
- "It appears to have a stigma".

When asked about ABL there was a favourable response from those who understood it and its purpose, but it was very apparent that there is a long way to go in developing a real understanding amongst either potential users or intermediaries:

- "This is shrouded in mysticism. There is only a basic understanding of this product";
- "Not sure that they would really understand it at all. There would probably be confusion with it seen as just HP or leasing."

The overall conclusion as a cause for action is summarised by one respondent on ABL: "There is a lack of knowledge regarding the different products available and education is key".

So, for the future, if the market for invoice finance is to grow in the UK, the invoice finance industry needs to work together to educate all stakeholders – government, accountants and other advisors, as well as potential users themselves – on the key advantages of invoice finance and ABL for growing businesses.

---

[8] Asset Based Finance Association Survey 2016.

The message must be conveyed that invoice finance is a relatively cheap form of finance which is an ideal solution for solving the cash flow and working capital needs of businesses of any size.

The growth of alternative finance in the UK could be considered a threat to the Industry going forward. However, it is arguably not the specialist single invoice finance platforms which have or will cause a threat, but the providers of "indiscriminate" cash who offer funds to SMEs without the SMEs necessarily getting the most appropriate form of finance to meet their specific needs. These alternative providers are springing up almost every day and there has to be a period of consolidation when some (and we are already seeing this) are unable to meet the needs of their clients or their forecast profits and are forced to sell and/or close. Their business models have yet to be tested by a slow down or recession and should this happen in the UK following on from Brexit, then the consolidation and failures will be rapidly accelerated.

Moreover, the alternative finance providers also create an opportunity for our Industry as they have so far tended to offer facilities to businesses that would not otherwise have looked at invoice finance as an option. This overall increase in awareness and in the product has to be a good thing for invoice finance providers and businesses alike.

We are already beginning to see businesses move from the platforms to ABFA Members. They have tested the benefits of invoice finance through using the platforms for single invoice finance and realised that a whole turnover facility can meet their cash flow needs more effectively and more cheaply.

Within the UK, there are moves afoot to bring the invoice finance industry more into the mainstream. The ABFA has recently merged with the British Banking Association, The Council of Mortgage Lenders, Payments UK, UK cards and Fraud Action UK into one large financial services trade association, UK Finance. Although this has meant the assimilation of the ABFA into that one organisation of over 250 members, it may also mean that invoice finance becomes recognised finally as a core product within the UK banking community with resultant increased awareness amongst staff and clients.

VI. Conclusion

Invoice finance and ABL will continue to grow in the UK. The merging of the ABFA with the other associations may lead to a step change in the development of the Industry.

Regulation may be imposed on the Industry in the medium to long-term and if it is, then, provided it is not too bureaucratic and intrusive it should assist in ridding the Industry of the stigma of "lender of the last resort" to SMEs.

Alternative finance can be seen as a means of growing the market for finance for SMEs but "traditional" invoice finance providers need to keep up with the fintechs and ensure that their own systems are simplified to meet the requirements of IT savvy businesses whose owners expect immediate responses and decisions to applications for finance.

And, of course, the Industry needs to work together to educate stakeholders and advocate the use of invoice finance through consistent language, highlighting the significant benefits of the product without the use of confusing jargon.

11. Factoring in the United States since 1960[1]

Stuart BRISTER

President, Wells Fargo Commercial Services

Brian MARTIN

Southeast Regional Manager, Wells Fargo Factoring Unit

In this chapter, we will explore trends and developments in the US factoring sector since 1960, a period in which there was enormous growth and change in the factoring sector due to:

- acquisitions and later sector domination by US banks;
- consolidation due to subsequent divestments by many of the acquiring banks;
- increasing automation, which allowed for more effective management of much larger firms that would emerge from the consolidation wave;
- a resurgence of independent, entrepreneurial factoring firms; and
- in response to surging imports, growth in international factoring.

I. US Factoring Prior to 1960

As the American textile industry developed during the 19th century, textile mills came to rely on external (and in some cases internal) factoring firms that provided sales, financing, credit, and collection services. Textile factors in those days often also acted as cotton brokers making a market for cotton growers to sell their crops to the textile mills, and then as the mills' sales agent selling the cloth or yarn produced to apparel companies,

---

[1] The opinions herein of the authors do not necessarily reflect those of Wells Fargo (© 2018 Wells Fargo Bank, N.A. All rights reserved) Capital Finance or any other Wells Fargo entity.

thereby providing the textile mills with financing from purchase to payment. While the end-to-end factoring model was largely abandoned by the early 20th century in favor of factoring firms acting as their mill clients' financier and credit department, there was one factor, Joshua L. Bailey & Co., Inc., which through the 1980s acted as both factor and sales agent for its textile clients, which included now defunct manufacturers such as Arkwright Mills and Mayfair Mills.

Before the 1960s, factoring companies were overwhelmingly private family-owned firms not affiliated with banks. However, there were two notable exceptions to the prevalent private-company format: Commercial Investment Trust (the predecessor to today's CIT), an early player in the nascent sectors of ABL and consumer finance, went public in 1924 and James Talcott & Co. went public in the mid 1930s. CIT would first enter the factoring sector in August 1928 through its purchase of Peierls, Buhler. In 1931, CIT acquired Morton H. Meinhard & Company and Greff & Company, and merged the two into a new subsidiary, Meinhard-Greff & Co. The following year CIT purchased William Iselin & Co., which at the time was the oldest and largest US factoring firm.

The founding of James M. Talcott & Company in 1854 is illustrative of the typical development of US factoring firms in the 19th century. James M. Talcott founded his namesake firm as a selling agent for his brother's knitting mill and later added other clients in the textile industry. As a selling agent, Talcott's firm was in a position to determine the creditworthiness of its mill clients' customers. From that activity, it was a short leap to providing financing for its client mills by making loans against the receivables owing to its client mills by the customers which Talcott's firm knew, solicited and credit-approved. The firm would survive the many financial panics of the 19th and early 20th centuries, and even the Great Depression, all of which witnessed the failures of many depository banks. These crises actually benefited firms like James M. Talcott & Co. since its funding was not dependent on bank deposits which tended to quickly dissipate during the panics prior to the creation of deposit insurance.

Until passage of the Bank Holding Company Act of 1956, and its subsequent regulatory interpretations, factoring was generally not considered an appropriate activity for federally-insured US banks. In fact, in 1960, there were only two banks engaged in factoring, both of which entered the sector in the 1930s, before the advent of deposit insurance and its associated regulatory lean: the First National Bank of Boston and Trust Company of Georgia. The limited participation of banks prior to the 1960s is indicative of the risks, both real and perceived, associated with factoring. Perception and reality were often aligned before the adoption of the Uniform Commercial Code (UCC), and a unified bankruptcy code, which laws today underpin the very existence of factoring. Prior to the adoption of the UCC, security interests in accounts receivable purchased by a factor hinged on notifications to customers (a slow, uncertain and cumbersome process) and possessory liens as to the inventory and documents which gave rise or pertained to the purchased accounts. The lack of consistent laws made it difficult for factoring firms and other lenders to complete with confidence secured transactions outside of their local areas. It was not until the near-nationwide adoption (Louisiana did not adopt until 1995) in the early 1960s of the first version of the UCC that factors and other secured lenders could complete transactions with confidence in the various states.

Prior to the 1960s, factoring firms were concentrated in New York, but there were a few firms located in other large US urban areas, such as Chicago, Atlanta, Kansas City, Dallas and Los Angeles. In terms of company names, today's observers would likely react "who's that?" to a "who's who" list of factors in the 1960s and earlier, such as A.J. Armstrong, H.A. Caesar & Company, Hubshman Factors Corp., Goodman Factors, Joel Hurt Factors, L.F. Dommerich & Co., Inc., John P. Maguire & Co., The Slavenburg Corp. and Walter E. Heller & Company, just to name a few.

II. The 15th of January 1965

Some dates in history stand out as significant turning points. For the US factoring sector, the 15th of January 1965 was a seminal date because it was announced that the directors of Hubshman Factors Corp. of New York City, a wholly-owned subsidiary since 1961 of vending machine pioneer Automatic Canteen, had agreed for the company to be acquired by First National City Bank of New York (now Citibank) for just over USD 12 million. Why is this date monumental in the history of US factoring? During the rest of the 1960s, and continuing in the 1970s, the competitive landscape in the US factoring sector would quickly and inalterably change as nearly every major independent factoring company would be acquired by or merge with a bank. In understanding the timing of this historic event, it is important to note that the (a) Bank Holding Company Act of 1956 and its subsequent regulatory interpretations had by 1965 clearly come to support factoring as a permitted commercial banking activity, and (b) by 1962, the first version of the UCC had been enacted by 49 states. First National City Bank of New York in the 1960s had established itself as the largest and most innovative US bank (in the same year, the bank bought consumer charge card issuer Carte Blanche as an entrée into the then nascent consumer credit card business), so it is not surprising that the bank was the first US bank to dive into factoring. First National City's factoring acquisition was probably motivated in part by the attractive yields that factoring offered. During the 1960s, inflation was increasing due in part to rapidly expanding GDP and high governmental expenditures related to expanding social programs, as well as heavy military spending. At a time when banks were paying 4¾% on passbook saving accounts, and with a Prime Rate of 6% by December 1965, US banks were in search of business segments like factoring which offered better yields compared to prime US commercial loans. Moreover, banks by 1965 were competing with the commercial paper markets for the funding needs of some prime US commercial borrowers, making yield-enhancing moves such as the Hubshman acquisition even more alluring.

First National City was first, but its factoring acquisition was not the last or even the largest. In the next five years, the following independent factors were among the firms acquired by banks in pursuit of adding factoring as a profitable line of business: Joel Hurt Factors (Citizens & Southern Bank 1965), Shapiro Brothers (Chase Manhattan Bank 1966), L.F. Dommerich & Co., Inc. (Chemical Bank 1968), Factors, Inc. (North Carolina National Bank 1969) and H.A. Caesar & Co. (First Union National Bank 1970).

Independent factoring concern Standard Factors and CIT went slightly different routes in their bank affiliations. Standard Factors jumped into the banking business by acquiring Sterling Bank in 1969, and the present-day Sterling Factors is successor of that firm. In 1965, CIT purchased Mead Brook National Bank, then a dominant bank in suburban New York City and the 45th largest US bank. CIT in 1967 acquired First National Bank & Trust of Freeport, and New York City-based National Bank of North America. Then in 1969, CIT purchased Trade Bank & Trust Company. The acquired banks, which by 1970 had USD 2.2 billion in assets, were ultimately merged, and adopted the National Bank of North America name. In the mid 1970s, CIT became troubled with loan losses and otherwise poor operating results, with earnings dropping a cumulative 60% between 1974 and 1976. Ultimately CIT was forced to divest its banking unit, selling the bank in 1979 to United Kingdom-based National Westminster for USD 430 million. In 1982, NatWest acquired the factoring unit of nearly-failed First Pennsylvania Bank, but would exit the factoring business in 1989 by selling it to Heller Financial.

Banks, with the advantage of deposit bases, would bring a cheaper and more stable source of funding to the acquired factoring firms, and for a time it was thought that the banks, which had commercial clients in a variety of industries, would also usher in a clientele diverse from the traditional textile, apparel and furniture industries that were closely associated with US factoring. While many factoring companies did see some diversification, particularly through growth in international, factoring today still remains most closely associated with its traditional industries. While the initial impetus for acquisitions included the higher yields that factoring offered, the increased competition resulting from the entry of banks in fact dramatically and permanently reduced factoring yields. Commissions, which are the fees charged by factors to purchase receivables and accept credit risk, were well above 1% in 1965. By 1980, the average commission rate was on its way to 0.75%, and today the average commission rate is well under 0.50%. Similar yield compression has occurred in interest rate spreads, which declined from over 4% in the mid 1970s to 2% today. Banks saw the need, and had the expertise to invest in data processing, which was essential for both growth and lower costs given the highly transactional nature of factoring. In the mid 1960s, at the advent of main-frame computing, a factoring firm with USD 200 million in annual purchases would have had to employ approximately 100 people to support its needs; by 1985, a factoring firm with USD 1 billion in annual purchases would have employed about 250 people. Today, after 50 years of technological advances, those same 250 employees could support more than USD 40 billion in annual purchases.

The entry and later partial exodus of banks would forever change the landscape of US factoring. To illustrate, in 1970, just after the first surge of acquisitions, there were 30 major factoring firms in the US. By 1990, that number would fall to 15, with the 10 largest firms representing about 75% of the aggregate annual US factoring volume; today, major US factoring firms number less than ten, with the two largest participants (Wells Fargo and CIT) representing in excess of 50% of today's US factoring volume.

III. 1985-Today

While certainly more adventurous than staid commercial banking, factoring in the mid 1960s had come to be viewed by banks as a fairly stable, safe and profitable sector. And while that is a fairly accurate depiction, a few well-publicized frauds in the early 1980s would remind banks of the risks of loss in portfolios which are not well-monitored. These well-publicized scandals, along with increased credit losses during recessions, and decreased yields due to hyper-competitive conditions, would lead to a period of rapid divestiture and consolidation.

In 1977, factoring concern J.P. Maguire & Co. was acquired by New York bank Irving Trust from Provident Bank, which had bought the unit in 1971 from Fieldcrest Mills. Like many acquirers, Irving likely hoped its new subsidiary could broaden its base of business beyond the textile and apparel industries. In March 1980, J.P. Maguire & Co. signed as a client Candor Diamond Company located in Manhattan, which was owned by Irwin W. Margolies. By July 1981, Maguire officials were having doubts about their new client and discovered that the USD 6 million owed by Candor was based on accounts receivable that were largely fictitious, and that the USD 2.3 million in diamonds Candor had represented as additional collateral could not be located. But the fraud and related loss were just the beginning. In an effort to silence witnesses who could testify in his related tax fraud trial, Margolies had his controller, Margaret Barbera, and her assistant, Jenny Soo Chin, murdered in April 1982, Mr Margolies, who later plead guilty to tax fraud and was sentenced to 28 years for that offense, was also convicted and sentenced to 50 years to life for his part in the murders of these two women.

The jarring news about Candor Diamond was still current in August 1983, when news articles reported that CIT unit William Iselin had sued Thomas Savage, its former president, and two other former employees, along with Irwin Feiner, a garment industry entrepreneur, charging that its former employees and Feiner conspired to obtain fraudulently some USD 20 million in advances from Iselin. But the bad news did not stop there, because Feiner also had additional companies factored by Chemical Bank, which had also duped that factor for an additional USD 20 million. As it turned out, Mr Feiner was using the money fraudulently obtained from Iselin and Chemical to purchase and operate a horse-breeding farm in Ocala, Florida. While most of his fraudulent schemes were directed at his factors, Feiner also defrauded several commercial

Factoring in the United States since 1960   167

banks which lent him funds based on two phony yacht builder certificates and excessive values on a Boeing 727 and two Gulfstream jets. The Iselin suit against Thomas Savage, who by that time was head of CBT Factors (owned by Connecticut Bank & Trust) was controversial, and resulted in a countersuit; Savage died in 1989 at age 70 before litigation was fully resolved.

By 1979, CIT was having financial challenges. The company rebuffed in 1979 a takeover attempt by industrial concern RCA, but RCA was back in 1980, and its second USD 1.2 billion acquisition attempt was successful. However, the debt-ladened CIT acquisition did not work out well. Moreover, a CEO change at RCA in 1981 resulted in a focus on debt reduction and operational simplicity after a decade of debt-fueled acquisitions including CIT, Hertz Rental Cars, frozen food maker Banquet and carpet manufacturer Coronet Carpet Mills. In late 1983, less than four years after its purchase, RCA announced that it would sell CIT to Manufacturers Hanover Corporation for USD 1.5 billion, which at the time was the largest single acquisition ever by a bank holding company. The "Manny Hanny" ownership was also to be short lived. By 1989, the financial condition of Manufacturers Hanover, along with some of its money-center counterparts, had weakened as a result of troubled loans to foreign countries. To reduce debt, increase liquidity and focus on cleaning up its troubled loan portfolios, Manufacturers Hanover in 1989 sold a 60% stake in CIT to Tokyo-based Dai-Ichi Kangyo Bank (at the time the world's largest bank) for USD 1.4 billion. Dai-Ichi Kangyo would ultimately increase its stake in CIT to 80% by 1995. Manny Hanny would ultimately merge with Chemical Bank, which in 1987 had sold its factoring unit to Citizens and Southern Bank, which three years later would also add Security Pacific's factoring unit (which was the product of two acquisitions, A.J. Armstrong & Company in 1981 and Citibank's factoring unit in 1984). The financial performance of Dai-Ichi Kangyo faltered in the late 1990s, and to raise capital, the Japanese bank spun-off its majority ownership in two offerings during 1997 and 1998, making CIT once again a public company.

Despite the many ownership changes during the 1980s and 1990s, CIT in the 1990s significantly expanded its market share in the US factoring sector. In 1993, CIT announced purchase of the US factoring unit of Barclays Bank, which had entered US market in 1980 by purchasing a factoring and ABL unit owned by Aetna Insurance. In 1999, CIT would again expand by buying the factoring unit of Heller Financial, which was originally founded in 1935, and since 1984 had been owned by Japan's Fuji Bank. The Heller purchase was followed quickly by CIT's acquisition of the factoring unit of Congress Talcott, which First Union had acquired through its 1998 acquisition of CoreStates. While the Heller and Congress Talcott acquisitions would at the time solidify CIT's role as the largest US factor, CIT's acquisition of troubled Canadian lender Newcourt Credit resulted in a share price decline, and in March 2001 acquisition-hungry Tyco International (best known for its ADT security and electronics component business) announced an offer to buy CIT for USD 9.2 billion. By early 2002 Tyco was the subject of a massive scandal amid rumors of accounting fraud and lavish spending by its CEO Dennis Kozlowski and CFO Mark Swartz. In February 2002 Tyco announced that it would sell CIT, but when an immediate buyer was not forthcoming, Tyco spun off CIT to the public, raising USD 4.6 billion instead of the USD 10 billion it had sought. The spinoff was completed in July 2002, and CIT was once again a stand-alone public company. After its third emergence as a public company, CIT embarked on another factoring acquisition spree, acquiring factoring units owned by General Electric (2003), HSBC (2003) and SunTrust Bank (2005). In each case, the "seller" was motivated by lackluster results that had been dented by the 2001 recession, poor growth prospects, and outsized losses stemming from failed retailers such as Ames Department Store and K-Mart. But CIT's growth as a whole was not fueled by its old line factoring business, but by its rapid growth through acquisitions and expansions in sectors such as student loans and subprime mortgages. On the 1st of November 2009, the parent company CIT Group filed for bankruptcy, and its liabilities included USD 2.3 billion owed to the US Government's Troubled Asset Relief Program. CIT quickly emerged from the proceedings but the bankruptcy definitely affected the factoring unit. The year following its parent's bankruptcy filing, the CIT factoring unit reported that its factoring volume had declined by USD 4.4 billion or 16.5%; further declines would follow in 2011 and 2012. While CIT's market share by 2015 was still considerable as the second largest factor in the US, it no longer had the overwhelming dominance that it enjoyed in 2005, when it held over 50% of the US factoring market.

Here are a few of the period's many transactions involving the sale/purchase of major US factoring businesses:

- Union Planters acquired the factoring unit of Florida-based Capital Bank in 1998 - Union Planters was later acquired by Regions Bank in 2004 and the factoring unit, which by that time was having portfolio issues, was sold in 2005 in a transaction led by Andrew

Factoring in the United States since 1960 169

>   Tananbaum (whose family started and who ran Century Business Credit until it was sold to Wells Fargo in 1998) with backing by private equity group Perry Capital;
> - From the Capital Factors sale arose First Capital, as former Capital Factors management team members with private equity backing purchased in 2005 First Capital, an Oklahoma-based independent recourse factoring company that would be converted to a non-recourse traditional factor and asset based lender – ten years later, First Capital was unwound, with its traditional factoring portfolio being sold to Sterling Bancorp, its recourse factoring portfolio sold to Seacoast National Bank, and its ABL portfolio sold to Ares Commercial Finance;
> - Irving Trust (which by subsequent hostile merger became part of Bank of New York) purchased the factoring units of Associates Commercial (1987), NCNB (1988), Slavenburg Corp. (1989), Banker Trust (1990), BankBoston (1993), MidLantic Factors (1996) and finally Bank of America (2000) – BNY would sell its by-then factoring conglomerate to GMAC for USD 1.9 billion later in 2000. GMAC also acquired a factoring unit from failed Finova in 2000. As previously mentioned, GMAC later exited the factoring sector by selling its unit to Wells Fargo in 2010;
> - Wells Fargo made a number of acquisitions on its way to becoming the largest US factor including Century Business Credit (1999), National Factors (1999), Commerce Funding (2006), Evergreen Funding (2006), Capital TempFunds (2009) and GMAC's factoring business (2010).

After all the deal making in the twenty year period ending in 2010, the US factoring sector would enter the second decade of the 21st century heavily consolidated, with the top two companies (Wells Fargo and CIT) having nearly a 50% market share, along with strong showings by family-owned independents Rosenthal and Rosenthal (founded and owned by the Rosenthal family since 1938), and Milberg Factors (founded and owned by the Milberg family since 1937), as well as the factoring units of BB&T, Sterling Bank and PEG-owned Capital Business Credit.

Table 5 (provided courtesy of R.S. Carmichael & Co., which has chronicled the US ABL and factoring sectors for many decades) vividly illustrates the massive growth and consolidation under bank ownership that has been wrought over the last 50 years.

Table 5: Factoring Industry volume & top players, 1965-2015

Year	Factoring Volume (USD billions)*	Top Players
2015	USD 100**	Wells Fargo, CIT, Rosenthal, Milberg, BB&T, Sterling
2005	113	CIT, GMAC, Wells Fargo Century, Capital Factors, BB&T, Rosenthal, Milberg
1995	61	CIT, BNY, Heller, FNB, NationsBank, Rosenthal, Milberg
1985	40	CIT, Security Pacific, FNB, Irving Trust, MHCC, BT Factors
1975	20	Meinhard-Commercial, Wm. Iselin, Heller, J P Maguire, FNB, Chemical, Citibank
1965	14	LF Dommerich, Hubshman (Citibank), FNB, James Talcott, AJ Armstrong, J P Maguire

* Total factoring volume as reported by US-based factors
** 2015 data includes only top 10 US-based factors
Sources: R.S. Carmichael & Co. estimates, CFA, Daily News Record, etc.

As the factoring sector has consolidated, so also has credit risk: the few larger participants now hold greater exposures to a consolidated retail sector. To mitigate this, many of the larger factoring participants lay-off risk through the use of credit insurance, hedges and other means. Despite all of the growth and deal-making of the last 50 years, the factoring in the US remains a financing niche that is not well known or understood. While factoring has been in existence much longer than the ABL sector, ABL over the last 50 years has emerged as a much larger and prominent form of financing for US businesses due to its applicability and acceptance by a wide array of industries.

During the mid-1970s following the initial wave of banks' forays into factoring, the management of many factors began to turn their attention to international opportunities. Originally responsive to the export needs of a few domestic client selling to foreign customers, international factoring was initially conceived as a way of approving foreign customers without taking undue credit and legal risks. For a slightly higher commission compared to domestic businesses, US factors would essentially subcontract to foreign financial institutions the responsibilities for credit approval, collection and risk of loss if the foreign customer was unable to pay for financial reasons. However, as imports from Asia and other countries grew during the 1980s, the rationale and flows of international factoring shifted from serving the occasional needs of domestic clients to a business segment dedicated to serving the credit and collection needs of foreign correspondents which were not familiar with, and did not want to take payment risk of US based customers. By the end of the 1980s, factoring volume inflows to US factors from international financial institutions aggregated in the billions of dollars, and at some factors came to represent as much as 10% of overall volume. For both the foreign supplier and its US customer, factoring invoices with payments terms of 30-90 days was both cheaper and easier than selling on terms requiring documentary LCs, which were both costly and cumbersome to administer. International factoring volumes continued to increase in the 1990s, and into the first decade of the 21st century, in conjunction with the growth of US imports. International factoring growth was also aided by the rules and procedure set down by the FCI cooperative, which served as both a rule-making body and communications platform for participating factors. While much of the international factoring volume is conducted under the auspices of FCI, there are significant volumes which are conducted via one-on-one relationships between a US factor and its foreign correspondent. According to FCI statistics, international factoring volume in the US in 2015 was nearly USD 16.4 billion or some 16% of total US factor volume. Unfortunately, the figure dropped to USD 7.2 billion in 2016 (7.6% of the total). Yet the market share leader in international factoring since 2013 has been Wells Fargo Bank, with much smaller shares by BB&T and CIT.

IV. Conclusion: the Overlooked Growth of Small Independent Factoring Companies

The final topic in this review of US factoring trends and developments since 1960 is the often overlooked growth of small independent factoring companies. Since most participants in this sector are private, accurate data is incomplete and scarce – some estimates put annual volume of small independents as high as USD 150 billion. Notwithstanding the lack of solid, vetted data, anecdotal evidence is very strong that both the number and volume of small independent factoring companies in the US has rapidly increased since 1960. Part of this increase is no doubt related to bank acquisitions in, and dominance of the larger factor segment, which has resulted in lucrative markets for the smaller independents (a) for companies with USD 10 million and less in revenues, as many of the larger factors often do not find it economical to pursue the factoring needs of smaller companies and (b) factoring prospects that cannot meet the more stringent due diligence and financial profile standards required by bank-owned factors. Further, the upheaval that followed interstate bank mergers and acquisitions from 1975 – 2000 put both former bankers and capital in play that led to the formation during the period of many small independents including Advance Financial, Presidential Financial (acquired by MidFirst Bank in 2013), Federal National Funding, JTA Factors (acquired by Canada-based Accord Financial in 1996) and North Mill Capital, to name a few. The sector has even attracted private-equity-backed "FinTech factors" such as BlueVine, 48 Factoring and Fundbox which have entered the fray over the last few years seeking to solicit and sign factoring clients via on-line and social media marketing versus the traditional referral, word-of mouth or local advertising used traditionally by small independents. Like their larger factoring brethren, small independent factoring companies have occasionally been the object of acquisitions by banks, including Goodman Factors (acquired in May 2014 by Independent Bank in Memphis), Bayview Funding (bought by California-based Heritage Bank of Commerce in October 2014) AmeriFactors Financial (purchased in September 2015 by Florida-based Gulf Coast Bank and Trust), and the purchase by Wells Fargo of four small independent factoring companies between 1999–2009. And though typically not well publicized, the sector has occasionally had its share of disruptions, such as PrinVest Financial or Liberty Financial just after the turn of the century. Despite the challenges of maintaining adequate capital and a volatile client base, small independents have achieved many successes, including broadening factoring's applicability to diverse industries, such as staffing, trucking, governments services, medical services, and industries other than textiles, apparel and furniture.

B – Enlarging to Continental Europe

12. Secured and Highly Regulated, the French Factoring Model

Patrick DE VILLEPIN

Global Head of Factoring, BNP Paribas

The success of factoring in the Anglo-Saxon world was no guarantee that it would flourish similarly in France. Situations were different. In France, this new concept called factoring brought in from abroad was far from self-evident. The penetration of this foreign financial technique was all the more visible given than it faced head-on competition with the classic forms of short-term credit issued by commercial banks (discount, promissory note or overdraft).

If not quite "behind the times", France is certainly "different". Cumbersome but effective, its system of discounts and rediscounts at the French central bank (Banque de France) is part of a very French tradition of centralisation and control. Many constraints still pose an obstacle to the flourishing of a factoring "made in France".

During the 1960s, resistance to factoring was high and not limited to banks. SMEs feared compromising their reputation with their clients (giving the impression of financial difficulties). Three arguments were made against factors:

- A psychological brake: gradual loss of commercial information, violation of trade secrets, intervention in management decisions, loss of buyer relationships and loss of control over sales policy;
- A managerial brake: fear of having to use strong-arm and insensitive collection methods in the event of non-payment, fear of putting all their eggs in one basket by using a bank's factoring service and becoming dependent on it;
- Lastly, a financial brake: the cost of factoring was deemed disproportionate and a disincentive compared to bank loans.

I. A Model Based on a Strong Regulatory Framework, Despite the Absence of Any Law

It took two years for a factoring company to be established in France. When a request was made in 1962, the National Credit Council (CNC) and the Banque de France immediately expressed two objections: 1) Fear of inflation in short-term credit: the financing should therefore be secondary to guarantees or management; 2) Risk of depersonalising credit: hence the requirement for a monthly statement of the buyer's amounts outstanding in order to trace the operations' beneficiaries.

At the end of a long debate, the decision was taken to make the regulation of financial institutions a requirement. Factoring French-style would be regulated or would not exist.

A Strong Regulatory Framework

In a centrally managed economy that was slow to adopt new ideas, the first factors played the role of precursors. At the outset, companies focused on international financing and exports. But very soon, the predominance of domestic demand redirected their energy towards the home SME market.

Founded on the 5th of May 1964, SFF (or International Factors France SA) was started by FNBB (with 50% of the capital). Among the other shareholders were SFAFC (a French credit insurance company, the future SFAC), joined later by International Factors AG (15%) and the Banque de Paris et des Pays-Bas (the future Paribas). Initially, things were difficult. After two years of operation, SFF had only 20 clients, mostly of medium quality. Completely unknown, the product was hard to sell. The brokers' channel (already active in credit insurance) soon became the preferred one. From the 1970s to the 1990s, the company ranked second in the French market, behind Factofrance Heller (FFH).

Established in October 1966, FFH was a 50/50 subsidiary of Heller Financial (formerly Walter E. Heller & Company Inc., founded in Chicago in 1919) and of the French American Banking Corporation of New York, an American company in which BNP and Suez Group were shareholders. Very soon, FFH took the lead in the French market. For decades, this Franco-American company promoted an original model of factoring, independent from banking networks. Whether generalists or specialists, the first factors all struggled to find their feet within the constraints of the French system.

Despite the absence of any law or set of rules, the strong regulatory constraint (guidelines, audits and controls) imposed by the Commission Bancaire (part of Banque de France) increased over the years.

A Pragmatic Professional Practice without any Law

If, in 1973, the French authorities adopted a highly empirical approach to this business, the 1984 banking law introduced a more precise domestic framework, while the Ottawa convention (1988) sought to give factoring a suitable international basis so as to develop exchanges.

On the 29th of November 1973, a decree by the minister of economy and finance determined that in future, the term "factoring" would be translated into French as "affacturage", the term approved by the Académie Française in 1974. Beyond the form, the text provided a new, economic definition orientated towards managing business clients' accounts. But the codification of "affacturage" only came twenty years after the creation of SFF, the first French "factoring" company.

Born of practice, the factoring contract was therefore not defined in French law, unlike Germany or Italy. The Dailly law of the 2nd of January 1981 (named for its drafter, Senator Étienne Dailly) was intended to provide a legal basis for factoring operations. But the technique took time to catch on. Although factoring was not mentioned in the banking law of the 24th of January 1984, the first version of its article 3 was subsequently amended to include this specific technique within the scope of banking activities and thus regulation. In application of that article, the purchase of receivables not yet due was included among credit operations by means of subrogated payment. Defined in art. 1249 and 1250 of the Civil Code, a contractual subrogation, the method preferred by factors, allowed a third party to collect the rights, shares, privileges or mortgages of a creditor against its debtor. Subrogation had to be made expressly and simultaneously to the sale of the receivable.

In the early 1990s, domestic operations still represented 95% of the French market. International operations were still in their infancy. Two legal provisions contributed to its expansion:
- At a European level: the Single European Act (1986) set the date of the 1st of January 1993 for the arrival of a vast European "internal market". This unique free trade area favoured the free movement of capital, services and goods within the European Economic Community, and later the EU;

- At the global level: the Unidroit convention on international factoring, known as the Ottawa convention (28th of May 1988), endowed this activity with a legal framework. On the 23rd of September 1991, France ratified its 23 articles.

Before these national and international frameworks had even been clearly delineated, factoring began at last to develop in France and in Europe generally: practice preceded theory, just as "factoring" preceded "affacturage" in French legal language.

II. The Golden Age and Dominance of Specialised Factors

None of the companies founded in the 1960s survived under their original names: SFF, Credit Factoring International, Slifac, Sofinter, Finimpex and even Universal Factoring have now disappeared from collective memory. Of these, Sofinter was the only one to have been liquidated. The other companies were all absorbed into the current market leaders.

The Dominance of Specialised Factors: SFF and FFH

Both of the first factoring companies, SFF and FFH, remained market leaders as specialised factors for nearly forty years:
- SFF (market leader in 1964) with Credit Factoring International (1971 market leader), renamed Slifac (1982 market leader), were at the origins of Eurofactor (2000), the number one on the market for ten years, in 2000-2001 and from 2006-2013. Incorporated into the AGF insurance group (1996) and annexed to Euler, the company became more robust. From 1998 onwards, the association between Slifac and SFF aroused the interest of the shareholders of the two Groups. Established in 1982, Société Lyonnaise d'Affacturage (Slifac), a subsidiary of Crédit Lyonnais, was the third largest factor on the French market and a high-quality competitor. In May 2000, the merger was decided: owned 50/50 by Euler Hermes and Crédit Lyonnais, Eurofactor became a temporary leader in France (ahead of the FFH Group and its 25% market share) and in Europe. But in June 2005, Crédit Agricole acquired the shares of Eurofactor before merging with Transfact (October 2005). Incorporated into Transfact, in 2006, Eurofactor once again became number one on the French

market. GE Factofrance, the traditional leader, was dethroned. For eight years (2006-2013), although under the impetus of this combined group, they lost some momentum. With more than 30% of the cumulative market share in the early 2000s (31.2% in 1999), the addition of SFF, Slifac and Transfact fell to under 20% in 2010. The erosion was considerable. In the early 2000s, Eurofactor was the new leader. But it proved a fragile lead: just like SFF in 1964-1966, it retained its lead for only two years, 2000 and 2001;

– FFH (market leader in 1966), but also Sofirec (1969) and Finimpex (1968) which became Cofacrédit (1974), gave birth to GE Factofrance (2001), the market leader from 1966-2006 (with the exception of 2000-2001), and once again from 2016 via its acquisition by CM-CIC Factor. Following the acquisition of Heller Financial by the Japanese Fuji Bank (1985), FFH continuously raced ahead throughout the 1980s and 1990s, despite growing fragilities: while the group combined had 40% of the market in 1980, it held only 20% by the year 2000; a decrease masked by minority shareholdings in the subsidiaries of retail banks such as Transfact (1985) or Factocic (1992). Whereas the contribution of FFH to this nebulous array exceeded 80% at the end of the 1970s, it was down to 58% by 2000.

As the financial and banking subsidiary of the General Electric industrial group, GE Capital Finance nurtured the ambition of diversifying into an activity that was still very profitable. After the acquisition of Sofirec (in 1995), the seventh French factor, the American multinational went in search of new opportunities. On the 30th of July 2001, GE Financial Services announced the purchase of Heller Financial Services and, via GE Capital Finance, acquired the factoring market leader in France. From the seventh place (after the acquisition of Sofirec), the subsidiary of GE rose fiercely again to top position in 2002!

In the continuity of FFH, GE Factofrance remained a specialised company. What distinguished it from the other factors in the banking sector was the continued absence of a network that could bring in business. The American company was committed to transforming a weakness into an opportunity. Until the 2000s, the model of independent factor proved to be solid and profitable. Direct marketing and the support of a network of loyal brokers perpetuated its initial aim. But the model was running out of steam. The well-known saying ("do not put all your eggs in one basket") ended up persuading companies, under pressure from bankers, to contract only with the "house factor". Profitability was no longer to be had (overstaffed with high operating ratios). One social plan after the other was put forward. In 2006, the supremacy of Eurofactor, newly bank-owned, definitively marked the decline of specialised factoring companies.

Banks as Factors

In the face of the declining hegemony of the specialised companies (60% of the cumulative share in 1992, compared to 87% in 1982), banks mounted an offensive. The game remained wide open and growth in the market attracted public banks:

- In 1974, Société Générale took 65% of France Factoring Group (FFG sarl), the French subsidiary of a German factor. Renamed Sogéfactoring and later Compagnie Générale d'Affacturage (1992), it became a 100% subsidiary of the French bank. At the beginning, its success remained modest. Doubling its market share (from 6.3% to nearly 12%) between 1999 and 2003, CGA became the fourth factor in the market and the third among the banks. In April 2004, CGA was the first French factor to obtain ISO 9001 certification solely for its factoring business. A few months later, the company was joined by BNP Paribas Factor, this time certified for the entire subsidiary (December 2004). Both remain to this day the only ones in Europe to hold that valuable label.

- From the time of its inception in 1984, Factorem proved to be a strong competitor: it held 8.6% market share in 1994, ten years after its creation. The surprisingly fast symbiosis between Banques Populaires' factor and SMEs contributed to this company's fine success. A result of a merger between the Banque Française du Commerce Extérieur (BFCE) and Crédit national (in 1996), Natexis SA, acquired by Banques Populaires (in 1998), led the group's factoring activities. After fifteen years of existence, Factorem became Natexis Factorem. This combination boosted the performance of the subsidiary, exceeding 10% market share from 1999 onwards, behind FFH, SFF and Slifac. In the summer of 2004, rumours of an upcoming merger with Coface (subsidiary of Natexis since 2002) were quickly denied. At the time of the creation of the Banques Populaires Caisses d'Epargne (BPCE) Group (in March 2006), Natixis became the new entity's financial services bank (in October 2006). Natexis Factorem was renamed

Natixis Factor. Its solid foundations allowed posting a highly stable market share of around 13%.
- During the pioneer period, BNP's subsidiary was still not in place. Shareholdings in Sofinter and FFH began, little by little, to unwind, the addition of Universal Factoring (from 1982) and BNP Factor SNC (1990) contributed to creating BNP Factor (in 1994). During the 1990s though, market share remained pretty low (around 5%), even temporarily pushed by a major IBM contract (1995-1998). In 2000, the rapprochement between BNP and Paribas was accompanied by a merger of BNP Factor and UFB Locabail's Factoring department. Changing its name to BNP Paribas Factor, the company was certain to succeed.

The End of the Golden Age

The golden age of factoring in France remained unique: a niche business, high profitable, attractive remuneration for salespeople, a fine conviviality among executives within their association's 'club': all in all, a moderate competition within a rapidly expanding market. In short, the period was an exceptional *El Dorado* that the turning point in the 2000s was to completely overturn. After the pioneering days (the 1960s) and the arrival of new actors (1970s and 1980s), the age of consolidation was approaching. Between 1990 and 2000, factored turnover had increased sixfold, from EUR 10 to 60 billion. The pause in 2002 (+0.4%) and 2003 (+3.8%) was only a temporary phenomenon: the market reached EUR 70 billion in 2001, 50 billion more than in 1994 (a multiplier of 3.5).

By a large majority, the clientele consisted of small and medium-sized enterprises: 80% of them assigned less than EUR 3 million in receivables annually, 39% of them less than one million euro. Contracts for more than EUR 75 million per year represented less than 0.2% of the clients.

III. The French Factoring Model and the Turning Point of the Crisis

Built on a strongly secured full factoring product to cope with the risky SME segment, from 1964-2000 the French factoring model evolved towards a more open, off-balance sheet, undisclosed and non-notified receivables finance product for large corporates (2000-2017). The turning point of the crisis required French factoring companies to change.

Solvency and liquidity issues as well as cost constraints resulted in some of them deciding to pass through strategic changes.

The French Factoring Model: From Secured Full Factoring to off Balance Sheet, Undisclosed and Non-notified Factoring

For many years, France remained a highly classic, secured full factoring-based market, very much focused on poorly rated micros (professionals) and SME clients (1964-2000). After the year 2000, the launching and repositioning of Eurofactor and GE Factofrance led the competition to develop a new product range for well-rated corporates and large corporates. From that period, the number of multinational clients grew to become the most important part in terms of turnover and funds in use: in 2016, 66% of factored turnover was undisclosed, 27.4% in full factoring and 6.6% of reverse factoring.

Mostly inspired by Eurofactor's innovative spirit, such a trend led the best players (Eurofactor, GE Factofrance, BNP Paribas and CGA) to develop off-balance sheet, undisclosed and non-notified receivables finance solutions.

In the beginning, everything went well. But significant fraud cases (Champagne Bricout being the largest one) in 2002-2003 alerted the regulator who decided, in 2004, to impose strict guidelines on "Affacturage en gestion déléguée" to the Industry: a mandatory external audit before signing the contract and quick cash collection capacity.

After 2005, huge contracts appeared in the market and the large corporate segment continued to grow again with impressive deals of up to one or two billion euros. The best factoring companies were the very first ones to impose those pan-European programs and to extend their offering far beyond their domestic borders, to the perimeter of the whole EU thanks to the European passport. A new French factoring model was born which today explains the success of the national top five being part of the European top 10.

French supremacy in factoring in Europe is proved on at least five fields:

- Fast growing, the French market is number one in continental Europe (21%), the second in Europe (17%) and third worldwide (11%);

- International factoring is the largest in the world (EUR 79 billion in 2016), before Germany (EUR 68 billion) and China (EUR 65 billion);
- Potential is still huge since factored turnover/GDP (12.1% in 2016) is just above the European average level (10.1%), mostly non-notified (56%) and with-recourse (57.5%);
- In terms of number of clients, the French market is the largest in Europe with 24% market share (43,000 clients out of 180,000 in 2017);
- Since 2016, factoring has become the largest short-term financing product (44%), far ahead of bank overdrafts (36%) and other short-term credits (20%).

The only weakness remaining is reverse factoring. Unlike Spain where 50% of the total factoring market is confirming, or Portugal (36% of the market), factoring solutions for suppliers in reverse factoring arrangements do not account for more than 6.6% of the French domestic market, declining by 3.8% in 2016 compared to 2015. Programs are very slow to reach maturity and take a long time and effort to become operational.

Generally, French factoring is one of the most balanced in Europe (SMEs/large corporates, domestic/international, full factoring/undisclosed), generating a nicely optimised business mix in terms of revenue. Cross-border fraud cases encountered in 2016 as well as the negative interest rate environment should not question, nor change this strong, ambitious and growing model.

Between Credit Insurance and Leasing, Mergers and External Growth, France Is Seeking its Factoring Strategy

Starting in the summer of 2007, the subprime crisis in the US and then the financial storm in the autumn 2008 gave a global dimension to the crisis and increased solvency and liquidity constraints. Unprecedented since the Crash of 1929, it showed the excesses of a virtual financial system disconnected from the real economy. For factors, the crisis was an opportunity to be seized as much as a challenge to be met. The crisis revealed the disparity between operating visions that resulted as much from the choice between credit insurance, leasing and factoring as from organic or external growth.

In terms of business, the factoring/credit insurance relationship gradually increased in clarity. For forty years, the endogamy between the two remained ambivalent: factoring had to guarantee clients against unpaid buyers, and credit insurance found, via this emerging activity, a way of diversifying its monochannel relationship with its brokers. What form should these ties take? Shareholder/subsidiary or client/supplier? For a long time, the SFAC and Coface wavered between one or other solution before their new shareholders, Euler Hermes and BPCE, put an end to the ambiguity:

- SFAC: minority shareholder (1964-1996) and subsequently sole shareholder (after 1997) of SFF, the company became Euler Hermes SFAC in 2002 and then Euler Hermes in 2012. It divested itself of 50% of its shareholding at the foundation of the first Eurofactor company (2000) and then completely disengaged when the second one was formed (2006). In the hands of a credit insurer for forty years, the new leader became a pure banking factoring service, a subsidiary of a large mutual group;
- Coface: founded at the initiative of the French State, specialised in credit insurance for export (1946-1994), the company privatised in May 1994 and became a majority subsidiary of Natexis Banques Populaires (in 2002). Then 100% owned by Natixis BPCE (2006), it diversified until 2010 into factoring before refocusing entirely on credit insurance.

Yet credit insurance and factoring are first cousins, called upon to cooperate in a partnership more than in a shareholder relationship. Two major arguments for such a choice: credit insurance is not a specialised finance activity and it does not have a network that can refer clients. As a result, credit insurers limited themselves to their core business of supplying and providing essential services to factors. The debate is closed. Other boundary questions have, by contrast, proven to be more critical.

Coexistence between leasing and factoring has come to a new reality: in 2002, the birth of GE Factofrance announced a synergy between two specialised financing businesses which are fundamentally different: one short-term, the other medium-term. The crisis was not without effect on this convergence. Initially, it was limited to bringing together support functions (IT, finances and human resources); in a second phase, the merging of the two businesses extended to the entire range of sales, prospecting and management activities. Curiously enough, this development only affected the two leaders (Eurofactor and GE Factofrance), engaged in a strategy of combining forces.

The disparity in strategic vision among factors was not limited simply to a technical question, that of combining credit insurance or leasing. Many other considerations came into play, notably company mergers and external growth:
- Mergers: SFF-Slifac (2000), BNP Factor-UFB-Locabail (2000), GE Factofrance (2002), FCF-Étoile commerciale (2005), Eurofactor-Transfact (2006), BNP Paribas Factor-FCF France (2012);
- External growth: the champion of acquisitions in France, GE Capital purchased Sofirec (1995), FFH (2002), RBS's factoring business (France, United Kingdom and Germany, 2010), and Eurofactor UK (2011). It ran far ahead of the other players, Eurofactor, FCF Holding (De Lage Landen, Étoile commerciale) and, more recently, BNP Paribas Factor (FCF Holding, 2012). After the acquisition of GE Factofrance by CM-CIC Factor (2016), the market is now completely concentrated in the hands of banks.

If, over the years, the number of factors has fallen (the factoring division of the ASF comprised only thirteen members in 2016, whereas it had some 25 at the beginning of the 2000s), the concentration is far from excessive. With almost 30% of international turnover, the French factoring model has been built on a status of credit institution, with a large EU perimeter thanks to the "European passport", whereas in the UK, a factoring company is often a commercial company, unregulated and domestic based. Contrary to a wide spread idea, the French market remains one of the most open to competition: in 2017, five actors exceed 15% of the market, whereas in 2000 only two factors held 55% of the market! France has true professionals who would stand to gain from greater recognition in their own country.

IV. Conclusion: a Mature and Highly Competitive Market

As in Italy, France remains definitively dominated by home grown players with no foreigner in the top five (compared to four out of five in Germany) and only three in the top 10. Historically, the American, Belgian, English or Dutch players have nevertheless stood out: FFH, GE Factofrance, FCF France, RBS Factor, ING Lease France, IFN Finance France (created in 1997, renamed in 2010 ABN AMRO Commercial Finance France), HSBC Factoring (established in 1997, Élysées Factor was renamed HSBC Factoring following acquisition by HSBC in 2005) and, more recently, Bibby Factor France.

There is no small or large factor, only professionalism and quality matters. In a few years, two Tom Thumbs – BNP Paribas Factor and CM-CIC Factor – entered the playground of the big boys:
- BNP Paribas Fortis acquired Fortis Commercial Finance (FCF) holding company on the 3rd of October 2011. The creation of the factoring competence centre in Brussels gave rise to a French and European champion. Because it did not reach the critical threshold of 10% of market share until 2009, the road travelled is simply enormous. A European factoring leader since 2011 (8.1% of market share in 2015), the BNP Paribas group benefited from the merger of FCF France and BNP Paribas Factor (2012) to rise to the top French position in 2014 and 2015, for the first time in its history;
- The sixth player in France, Factocic has long focused on the SME market. A 66% subsidiary of CIC (until 1998), the Crédit mutuel-CIC group held 100% of its capital in 2010, after purchasing 34% from GE Factofrance. Constant in its results, the smallest of the "large factors" had a flawless trajectory. Born of the combination between Factocic and CM-CIC Laviolette on the 2nd of January 2012, CM-CIC Factor thus proved its ability to accompany large companies as well as SMEs. In 2014, the company crossed the 10% threshold of market share for the first time in its history. In July 2016, it acquired GE Factofrance to constitute the new leader of the sector.

50 years after its birth, the French market, definitely mature with its five champions, has reached a universally recognised standard of quality. It is, furthermore, essential to create the conditions for loyal and transparent competition among actors when it comes to status and regulation. Distributed since 2014, mostly across specialised credit institutions (a status that is almost unique in Europe, for which no country envies France), the French factors have called for a harmonised, unified or even adapted legal and prudential regime across the EU. There are several subjects (access to the European passport; access to medium-term financing from the ECB; whether or not to be subject to a deposit and resolution guarantee fund or to the single resolution fund; treatment in terms of solvency or liquidity ratios; compliance with the rules of conduct, financial flow traceability or KYC) on which the new European regulator, the ECB, will sooner or later have to take a position in order to prevent market distortions and the emergence of unsupervised fintech platforms.

13. Prussian Thinking as the Basis of Made in Germany

Joachim Secker

CEO, Targo Commercial Finance
Chairman, German Factoring Association

In Germany, factoring has a unique history, one that makes the topic here interesting because Germans are known internationally for being diligent and correct, especially when it comes to paying on time. After 1945, Germans had to rebuild not only their country, but also their view of the world – into one of outstanding open-mindedness in Europe. When it came to factoring however, the Germans were, at the outset, very reserved. Laws making factoring extremely difficult existed well into the 20th century, which left company financing to so-called house banks. Today, Germany is profiting as an export nation and is the international flag bearer for strong small and medium-sized companies, especially when it comes to factoring as a form of finance that provides liquidity for new ideas and success in markets.

History shows us why, for a long time, the concept of morally binding duty also applied to the payment of invoices in Germany, i.e. to accounts receivables and, in part, still applies today. Germans pay invoices immediately, not just "punctually" on the final due date. For our fathers or grandfathers born before World War Two, this was a matter of course. For this generation, it was equally a matter of course not to go into debt except in emergencies. People purchased what they could afford, or they saved and purchased later. These old "virtues" also had very positive side effects that still apply today: those who are economical pay attention to the quality and longevity of products, a fundamental aspect of products "Made in Germany".

I. German post-war Economic Miracle: from the Dominance of House Banks to the First Factoring Pioneers

While the post-war period brought open mindedness and a needed break from absolute adherence to power, the old "virtues" were carried over and helped when it came to rebuilding. The German economic miracle of the 1950s and 1960s was based on hard work and discipline. And suddenly a lot of money was back in circulation, especially with the banks because, given their new prosperity, Germans could save money again and deposit it. Anyone who, as an entrepreneur of a small or medium business, needed capital for investments at that time, simply went to their local house bank. And of course, they were granted credit, sometimes on a simple handshake with the branch manager. In addition, large-scale industry grew, especially on the Rhine and Ruhr in North Rhine Westphalia. One of the first major banks – Commerzbank – did not have their first headquarters in the future banking centre of Frankfurt but in Dusseldorf, close to the coal producers and steel forgers, in essence, a large "house bank". This amount of detail is necessary to understand the special situation in Germany. On the one hand, the house bank system with classic bank financing applied here for a very long time. On the other, unlike in other countries, small and medium-sized companies were able to grow alongside large-scale industry thanks to the opportunities available from the years of the economic miracle. Today, these SMEs form the backbone of the German economy. These companies – primarily suppliers to industrial concerns or concentrated on the construction of special machines – have been particularly suited to alternative financing options because of their rapid growth.

Factoring in Germany Starts in "Warehouses"

Germany "discovered" factoring relatively late. More precisely, at the height of the economic miracle. This highpoint can be defined in different ways but 1955 was a particularly special year – Germany no longer had sufficient workforce for its boom and had to recruit so-called "guest workers" from abroad. In 1955, the millionth VW Beetle rolled off the production line. The peak period of the economic miracle can be considered to be from 1955 until well into the 1960s. In 1958, the scene was set – the complete utilisation of economic capacity prepared the ground for the first companies to look for alternatives to their classic house banks for investments and export business. And that was factoring.

In 1958, the Mittelrheinische Kreditbank Dr Horbach & Co. KG in Mainz, close to Frankfurt on Main, concluded its first factoring contract.[1]

According to the accounts published at the time[2], the Horbach Bank's balance sheet grew from DEM 42 million in 1959 to 180 million by the middle of the 1960s. A part of this growth can be attributed to factoring. The then private bank transferred its fast-growing factoring business to its subsidiary, Inter-Factor-Bank AG, in 1963.

In a 1965 article titled "Cash in the Till", the news magazine *Der Spiegel* wrote: "Slipped into a large, run-down warehouse at the end of the Mainz suburb of Mombach where the cabbage fields start, the Inter-Factor-Bank can be found. (…) Inter-Factor purchased accounts receivable valued at almost DEM 100 million from West German companies and paid cash for them."

Banker Dr Josef Horbach had entered into a risky business at the time "because several factors that had made the rise of factoring in America possible in the first place were missing in Germany. Those that purchase accounts receivable and take on the liability (*del credere*) must know the exact creditworthiness of the debtor. In America, it is easier because the company's balance sheet usually indicates the true intrinsic value, while in West Germany the amount of the operating profit that disappears into hidden reserves remains opaque", noted *Der Spiegel*.

First International Provider in the Market

Despite the lack of legal conditions, the story of factoring in Germany continued. Soon the second provider followed, this time from the home of factoring, the US. The German born factoring pioneer, Walter E. Heller, founded Walter E. Heller & Co. in Chicago in 1919.[3] Just like Horbach, Walter E. Heller opened the Heller Factoring Bank AG in Germany[4] in Mainz. Thus, the old trading city on the Rhine, where Johannes Gutenberg invented printing in the 15th century, became the first "capital of factoring" in Germany.

---

[1] Hagenmueller K.F., Sommer Heinrich Johannes, Brink Ulrich, "Factoring Handbuch", Frankfurt/Main, Fritz Knapp Verlag, 1997, p. 61.
[2] http://www.spiegel.de/spiegel/print/d-46273040.html.
[3] Deogun Nikhil, Murray Matt, The Wall Street Journal Online, 30.07.2001; http://www.wsj.com/articles/SB996441111697437428.
[4] Hagenmueller K.F., Sommer Heinrich Johannes, Brink Ulrich, "Factoring Handbuch", Frankfurt/Main, Fritz Knapp Verlag, 1997, p. 50.

By the start of the 1960s, the major banks in Germany could no longer leave the successful trend in financing to the newcomers. In 1962, the factoring concern Factoring-Gesellschaft für Wirtschaftsförderung KGaA was founded in Hannover as a majority-owned subsidiary of the savings bank Neuen Sparkasse von 1864 Hamburg and Norddeutsche Finanzierungs-AG, a subsidiary of Bremer Landesbank and the Sparkasse in Bremen. Both North German providers and the two factoring pioneers from Mainz, Horbach and Heller, joined forces in 1966 to form the "Arbeitsgemeinschaft Factoring-Banken" (Consortium of Factoring Banks) headquartered in Mainz.[5]

Misplaced Embarrassment as Factoring Flaw

There were still obstacles to an accelerated expansion of factoring: "Others (companies) cultivate personalised client care and fear that the factor collects money on a large scale like a bailiff", wrote *Der Spiegel* in 1965. "Above all German companies are embarrassed to inform their debtors that the accounts payable have been assigned to a factoring bank."[6]

Nevertheless, in 1969, another major provider entered the factoring business in the form of Wuppertaler GEFA Gesellschaft für Absatzfinanzierung GmbH, a subsidiary of Deutsche Bank that, additionally, was focused strongly on international factoring and accordingly joined FCI. In 1971, the number of factoring institutes in Germany was still limited: twelve in total. According to estimates, these had a transaction volume from factoring of DEM 1.5 billion.[7] The small industry was, however, already diversified. The factoring providers were, in part, specialists with parent companies abroad such as the Heller Factoring Bank; subsidiaries of large banks or savings banks; local private banks and industry providers – such as Bertelsmann Distribution GmbH which, as a subsidiary of the media group Bertelsmann, offered this service.[8]

In contrast to the US, factoring in Germany in the 1960s and 1970s was primarily offered as an instrument for financing sales. Factoring dominated without *del credere* protection and was also known as "false

---

[5] Mueller Gerhard, Loeffelholz Josef, "Bank-Lexikon: Handwörterbuch für Das Bank- und Sparkassenwesen", Heidelberg, Springer-Verlag, 2013, p. 687, 688.
[6] http://www.spiegel.de/spiegel/print/d-46273040.html.
[7] Hagenmueller K.F., Sommer Heinrich Johannes, Brink Ulrich, *op. cit.*, p. 61.
[8] *Ibid.*, p. 64.

factoring".[9] Despite this exceptional position there was, from the very beginning, no problem with the word factoring in Germany. At that time, the word "Absatzfinanzierung" (sales financing) was commonly used for factoring albeit not predominantly.[10]

II. Special Characteristics: Disadvantageous Legal Situation and Prohibition of Assignment

There was a very serious legal reason why factoring in Germany gained ground so slowly before the end of the 1970s: factoring did not initially fit in the German legal system. In 1959 – the same year that the factoring market was established – the Federal Court of Justice (BGH) judged that "Blanket assignment of future customer (client) debts agreed for securing credit is unlawful and void insofar as, in accordance with the intention of the parties, they also cover such accounts payable that the debtor must assign to their suppliers because of extended retention of title." It was, therefore, about protection of suppliers – i.e. that companies could not use their goods to guarantee credit while the supplier remained unpaid.

Providers Get Organised in 1974 and Bring down Obstacles

Against this background, leading German factoring institutes founded, amongst other things, the German Factoring Association (Deutscher Factoring-Verband e.V.) in 1974 to represent the interests of German factoring companies at a national and international level. Major successes for the Industry and the association came in 1977 (Az.: VIII ZR 169/76) and 1978 (Az: VIII ZR 80/77) with two judgements by the BGH which ruled that "genuine" factoring, in which the factor takes on *del credere*, the blanket assignment agreement is not unlawful. This is because with genuine factoring, the factor buys the accounts payable irrevocably and the seller of the debt can satisfy the supplier from the proceeds as if they had collected the debt themselves.[11]

---

[9] *Ibid.*, p. 61.
[10] Knopig G., "Factoring – Neue Wege der Absatzfinanzierung", *Zeitschrift für das gesamte Kreditwesen*, 1957, p. 61 ff.
[11] Source: Dr Cornelia Nett, General Counsel at TARGO Commercial Finance.

Market Success 20 Years Later

With immediate effect, factoring in Germany could be conducted as in the US and most other European countries. From 1978, full-service factoring (also known as standard or old-line factoring) became a success in Germany, some twenty years later than that in most industrial nations.[12] It became established and, slowly, ever more companies became interested in this form of financing.

With the further development of mid-range computer technology in the 1980s and its adoption in medium-sized companies, factors also developed a process based on the delivery of data by the client. While information was initially transferred in list form, today fully automated data transfer is the norm. This process, intercredit factoring (also known as bulk or in-house factoring) has become the preferred version of factoring for clients. The service aspect has become less important. The added value for the client lies in the financing and taking on of *del credere*. It was, however, only with the reunification of East and West Germany in 1990 and the fall of the Iron Curtain that the factoring business – and especially later with cross-border factoring – that factoring took off. In the period between 1990 and 1993, with the development of trade with Eastern Europe, cross-border factoring accounted for between 27% and 31% (DM 3.6-6 billion) in Germany. Compared to before, the figure was around 20% in 1986. This high proportion of foreign to domestic factoring flattened out again in the following years because of increased domestic demand.[13]

Large Companies Temporarily Enforce a Ban on Assignability

One final hurdle for factoring still existed at the beginning of the 1990s, once again, a German characteristic. Market-dominating companies who could dictate purchase conditions mostly insisted on a ban on assignment of accounts payable by their suppliers. These in turn were mostly medium-sized companies that needed to continuously purchase materials and produce cost-effectively. As such, they were predestined to be clients of factoring, but they were required to sign purchase conditions that included a ban on assignment and had to refrain from factoring. The legal basis for this was paragraph 399 of the Civil Code (BGB) which

---

[12] Hagenmueller K.F., Sommer Heinrich Johannes, Brink Ulrich, *op. cit.*, p. 62 ff.
[13] *Ibid.*, p. 60.

permitted free assignability to be limited if both sides – creditor and debtor – agreed to it.

One reason for the exception to the ban on assignability was the large companies' unjustified concern that it would not be possible, from an organisational point of view, to ensure that payments would be made to the factor rather than the supplier. And surely, in the back of their minds, there was a concern of being drawn into demands for payment more often. Given this scenario, the factoring companies in Germany, represented by the German Factoring Association, tried to get large companies and the government to rethink.[14] With success, in 1994, on the initiative of the association, the government added paragraph 354a to the code of commercial law (HGB). This stipulates that debts can be assigned despite a ban on assignability. It also allows, however, the debtor to pay the original creditor even if payment is due to the factor on account of the assignment. What remains is the German peculiarity that a debtor may make payment to the original creditor despite the invoice being submitted by the factor.[15]

Factoring in Germany was therefore freed from obstacles. According to the 1997 factoring handbook (Fritz Knapp Verlag, published by Hagenmüller, Sommer, Brink), clients who used factoring came from over 25 industries, in particular from processing industries as well as trade and service sectors. As opposed to America (textile and clothing industries), there were, and are, no "classic" industries that use factoring. A compilation by Heller Bank AG in 2006 listed metalworking and other industrial companies (30% in total) above textile and electrical industries (12% each). Factoring users in Germany generally have one key feature: they come from the *"Mittelstand"*.

III. The Triumph: Economic Change Favours Factoring Despite all the Crises

These clients had to adapt in many ways in the 1990s: rapid progress was made in the development of information technology; companies became ever more international and larger inventories had to be made available for just-in-time delivery. All this required liquidity. In factoring

---

[14] Secker Joachim, Weimer Hermann, "Factoring und ergänzende Finanzdienstleistungen", Heller Bank AG, Universitätsdruckerei H. Schmidt, Mainz, 2006, p. 55.
[15] *Ibid.*

providers, the companies found partners that gave them the necessary funds.

Against a background of medium-sized companies and suppliers being forced by their buyers into faster and slimmer production processes because the buyers tightened the price screws, the head buyer of Opel/GM and later Volkswagen, José Ignacio López, made headlines in Germany. On the one hand, because of a legal process about company secrets that was later dropped; on the other, because of a significant drop in the quality of components delivered by suppliers because of extreme price pressure. It was named after him as "the López effect".[16]

As a result, the factoring scene in Germany recorded a sharp increase in demand in the 1990s. Accordingly, ever more international providers entered the market. Dutch finance houses in particular, such as Rabobank with De Lage Landen Factors, Fortis with FMN Deutschland GmbH and ABN AMRO with IFN Factors expanded to Germany after 1990.[17] The major credit insurance companies also entered the market in various ways but then left again. As of today, only Coface Finanz GmbH is still active.

In 2001, the General Electric subsidiary, GE Capital, acquired 50% of Heller Financial Inc., the oldest of the remaining factoring providers in Germany from Heller Bank AG. In 2005, it increased its stake to 100%.

SMEs Overcome Crisis after the 11*th* of September 2001

From the end of the 1990s to the beginning of the year 2000, the German economy – as with the global economy – showed strong growth. In addition, under Chancellor Gerhard Schröder's government, Russia became an increasingly important trading partner. However, when the so-called dotcom bubble burst in 2000, combined with the events of the 11th of September 2001, the German economy was plunged into a deep crisis with high unemployment. Of special consequence in Germany was increased migration of qualified workers from the reunified former East Germany, with its already weaker economic development, to the "old" states of the former West Germany. For factoring providers, this meant increased hedging of defaulted payments and a decline in international business.

---

[16] http://www.spiegel.de/spiegel/print/d-9134366.html.
[17] Hagenmueller K.F., Sommer Heinrich Johannes, Brink Ulrich, "Factoring Handbuch", Frankfurt/Main, Fritz Knapp Verlag, 1997, p. 65 ff.

In this critical phase, the small and medium enterprises prevented the economy from collapsing. Thanks to the strength of these enterprises, the German economy recovered well from 2004 and set off to new highs. At the same time, trade relations with China expanded strongly from which, above all, the German car manufacturers and their mostly middle-sized suppliers profited. The companies had fully embraced globalisation and cross-border factoring was accepted as an effective instrument by many of the companies. Transactions with foreign clients and subsidiaries abroad were secured through internationally experienced factoring providers and handling of foreign regulations and modalities was put in their hands, allowing the companies to concentrate on expansion.

Factoring has finally arrived in the German economy. Today, it is above all about adjusting to the special needs of the clients – national, international and, increasingly, digital.

Basel II Encourages Alternative Financing

A further driver for factoring at that time was the Basel II directive. The Basel framework agreement was published in June 2004 and came into force at the end of 2006. On a European level, the implementation of Basel II was made law by the publication of Banking Directive (2006/48/EC) and Capital Adequacy Directive (2006/49/EC) in June 2006. In Germany, the implementation of Basel II was passed into national law through changes in the banking act and through supplemental regulations, also in 2006.[18] For banks, Basel II means that potential credit risks with business clients must be taken into account by the banks in their ratings, such that conditions of credit must progressively be tightened according to the level of risk. The result was a decisive argument in favour of factoring: the sale of accounts receivables leads to a reduction on the balance sheet for the same amount of equity, resulting in a higher equity ratio and thereby, usually, to a better rating.[19]

It is therefore not surprising that, between 2004 and 2008, factoring in Germany received a significant boost. The Factoring Industry

---

[18] https://www.bundesbank.de/Navigation/DE/Aufgaben/Bankenaufsicht/Basel2/basel2.html.

[19] Kelm Michael, "Anforderungen an die Kreditinstitute und Möglichkeiten der Mandantenunterstützung durch die Steuerberater zur Optimierung des Ratings", Hamburg, Diplomica Verlag, 2007, p. 62.

doubled its turnover at that time.[20] Meanwhile, almost all providers had diversified their offering in Germany to meet the needs of their clients. Along with the classic full-service factoring, variants such as smart-service factoring, where the client retains control of the collection process, were in demand. On the other hand, total financial solutions, where factoring is a component (known amongst others as "factoring plus") became more important. Here, together with the client, the factor checks the asset side of their balance sheet to generate additional scope for financing. In Germany, the factor needs a banking license for this.

Lehman Crash Creates New Supervisory Regulations

In September 2008, the global economy slid into its next crisis through the collapse of Lehman Brothers. As a result of the recession, factoring turnover in Germany also declined. But it would only be a short dip because once again the results of an economic crisis – rigid credit lending by the banks, higher risk of default by borrowers – led to even more reliance by clients on factoring. Because of the changes in the banking act (KWG) in 2009, companies that provide factoring within the meaning of § 1 Abs. 1a Satz 2 Nr. 9 KWG to the extent that authorisation is required must, since the 25th of December 2008, be approved and are subject to supervision. They are thereby subject to restricted governance by the federal agency for financial supervision (Bundesanstalt für Finanzdienstleistungsaufsicht or BaFin).

Security and supervision were and are for the domestic factoring providers nothing new. In Germany, high standards apply – in part, excessive as explained, for example, in relation to the ban on assignability. One event shocked the scene before the BaFin regulation: the world leader in sport surfacing, Balsam AG, was found guilty in 1994 of submitting false, excessive invoices to its factoring provider and as a result profited. The bankruptcy of the factoring company, Procedo GmbH, made headlines. It made a spectacular business trial.[21]

From 2010 to today, the low interest rate in Europe associated with the Euro crisis has been another aspect that has influenced factoring. Companies now receive very favourable loans from their house banks if they fulfil the rating conditions. On the other hand, factoring remains attractive, amongst other things, because companies can pay their supplier

---

[20] https://www.svea.com/de/deu/News-Archiv/Factoring-Geschichte-Eine-4000-Jahre-lange-Tradition/

[21] http://www.spiegel.de/spiegel/print/d-13686447.html.

invoices faster and thereby take advantage of discounts for early payment. Today, two to three percent discount is a better yield than 0.1% interest on a bank balance.[22] In addition, German companies are now familiar with all the benefits of factoring, especially speed and flexibility.

Factoring as a Controlling Instrument

Factoring is increasingly becoming a controlling tool for company management; digital capabilities provide managers with an overview of existing and assigned accounts receivable as well as the liquidity freed up for new ideas "with just one click". This enables market opportunities, for example, to be used faster and with greater success.

Thanks to global connections with relevant IT expertise, GE Capital was one of the first factoring providers in Germany able to cover a complete factoring process for clients (System "FactorLink"). With "FactorPulse" GE Capital brought an additional solution to market for mobile applications with which company managers can quickly call up the status of factoring engagements in real time via a smartphone or tablet – whether they are in a meeting, travelling or with clients.

The requirements of SMEs in industrialised countries in Europe were researched by GE Capital annually up to 2015 with the help of GE Capital's CAPEX-Reports – a barometer of the mood of European medium-sized companies. Since the 2000s, an important criterion for German companies when choosing factoring providers is whether these understand their specific requirements and have experience in their industry. In August 2016, the leasing and factoring business of the German GE Capital was taken over by the French Bank Crédit Mutuel and since then has operated under the name TARGO Commercial Finance.

Industry 4.0 and Fintechs as Current Drivers

In Germany, as in the rest of the world, the latest trend in factoring is digitalisation. Factoring is increasingly being used as a tool in upgrading for Industry 4.0. At the same time, in Germany, the digital trend is also producing a growing number of so-called fintechs that are developing out of the Berlin start-up scene. Along with lending at the click of a button, they have factoring in their sights, which will drive the market further.

---

[22] Secker Joachim, Diewald Jörg, "Mittelstandsfinanzierung", *Börsen-Zeitung Spezial*, 19.05.2016, p. 15.

From the German Factoring Association's point of view, these fintechs will have a positive effect on factoring business. Inspiration will come from this sector and cooperation is conceivable.

Despite this backdrop from low interest rates to fintechs, the German Factoring Association, with 33 member companies representing around 95% of the Industry, was nevertheless able to report a further increase in volumes of 3.8% to EUR 217 billion for 2016 over 2015 after a strong two digit growth the previous year.[23] The top 5 industries for factoring providers are currently trade and trade brokerage, vehicle construction, metal product manufacturing, machine building, services and electronics/electronic components. In comparison to 2015, the number of clients increased to over 27,000 in 2016 (+3.4%). This shows that factoring in Germany is a successful product, despite ever more challenging conditions, especially in relation to international expansion and digitalisation.

---

[23] http://www.factoring.de/factoring-branchenzahlen-1-halbjahr-2016.

14. The Italian Way, a Creative Business under Legal and Regulatory Constraints

Mario Petroni
Past General Manager, IFITALIA

Liliana Innocenti
Past International Manager, IFITALIA

Before the 1960s, factoring as a financial system, with the exception of a few isolated cases, did not seem to have any future in Europe. However, due to the growing need to expand overseas, American factors increased their operating business at an international level, by setting up their financial institutions outside their national borders.

In November 1960, Charles Harding, chairman of Meinhard & Co. (future CIT Group), leader in "Old-Line factoring", decided to set up a subsidiary in London introducing a "New Style factoring". Following this, FNBB, in collaboration with the Commercial Bank of Samuel & Co. and the confirming house of Tozert Kemsley & Milbourne Ltd London, founded in Coira, the IF Ag Swiss holding company with the aim of developing factoring companies in various European countries.

After IF Ltd in London, the first affiliate to IF Ag holding, many European banks and financial institutions became interested in having a subsidiary of that kind in their own country. At the beginning of the 1960s, Italy was facing an economic boom and badly needed to build its productive capacity as well as to finance SMEs, most of which were family owned, by way of short-term credit facilities. In this context, factoring was only considered as an alternative to classic forms of short-term bank loans: an additional way to increase the availability of finance by obtaining advance payment on invoices.

At that time, factoring was quite unknown in Italy. Only Banca Nazionale del Lavoro, one of the main Italian banks, accepted the proposal of cooperation made by the FNBB. It therefore became the first Italian bank to adopt these new financial tools, setting up on the 12th of December 1963 as IFITALIA (IF-Italy) in a joint venture with FNBB, IF Ag Holding and Efibanca. The new company soon became a founder member of IFG and the forerunner of such a business, offering both old-style and new-style factoring. At the beginning, the volume of transactions was very low.

I. The Expansion of Factoring Without Any Legal Framework

From the 1960s to the early 1980s, factoring in Italy made its first steps, encountering some difficulties as a result of lack of knowledge and trust. Despite that situation, it began to flourish thanks to a very open market. Because of the absence of any legal or technical constraints, no barriers prevented its development. The results soon began to be positive.

The Original Operating Modes: Lack of Knowledge and Distrust of Factoring

During the 1960s, factoring faced great resistance in Italy as in other countries. There were mainly three arguments against the product:
- The reluctance of companies to accept unknown solutions which seemed to be in competition with the standard bank products;
- An unfounded fear from many companies that notification of assignment of receivables to the debtors would arise suspicion of financial weakness;
- The fear of damage to business relationships with clients because of the lack of confidence in the factors' managerial ability, particularly with regard to their doubtful collection methods, in the event of unpaid receivables.

In addition, the cost of factoring was higher than the one applied by the banks for their standard loans. This was deemed to be a disincentive for SMEs, who did not realise that a part of the fee was not fixed and that therefore the real cost would undoubtedly be lower.

Initially diffident because they considered factoring as a competitor instrument referring to "with recourse notification business" (*Pro solvendo*), banks changed their approach when it began to be "non-recourse" (*Pro soluto*), considering it to be a complementary product because of the advantages offered in the collection of receivables and the assumption of commercial risk in the event of default.

As a consequence, the Italian market has seen a large increase in the number of factoring companies owned by the Banks or their subsidiaries.

Market and Actors' Evolution Throughout the 1970s and Early 1980s

After the first years of uncertainty and doubts, pushed by factoring companies, business flourished and developed both on the domestic and international side.

IFITALIA, Pioneer of Factoring in Italy

IFITALIA first started to offer standard products and services in the Italian domestic market, mainly with recourse solutions, including financing and collection, studying from time to time and launching new products, according to the evolution of the market. In order to develop the business more and to better understand companies' needs, it opened branches in Rome, Turin, Padua, Florence and Bologna. As one of the founder members of IFG, the company was in a strategic position to offer international factoring, "export and import", in Europe and in major countries around the world, by using the high professionalism and ability of IFG members, thus granting high quality services to its clients. For many years, BNL's subsidiary remained the leader in international business.

The First Operating Factoring Companies in Italy: "the Trailblazers"

Over the years, IFITALIA became the trailblazer of the Factoring Industry. It was followed by:

- ItalFactor SpA (Heller Factor Italia), founded in 1968 by Banca Commerciale Italiana (50%) and Walter E. Heller (50%);
- Credit Factoring International, founded in 1972 by Credito Italiano (50%) and Westminster Bank London (50%);
- Centro Factoring International, founded in 1972 by Centro Leasing (Cassa di Risparmio di Firenze) for 90% and Banco di Sardegna (10%).

After these three companies, many others were created including Factorit (1978), Barclays Factoring International (1980) and CBI Factor (1981).

In the beginning, the majority of factors were concentrated in Milan (Lombardy), a region that has been and still is Italy's main business and financial hub. Later on, others were created in other regions such as

Piedmont, Veneto and Marche. Only in 1982 when Sud Factoring was founded, was the first one located in the South of Italy (Puglia region).

Despite the Economic Crisis, Factoring Business Experienced Incredible Growth

The Italian economic crisis, which began in 1973, changed the scenario and objectives of the previous period. The government subordinated economic development and growth with a tight monetary policy by imposing stringent constraints on banks' transactions and credit institutions. However, the crisis proved to be a great opportunity for factors providing the Italian market with great experience and strong development, both in terms of quality, as well as quantity, during the period from 1973 to 1983.

The volume of business thus increased from ITL 413 billion in 1976 to over ITL 10,000 billion in 1984 in a potential market of around ITL 50,000 billion, which meant very high availability to the Factoring Industry. In percentage terms, the development of business increased during 1978 to 1982 from 12% compared to the previous year to 100%.

The road was opened: in the field of financial techniques, factoring was one of the tools best suited to the needs of companies looking to solve cash flow issues. The slogan "invoices equal money", coined by some players to advertise factoring techniques, highlighted its salient aspect.

The demand for domestic business was predominant, in spite of the fact that most factoring companies, including merchant factors whose core business was international, were also offering international services. With a total amount of ITL 6,900 billion in 1983, international transactions represented a small part of the whole market, only a 3% share.

A major reason for the rise of factoring was the offer of a package of services which included ledgering, trade policy, financial and loans management, organisation, and last but not least, the ability to expand in to new forms of funding, which was very much appreciated in markets like the Italian one. The lack of available credit lines was often a great problem for SMEs. The consumer goods industry (especially in the textile and clothing areas) with short-term payment terms of 30-90-120 days, a fixed stock portfolio and revolving supplies, were viewed as the most attractive sectors for factoring business. The typical Italian practice of postponing payments, of which the public administration was also guilty, served to push factoring to the top of the world rankings in the Industry. A considerable number of agreements were signed with the institutional players, insurance companies and regions, in addition to the already existing joint ventures with leading private and public industrial entities, allowing SMEs to enter international markets by taking advantage of these financial products.

II. The Golden Age of the Factoring Industry: Bank Subsidiaries and Captive Entities

In Italy, not only did the banking world, which had its own factoring company or specialised internal department, show great interest in factoring, but the industrial world did too. During the 1980s and 1990s, there was a proliferation of "captive or finalised companies", controlled by public and private industrial groups in joint ventures with leading factoring companies or banks. These companies joined with those of the banking sector, which had a dominant role within the Italian factoring market.

First Captives in Industry and Agriculture Before Specialisation in the Health Sector

The first captive, Olivetti Factoring SpA, was founded on the 1st of March 1980, between the group from Ivrea and IFITALIA. It was followed afterwards by 18 other factoring captives, in which BNL's subsidiary had a partnership. Among the others, three main ones need to be mentioned because of the importance of the industry involved:

- Agrifactoring (Federconsorzi, BNL, Efibanca, IFITALIA, Banco S. Spirito) was the first captive in Italy to offer factoring to the agricultural field;
- Factor Coop SpA assisted the cooperatives in all the sectors, mainly in the consumer field;
- Farmafactoring, today Banca Farmafactoring, specialised in the pharmaceutical industry.

These factoring companies were located in various Italian regions, from North to South, and each one had its own specialisation, depending on their parent industrial group.

The growing number of factoring companies and the various operating and economic sectors involved required a high specialisation, which implied setting up specialised departments to manage receivables concerning both the private sector and public administration. In fact, it should be emphasised that this sector is subject to its own rules and particular procedures. Not all factors operated in the same way. Farmafactoring, founded in 1985 by a group of Italian and multinational pharmaceutical companies, was set up with the aim of working in a single and specific sector.

The Main Playing Fields of Factoring Development

As a product for all types of industries and company sizes, factoring expanded more and more in some fields, such as the IT industry, motorcycles and tyres, where "maturity factoring" was of interest.

The health sector and public administration also played an interesting role in its development.

IT Industry and Maturity Factoring

As aforementioned, the factoring market evolved by increasing the services offered. IFITALIA not only sold the product directly but also offered what the experts call in jargon "service" i.e., placing "in house factoring" at the full disposal of users.

Giant IBM, its long-term client, was one of the first companies to take advantage of the factoring company's flagship "maturity without recourse", thus creating a snowball effect in the market:

- IFITALIA managed the receivables issued by the IBM Group to IBM's dealers;
- On the maturity date, it would pay the claims without recourse to the IBM group.

The situation changed when IBM decided to manage this new product on its own, in order to improve its managerial autonomy and flexibility to allow more market growth. In May 1992, IBM formed a company, IBM Factoring, in partnership with a factoring company in the role of back office within a Service Level Agreement (SLA).

Credits to the Health Sector and Public Administration

The peculiarity of the public administration sector (that has a complex and specific discipline the Italian factors are obliged to comply with) is the delay in payments, which firmly limits the financial liquidity of SMEs preventing them from meeting their short-term commitments. Over the years, many worthy and reputable firms needed economic support to avoid liquidity problems that could affect their business life. Factoring has been the operational tool able to meet the needs of businesses thanks to the high customisation of relationships between factors and the public administration. Factors have been able to support firms by managing payment delays that could exceed 1,000 days in some regions (these delays have been reducing sharply in 2016 and 2017). The importance of the assignment and the notification of debts have been such that the Italian legislator dictated a specific rule that provided for the "non-recourse" transfer of certified credits to encourage businesses and reduce the timing of payments by the public administration and public health service.

A special mention must be made on "split payments", i.e. splitting of VAT payments, where, for certain firms belonging to the public administration and some companies listed at the Milan Stock Exchange, the VAT on invoices is paid directly to the tax office by the buyer. Therefore, VAT is deducted from the invoice balance resulting in a reduction in turnover and therefore in the contribution margin of the individual report.

Factoring Industry: Evolution, Refinement and Improvement

The factoring product, far from being static, permanently moves to suit the needs of the economy and finance, based on the changes that occur over the years.

The Refinement and Improvement of the Operating Model

In the 1980s, factoring was a pure financing activity mainly addressed to small and medium-sized firms not adequately capitalised. During the 1990s, there was a change in client types, with a switch from SMEs to corporate and large corporate companies. This meant attending to different needs and a larger offering of products, such as reduction of assets, outsourcing, financing to the sales' network and/or to the supplier. To minimise the risk in this segment, factoring companies further developed the use of syndicated business.

The factoring market in Italy today still retains its significant size despite the fact that the contractual forms widespread in the country differ from those abroad. Financing and services are two sides of the same coin.

Business Growth in the 1980s and 1990s

In Italy, at the end of 1984, there were 36 active factoring companies. The main banking factoring subsidiaries were: IFITALIA/BNL Mediofactoring, Factorit, Italfactor Italia, Centrofactoring, Credit Factoring, Barclays Factoring International, C.B.I Factor, Comfactor and Merchant Factor. Over the years, the number of factors reached 80 thanks to captives, and the market steadily increased.

By 1989, the Italian factoring market had outgrown that of other countries. For the first time, it surpassed the US and jumped to the top of the world rankings. The 80 Italian companies made business volumes of USD 51.2 billion, equivalent to 27% of the world market. Such an increase was caused by various reasons:

- Extremely long payment terms, sometimes exceeding one year or more in public administration business;
- Better knowledge and confidence in the factoring product;
- Valuable funding instrument to overcome credit crunch times.

It has been historically proven that, in crisis situations, factoring increases its volumes as a business support tool to enterprises. In most cases the contracts were "with recourse" (*Pro solvendo*). A report by Banca d'Italia stated that, in 1985, non-recourse transactions amounted to only 20% of the total business, increasing to 31% in 1988, far below that of other countries.

In 1990, factoring business turnover exceeded ITL 80,000 billion, still placing the Italian market at the top in Europe, number one ahead of Great Britain. Afterwards, it remained number two for sixteen consecutive years. From that date, the expansion of the market remained at sustained levels of growth, in spite of a decline in the growth of non-recourse business (down to 27.8%, from 32% in 1989). This was because of an economic downturn caused by the constraints imposed by the authorities on the provision of domestic credit.

In 2007, factoring business accounted for approximately 11% of trade receivables, still placing Italy number two worldwide, after Great Britain and ahead of France, the US and Japan, connected to the national prevalence in deferring payments, which corresponded to a high amount of trade receivables.

From 2008, the market began to decrease sharply in line with the economic and financial crisis which had a deeper impact in Italy than in most major countries. At the end of 2013, the Italian market had a huge increase but remained only in fourth place in the world in terms of purchased receivables.

In 2016, factoring turnover exceeded EUR 209 billion, equal to 11% of national GDP. The increase of 9.5%, which was higher than the average (2.3%), placed Italy among the top in the European market, a positive trend resulting in a valuable tool for supporting businesses and the real economy, particularly SMEs.

Concentration in the Market

From 1964 to 1993, IFITALIA remained the Italian market leader by volume, profit and its partnerships with various captive companies. However, in 1994, Mediofactoring, a subsidiary of the Banca Intesa San Paolo group, took the leadership, thanks to a double advantage:

- Greater impact after the mergers with other factoring companies whose shareholder banks had already merged with its parent company;
- Greater number of branches of its parent bank in the Italian territory.

After the acquisition of BNL by the BNP Paribas Group in 2006, IFITALIA decided to concentrate on profitability more than on turnover. For the first time, in 2012, the company was surpassed by Unicredit Factoring. In the Italian market, Mediofactoring jumped from 26.5% in 2001 (turnover of EUR 28 billion) to 32.5% in 2013 (EUR 55 billion), while Unicredit and IFITALIA had, at that date, a share of 16.7% and 14% (EUR 28 and 25 billion respectively), followed by Factorit, Italease and UBI Factors. In recent years, Banca IFIS also took an important market share. In July 2014, Mediofactoring was merged by incorporation into Mediocredito Italiano SpA, becoming a department of it.

Altogether, the top three companies reached, in 2016, 57% of the national business (EUR 122 billion, compared to the total market turnover of EUR 202 billion based on a study of 31 factoring companies), reflecting a high degree of market concentration:

- Mediocredito Italiano: 28.7% with a turnover of EUR 58 billion;
- Unicredit Factoring: 17.3% (EUR 35 billion);
- IFITALIA: 14.3% (EUR 29 billion).

As already mentioned, in Italy there was a huge fragmentation of factors with quite a few with adequate means and sufficient IT development. Over the years, the panorama of factoring companies has changed: captive companies decreased for various reasons, mainly because of the stringent requirements that financial institutions were called upon to perform – transparency, privacy, anti-money laundering, complaints, supervision, ICAAP, rules of Banca d'Italia, strict internal procedures, solvency, liquidity issues as well as cost constraints concerning human resources in particular. Financial markets also recorded significant mergers among major banks and the effects of these mergers involved factoring companies, reducing the number of companies. Some financial intermediaries changed their status to become banks with the aim of gathering public savings as funding.

III. A Creative Business under Constraints

From a pure technical tool, the Factoring Industry in Italy morphed into a managing and financial service able to comply with several needs related to trade credit policy.

An original Business in Terms of Products and Organisation

While factoring was consolidated over the years, it lacked an independent structure and organisation able to aggregate, manage data and bring the actors under the same umbrella. This lack was filled by the constitution of the *Associazione Italiana per il Factoring* (Assifact).

Assifact, a Proactive Organisation

Assifact was founded in 1988, bringing together factoring operators in order to promote a stable and orderly development, as well as to provide relevant information regarding factoring in compliance with antitrust rules. Assifact is characterised by its commissions to study the most diverse issues. Able to interact with Regulators (Banca d'Italia and *organi di vigilanza*), the association is very useful for discussing standards and principles that are often specifically dictated or dedicated to banks but are not convenient for factoring companies. Over the years an attempt was made to align the regulatory principles that banks and factoring companies have to observe.

An innovative Range of Products

During the 2000s, non-notification or undisclosed factoring became more and more attractive to corporates, large corporates as well as to multinationals. Also pan-European factoring enabled companies with subsidiaries, holdings and partners located in various countries, to uniformly manage these units with a single master contract.

To the standard product "with or without recourse" gradually more complex products were added to comply with the needs of the industry: maturity factoring, reverse factoring, non-notification and undisclosed factoring.

Maturity factoring is an Italian innovation, not familiar in other countries. It found wide acceptance and performed well as it offered an additional form of financing to the buyer, without any impact on its financial ratios. The main sectors involved were pharmaceuticals, motorcycles, IT (hardware) or the tyre industry.

Reverse factoring was particularly appealing to medium and large enterprises. By making special agreement with factors, it allowed their suppliers, particularly the smaller ones, to easily access invoice financing, thus improving their liquidity situation in the years of crisis when the "credit crunch" strongly constrained the ability of SMEs, that are the "engine" of Italian economy, to obtain credit facilities. Reverse factoring also had a great impact in the public administration field, certifying the debts of public entities and allowing their suppliers to collect money at due date despite huge delays. Throughout the years, "tailor-made" products created to satisfy the client's needs remained a strong issue.

A Business Under Pressure Due to Specific Rules, Legal and Regulatory Constraints

In the beginning, lacking rules for factoring business, Italian factors made bilateral agreements with their clients that in some cases created controversy, thus the need for a specific law.

Specific Rules: The Factoring Contract

Factoring is an atypical contract, pursuant to art. 1322 of the Civil Code, a tool for financing trade receivables able to satisfy a range of client needs: financing, warranty and management. Due to the lack of relevant legislation regarding this financial instrument, the legal framework was borrowed from the one provided for the assignment of credit by Civil

Code (art. 1260 & seq.). Progressively, such a legal gap has been filled by the contribution of Italian jurisprudence and international law. The key features of factoring were:
- The transfer of non-recourse credit with the factor's assumption of the debtor's default risk;
- The whole client's portfolio assignment (including future receivables assignment).

The Necessity of a Legal Framework: Genesis of the 1991 Law (Regulations Concerning the Assignment of Receivables)

Thanks to some proposals made by the three leading factoring companies (IFITALIA, Factorit and Credit Factoring) the legislator finally intervened by dictating a specific discipline for factoring with the law n° 52 dated of the 21st of February 1991 entitled "discipline of purchase of business receivables".

The Constraints of the Factoring Legislation

Today, the factoring business has two sets of legislations that every player has to apply: the Civil Code and the 1991 special law.

The general framework is contained in the articles of the Civil Code dedicated to the assignment of receivables, compatible with the special legislation, in particular regarding the following provisions:
- All trade receivables are transferable without the debtor's agreement as long as the assignment is not prohibited by law (art. 1260-1262-1263 cc);
- Prohibition of assignment, legal or conventional (art. 1261 cc);
- Notification of the assignment to the debtor who must be informed of the new beneficiary by a communication of the assignment or by his acceptance of the transaction. In case of lack of communication of the assignment, the assignee validly pays the party that appears to be the creditor of the sum (art. 1264-1265 cc);
- Effectiveness of the transfer against a third party.

The 1991 law introduces the following new features for factoring:
- The transfer may also take place in bulk and for future receivables, it is assumed "with recourse", unless the assignee waives in whole or in part to the guarantee;

- The transfer may relate only to receivables arising from contracts to be concluded in a period not exceeding twenty-four months, with a certain object, as well as with identified debtors in regard to future claims;
- As to the effects of the assignment of future receivables, the same is characterised as a mandatory act deferring the transfer to the very moment in which the credit arises.

Finally, the law provides the effects of the assignment of receivables in case of bankruptcy.

"La Revocatoria"

The law makes a clear distinction between two different situations:
- Debtor's bankruptcy: The payments made by the debtor to the assignee are not subject to the Revocation according to relevant rules. Such action may be proposed to the assignor if the receiver proves that he was aware of debtor's insolvency status on the date of the payment to the assignee, in any case within a year (art. 67 of bankruptcy rules);
- Supplier's bankruptcy: The effectiveness of the transfer against third parties cannot be opposed to the supplier's bankruptcy unless the receiver proves that the assignee was aware of the assignor's insolvency status at the moment of the payment and provided that such payment was made in the year preceding the bankruptcy and before the due date of the claims.

Over the years, conflicts, trials and jurisprudence have proven that the *Revocatoria* was a huge constraint for factoring companies, constraint not existing, at least at such a level, in many other European countries.

A Strong Regulation

In Italy, factoring can be operated by banks or "Intermediari Finanziari" (financial intermediaries) enrolled in the relevant "Register of financial intermediaries" and supervised by the Bank of Italy.

To comply with the Basel II directive, Banca d'Italia promulgated some circulars specifying some duties to be respected, such as to provide:
- Monthly aggregated data concerning the rates applied as well as transactions done in the period;

- Data concerning anti-money laundering to the Archivio Unico Informatico (AUI), sole data base;
- Data useful for the financial institution's supervision.

In addition, Banca d'Italia requires a lot of controls to be in place in factoring companies and pays a lot of attention to the board's role and its members.

IV. Conclusion

Today, we understand better that factoring is a more comprehensive solution than the simple advance payment of receivables. Indeed, in times of a credit crunch, such a solution becomes the winning model, transforming invoices with deferred payments into prompt cash.

Factoring is becoming more and more familiar, especially to SMEs, as a form of complementary financing and credit risk cover. The management of receivables is also very much and increasingly appreciated as it allows businesses to reduce their own managements' cost and to save time, thus allowing them to focus better on sales. Clients' satisfaction is there to prove the progress made: 63% of medium sized, corporate and large corporate companies consider that the Factoring Industry has a different approach to client valuation from banks when 58% of them consider factoring as a good solution to improve their financial status, their cash position in respect to lenders by improving the balance sheet index and working capital.

Therefore, factoring is now firmly established as a strong bridge between banks and non-banking activities.

Part III

Future – Factoring Tomorrow (The 21St Century)

Introduction

Patrick DE VILLEPIN

Global Head of Factoring, BNP Paribas

In the era of globalisation, European domination of the factoring market may appear to be under threat, from both the inside (lack of uniform framework within the EU) and from the outside (Asian competition). Yet European leadership remains vital to ensure that a secure model is promoted on a worldwide basis, based on adherence to compliance rules and on risk management, notably in the operational sphere.

It has to be admitted that globalisation is a new idea in such a business. In Asia, America, and Russia, since the start of the 21st century, the economic superpowers have seemed to want to define global trade and receivables finance. In reality, this has been affected by the ebbs and flows of financial crises and geopolitical upheaval.

A recent phenomenon of the last decade, the penetration of Asia (see chapter 15) appeared to be irretrievable and irreversible, given the transfer of power from the Atlantic coastlines to the Pacific Rim. In the early 2000s, the continent accounted a small percentage of the global market. With the exception of Japan, no country had a significant market share at the time. In 2010, the market share exploded to 21.5% (against 16.3% in 2009) and culminated at 26% in 2014. The penetration is concentrated in five countries: China, Japan, Taiwan, Hong Kong and Singapore.

The rise of China (see chapter 16), which has enjoyed phenomenal growth since 2006 (EUR 14 billion turnover in 2006, EUR 155 billion in 2010, and EUR 378 billion in 2013), has been accompanied by equivalent decreases on the old continent. Evidently the drivers of growth in the 21st century are located in Asia. "Greater China" (Peoples Republic of China, Taiwan and Hong Kong) represents a reservoir of great potential. Having become in 2011 global market leader in factoring after six years of exponential growth, China saw slower growth in 2014 (EUR 406 billion) before falling back significantly in 2015-2016 (EUR

353 billion and EUR 302 billion respectively), a fall of over 25% versus the high point in 2014, during years of credit crises and failures associated with growing levels of fraud.

Severely affected by an unprecedented liquidity and debt crisis, paradoxically Europe exits a decade of doubt, stagnation and deflation in a strengthened position. Although diminished, it once again covers over two-thirds of the global market. Such is the power of this profession of secured financing: year after year it demonstrates its ability to bounce back, even during periods of crises. A symbol of this resilience, in 2016 France replaced China at the top of the global rankings of international factoring!

So, who can now threaten European domination? Obviously, the predominance of the American continent – or rather of the United States (see chapter 17), Canada (still a relatively marginal player) and above all Latin America (see chapter 18) having only recently been converted to this technique – may appear to be of long standing and even preeminent over any other nation or region of the world. Although at the origins of the IFG, the US had never exerted the slightest supremacy over global factoring during the past 50 years. Today, the American continent accounts for less than 10% of the global market (8.4%). Since the start of the 21st century, it appears that the US has never managed to sustainably break through the turnover barrier of EUR 100 billion! However, there might be a debate about this claim: the turnover figures collated by the CFA do not include many of the large number of smaller banks and independents that comprise the membership within the International Factoring Association (IFA) – which unfortunately does not collate its volumes. It is therefore possible that the value of the overall US factoring market could be perhaps twice that reported by the CFA.

An immense country jammed between Europe and Asia, Russia (see chapter 19) had not re-established in 2016 its volume of 2013 (EUR 42 billion). The old soviet superpower has never managed to make its mark in the global rankings. Blow by blow, it has become a victim of the financial crisis and sanctions following the invasion of Crimea and part of Ukraine. Similarly, Oceania only enjoys a marginal share of the factoring market, although market volume in Australia is nearly twice that of Russia.

The rise of the emerging countries constitutes a mitigation factor vis-à-vis current European supremacy.

Introduction

Does the concept of emerging country (see chapter 20) still hold any relevance? What do Brazil (EUR 45.3 billion), Russia (EUR 28 billion), India (EUR 3.8 billion) and China (EUR 302 billion) have in common? In factoring, it has to be stated that the BRICs are not even in the same ballpark.

In spite of internal political instability and geopolitics that have significantly affected its economy and exchange rate, it has to be said that Turkey (see chapter 21) represents a model emerging country and bridgehead between the continents, in terms of both the organisation of its strong community of factors and its dynamism in export factoring.

In spite of a not negligible presence in the Maghreb and the Middle East countries (see chapter 22), without a doubt due to the inaccessibility of Algeria and the end of cash surpluses of the Gulf monarchies, Africa (see chapter 23) remains a continent in the making with less than 1% of global volume, 80% of which is concentrated in South Africa. However, InvoizPaid, a brand new fintech has just been launched in Nigeria!

Today and in the future, the economic reality of factoring invariably seems to bring the observer back to the shores of old Europe; it is a reality that only further education and professionalism, based on the keys to success of the European market, would allow these emerging markets to challenge and counteract the success of this model. But this does not mean that Africa and Asia do not represent the future of secured financing.

A – Globalisation

15. Factoring in Asia, a Promising Future

Ilyas KHAN

Head of Receivables Finance, Standard Chartered Group

Factoring started in Asia during the 1980s, which took place approximately 20 years after the arrival of the modern era of factoring in the 1960s into Europe from the US. Japan is among the first of the Asian countries to have started factoring, and was the world's leading export factoring market for seven years straight, beginning in 1994. Taiwan surpassed Japan as the leading export factoring market in 2001 and Hong Kong showed significant growth during this period as well. The success of Taiwan and Hong Kong had a big impact on mainland China, which took over from Taiwan in 2008, becoming the world's largest export factoring country:

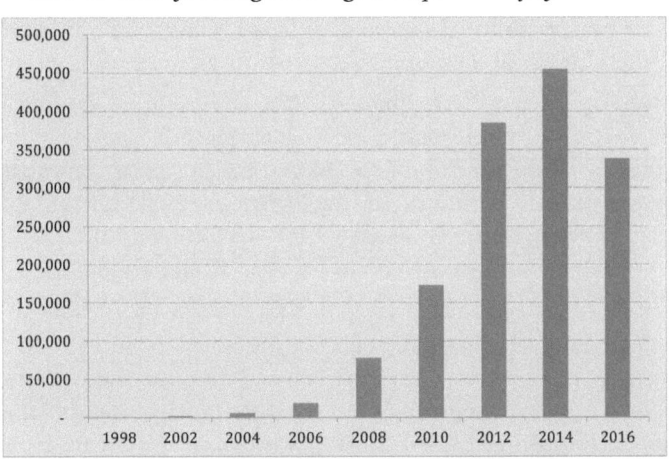

Table 6: China factoring volume grows exponentially after 2006

(Source: FCI, in USD million, exchange rate: EUR 1 = USD 1.12)

Although the Factoring Industry in Asia is less than 40 years old, it became the second largest market in the world just behind Europe. During the past 30 years, despite the continuous challenges in the global economy, the growth rate of business volumes was four times faster compared to the growth rate of the world economy. Even right after the global financial crisis in 2008, the Industry grew at its fastest pace yet, compared to traditional bank lending, which saw a reduction, and helped in part to stimulate the world economic recovery.

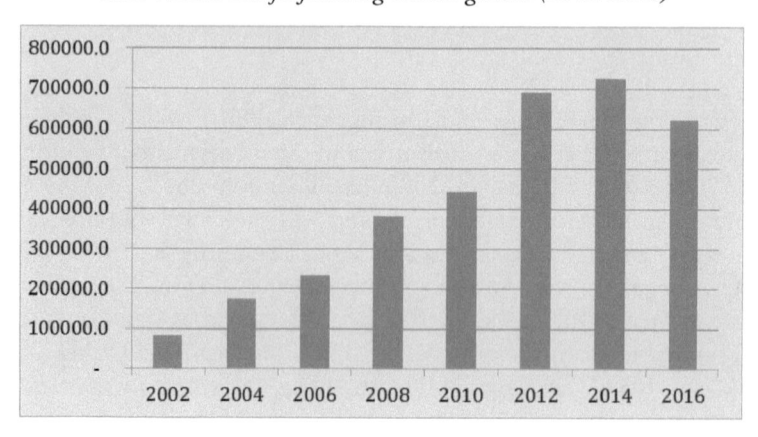

Table 7: Asia-Pacific factoring volume growth (2002-2016)

(Source: FCI, in USD million, exchange rate: EUR 1 = USD 1.12)

Apart from traditional players like Japan, China, Taiwan, and Hong Kong, there are rapid developments across Asian markets as well.

Singapore, as a regional financial hub, is a mature factoring market mainly focusing on big-ticket receivables finance programs for large corporates. Volume continues to grow since the crisis, especially after comparing the performance of the other more developed factoring countries in Asia. Turnover reached EUR 40.5 billion (USD 45 billion) in 2016, with a 7% market share in the Asia-Pacific region.

Factoring was introduced to Korea as early as the 1980s. With the increasing volume, the Commercial Act was amended in 1995 to include factoring as one of the basic commercial activities together with financial leasing and franchise finance. One of the disadvantages was that under the Korean GAAP, non-recourse factoring was considered a loan. However, a significant change took place in 2011, when the government switched its accounting standard from the Korean GAAP to the IFRS, which views non-recourse factoring as a receivables purchase, and therefore subject to beneficial "off-balance sheet" accounting treatment to Korean corporates. Since then, the Factoring Industry in Korea has witnessed a significant growth. However, Switzerland's ABB South Korea subsidy was hit by a USD 100 million fraud case in 2016. A senior executive was forging documents and colluding with an important third party to embezzle funds from the company. This had a negative effect on the Factoring Industry and the Central Bank of Korea tightened its policy afterwards. Now it takes months for financial institutions to on-board a factoring client, requiring enhanced due diligence on the parties involved. At the transaction level, more supporting documents are required to prevent fraud. Hence, factoring volume has remained flat in the past year.

India is transforming from a nascent market to a more developed state. When the Banking Regulation Act of 1949 was amended to include factoring as a form of business, it was expected that most banks would engage themselves in the business. But the Industry was developing slowly with the absence of a factoring law and low awareness amongst the corporates. To further promote the Industry, the government of India enacted the Factoring Act in 2011. This provided greater clarity to the factoring business and set the norms to regulate the market. Per FCI statistics, factoring volume in India surged in 2012 and 2013 with a +30% and +44% annual growth respectively. And it continues to see progress.

Factoring in Malaysia, Indonesia, Philippines, Thailand, Cambodia, Sri Lanka, Bangladesh, Vietnam, and Mongolia has also gained increasing attention. Government authorities are generally supportive and have interest in facilitating cross-border trade and SME business via factoring.

I. Commercial Factoring Companies: New Growth Area

Although banks dominate factoring business in terms of volume, they normally include more stringent underwriting requirements on sellers and buyers which SMEs normally have a hard time to meet. Besides, due to the de-risk strategy adopted by most banks after the financial crisis, those companies that would be eligible for financing could no longer pass the existing rigorous risk assessment criteria. Meanwhile, what banks can offer is normally limited to providing a bank account and a line of credit. But for SMEs, running a successful venture goes beyond a bank account into other vital aspects of business operations like ledger management, payment collections, risk management, etc.

Hence, there is a growing trend for a number of commercial factoring companies in the region to develop and support the financing needs of SMEs, including in those industries that the banks might not easily be able to finance. Factoring companies normally specialise in a few selected industries and provide customised solutions to their clients. They are able to adapt to the latest market trend or technology innovation more quickly due to the manageable size of business.

Table 8: Brief comparison of banks and factoring companies

	Banks	**Factoring companies**
Service	Focus on financing.	Normally specialised in one industry. Provide value-added service beyond financing: buyer due diligence, collections. Settlement, guarantee, ledger management services etc.
Credit assessment	Credit assessment is mainly done on seller and internal credit limit is required to facilitate factoring.	Assessment on seller, buyer and receivables. Work with third party to acquire more information for credit assessment.
Target client	Large corporate.	Any corporate.

Despite the short history, factoring companies expanded rapidly over the last five-year period. Total paid up capital is approximately CNY 400 billion (USD 59 billion). In fact, 84% of all registered factoring companies are registered in one of the following three provinces: Guangdong (Shenzhen), Tianjin and Shanghai. However, the largest percentage of inscribed companies is located in the Shenzhen region, due in part to the lowest capital threshold required by Chinese entrepreneurs today. Commercial factors are regulated by the ministry of commerce. However, change is underway. It is reported that the China Banking Regulatory Authority (CBRC) will soon be responsible for all factoring activities in China, including the commercial factors, which may have a significant impact on the rules regulating the commercial factoring market there. Nonetheless, it is estimated that within the next three to five years, commercial factoring volume will reach CNY 500 billion (USD 74 billion).[1]

Factoring companies are innovative in many ways:

Involvement of Banks

Many banks collaborate with commercial factoring companies and utilise them as their sales channel. Based on the banks' requirements, factoring companies source suitable clients in the market and refer them to the banks. The banks either offer factoring facilities directly to sellers or purchase those receivables from the factoring companies. This way, banks can expand their sales channel to cover all the markets, reduce sales and marketing costs, and improve factoring facilities' approval rate. At the same time, factoring companies benefit from the agency fee and pricing arbitrage. Banks will also provide re-factoring services to these commercial factoring companies, offering financing and best in class service for their clients, in the form of outsourcing and white labelling.

Cooperation with Third Party Platforms

There is a new trend for factoring companies and third-party platforms to collaborate.

For instance, Alibaba.com is an online trading platform with its own payment system, Alipay. For the purpose of fraud prevention and eliminating commercial disputes, buyers must pay to Alipay first. Only afterwards, the seller will ship the goods to the buyer. When the buyer accepts the goods, Alipay will then release the payment to the seller. In this trade flow, the receivables tenor is quite short, and the payment risk is very low. In case the seller has financing needs during this period, factoring companies make a quick assessment based on historical data provided by Alibaba.com. If a factoring company decides to offer factoring facilities to the seller, Alipay will transfer the buyer payment to the factoring company directly, once the buyer confirms the acceptance of goods or services.

There are also instances when factoring companies finance receivables of airlines. After flight tickets are sold, travel agencies will make payment to the International Air Transport Association (IATA) first. Then IATA will transfer the money to designated airlines, which takes approximately

---

[1] China Factoring Association.

fifteen days. During this period, factoring companies provide financing to airlines after IATA confirms that payment has been received from the various travel agencies. Once factoring facilities are extended, IATA will transfer the payment to the factoring companies directly.

In such a business model, the third party is critical for the purpose of risk assessment and portfolio monitoring. It requires a third party to provide accurate receivables information, a controlled collection process, and ongoing transaction monitoring. These receivables are normally of low value, high volume, shorter tenor, and the process requires an automated system as opposed to manual processing to ensure accuracy and efficiency.

Reverse Factoring

A number of factoring companies are set up to factor suppliers' receivables by way of a "reverse factoring" procedure, where a contract is signed between the bank and the anchor buyer, financing the various suppliers on O/A terms leveraging the strength of the anchor buyer's balance sheet. Reverse factoring, also referred to as confirming or payables finance, all under the heading of SCF, is one of the key products offered to all of the participants in their ecosystem to help improve working capital and profitability. This concept is particularly popular in markets like China. However, today they remain mainly domestic in nature.

II. Factoring and Fintech in Asia

Faced with increasing pressure to meet short-term liquidity needs, compressed margins, and growing counterparty credit concerns, the industry is looking for easy, convenient, and more cost-effective ways to manage receivables financing. Fintechs are one of the most popular solutions to improve the financial efficiency, and enhance the working capital, of both buyers and suppliers. This is promising in markets like Asia due to its fragmented nature and large number of SMEs.

Overview

Corporates, both upstream and downstream, benefit from fintechs mainly via integration and automation.

Seamless connection and integration of physical and financial supply chains bring together suppliers, buyers, and other supply chain partners in one marketplace. This provides end-to-end connectivity, visibility and loyalty along the supply chain.

According to the Association for Image and Information Management, automation leads to an average of 29% reduction in invoice processing costs, which can translate to USD 300,000 per year for an organisation that processes up to 10,000 invoices per month. The Institute of Finance and Management emphasises that implementing a high level of automation enables businesses to reduce the average cost of processing a purchase order-based invoice to USD 7.03 compared to an average of USD 9.62 for businesses with little or no automation. Besides cost reduction, automation can also minimise errors, fraud, and onerous invoice processing involved in the manual work.

In view of the benefits brought by the fintechs, financial institutions started to invest in technologies in one way or another to stay ahead of the market.

Banks in general focus more on developing their own internal systems to facilitate their clients' ecosystem. Currently, top tier banks and most tier two banks in the region have their own online supply chain financing platform to provide auto-financing and cash flow management services.

As for factoring companies, they are usually participating in these third-party platforms. For example, JD.com, the second largest B2C online retailer in China, started its own factoring company in 2013. It provides end to end supply chain management to more than 2,000 retailers on JD.com. In 2016, its factoring volume reached CNY 40 billion (USD 5.9 billion). Turnaround time of disbursements is only three minutes after the financing request is submitted. Besides, factoring companies are using fintechs and third-party data to complement their risk assessment. Factoring companies make analyses based on companies' financials, production cycle, cash flow, balance sheet, inventory etc. provided by these third-party platforms. It is an effective tool to assess SMEs who are the main clients of these factoring companies.

Apart from financial institutions, government bodies also actively promote fintechs in the Factoring Industry. For example, the government of India is in the process of establishing an electronic trade receivables discounting system to be governed by the regulatory framework put in place by the Reserve Bank of India. This is to finance trade receivables of

Micro, Small and Medium Enterprises (MSMEs). This will significantly improve the liquidity of these smaller corporates in all different sectors.

E-commerce Financing: a New Form of Factoring

With the development of fintechs and the evolution of e-invoicing, the creation of e-commerce platforms may be one of the major factoring service offerings in Asia in the future.

First of all, e-commerce platforms have a natural advantage for credit assessment and risk control compared to traditional factoring companies and banks. They can make use of their own database of trading details to assess the seller, buyer, and receivables quality, as well as to monitor payments and transaction flows.

Besides, Asia-Pacific accounts for 40% of global e-commerce sales in Q1 2017 and the volume is expected to grow further. This is a good sign for the Factoring Industry as it translates to a bigger share of the pie in terms of the financing of accounts receivable. Today, the vast majority of e-commerce sales go to larger or more mature markets in the region like China, Japan, South Korea, and India. In the coming years ahead, Southeast Asia might be the next major boom market due to a growing middle class and expanding internet access.

Hence, the promise of fast growth has lured e-commerce companies to explore solutions to monetise their suppliers' receivables and use fintechs to build a robust risk framework around it. Asia's two e-commerce giants Alibaba and JD.com have already started to build their own factoring capabilities and expect to be one of the critical players in the Factoring Industry in the near future.

III. Industry Regulations

Factoring is a comprehensive financial service that involves transfer of receivables by creditors to third parties and is associated with various inherent risks. Lack of regulation and supervision could hamper the rapid growth of the factoring segment.

Legal Basis of Factoring

Most markets in Asia have factoring regulations such as in India, China, Hong Kong, Taiwan, Korea, etc. In the mature markets like Singapore, factoring is better recognised and widely accepted even though there is no specific law governing it. All of the financial institutions and factoring companies are already properly licensed and regulated under the existing legal system and banking laws. In case of default, the recovery rate is relatively higher in those advanced markets, due to faith in their legal jurisdictions to resolve conflicts and adjudicate factoring cases properly and expeditiously, which gives factors the confidence and comfort in the Industry. However, just the opposite is true in those markets where the rules are weak or have never been tested, especially in the developing markets. The common concerns of factoring with regard to conduct or behaviour of the parties involved include the lack of transparency in the transaction, the inability to assign claims and have effective ownership in the receivables, and the rise of fraud and dispute risk, especially when the courts do not know-how to resolve such cases. Hence, there is an urge for those markets to introduce adequate regulations to promote the healthy development of the sector.

For example, factoring started in India in the 1940s. However due to the absence of a robust legal framework, the Industry remained at a nascent stage. The government in tandem with the Reserve Bank of India has recognised the issue and enacted the Factoring Regulation Act in 2011 to give an impetus to factoring activity.

In China, the legal environment is also improving over the years. In October 2016, China revised factoring business norms for the Chinese banking industry to further ensure the Industry standard. Besides, based on the legal precedents, it shows that the law admits the bank's ownership of the receivables, and supports the bank to collect the money from the buyer. Also, for insurance companies, if the terms and conditions in the insurance policy are unfair or not disclosed properly, the insured party is entitled to the claim even if there is an indemnity clause in the policy. However, it is noted that the profession was deluged with factoring fraud cases between 2014-2016, which created great strains within the lower courts. Nonetheless, the positive evolution of the legal foundation for factoring in China has provided greater confidence and impetus to the Factoring Industry there.

However, certain regulations may at the same time have negative consequences on factoring business. For example, effective from October 2016, corporate tax was replaced with Value Added Tax (VAT) in China. There is no final decision yet on the tax treatment on factoring companies. In the event that the tax is charged on the interest amount instead of the difference between interest income and cost of funds, taxes may be much higher for factoring activity. This would have a significant adverse impact on the profitability of the Industry.

Financing Environment

In Asia, the cost of funds, especially in USD, is relatively high for both banks and factoring companies. There are thousands of them in the region looking for sustainable funding to expand their business. Hence, providing a reliable and ongoing funding source is critical for the further expansion of the Industry.

Asset Backed Securities (ABS) could be a solution to provide liquidity as well. Banks and factoring companies can turn their receivables portfolio into marketable securities. Receivables ABS have attracted high attention recently. Government authorities are also supportive. In China, receivables ABS are allowed to be listed on the exchange and regulated by the authorities. In 2016, China exchange listed 77 receivables ABS with a total amount of CNY 80 billion (USD 11.8 billion). Among which, 14% were issued by banks, and 86% were issued by factoring companies.

Credit Rating System

Unlike most lending facilities that focus on seller credit assessment, factoring requires analysis of the seller, the buyer and an examination of the quality of the receivables. Quite often, buyers/debtors are not the customers of the bank or the factoring company. There is a significant demand for a robust client rating system and database to assess the credit risk.

The credit rating is more readily available in developed markets like Japan, Singapore, and Taiwan. The government authorities usually play a key part in building such a comprehensive and transparent rating system.

However, the credit worthiness and rating systems in developing markets evolve at a much slower pace. There is no mature external rating system and there is limited data available via government official credit bureaus. Moreover, the credit insurance companies involved in international factoring usually have limited capabilities in these markets. Most of the time, SMEs are not covered by insurance companies simply due to the lack of financial data. Hence, development of credit databases and rating systems is crucial and imperative for the further growth of factoring in the region.

IV. Conclusion: Factoring Outlook in Asia

Due to the recent economic downturn and more restricted regulations of financial institutions, factoring volume in Asia encountered a decline in 2015 and 2016. The downturn happened mainly because of the performance of traditionally strong players like Taiwan and Japan, as well as China. However, there are some markets with positive growth such as Hong Kong (+28%), Australia (+14%), and Singapore (+4%) in 2016.

In the coming years, Japan and Taiwan will continue to be the top Asian countries but volume may decline slightly. In Japan, more invoices will be financed by electronic platforms, which is a new trend. Hong Kong and Singapore are recovering from the financial crisis, and the volume will pick up further. India, as a new growth area in the region, is expected to grow fast with the factoring market opening to the foreign banks, relaxation of regulations by the Reserve Bank of India, as well as increasing awareness and confidence in the Industry.

China, being the largest factoring market in Asia, and the second largest in the world, still has great potential to grow as shown with the strong increase in the number of factoring companies. As in 2016, there were 5,584 registered commercial factoring companies in China, which is 102% more than compared to 2015:

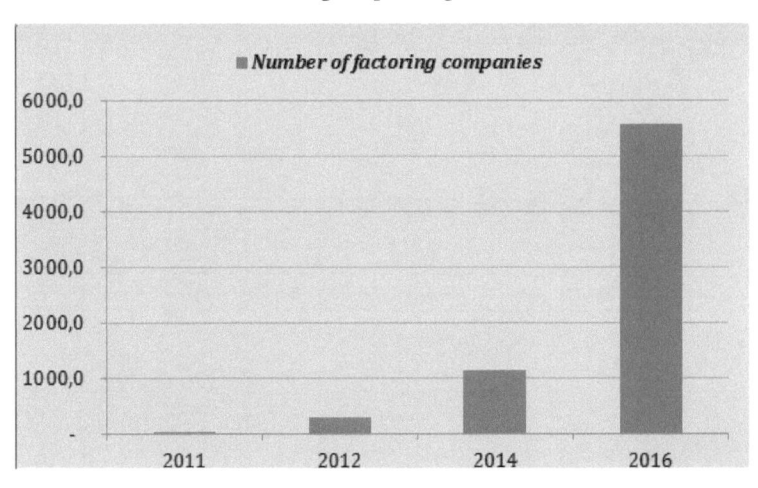

Table 9: Factoring companies' growth in China

(Source: Factoring company development report, Ping An Securities, 2013)

As of December 2016, accounts receivable of enterprises above a designated size has reached a record CNY 12.6 trillion[2] (USD 1.9 trillion), which is 9.8% higher compared to last year, out of which less than 20% is factored. This promises a steady growth of factoring volume in the coming years.

---

[2] China National Bureau of Statistics.

16. Factoring in China, an Ambitious Tiger

Jiang Xu

Deputy General Manager, Global Trade Services Department, Bank of China

Since the adoption of the reform and opening-up policy nearly 40 years ago, China has conformed to the trend of economic globalisation by opening up to the outside world and promoting economic and trade cooperation with other countries. During the opening-up process, factoring entered China in 1987, and gradually developed into a well-established Industry through 30 years of evolvement. Now China has become one of the world's leading factoring markets with trillions of RMB factoring volumes and thousands of factors. After a slow start during the late 1980s and 1990s, factoring grew tremendously during the first ten years of the 21st century with the rapid development of China's economy and foreign trade. After China entered the "new normal" in 2012, the Factoring Industry also began to consolidate and readjust to the changed economic environment. Although the speed of development is somewhat slowing down, there is still great potential for factoring to grow in China and the prospects are favourable.

I. Different Stages in the Development of China's Factoring Industry

The development of factoring in China can be divided into three stages. In the first two stages, banks were almost the only players. Non-bank factors (commercial factoring companies) have jumped on the bandwagon in recent years but banks still dominate the market.

The Initial Stage (1987 to 1999): Slow Start

The origins of factoring in China can be traced back to 1987, when Bank of China signed a "Master Factoring Agreement" with Disko

Factoring Bank in Germany, and for the first time introduced the concept of factoring into China. In 1992, Bank of China officially launched international factoring services, and joined FCI in 1993. Domestic factoring started even later. In 1999, again it was Bank of China that took the lead, this time in launching domestic factoring services in China. During the 1990s, there were only a handful of factors, all of whom were banks, and a big gap between China and the developed markets in terms of business volume, types of factoring products offered to clients and service quality. FCI statistics show that from 1993 to 1999, annual factoring volume[1] in China was less than USD 100 million.

The Second Stage (2000-2011): Rapid Growth

China's entry into the WTO in 2001 marked a watershed for the country's Factoring Industry. Since then, and for the next ten years, China's economy and foreign trade grew at a solid pace, providing fertile ground for the sustainable rapid growth of China's Factoring Industry. For Chinese exporters, while the rewards of selling in an international marketplace could be substantial, success could also bring its share of problems. One of the greatest problems facing Chinese exporters was the increasing insistence by importers that trade be conducted on O/A terms, which could cause severe cash flow problems and the more serious problem of buyer default. Factoring solves just these problems and was welcomed by the Chinese exporters. On the supply side, during this period, more and more Chinese banks began to offer factoring services and successively joined FCI. They formed their own industry organisation in 2006, known as the Factors Association of China (FAC), which later became a sub-committee of the China Banking Association (CBA). There also appeared a few commercial factoring companies, but their business volume was trivial. According to FCI statistics, in 2012, China's factoring volume[1] totalled USD 453 billion, and the compound annual growth rate (CAGR) for the period was nearly 60%.

---

[1] There are two sets of data for China's factoring volume. One is the statistics by FCI, which include factoring volume by country and have been published every year for decades. The other set of data is the statistics by Factoring Industry organisations in China such as FAC, which only got started a few years ago. The two sets of data vary to some extent, but not significantly, and may both be used in the text in different contexts.

The third Stage (2012-now): Consolidation and Readjustment

Since 2012, China's economy has shifted to a "new normal" with a slower growth rate, with risks emerging in some sectors of the economy such as iron and steel, cement and electrolytic aluminum. China's Factoring Industry felt the impact both in terms of business volume and risk exposure. According to FAC statistics, in 2013, China's bank Factoring Industry generated CNY 3.17 trillion in factored volume, which was the highest figure ever recorded, but with a much lower year-on-year growth rate (12%) than in previous years. In 2014, the total factoring volume for Chinese banks was CNY 2.92 trillion, decreasing for the first time in history. In 2015, the volume was CNY 2.87 trillion, dropping for the second consecutive year. With regard to risks, most Chinese bank factors have experienced downward pressure of factoring asset quality from 2012 to 2015 although the pressure has somewhat eased since 2016.

Commercial factoring has achieved remarkable growth in this period. Although China's first commercial factoring company was founded in 2005, it was not until 2012 that commercial factoring began to flourish. In June 2012, the ministry of commerce was designated to be the regulator for commercial factoring companies. The ministry of commerce did a lot to promote commercial factoring. With its help, China's commercial factoring companies formed their own trade association, Commercial Factoring Expertise Committee (CFEC). According to statistics by CFEC, the number of commercial factoring companies exceeded 5,500 at the end of 2016, compared to 50 in 2012. Around 1,100 commercial factoring companies (20%) have conducted business. The volume of commercial factoring in China was estimated to reach CNY 500 billion in 2016 compared to less than CNY 10 billion in 2012, growing at a CAGR of 160%.

II. Future Trends: the Prospects are Still Favourable

Although confronted with many challenges, the winds of change are blowing in favour of China's Factoring Industry, mainly stemming from ongoing demand, the nation's economic restructuring, the trend towards transaction banking and support from the government.

The Ongoing Demand for Factoring

In today's trading environment, the LC is diminishing and being replaced by O/A payment terms. It is estimated that more than 70% of global trade is conducted on O/A terms, and the percentage might be even higher for domestic trade in China. Statistics by the National bureau of statistics of China show that the accounts receivable of industrial enterprises above designated size[2] are increasing every year, reaching CNY 12.6 trillion by the end of 2016. Where there are accounts receivable, there is demand for factoring. National strategies such as the One Belt, One Road (OBOR) initiative, RMB internationalisation and the launch of free trade zones will also bring more business opportunities for factoring in China.

China's Economic Restructuring

Under the "new normal" state, as an important aspect of the economic restructuring, the Chinese government is strongly encouraging SMEs to play a more significant role in the economy. Factoring is universally accepted as vital to the financial needs of SMEs. It can be expected that factoring will contribute in its own way to the development of China's SME sector.

The Trend Towards Transaction Banking

Transaction banking is becoming a strategic business for many Chinese banks. Although the nature and scope of transaction banking varies across different organisations, most definitions feature some common components, among which cash management and trade finance are core to the business. By providing clients with a package of services including financing, accounts receivable management and payment settlement, factoring is indispensable in transaction banking and is bound to be more widely used in China.

Support from the Government

On the 27th of January 2016, it was decided at the State council executive meeting, chaired by Premier Li Keqiang, that the Chinese government would develop policies to create more diversified financing

---

[2] In China, "industrial enterprises above designated size" is a term used by the National Bureau of Statistics and it refers to enterprises with annual revenue of CNY 20 million or more from their main business operations.

channels for the real economy through measures such as "vigorously developing receivables finance". This was the first time in history that the chief administrative authority of China officially promoted receivables finance. Soon afterwards, eight cabinet level departments, including the People's Bank of China (the central bank), the China Banking Regulatory Commission (CBRC) and the ministry of commerce, jointly issued policies on concrete measures. At Industry levels, in April 2014, CBRC promulgated "the Interim provisions for factoring business of commercial banks", in an effort to regulate and promote the healthy and orderly development of China's bank Factoring Industry. And since 2012, the ministry of commerce has also issued various policies, rules and regulations to promote commercial factoring. Support from the government and regulators will certainly lead to a more sustainable development of Factoring Industry in China.

17. Future Trends for Factoring and Commercial Finance in America

Andrew Tananbaum

CEO, Capital Business Credit

The legendary management consultant Peter Drucker famously said, "The only thing we know about the future is that it will be different." Today he might add, "The future we're entering is likely to be more different than we can imagine."

Some things about the future are fairly linear and therefore easy to predict. For example, the inexorable march of e-commerce means there will be fewer and fewer invoices and more and more direct to consumer business, including disintermediation of the bricks and mortar retailer.

How can an industry factor invoices that are never issued? In a world with no invoices to factor, the business would shift partly, or entirely, to what amounts to secured loans against inventory (aka ABL). Will companies continue to buy and own the receivable? The trend is already against it: ABL in the US is already much larger than factoring in terms of funds employed.

What is harder to predict is what will arise from the application of technologies like artificial intelligence and blockchain. These promise to usher in an era of non-linear, transformative change. This word, "transformative", is routinely misapplied to changes that are merely important. Here it is meant in the literal sense: changes that feel more like a revolutionary step forward. The WHAT of "Supplier X offers financing to Buyer Y" will remain the same – the Trade Finance business is about three thousand years old for a reason – but the HOW is what will be transformed.

When thinking about a future with the potential to be that different, making concrete predictions is neither wise nor particularly useful. Instead, this chapter will focus on five key developing trends that, synthesised, appear likely to shape the future of factoring.

It is important to note that these trends will be mutually self-reinforcing. The more and faster that technology improves, the more powerful the other trends driving change will become.

The five trends:

1. Technology radically enhances (and continually refines) the ability to predict defaults and price risk;
2. Sea changes to cost structures;
3. Everybody is a factor and nobody is a factor: disintermediation (Who does what to whom?);
4. Marketplace expansion and the interconnectivity and emergence of powerful networks;
5. Whither the incumbents? The innovator's dilemma.

What is not likely to change, at least in the foreseeable future, is that business will have a continuing need for financial leverage and working capital.

I. Technology Radically Transforms (and continually refines) the Ability to Predict Defaults and Price Risk

All finance relies on some calculation of trust, risk and return. In the earliest days of handshake deals, and only a gut feeling about a borrower's character, the number of years in business and reliability might have informed this calculation. Today, complex (but still rules based) algorithms and credit ratings inform decisions – and even social media data[1] plays a role. In the future, financiers will have access to near perfect real time information (both from the client and its buyer) and Artificial Intelligence (AI) will track billions of sets of data and attributes to continually refine and improve its ability to predict outcomes.

The rise of AI, interestingly, represents a kind of return of "gut feeling" – but heavily informed and validated by data. A major strength of AI is its ability to evaluate unstructured data. For example, Natural Language Processing is already being used to perform sentiment analysis of news stories about a company or industry.

It is not hard to imagine the same tools being leveraged to glean insights from blog posts by a company's top leaders about their character and reliability. For example, imagine that an analysis of hundreds of

---

[1] https://www.wsj.com/articles/borrowers-hit-socialmedia-hurdles-1389224469.

thousands of deals reveals that company CEOs who write in a passive voice are 85% more likely to be late in payments by five days.

Even the time-honoured practice of "looking a prospect in the eye" is already taking on new meaning. A start-up called Lapetus analyses "selfies" to predict life insurance risk. By studying hundreds of points on a human face and thousands of regions, Lapetus can estimate the person's BMI (body mass index) – is this person fit or not? Is this person a smoker, or a non-smoker? It can even tell how fast or how well someone is aging. Imagine comparing selfies taken a year apart, to estimate how much stress a company leader has been under.

The combination of structured and unstructured data and the ability of AI to evaluate new deals against thousands or millions of previous outcomes means that deals that today might appear identical will be shown to have different risks. What is more, every new deal continually improves the ability of the AI to predict and price risk.

The speed of funding is likely to rise dramatically, and the cost is likely to fall.

The more precisely you can predict and price any given bundle of risks, the more it changes the credit business and the more scalable it becomes.

More precise prediction of risks will lower credit spreads and commissions. On one hand, we might expect to see lending become like a game of limbo: "how low can you go?" How small of a return are you willing to accept for what is predicted to be a 99.76354% sure thing? At the other end of the spectrum, it seems logical to expect turbo charged risk and lower required equity. For example, a securitisation might have six or more tranches of risk rather than just two.

Still, markets can never be fully inoculated against risk. As Peter Bernstein put it in his book *Against the Gods: The Remarkable Story of Risk*, "The prevalence of surprise in the world of business is evidence that uncertainty is more likely to prevail than mathematical probability." There will always be some urge to rub the Buddha's belly for comfort.

II. Sea Changes to Cost Structures

Despite real progress, much of the cost structure in factoring today would be instantly recognisable to the leaders of factoring firms from a half century ago.

Origination costs remain high – and are often still driven by individual relationships nurtured over time by business development executives. For companies in traditional factoring, this may seem like a cost that cannot be significantly reduced: where else will the business come from? The reality is that those costs can and will be reduced significantly – and in some cases, eliminated entirely. It seems likely that there will be at least two means of accomplishing this. First, the rise of networks (more about that later), and second, the increasing ability of lenders to offer financing to businesses that the lender already has a great deal of data and insight about.

These networks, along with previously unobtainable levels of transparency, should also shrink the significant costs that still exist in underwriting, administration, liability management, and every other aspect of the factoring business.

Blockchain has vast promise to change the nature of trust, which again impacts cost structures for the better. For example, a January 2017 analysis from consultancy Accenture and operations benchmarking company McLagan, "Banking on Blockchain: A Value Analysis for Investment Banks", estimates that blockchain technology could save leading investment banks up to USD 12 billion a year in back office costs. Where do they foresee those savings occurring? Up to 70% in financial reporting. Up to 50% in compliance. Up to 50% in settlement and clearing and other business operations.[2]

The rise of Ethereum – which builds on blockchain but differs in its ability to embed complex contracts and operate more at the speed of financial services – has even greater potential. In fact, Ethereum could become the application platform that most of the emerging financing networks will run on.

III. Everybody Is a Factor and Nobody Is a Factor: Disintermediation

In the recent past, traditional factoring had shifted toward being more of a bank product than a specialty finance product. In the future, we should expect technology to enable entirely new competitors everywhere up and down the entire value chain, including point solutions seeking to cherry-pick the most profitable niches.

---

[2] http://www.businessinsider.com/accenture-blockchain-could-save-top-10-investment-banks-up-to-8bn-a- year-2017-1.

Future Trends for Factoring and Commercial Finance in America 239

As technology transforms the ability to predict and price risk and emerging platforms find they can be more efficient than traditional factoring businesses, the typical barriers of entry to the factoring business will continue to erode – or vanish altogether.

What is more, it can be argued that any of the digital giants – Google, Apple, Facebook, Amazon, or Alibaba – has the depth of data, the depth of AI talent, and sufficiently deep pockets to become a financing company if they chose to be. In fact, Amazon is already in the business in a small but very smart way.

Orchard Platform has created a useful graphic that helps map the relationships within this emerging ecosystem. This is how that ecosystem looked as of January 2017.

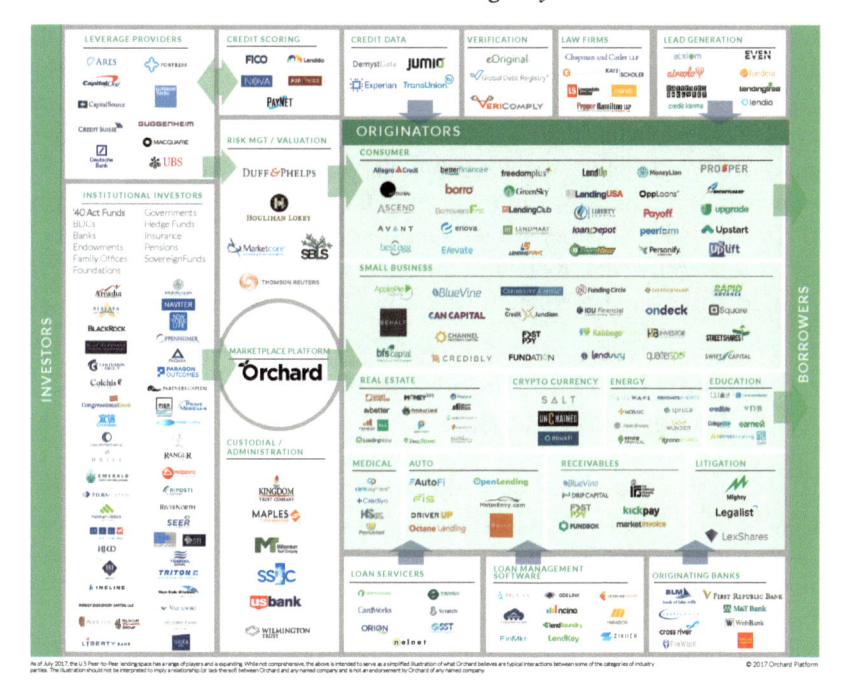

Table 10: Online lending ecosystem

What is driving these changes is more than simply raw capitalism or a desire to push innovation. There's a cultural imperative as well. The early digital era has trained people to believe that whatever they want should be easy to obtain, and with as painless a process as possible. Already, pushing a button on a device feels as needlessly onerous as filling out a stack of paper forms did to our grandparents. People want what they want, and they want it now.

Amazon, which probably knows as much about real-time access to goods as any company on Earth, agrees. Remember the problem of origination costs? Amazon has found a factoring method that eliminates those costs entirely. They lend only to the very top sellers in their Amazon marketplace. You do not ask Amazon for a loan – Amazon offers you a loan if their algorithm judges you worthy.

In a way, this is an echo of the past. For a time, GE shifted from being a manufacturing firm to relying heavily on financing. At one point, nearly half their profits were generated from GE Capital before they ultimately left that business.

Disintermediation begins from all sides at once: for traditional factoring firms this may feel like getting pecked to death by ducks. Many of the start-ups are squarely aimed at solving a very specific problem or serving a specific niche, while reducing, avoiding, or altogether eliminating the typical legacy cost structures. Some are focused on SMEs with occasional short-term cash flow gaps. Others seek to be a marketplace lender for commercial receivables. This niche orientation makes sense at the outset: the focus makes it easier to get venture or angel funding to start, and easier to identify what niche the companies will sell into. But if history is a guide, this disintermediation will evolve into something different.

IV. Marketplace Expansion and the Emergence of Powerful Networks

As venture capitalist Mark Andreesen memorably put it, "Software is eating the world". Financial services – including factoring – will get "eaten", too. It seems likely we will see the rise of "Credit-as-a-Service", both because technology makes it possible and because the potential will be obvious to both lenders and borrowers. CEO Michael Finkelstein of The Credit Junction summarises this ethos neatly: "We continue to move to a real-time access to goods and services society and capital should be no different."

In 2016, global investment in fintech companies hit USD 24.7 billion across 1076 deals. Dozens of alternative funding start-ups are vying to win business from traditional factoring firms and other providers. Each will race for growth and take advantage of network effects.

Typically, as winners seek to leverage network effects, a wave of consolidation will hit.

What are "Network Effects"? Mark Andreesen's firm, a16z, offers a clear definition:

> "Simply put, a network effect occurs when a product or service becomes more valuable to its users as more people use it." (*Also known as: demand side economies of scale*).

They go on to note that network effects create barriers to exit for existing users and barriers to entry for new companies, and can help create or tip winner-take-all markets.[3]

Imagine a "Big Bang Theory" in which the marketplace radically expands – serving entirely new clients in entirely new ways – and consolidates power at the same time.

It is not difficult to imagine a future in which two or three robust, well-functioning networks – stripped of most of the Industry's old cost structures and including only the features which are essential for modern business – would exist to match buyers and sellers. This sort of positive consolidation would boost already powerful network effects: the more funders and businesses that need funding, the more value each large network would gain. As dominant networks emerge, any company seeking to provide funding would have no choice but to fight to be a supplier of money to those networks.

Already, there are companies angling to create powerful platforms. A post on the 23rd of July 2017 in TRF news notes:

> "FCI is launching a buyer-centric approved payables finance platform for its growing global membership. Called FCIreverse, it uses a platform designed by Demica, a leading provider of technology-based alternative finance solutions and together offers FCI members the opportunity to develop buyer-led "reverse factoring" programs."

With all platforms, improved ability to predict risk promises to enable loan sizes to shrink. This would mean a far larger quantity of far smaller deals. Presumably, this will tend to reduce concentration risk by industry or client. Yet oddly, it is also possible that the same kinds of network effects will tend to create more concentration risk. If a company like Amazon all but replaces all other retailers. In that scenario, how much

---

[3] https://a16z.com/2016/03/07/all-about-network-effects/.

"future Amazon" risk can a network or company hold without needing to spread some of that risk to others?

The primary reason powerful networks seem so likely in the long-term is because they would be the most efficient way to bring buyers and sellers together. This does not mean they will be immune from challenges in the near term, however.

Skeptics can – correctly – point to The Receivables Exchange, which was the first major US based invoice trading platform and say: "this idea has been tried and it did not entirely work". This is true, but it is also typical. Gartner's Hype Cycle illustrates the usual path of progress: disillusionment nearly always arrives before enlightenment.

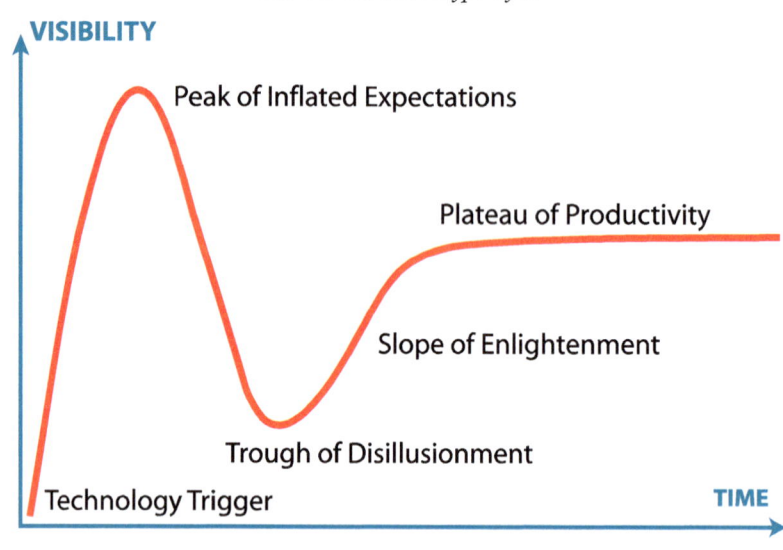

Table 11: Gartner's Hype Cycle

It also pays to remember that first-mover advantage does not always mean that first-movers win. Google was not the first search engine, nor was Facebook, the first social network. In these things timing, leadership, and a certain amount of luck are always a factor. As Microsoft's Bill Gates sagely put it: "We always overestimate the change that will occur in the next two years and underestimate the change that will occur in the next ten."

V. Whither the Incumbents? The Innovator's Dilemma

If the trends outlined in this chapter turn out to be directionally accurate and mutually self-reinforcing, it will put a fair amount of pressure on traditional factoring firms.

A very real challenge for incumbents in the traditional factoring business is that there is a lot invested in the traditional way of doing things – both in the literal sense as well as the cultural sense. In many ways, it may be easier for a start-up to take a blank page approach to business and eliminate them from the outset than it will be to reduce those costs over time.

The net impact of the shift in cost structures will be to democratise lending, encourage new entrants to the business, and put pressure on traditional business to adapt quickly. However, it seems clear that this process has not only already begun but is quickly accelerating.

TechCrunch describes the difficulty for incumbents well:

"As disruptive products continually address markets that previously could not be served — a new-market disruption — or offer simpler, cheaper, more convenient alternatives to existing products — a low-end disruption, incumbents will find it almost impossible to respond. In a new-market disruption, the unserved clients are unserved precisely because serving them would be unprofitable given the incumbent's business model. In a low-end disruption, the clients lost typically are unprofitable for the incumbents, so the big companies are happy to lose them.

Thus, we have the innovator's dilemma. Incumbents appropriately ignore the new product because it is uneconomic to respond, but the incumbents' quiescence can lead to their later downfall."[4]

VI. Conclusion: a Final Note

Is the future bright, or bleak? It depends on what exactly the future turns out to be, and what place your company has in it. The companies that unlock the formula to create powerful networks will find the future incredibly bright. The incumbents who find their traditional business disrupted will view that same future quite a bit different.

---

[4] https://techcrunch.com/2013/02/16/the-truth-about-disruption.

The trends outlined here feel instinctively right, although obviously it is impossible to predict with any precision. Readers are encouraged to think critically about the trends in this chapter and imagine their own vision of the future.

This chapter opened with a quote from Peter Drucker, and so it seems only fitting to close with one: "The best way to predict the future is to create it."

18. Factoring in Latin America and the Caribbean, a Sleeping Region

Alberto WYDERKA

Latin America and The Caribbean Chapter Director, FCI

Baptized for the first time in 1507 after the discovery of Amérigo Vespucci, "America" is a contrasted continent with its different culture and mixed races, with immigrants and economies at different levels of development. A clear distinction should be made between its two regions: North America on the one side, Latin America and the Caribbean (LA & C) on the other side, the latter including Central and South America, although in some of the countries, spoken language is Portuguese, English, French or Dutch and not Spanish: 33 countries in all.

In his book, *El Continente Dormido* (The Sleeping Continent), Mr Alberto Padilla, one of the most renowned economic and financial journalists of the continent, summarises the global evolution of the region:

"In the middle of the second decade of the 21st century, while the world is talking about drones ready for home deliveries, cars with the ability to handle themselves, space tourism and the internet of things, Latin America lives at the mercy of the price of its commodities: corn, wheat, soy, coffee, copper, petroleum. In fact, for several centuries we have depended on the same things to survive; our continent sleeps in a slumber that rests on its natural resources and to which economic development seems to be eternally elusive. When the exploitation of raw materials no longer guarantees anything, the challenge is to quickly transform stability into growth and growth into development".

North America, – Canada and the United States – enjoy a higher level of economic development, whereas the countries that make up LA & C are developing at very different levels. Those who are knowledgeable attribute such differences to many circumstances, like the origins of the first and successive immigration flows, different weather conditions, laws, social, cultural and economic trends, etc. However, LA & C is crossing a momentum in its political, social, financial and economic fields, which by looking at the future, opens new business opportunities for all of them. Many countries of the region, to a greater or lesser extent, are taking advantage of such a trend and have started to draw strategies for long-term development. Except Venezuela, the democratic systems are strengthening and consolidating, and most of the region has better resisted the effects of the economic and financial crisis, thanks to sound and responsible macroeconomic management and to structural reforms carried out in recent years.

There is no doubt that the economic dynamics of each LA & C country generates multiple business opportunities, not only within each country, but also among the countries of the region and, finally, between them and the rest of the world, as a result of the growth of demand and supply of products. So, it would be logical to think that, on the one hand, the domestic Factoring Industry will find an appropriate environment to grow in volumes, and, on the other, more opportunities will flourish in the international arena for current members, encouraging those banks and other financial institutions that today do not offer international factoring, to understand the contribution of the service to the growth of trade and new business opportunities.

Young and dynamic, this sleeping region has a lot of positive opportunities in its game to start a new development in the years to come.

I. A young History and a Positive Evolution Despite Risks and Barriers

Effectively launched since the last quarter of the 20th century, the Factoring Industry is mainly concentrated in domestic business and suffers from some risks and barriers to ensure a sustainable and strong development.

Birth and Growth of the Industry

LA & C is one of the richest regions in the world, with enormous opportunities and economic growth. This framework presents a proper field for the expansion of domestic and international factoring, invoice discounting and reverse factoring as tools for financing and risk mitigation. Nevertheless, it is still a virgin region in the use of these tools. Why?

– Unfortunately, there is still limited knowledge and availability of domestic factoring;

- The lack of a legal framework or specific law in some countries that could support the product. This is one of the reasons why banks, in those countries, are not willing to offer domestic factoring on invoices whereas financial companies are the ones who become active players in this niche market;
- Bank risk managers are concerned about the product because of misconceptions about the Industry;
- In general, regulators only have a vague idea of the product, and as a result, there is a lack of support.

For the first time in 2012 and again in 2013 and 2016, the global turnover of the sub-continent has been higher than in North America: EUR 104 billion compared to 95 billion in 2016 respectively, which LA accounts for more than 52% of the total continent and 4.4% of the global factoring volume; a nice achievement considering the gap between economies. But the growth has been rather stable in the last five years (only + 2.8% in 2016/2012) and very much concentrated in four main countries:
- Brazil: EUR 45 billion (43.5% of the total in LA & C), coming from 12 billion in 2000 but 49 billion in 2010;
- Chile: EUR 25 billion (24%), coming from 2.6 billion (2000) and 16 (2010);
- Mexico: EUR 22.5 billion (21.5%), coming from 5 billion (2000) and 14.5 billion (2010);
- Colombia: EUR 7.6 billion (7.3%), coming from almost nothing in 2000 and 2.8 billion (2010).

In 2000, the global turn over of LA & C reached no more than EUR 22 billion. It proves that this market was at the beginning of its birth in the 20th century and grew by a multiple of five since the beginning of the 21st century.

Risks and Barriers for the Development of Factoring in the Region

The lack of adequate tools such as the availability of risk data providers in many countries and the lack of credit insurance policies covering buyer credit worthiness are clearly an obstacle for a strong and sustainable growth of the whole sub-continent.

Risks and barriers still remain. Although education is highly valued, in practice it is not reflected, and this impacts not only the knowledge of these products but also the quality and efficiency of the service. Probably at the level of the whole region, a transversal approach should enable the launching of master contracts on a multidomestic base.

I believe that Federacion Latinoamericana of Factoring (FELAFAC), of which FCI is member, should pay a more active role in the region in order to help the development of domestic laws and its standardization, advocacy and education.

A Dynamic and Positive Evolution for the Development of Domestic Factoring

Due to closer governmental tax controls, a progressive conversion of "paper" invoices into electronic invoices is being experienced in Mexico and in the largest South American countries (Chile, Peru, Colombia and Argentina), as well as in some other countries in the rest of Central America.

In conjunction with that, several regional IT companies developed e-factoring platforms, and all together are strongly influencing the domestic factoring business in those countries.

Players are seeing e-factoring as an opportunity for growth, due to a more secure way of doing factoring and invoice discounting. Chile and Mexico lead this process which has now set foot in Peru, already well advanced, and Colombia, where there is steady use. The same development is being followed by other LA countries.

This situation, combined with a proper law for financing invoices (with different names according to the countries: in Chile, "Ley de factura", copied by Colombia and Peru), fuelled the domestic industry, and lowered risks in processing and disputes. A clear example of this growth is Mexico, Chile and the Dominican Republic, where we find banks transacting invoices in locally developed e-factoring platforms.

Brazil is a special case, where the "Duplicata", a particular law for invoice financing is very well established and offered by banks, leaving factoring of invoices to factoring companies.

One of the main important sources to finance domestic invoices in Brazil is the so called FIDIC (a fund). Big factoring companies created their own FIDIC and this improved their competitiveness with banks.

Regarding factoring law, other countries are learning that it is necessary to sanction it in order to provide the service in safer conditions. Guatemala is a good example of that, where they are in the final stages.

II. Confidence in International Factoring Today and Tomorrow

The difficult Start of International Factoring

To launch international factoring, it certainly would be helpful to take advantage of the knowledge and experience of a sustainable domestic factoring base, at least this is the logical progression in the evolution of a traditional factoring market. Whilst the prior existence of a factoring law is not required, it needs to be stressed that in countries where a factoring law has been sanctioned, it has led to the strengthening of domestic factoring business. Such success stories can be witnessed in countries like Peru, Chile and Colombia. This is also the experience in Mexico, which has low domestic factoring volumes. But what we see as a common denominator with larger domestic factoring markets is the eventual development of large international factoring activity. However, compared to other countries in other continents, and compared to the potential factorable trade in Latin America, international factoring volumes still remain weak and rather minimal.

The figures are clear: in the whole region, international factoring reaches no more than EUR 2.2 billion in 2016 (4.3% of the market worldwide) when it was negligible in 2000, except Chile (EUR 400 million), Cuba (EUR 200 million) and Mexico (EUR 150 billion). The main countries today are Chile (EUR 1.1 billion), Mexico (EUR 460 million) and Peru (EUR 350 million).

Still, in 2012, international factoring reached EUR 1.5 billion in Chile. Clearly, turnover was pushed at that time by a Pescanova bankruptcy filing and declined dramatically after the bankruptcy of the Spanish giant of frozen fish in 2013. Surely, the dynamic trend of international factoring has been damaged by this risk issue and in consequence between factors themselves.

More globally, the exchange regulations play an important role in the expansion of cross-border factoring. Currently, the vast majority of LA countries have foreign exchange regulations which allow cross-border factoring development without major problems. Venezuela, and to a larger extent Brazil, whose FX framework is more regulated, of course have a much more difficult environment for service development.

Notwithstanding the abovementioned issues, that explain the small growth of international factoring. LA & C is still a region with a huge growth opportunity for the service, because of:

- Low product expansion;
- The needs of importers and exporters to have a secure solution to develop their businesses;
- Economic growth in LA as well as the growth of intra-regional and global trade.

These facts are increasingly perceived by banks and financial companies. With regard to banks, beyond the confusion that may exist regarding international factoring, they specifically realise that factoring is one of the most secure ways to finance SMEs, which otherwise they would not finance. And so, it opens new market segments and new business opportunities.

What is still lacking is for governments and regulators to realise and understand that 80% of world trade is performed on O/A, and that the financial solutions that FCI promotes minimises the risks for exporters, with the final positive outcome being the growth and expansion of their countries' exports.

Cross-border Factoring Today

After 50 years of existence, FCI has around 30 members in LA & C, with around 50% having ongoing two-factor business, including those who operate at an extremely low volume. This turnover represents slightly over 1% of the total two-factor turnover of FCI. That is why I see LA & C as still being a virgin region… *a Sleeping Continent* in our Industry.

Why is that? Why is the development, the expansion of our cross-border Industry at such a slow pace? And I am focusing my question on cross-border rather than on local factoring, because in the local field, factoring has achieved – in general – greater growth; as it was previously mentioned, some countries like Chile, Colombia, Peru and Mexico could be considered mature markets. The development of platforms and the increasing effectiveness of the electronic invoice have facilitated the consolidation of domestic factoring. However, cross-border is still lagging behind.

My perception is that in LA, export companies in general, and SMEs in particular, are not well served by banks in their trade businesses and needs. And I am focusing on banks, because in general there are not too many factoring companies in the region neither specialised nor willing to be active in financing international trade, at least today, with the exception of companies in Chile, to some extent in Brazil and a few in some Central American countries, like Guatemala and Nicaragua.

There is a shallow culture in financing O/A international sales, as opposed to a deep culture in financing working capital. In other words, banks in general are accustomed to, and prefer, providing working capital (which will be somehow directed to international trade) rather than financing international sales in themselves. This is not a play on words, it is a conceptual issue. Unfortunately, this is one of the core reasons why it is so hard to get banks into cross-border factoring. Such barriers argue against the desired expansion and penetration of our product.

However, those banks willing to enlarge their services in favour of export clients, and which understand that cross-border factoring is a tool that allows them to serve exporters in general and SMEs in particular by financing their exports in O/A with mitigated risk, are the ones that incorporate the service more quickly. In other words, they realise that cross-border factoring opens a new client segment (SMEs) which they would not be willing to finance by using traditional tools (working capital financing, with recourse) because of their reluctance to assume such risks.

Cross-border Factoring Tomorrow

So, what about the future then, what about the expansion of cross-border factoring, reverse factoring, etc.? Can we expect expansion and growth of those services? And who will be the main players? The answer is yes. I am convinced, and very optimistic, because the region is on a good path; FCI is also on a good path, contributing to such an expectation.

In countries like Peru, we observe an important degree of evolution and maturity. Currently, a Peruvian bank (Banco Credito del Peru) is contributing the largest volumes. In Chile, we find a bank, Banco de Chile, that developed a four-corner international confirming SCF model, in part transacted through the FCI platform. Such examples justify an optimistic view of future trends.

The new product that FCI is developing aimed mainly to national entities, I am referring to FCIreverse for domestic and international O/A financing, aroused a strong interest among national banks and companies in the region. Why? It is a matter of risk. As the product is buyer centric, entities feel much more comfortable assuming risk on big corporates, and as a large number of countries have an importing profile, it is an excellent tool to serve large chains and big importers.

Additionally, FCI is giving support with education to those members who still have not set up factoring services, providing follow-up and mentoring. In the field of expansion, the chain continues to fuel the Industry and to seed meeting prospects, as well as promoting best practices among members, preventing financial delinquency and respect for compliance and normative behaviour. All of this will contribute to retention of current members and will help to stabilise the region by providing knowledge and showing the benefits of cross-border factoring. It will facilitate a stable growth.

However, banks from other regions of the world should work on understanding and knowing the LA & C banks much better and more deeply, both the current and future members of FCI.

There is a perception in local LA banks of a sort of reluctance or unwillingness to develop cross-border factoring business from some members of other regions, to accept risk coverage offered by them, but also to provide credit cover to them. The main reason is compliance, which can be understood. No one can force a bank, as a free agent, to start working and establishing a correspondent relationship with another one.

It is true that the issue of the "Panama papers affair" has brought these concerns to the surface. Certainly, it is a very delicate issue, which has raised an alarm. But this issue has mainly affected prominent people not only from some LA & C countries, but also from many European and Far East countries.

All LA & C member banks have their compliance policy in place. Should it be reviewed by their correspondent members? Absolutely, yes. But how many of our LA members were suspected of being involved or even facilitating corruption or money laundering? None. So where does the concern and the reluctance come from?

The growth of cross-border factoring in the region will require more willingness from banks of other regions to establish a correspondent relationship, of course subject to a better and deeper understanding on both sides, with proper due diligence to develop more knowledge, confidence and trust between them.

As the above-mentioned barriers are gradually removed, I have no doubt that the different versions of cross-border factoring, promoted and supported by FCI, will flourish. Then yes, we will be able to say that in LA & C countries, the Factoring Industry will consolidate and grow with a sustained and non-stop trend.

III. Conclusion: LA & C, Ready to Awake?

The *sleeping continent* is now ready to awake in international as well as in domestic factoring, if all actors, in North America, in Europe or in Asia give their chance to a new future within a responsible and secure partnership.

19. Factoring in Russia, a Self-Sufficient Market

Mikhail Treyvish

CEO, Universal Crowdsourcing Agency Omnigrade

The Russian factoring market began to develop shortly after the appearance of the market economy in Russia, after the collapse of the centrally planned economic system of the Soviet Union. This forced the first players in this market to create all the key functions necessary for the successful operational functioning of the factoring business by themselves, without reliance on the appropriate infrastructure.

In Russia, initially there were no suppliers of factoring software – the factors had to hire programmers and develop it by themselves. There were no credit bureaus – it was necessary to establish a system for collecting credit information about clients and their debtors. There was no credit insurance – they had to build their own credit underwriting system.

However, the result of building such a self-sufficient system was that many clients began to apply to factoring companies not only for financing, but also for insurance of credit risks, selection of debtors and collection. This increased the added value of factoring services and allowed factors to keep the level of margin and return on assets at a high level for a long time.

I. The Development of Factoring Prior to 1998

For more than 50 years – after the cancellation of the new economic policy in the USSR in the early 1930s to Gorbachev's reforms in the mid-1980s, no market economy and, accordingly, factoring existed in the USSR.

The changes began with the adoption of the USSR law on the 26th of May 1988 on "Cooperation in the USSR," allowing the creation of the first non-state companies and enterprises. Soon, State enterprises also obtained the right for independent economic activity and the first private banks began to appear.

For the first time, the monetary authorities of the country mention the word "factoring" in a letter of the State Bank of the USSR of the 12th of December 1989 "on the procedure for conducting transactions on assignment by suppliers to the bank of the right to receive payment on claims for goods delivered, work performed and services provided", where banks were allowed to carry out factoring transactions. But the definition of factoring quoted there was very strange – as an operation for the assignment of overdue receivables. Specifically, the letter provided that the assignment of claims to the debtor is made only after the supplier receives from the payer's bank a notice that the payer does not have the funds and transfers the claim to the so-called card index number 2, keeping the payment documents that were not paid in time.

Such an unusual interpretation of the concept of factoring is associated with a deep economic crisis that raged in the last years of the existence of the Soviet Union. Mass insolvency of enterprises had become a scourge of the economy, the legal procedure of bankruptcy did not exist yet, and the authorities tried to fight the problem by all possible means. Moreover, no one knew what factoring really was in the conditions of the recent "iron curtain" and there was a lack of knowledge about financial mechanisms in the market economy by government officials.

Soon (in December 1991), the Soviet Union ceased to exist and on its base fifteen new States appeared, including the largest – the Russian Federation.

In the Russian Federation, the word "factoring" again started to be used, in 1994, by the private bank TverUniversalBank, large for that time, and again in a rather unusual form. It was exclusively for import factoring and to be able to implement it TverUniversalBank joined FCI. The scheme was as follows: The bank persuaded Russian importers to use O/A when purchasing imported goods instead of prepayment or LC. In order to give the guarantee as import factor, TverUniversalBank took from the importer a deposit in the amount equal to the amount of the contract. At that time, the deposit rates were very high and exceeded 10, and sometimes 30% p.a., even in USD and European currencies. When translating the contract into the O/A terms, the exporter often raised the price, but this was more than compensated by the high interest on the deposit. Thus, both the bank and the importer could earn extra money.

The Rossiysky Kredit Bank, in which the factoring department appeared in June 1996, found another way. The Rossiysky Kredit Bank relied on domestic factoring and on the maintenance of food supplies and Fast-Moving Consumer Goods (FMCG) in small stores. At that time, neither credit insurers nor credit bureaus operated in Russia. At the same time, as there were no large retail chains, most consumer goods were sold through small stores, the number of which in Moscow alone amounted to several tens of thousands, and the debt of one store to one supplier did not exceed USD 3-5,000. In such circumstances the factoring department of the Rossiysky Kredit Bank took a decision to set a credit limit for each store on the basis of credit history on payments for earlier deliveries.

The most important event for the factoring market in Russia was the adoption, in March 1996, of the new Civil Code, namely chapter 43 "Financing against assignment of receivables", which contained a very liberal regulation of factoring. In particular, it allowed the assignment of future receivables, and prohibition of assignment on the contract between the supplier and the buyer was considered negligible. The emergence of a liberal legal regulation became a major impetus for the growth of interest in factoring in Russia and predetermined the rapid growth of the market in the 21st century. At the same time, the new Civil Code left unclear the question of whether a factoring license was needed. In accordance with one of the interpretations of the Code, a banking license was required for factoring activities, according to another interpretation – no license needed at all. This ambiguity predetermined the development of factoring for years ahead on behalf of the banks except for one vivid exception, which will be discussed below.

In 1997-1998, several Russian banks announced their intention to start providing factoring services, getting accustomed to the experience of the Rossiysky Kredit Bank, TverUniversalbank or trying to find their own business model. But the severe financial crisis, which began in August 1998, suspended all factoring activity in the country for more than six months.

II. The Economic Crisis of 1998: a Turning Point for the Russian Economy and the Factoring Market

Started in 1997, the so-called Asian financial crisis, which led to significant shocks in currency and stock markets of Thailand, South Korea, Indonesia, Malaysia and other countries, reached Russia in August 1998. The result of the financial crisis in Russia was:
- Default on government debt obligations;
- five-fold devaluation of the Russian rouble;
- Bankruptcy of most major banks.

As a result, all Russian banks that had factoring business or tried to start it went bankrupt. This led to a complete halt of factoring business in the country. However, in general, the financial crisis has had a long-term positive impact on the Russian economy:

– The devaluation of the rouble has led to the growth of competitiveness of goods and services of Russian companies;

– The bankruptcy of many enterprises founded in the Soviet era cleared the way for new, more efficient companies. And managers of the new generation, often with experience of work or study abroad, came to management positions in the surviving companies;

– The surviving large banks began to expand the range of financial transactions that had previously been largely limited to operations with currency, government securities and interbank loans. This wiled to the rapid development of consumer lending, and a little later – of factoring.

Combined with the rising prices of Russia's major export commodities (oil, gas and metals) and a number of reforms (in particular, reducing the income tax rate to 13% flat), this led the Russian economy into a decade of rapid growth (until the global economic crisis of 2008-2009), and the factoring market – to sustainable development and transformation into an important sector of the Russian financial industry.

III. 1999-2003: Oligopoly and Rapid Growth

In February 1999, after a six-month break in Nikoil Bank (later, after several mergers and acquisitions turned into the bank Uralsib) a factoring division appeared. In the summer of 1999, Probusinessbank started the provision of factoring services. Over the next four years, these two banks, to which the former employees of the factoring department of the Rossiysky Kredit Bank moved, were the only players in the Russian factoring market, but the business of each of them developed very dynamically.

Each of the factoring departments of these two banks had its own IT department, which developed and implemented specialised factoring software, named Doctor Factor in Probusinessbank and Nikfactor in Nikoil. This became one of the specific features of the factoring market in Russia – the first players, because of the limited budget and time deficit in setting up business, preferred not to buy software from foreign software providers, but to develop their own. This, among other things, offered the necessary flexibility, as IT staff could quickly adapt the software when changing legislation, introducing new products and services, or to the requirements of individual clients. Later several factoring software suppliers appeared in Russia.

In the autumn of 1999, Nikoil Bank joined the IFG and in 2000 began to provide services for export factoring and later also for import. In 2002, the factoring department of Nikoil Bank started expansion into the regions (before this time, domestic factoring was limited to transactions with trade receivables, related solely to the supply of goods inside Moscow). Because of a certain interpretation of the Civil Code, it was possible to conclude that a banking license was required for factoring, so the following scheme was implemented. An operational factoring company Nikoil was established, which did not have a banking license, but could open branches in the regions. Each branch recruited staff responsible for:

- Sales to new clients;
- Maintaining relationships with existing clients;
- Collection of information on solvency, business reputation and other information important for making decisions on credit operational risks.

The latter was particularly important given the fact that the credit insurance and credit information industry were still absent in Russia. Nikoil Bank received the necessary information under a contract with Nikoil Operating Company and financed clients from its balance sheet. Thus, factoring began to spread throughout Russia, which, taking into account the huge size of the country (Russia ranks first in the world in terms of the size of the territory) was a critical factor for the development of the market.

IV. 2004-2008 – Increased Competition and New Formats

2004-2009 was a five-year period of serious changes in the Russian factoring market. In April 2004, the bank "National Factoring Company UralSib-Nikoil" was established, later renamed into the bank "National Factoring Company" (NFC), created on the basis of the former factoring division of Nikoil Bank. It became the first and only specialised factoring bank in Russia. Having received greater independence, the NFC factoring business started to develop rapidly. In the first year of independent work, the number of clients increased three-fold.

In addition to independence, the growth of the number of funding sources contributed to the development of NFC, which now included the issue of bonds, interbank loans and loans from the Bank of Russia. By 2008, the share of the parent bank Uralsib in the NFC liabilities was only 24%.

New players from among the Russian banks began to appear. So, Petrocommerce Bank, Alfa-Bank, Moscow Credit Bank and some others announced the start of factoring business around this time. A separate story is the development of Eurokommerz factoring company, established by a group of entrepreneurs from Russia and Kazakhstan. Initially, the company Eurokommerz created joint ventures with banks – three joint ventures were established: with the banks Stroycredit, Transcredit and Trust. However, in 2006, all three companies were consolidated into one – the factoring company Eurokommerz. In the same year, its main shareholder became the Russia New Growth Fund, managed by Troika Capital Partners, whose beneficiaries were the European Bank for Reconstruction and Development (EBRD), Temasek Holdings, Goldman Sachs, Troika Capital Partners, LGT Capital Partners, AXA and others.

Eurokommerz became the first factoring company in Russia without a banking license. Among lawyers at that time there were disputes about the legitimacy of this status, however, no court actions against Eurokommerz were filed. Eurokommerz began an aggressive campaign aimed at ensuring a rapid growth in the number of clients and assets. This campaign was accompanied by massive advertising in mass media and other marketing actions, as well as an extremely liberal approach to risk management, an almost complete absence of selection of clients. As a result, in 2007, Eurokommerz came out on top in the Russian factoring market, pushing the formerly leading NFC. In 2008, the number of clients of Eurokommerz reached 3,700 against 900 clients from NFC. However, as a result of the 2008 crisis, Eurokommerz lost its solvency and was eventually declared bankrupt. This was a very large-scale bankruptcy case, but so far it remains the only such case on the Russian market.

As a result of the increase in the number of players on the market, price competition arose for the first time. In response to price competition, the types of factoring with increased added value began to develop: non-recourse factoring and maturity factoring, which maintained the previous margin level. Since credit insurance in Russia was still not developed at that time, factoring services became its substitute in some cases. In addition, the technology of communication with clients was changing. Instead of processing paper documents, factors were actively moving to electronic document flow with suppliers.

The global crisis of 2008 could not but affect the Russian Factoring Industry, but its consequences were much milder than in 1998, except for the bankruptcy of Eurokommerz. The large amounts of liquidity that the Bank of Russia provided to the financial system of the country, as well as the joint struggle against the global financial crisis in other countries, primarily in the G20 countries, helped the main players of the factoring market survive the crisis without catastrophic losses.

V. 2009-2017: Matured Market and Liberalisation of Regulation

On the 26th of April 2009, an important change in the legislation occurred in Russia – a new edition of article 825 of the Civil Code of the Russian Federation was adopted, which completely abolished the requirement for a license to provide factoring services. This has led to a noticeable increase in the number of players. New factoring companies started to appear, banks began to transform their factoring departments into independent subsidiaries (though not in all cases, but in most cases), factoring companies began to appear in the regions of Russia: St. Petersburg, Yekaterinburg, Chelyabinsk, Saratov and some other cities.

In addition, the largest banking groups became interested in factoring. First, in 2009 the second-largest bank of the country – VTB Bank – created the subsidiary factoring company VTB factoring, and in 2014 the largest bank in the country – Sberbank – created the subsidiary factoring company Sberbank factoring. VTB factoring in the last few years held first place in the market. The first factoring company with foreign capital appeared – RB Factoring – a subsidiary of Rosbank, a member of the Societé Générale group, a factoring unit also formed in the Russian Unicredit Bank.

The stimulus for market growth was also the activity of the state bank in supporting SMEs, which implemented a program of refinancing of factoring companies and factoring divisions of banks where their clients represent the small and medium business sector.

The total number of players on the Russian factoring market is about 50. The exact number is unknown, since there is no single register of all factors. The Association of Factoring Companies (AFC) of Russia, combining the largest players in the market, has 22 factoring company members and two members who are software developers. The ratings agency Expert has, for the last thirteen years, conducted annual reviews of the factoring market in Russia based on a survey of key players. At the end of 2016, there were also 22 factoring companies reported, but their composition is slightly different from the membership of the AFC. Approximately 50% of the market for the last four years falls to the share of the three largest players: VTB factoring, Promsvyazbank together with its subsidiary Promsvyazbank factoring (they specialise in servicing large business and small and medium business respectively) and Alfa Bank. The share of the top 10 companies accounts for about 80% of the market.

Nevertheless, the process of new factoring companies appearing does not stop. Very often the initiators of their appearance are employees or teams of employees, leaving the old market players. They motivate private investors or banks (in Russia there are more than 600 banks and most of them are not yet involved in the factoring business – neither as factors' creditors nor as their shareholders) to open new factoring companies.

According to the data of the RA Expert, since about 2013 the market has experienced stagnation, which replaced the previous sharp growth of the market (37% growth in 2010, 77% growth in 2011 and 65% growth in 2012). Factoring turnover fluctuates near the mark of 2 trillion roubles (2.06 trillion roubles in 2014 and 2.08 trillion in 2016). The reason for this was the economic crisis caused by the fall in oil prices, economic sanctions from a number of foreign countries and the exhaustion of the previous growth model. In this situation, factors are in search of new ideas, but their ideas about what could be a driver of growth diverge.

A number of players see, as the main potential source of development, the possibility of financing public procurement contracts, which is currently prohibited by the current law, and are therefore lobbying for its amendment. Others are looking for opportunities for further expansion into the regions of Russia, including small towns and settlements. There is a further differentiation on the client base: the largest factoring company of the country, VTB factoring, and a number of other companies and banks target large and very large corporate clients, while others are trying to expand their client base through medium, small and even micro-businesses.

Another important trend is the use of modern IT technologies, which are becoming an increasingly important feature of the Russian factoring market. This applies to the almost universal introduction of EDI-technologies in the implementation of factoring transactions and document flow with clients and debtors. The players of the factoring market have also started to get accustomed to blockchain technology, and, in the beginning of 2017, it began to be used in the practice of Russian factors.

By 2017, the Russian financial market had an infrastructure not in existence in the 1990s: there are corporate collectors, credit insurers and credit bureaus. And new factors have a choice: to outsource a number of key operational functions to them or to develop their own as the first players on the market did before.

VI. Conclusion: In Search of New Niches in Russia and Abroad

The unique Russian experience of creating a full-fledged factoring market in the absence of a supporting infrastructure opens up certain opportunities for Russian factors for expansion into emerging markets with a weak level of factoring development, especially if it is a country with large territories and significantly different regions. For countries such as Indonesia, the Philippines, even India, the Russian experience would certainly be useful. And a number of factors and factoring professionals have already started to look closely at such markets, especially given the fact that the Russian trading and manufacturing business is also actively seeking new markets, as a result of the reduction of opportunities for growth in Russia. Another possible vector of development is the most distant regions of Russia itself, primarily Siberia and the Russian Far East, where the level of factoring promotion is still limited. And, finally, the third opportunity is connected to a departure from classical factoring and the development of new products within the framework of receivables finance.

The Russian factoring market, now for the first time in more than 20 years of development, is in a no-growth situation and needs new ideas. Ironically, this happened after a lot of new players, who believed in its huge potential, appeared in the market. Numerous discussions that are taking place in the factoring community of Russia show that work on new ideas is going on and is very hard and intense.

B – Emerging Countries

20. Factoring in Emerging Countries

Margrith Lütschg-Emmenegger

Past President, FIMBank
Past Chairperson, IFG

The first question that comes to mind when looking at the title is: What is an emerging market? This is from Wikipedia:

"An emerging market is a country that has some characteristics of a developed market, but does not meet standards to be a developed market. This includes countries that may become developed markets in the future or were in the past. The term "frontier market" is used for developing countries with slower economies than "emerging". The economies of China and India are the largest."

According to *The Economist*, many people find the term outdated, but no new term has gained traction so far. The four largest emerging and developing economies by either nominal or Purchasing Power Parity (PPP)-adjusted GDP are the BRIC countries (Brazil, Russia, India and China). The next five largest markets are South Korea (though considered a developed market), Mexico, Indonesia, Turkey and Saudi Arabia.

In the 1970s, "less developed countries" was the common term for markets that were less "developed" (by "objective or subjective measures") than the developed countries such as the USA, Western Europe and Japan. These markets were supposed to provide greater potential for profit, but, of course, also more risk caused by various factors. This term was thought by some to be politically incorrect so the "emerging markets" label was created. The term is somewhat misleading in that there is no guarantee that a country will move from "less developed" to "more developed", although that is the general trend in the world. Countries can also move from "more developed" to "less developed".

Julien Vercueil recently proposed a more pragmatic definition of the "emerging economies", as distinguished from "emerging markets", coined

by an approach heavily influenced by financial criteria. According to his definition, an emerging economy displays the following characteristics:
- Intermediate income: its PPP per capita income is comprised of between 10% and 75% of the average EU per capita income;
- Catching-up growth: during at least the last decade, it has experienced a brisk economic growth that has narrowed the income gap with advanced economies;
- Institutional transformation and economic opening: during the same period, it has undertaken profound institutional transformation which contributed to integrate it more deeply into the world economy. Hence, emerging economies appear to be a by-product of the current globalisation.

At the beginning of the 2010s, more than 50 countries, representing 60% of the world's population and 45% of its GDP, matched these criteria. Among them were the BRIC countries.

The term "rapidly developing economies" is being used to denote emerging markets such as the United Arab Emirates, Chile and Malaysia, which are all undergoing rapid growth.

I. Emerging Markets in the Context of Factoring

With all this information in mind, what does this mean for factoring? Do we see our factoring markets with the same viewpoint/evaluation? I believe there are some differences, but overall the definitions seem the same, i.e. in summary: difficult markets with huge opportunities and substantial growth potential.

There are, of course, some countries which are famous exceptions, disproving the rule, for example the above three countries, being called "rapidly developing economies" are good examples of how we differentiate product development in emerging markets.

For example, Chile has a well-developed factoring market already with several professional players, banks as well as non-banking financial institutions. The UAE has some activity, but it is still in its infant state, and Malaysia has hardly any activity in factoring despite its well developed and strong financial sector. Looking at other countries, South Korea, for example, considered a "developed" market and highly active in trade but at present still has a very small factoring market.

So, let us look at what the key ingredients are for a solid and strong factoring market in emerging countries – and indeed in general:
1. Clear laws and regulations for non-negotiable payment instruments especially for assignments. Self-regulation is often the best environment but that requires a fairly mature market/industry;
2. Transparent, reliable and actual financial information on companies, especially on SMEs;
3. A dispute settlement or conflict avoidance mechanism: The introduction of an invoice registry is ideal and should be supported and encouraged – authorities need guidance on how to best implement this. There are several countries, like Chile, which have a strong risk culture;
4. Improvement of technology to reduce transaction costs and increase financial security: Regulators should support/encourage competing providers and consumers to take advantage of technological innovations. For example, in India, the goal was to adopt an approach that was technology driven but neutral in terms of technology platform;
5. Talent and capabilities: It is absolutely critical to develop the pool of talent and create an environment to improve capabilities. We must create the possibility for staff to gain experience when dealing with these products including in compliance and monitoring.

Governments can and should play an important role in designing and implementing comprehensive policies to promote access to financial services such as factoring, receivables finance and SCF. This includes of course KYC/AML requirements. The work by the governments, however, must be supported by the private industry, the associations and networks.

Effective use and access of affordable, innovative and sustainable trade finance products is key for the healthy development of emerging markets and will not only improve economies but will contribute to poverty reduction and social developments.

It might be worthwhile considering a discussion on how the interaction between different networks/organisations of financial services could speed up and expand this important process between private industry and governments.

Risks in emerging markets for factoring remain high – most emerging market institutions pay little attention to risk culture, talent and capabilities. In many organisations, risk functions are relegated to a secondary role in the organisation, struggling to attract, retain and manage talent. They also have had little impact on increasing risk awareness, literacy and accountability in other lines of defence, including the business' front line. Risk management is seen almost as a hurdle rather than a true partner of the business or as a group that could play a steering role in the organisation. For example:

1. Act on the risk culture across the organisation – not just in risk and credit terms: Although credit is a major source of risk and revenue for the vast majority of banks/financial institutions in emerging markets, credit processes and underlying support mechanisms have remained largely unchanged in most institutions. For example, many still do not effectively use predictive statistical models (such as scoring models for behavioural scoring) in underwriting and monitoring, something which is, of course, highly recommended and an investment, even if quite significant, that will improve performance.
2. Build advanced risk models on qualitative and quantitative credit data: There is a lack of information on creditworthiness in emerging markets, so banks/institutions have a strong motivation to invest in creating risk models that incorporate both qualitative and quantitative factors.
3. Enhance collections processes to improve the bottom line: Collections have not been a priority area for emerging market institutions and there is significant room for performance improvements which will impact the bottom line significantly.

II. Way Forward – Best Products

There is a lot of work to do to create efficient and safe factoring products in emerging markets as the above issues demonstrate. Focus must be on education and training for all stakeholders (including the involvement of leading market players with local universities via Masters or even PhD programs in cooperation with reputable international and regional industry associations) combined with a wise product selection to support the development of a healthy industry.

Export and Import Factoring

The use of the two-factor systems of FCI is a good approach to reduce credit risks, facilitate collections and mitigate potential fraud. The import and/or export factor will assist in the handling of the transaction and be able to guide the emerging market counterparty/correspondent through the process, thereby ensuring good practice and enabling a certain learning process at the same time.

Reverse Factoring

Especially for domestic business it is a worthy way to start offering factoring in emerging markets.

Starting from the buyer credit worthiness (not only large companies, but also SMEs) and funding its suppliers, often SMEs with little or no access to funding or only at very high cost, it is a truly good way to support SMEs and reduce credit risk. While "on-boarding" the suppliers (SMEs) will be a fairly labour-intensive process, it will also create an excellent cross-marketing and business development opportunity.

It is a known fact that reverse factoring faces challenges penetrating buyers from the SME segment, which is mainly due to the high fixed costs of implementation for such structures (usually designed ONLY for very large companies).

In recent years the trend started to shift because of the latest technology developments and the possibility of also bringing in the mix of tools already available in the retail side of banking (e.g. credit cards, where it can be assumed that "it actually means the buyer is credit worthy", similar to the starting point of reverse factoring) – this is how some innovative banks have merged the capabilities of commercial credit cards into actual reverse factoring structures, opening new growth opportunities for an underserved segment of buyers, the SMEs. It remains to be seen if such an innovative approached can bring new dimensions into emerging markets where most of the buyers are SMEs.

III. Conclusion

An estimated 52-64% of the formal SME sector in the emerging markets are unserved or underserved, with an estimated credit gap of USD 1.6 trillion.

Effective access and use by firms of affordable and sustainable financial services like factoring products (including leveraging the latest technology and already existing credit tools in the financial industry) from recognised providers is essential to reduce poverty and youth unemployment in emerging markets.

But there is not only a moral obligation – there is no doubt that emerging markets need our products, but more importantly and often forgotten or disregarded, we, the Industry, need the emerging markets equally if we want to see growth in our business in the future.

Some actions are of course urgently required and that means commitment, dedication, devotion and investment by the participants of the developed countries that in my opinion is currently lacking.

21. Turkey, Bridging the Continents via Factoring

Çağatay Baydar

CEO, TEB Faktoring
Chairman, FCI

As the 17th largest economy in the world and eighth largest economy in Europe with a GDP of about USD 858 billion in 2016, Turkey has been an active member of the G-20, which represents the world's most powerful economies. Within this scope, per capita income measured at USD 11,000 in 2016.

In line with the policies implemented as part of the export-oriented growth model followed since 1980, significant developments have been observed in the market share held by labour-intensive industrial products such as textiles and clothing, iron and steel, or foodstuffs. However, in recent years Turkey's production and export structure has shown a substantial shift towards high-technology industries with products requiring intense research and development, such as electrical and electronic machinery, equipment and vehicles. In 2016, Turkey exported USD 143 billion and imported USD 199 billion, resulting in a trade deficit of USD 56 billion.

The EU remained the main export market for Turkey in 2016, with a share of 48%, followed by Middle East and North Africa (MENA) countries with a 26% market share. Turkey's major exports are vehicles (14% of total exports); boilers, machinery and mechanical appliances (9%); precious stones and precious metals (8.5%). China was the main import source for the Turkish economy. Imports from China accounted for about 13% of overall imports in 2016, followed by Germany (11%) and Russia (8%).

Mostly concentrated on SMEs and exports, the Factoring Industry in Turkey is part of a strong financial sector, well regulated, driven by law and quite innovative.

I. Factoring in Turkey Is Part of a Strong Financial Sector, Well Regulated, Driven by Law and Innovative

Thanks to the regulatory reforms and structural overhaul that the government implemented in the wake of Turkey's financial meltdown in the early 2000s, the Turkish financial industry proved resilient during the global financial turbulence in 2009 as well as in the ensuing economic crisis. Banking has a strong dominance in the Turkish financial industry, accounting for over 70% of overall financial services while insurance services, factoring, financial leasing and financing companies demonstrate significant growth potential.

A Structured Organisation Under the Umbrella of a New Regulation, a New Law and a New Association

Three main components have played a key role in structuring factoring business in Turkey: regulation, law and financial association.

The Role of BRSA Since 2006

Since 2006, the Banking Regulation and Supervision Agency (BRSA) is authorised for the regulation and supervision of the non-banking financial sector, including factoring. Its recognition as a major non-banking financial instrument is a milestone for the Turkish Factoring Industry. The BRSA carries out regulation, supervision and enforcement functions in order to ensure confidence and stability on financial markets, to make credit systems operate effectively, to protect the rights and benefits of savers, and to improve banking and financial sectors. With its sincere and effective approach, the BRSA fully cooperates with all the players for a steady and healthy development.

Since 2006, there has been continuous progress in factoring regulation driven by the BRSA. Between 2006 and 2010, all factoring companies were audited and relicensed by BRSA as well.

A New Law for Factoring in 2012

The second and more important milestone is the implementation of a new law, which is a welcome result of strong cooperation between the sector and BRSA and long-lasting lobbying of the former Factoring Association.

The law on Financial Leasing, Factoring, and Financing Companies, which went into effect with its publication in the official gazette on the 13th of December 2012, is quite important in many different aspects. One of the detrimental aspects is that factoring companies are now categorised as "Financial Institutions" and factoring has been specified with all its services.

Furthermore, the principles of governance have been redefined. For example, one part of the new regulation requires factoring companies to increase their minimum paid in capital from TRL 7.5 million to TRL 20 million. In short, the new law is helping the sector to be more institutionalised and to have a strong financial structure.

The Key Role of the Association of Financial Institutions for Factoring Development

Another vital change was the decision of the parliament to unite three sectors – leasing, factoring and consumer finance – in one establishment. By the end of 2013, the Association of Financial Institutions (AFI) was formed as the umbrella organisation of three sectors with its sector representative councils, which compose the board of the whole association.

With the new corporation identity, AFI has taken many actions. The first significant action for the factoring sector was to establish the Receivables Recording Centre (RRC), given as a duty to the association under article 43 of the law.

The RRC became operational in January 2015. Every factoring company in Turkey has joined this system, which also counts eighteen banks as members. For many years, the Factoring Industry had to contend with the serious risks inherent in such under-handed practices as duplicate invoicing and financing. That problem has at last been overcome by this centralised system, which the AFI set up together with the Credit Bureau of Turkey, which is under the association's control.

Additionally, the Department of Revenue Administration (DRA)'s e-invoice system has been integrated into the RRC. Under an agreement between the AFI and the DRA, personal identification numbers, tax registration numbers, e-invoicing obligations and e-invoice verification functions, were also linked into the RRC. These additions have made the RRC an innovative system that provides the means for the integrated querying, monitoring and reporting of all the information contained within it.

After intensive analysis carried out during 2015, the second phase of the RRC project, which became operational in 2016, information about payment instruments such as post-dated cheques, notes, and bills as well as their collection was also fed into the system. With these additions, the RRC became a data centre that allows invoices' payment performance to be monitored and whose importance to the country is second only to that of the Data Risk Centre (DRC) under the control of the Turkish Banking Association. The membership of factoring companies to the DRC started in 2010, where the credit information and payment performance of the clients of banks and financial institutions are recorded and shared among them.

In brief, the RRC should be used by factors and banks. Preventing multiple assignment and financing of invoices, it is integrated with the system of the revenue administration which verifies that the e-invoices have arisen from real trade and are valid, collects the payment information of the factored receivables, consolidates all data related to the assigned receivables of the Turkish Factoring Industry and provides reporting on all receivables data to the sector.

After the law, major projects and developments have started to be realised under the AFI, especially to bring more funding to the Industry. In 2014, funding opportunities on that Takasbank money market was provided to the association members. The Takasbank money market, which started activities under Istanbul Settlement and Custody Bank Inc. (Takasbank) in October 1996, currently responds to the bids and offers of banks and intermediary institutions having surplus funds and/or funding needs. Since 2014, AFI members have taken part in Takasbank money market operations, where they are able to invest their short-term excess funds and to fulfil their funding needs.

An innovative Sector

Fintech was born of the technology innovations supporting financial services companies by enabling the finance sector to reduce costs significantly, so that the clients that the finance sector serve, from large companies to SMEs, could also benefit. The Turkish finance sector is highly successful in using, as well as launching, new technologies. In accordance with the needs of both the economy and the sector, the Factoring Industry has focused on fintech solutions and digitalisation projects under the AFI such as supply chain and distributor chain finance systems, private integrator projects, core factoring software systems and receivables recording systems.

The Turkish factoring sector believes that the future of finance, including factoring, depends on digital integrated solutions such as e-signature, e-invoice, e-archive, e-ledger, e-assignment, e-factoring, e-factoring mobile, creating digitalised new technology based products such as SCF, distributor chain finance and giving traditional factoring and receivables/trade finance services under the IT platforms.

Trade Chain Finance Systems (Supply Chain/Distributor Chain Finance)

After RRC, another digital integrated project is to establish a centralised trade chain finance system for both supply chain and distributor chain finance solutions under the association to which factoring companies, banks, thousands of suppliers and buyers, creditors and credit insurers will have access. With the integration of the trade finance platform with RRC, e-invoices could be verified by the system of Gelir İdaresi Başkanlığı (GIB), the Turkish Revenue Administration as well.

A world-beating project as unique and as exceptional as the RRC, the AFI trade chain finance system is scheduled to become operational at the beginning of 2018. When this new market is added and becomes operational in the financial system, it is expected that SMEs' share of the total credit supply will increase from 26% to 35%.

Private Integrator Project

The private integrator project is a project that, since 2015, the AFI has been working on in order to help businesses adapt more quickly to the steadily increasing presence of e-invoices, e-ledger, and e-archives in commercial life.

Private integration in the search of forwarding the third-party obligators invoices and to receive them, refers to inclusion of data processing into the GİB system. So, the e-invoice setup is developed for enabling the secure transmission of invoices between parties. In Turkey, the sectors were obliged to adopt e-invoice application from January 2014 in accordance with the e-invoice legal statute related tax procedural law.

In July 2017, the AFI's factoring commercial enterprise received a "private integrator" license from GİB under the ministry of finance.

The AFI's main aim to be a private integrator is to provide e-invoicing, e-archive and e-ledger services to the clients of factoring companies. So, in the future, with the allowance of taxpayers, factoring companies will be able to connect to this system and reach the account ledgers of their clients directly as well as seeing their momentary balance sheet online.

Core Factoring Software System

Another project of the sector is to build a centralised core factoring software system under the Association. In Turkey, most factoring companies (approximately 40 companies among 61) are mainly using two factoring software packages. However, most of the members are not happy with those systems.

The current factoring solutions in Turkey are not fully compliant with the new factoring regulations. Moreover, the software infrastructure is lacking the digitalisation of the sector. Therefore, the factoring companies applied to the Association to have a new software solution that can meet the needs of today. If this project is realised, the aim is to integrate the core factoring software to the other fintech systems – RRC and the trade chain finance system – under the Association. That will create a link between all trade partners, financiers and other related stakeholders connecting multiple sellers, buyers, factors and banks, allowing e-invoices to be verified, therefore establishing confidence among the sellers and buyers of the finance industry, creating a high level, speedy, trustful service quality and cost efficiency.

In summary, the future of factoring in Turkey is being built as a trade finance product via fintech solutions. As a result of governmental support, access to critical information centres and the new projects with the support of the AFI, the non-bank financial institutions have shown steady growth in recent years. In Turkey, factoring is the second largest financial industry after banking.

II. Recent and Dynamic, the Factoring Industry in Turkey, Mostly Concentrated in SMEs and Exports, is Opened to the World

Turkey's brilliant contribution to factoring appears mainly in two sectors and shows a great openness to the world.

A Recent and Dynamic History

The first factoring transactions in Turkey started in 1988 in a bank division. Two years later in 1990, the first factoring companies were established. In 1994, the Factoring Industry started to be regulated by the Treasury and in the same year the Turkish Factoring Association was launched.

The growth trend continued in 2016 despite the challenging macroeconomic environment. It was a fairly profitable year with the industry ROE registering at 13.7% compared to 8.6% in 2015. The factoring business provides financing to the majority of SMEs and is, therefore, highly sensitive to fluctuations in economic activities.

At the end of 2016, the total assets of factoring companies in Turkey amounted to TRL 33 billion. Total factoring receivables grew by 24% reaching TRL 31 billion, and shareholders' equity increased by 11% to TRL 5.1 billion. In 2016, total borrowings rose by 30.5%. At the end of 2016, as a result of the smaller network of representative offices, the number of employees decreased by 2%, while the client base increased by 3.7%.

In 2017, there are 61 factoring companies, 375 branches all around Turkey and 4,800 professional staff working for the Industry. All of them are serving approximately 100,000 clients in every sector including their 300,000 debtors, and also providing TRL 31 billion in funding to the real economy. So, factoring is widely used by every sector in Turkey.

Moreover, Turkey's yearly factoring volume is growing faster than the rest of the world, with an average annual growth rate of 33%. With a total volume of EUR 35 billion in 2016 (29 in domestic and six in international), Turkish factoring is the 17th largest in the world and ninth in Europe.

A Factoring Business Concentrated on SMEs and Exports

The two main pillars of factoring in Turkey are the SME segment and export expansion.

Generally, the yearly increase of factoring volume is due to lack of liquidity and working capital, late payment practice and default risks, difficulties in obtaining bank credits for SMEs, and a high level of operational expenses for accounts receivable (A/R) management. Additionally, global economic turmoil and increasing levels of commercial risks in foreign markets, corporate, banking and sovereign bankruptcy risks due to a massive loss of assets, and a 60% share of O/A transactions in total, Turkish export volumes are the main factors creating the speedy growth of export factoring in Turkey.

The Huge Part of SMEs Based on a Post-dated Cheque System

Contrary to many European economies, factoring in Turkey is not, in general, dedicated to corporate and large clients. It is mostly based on the SME segment.

The main characteristics of the domestic factoring market in Turkey are:

- Bank subsidies dominate the sector with a 66% market share;
- 60% recourse, 40% non-recourse;
- Average maturity of 95 days;
- Transaction (invoice by invoice) basis financing;
- Post-dated cheques used as payment instrument and collateral;
- Invoice discounting with or without post-dated cheques is common;
- Traditional supplier financing is slowly being replaced with an IT based SCF;
- Use of e-invoices increasing speed;
- Mainly focused on construction, petroleum, manufacturing, wholesale and retail.

In fact, SMEs in Turkey play a crucial role in economic development. They account for 73.5% of employment, 55% of gross investment, 53.5% of value added and 99.8% of total enterprises. Moreover, a healthy SME sector is important to increase the resilience of the economy to shocks. However, SMEs in Turkey have different types of financial problems to deal with: difficult access to bank credit, higher interest rates with short-term maturity, insufficient access to capital market instruments, insufficient equity capital, and lack of professional financial management. In Turkey, several organisations address the financial bottlenecks of SMEs. Organisations such as the Small and Medium Scale Enterprises Development Organisation (KOSGEB), the Credit Guarantee Fund (KGF), and the Union of Chambers and Commodity Exchanges of Turkey (TOBB) provide financial and/or non-financial assistance for the development of SMEs. The backbone of the Turkish economy depends on SMEs as well as exporters. One of the national strategies for the Turkish economy is to grow exports, and the Turkish Export Assembly, which is the roof organisation of around 55,000 exporters, is focused on supporting the exporters.

The Key Importance of Export Factoring for the Turkish Economy

Turkey in 2017 ranks first in two-factor export business among the FCI members. Until 2016, Turkey was second after China in terms of such deals, but a surge in business volume boosted the country to first place. However, export factoring business still has great potential in Turkey as the penetration of export factoring business is only 7% in the total Turkish O/A export volume.

Mainly, Turkey exports to the EU (48%), near and middle East (22%), Africa (8%) and other European countries (7%), and imports come from EU (39%), other European countries (11%), near and middle East (7%) and Africa (3%).

The main characteristics of the Turkish export factoring market are:
– FCI members dominate the sector with a 98% market share;
– 35% recourse, 65% non-recourse;
– Average maturity of 75 days;
– Whole turnover on a debtor basis;
– Mainly focused on textile, automotive spare parts, petroleum and metal industries;
– Risk Protection service is the main driver;
– High level of educated staff and service quality.

Since 2015, in cooperation with the AFI and Turk Eximbank, factoring companies have started to provide exporters with the Central Bank of the Republic of Turkey (CBRT) sourced post-shipment export rediscount credits through Turk Eximbank. Channelling more financial support through CBRT to AFI member factoring companies generates significant cost advantages for exporters.

2015 saw the completion of a project which was conducted jointly by the AFI and Turk Eximbank and whose aim was to integrate Turk Eximbank's export credit insurance system into the operations of the

Turkish Factoring Industry. As a result, Turk Eximbank's short-term export credit insurance began playing an even greater role in Turkish exporters' ability to venture into global markets. With the addition of Turk Eximbank's export credit insurance added to its existing portfolio of factoring products and services, Turkey's factoring companies are now providing services to numerous countries in Africa, the Middle East, and elsewhere around the world.

An Industry Opened to the World: the FCI Success Story of Turkey

The FCI success story of Turkey started in 1987 with the FCI annual meeting held in Istanbul. The first factoring transaction was in export business and export became the main driver of the Factoring Industry in Turkey. In 30 years, Turkey has become the leader of the two-factor export factoring volume in FCI having 20 members in the Chain. Moreover, Turkish factoring companies are the ultimate winners of FCI annual awards for excellence in export performance categories, with TEB Faktoring chosen six times, Garanti Faktoring three times and Yapı Kredi Faktoring twice as best export factor among the FCI members.

Last but not least, Mr Çağatay Baydar, General Manager of TEB Faktoring was elected as FCI Chairman two times for the years of 2011-2013 and 2016-2019. Several Turkish members in management level participate in FCI technical committees such as marketing, legal, communication and SCF. The education manager of FCI is also a highly experienced Turkish colleague who worked in the Turkish Factoring Industry for many years.

III. Conclusion: Role Model in the Region and Bridge Between Continents

Many aspects of the Turkish factoring market for being a "role model" in the region can be emphasised:
- It is a regulated market;
- It has a high level legal environment and strong corporate governance;
- The rights and issues of factoring companies are represented in front of all governmental organisations by the AFI very strongly, as it was established according to the law;

- BRSA supports the Factoring Industry including understanding SCF as a factoring product;
- The Central Bank supports factoring companies by funding them in export business;
- New funding facilities for factoring companies are provided by Takasbank;
- There is access to the two important data centres for risk management and assigned receivables;
- There is cooperation with the governmental organisations such as Turk Eximbank, the Turkish Exporters Assembly, the association for SMEs etc.;
- Digitalisation projects of the AFI in accordance with the needs of the factoring sector.

The role of Turkey is best suited as a hub for international factoring due to its geographical position between more mature markets and developing ones. With Turkish industry's 26 years factoring experience, it has become a very good example for developing markets. This knowledge and experience is not only due to its geographical position and its success in export factoring and general global factoring expertise, but also to the work it has conducted in the legal and regulatory environment.

Turkey is a great example of how factoring industries can successfully work with governments and governmental organisations. The main reason for this success relies on the necessity to be one-voice in front of executive, legislative and judicial authorities.

As mentioned, after the law on financial services, the sector focused on building the future of factoring in Turkey with the new innovative IT based products such as supply and distributor chain finance, and on the centralised e-solutions under the Association.

As the Factoring Industry in Turkey is dynamic, developed very rapidly with the new centralised IT initiatives, and is very well connected with other countries, all those developments and its geographical position make Turkey a bridge between the continents for international trade and factoring, SCF, know-how transfer and Islamic factoring.

22. Factoring in Maghreb and the Middle East, Still a Limited Market

Fatma Bouraoui
Legal Advisor, Senior Counsel

Alexandre de Fournoux
Head of Factoring Emerging Markets, BNP Paribas

Haitham Al Refaie
Group CEO, Tawreeq Holding

Maghreb and the Middle East markets are not at the same pace of development. In Maghreb, factoring was launched in the 1990s, much influenced by French rules (subrogation). But in the Middle East it only emerged in the early 2000s, through an Anglo-Saxon environment (more invoice discounting or asset backed lending than classic factoring services).

Among the four Maghreb countries, factoring is available in three of them (Mauritania, Morocco and Tunisia) and it represented 12% of the African factoring market in 2016. Despite the introduction of the product in legislation (1993)[1] after additional laws and addendums[2], there is no factoring offering available in Algeria. One of the reasons suggested is that the economic actors rejected the concept because it would be inconsistent with Algerian businesses practices.[3] The two oldest countries to have launched factoring for over the last twenty years are Tunisia and Morocco. In 2009, Mauritania launched a factoring activity closely aligned with leasing business. It represented a total turnover of around EUR 200 million per year in 2016, contributing to less than 1%

---

[1] Décret législatif No. 93-08 du 25 avril 1993.
[2] Décret exécutif No. 95-331 de l'Aouel Joumada Ethania 1416 correspondant au 25 octobre 1995 relatif aux conditions d'habilitation des sociétés pratiquant le factoring. Code du commerce 2007, articles 543bis14 – 543bis18.
[3] « Remarques critiques sur la technique du factoring en droit algérien », *Revue Algérienne des Sciences Juridiques, Economiques et Politiques*, No. 1, 2007, p. 111-130.

of the total African market and provided by two factoring companies: Banque Populaire de Mauritanie and Commercial Factoring Limited.

The factoring market in the Middle East is nascent with great potential. However, market development has stalled in comparison to other global hubs. Despite available literature references to the early concepts of factoring dating back to ancient Mesopotamia, the fact is, it only re-emerged in early 2000. In the Middle East, the market is diverse and development across jurisdictions have differed. For instance, the factoring market in Egypt has seen rapid development and growth in comparison to the rest of the region, attributed mainly to regulation and market acceptance. However, the overview in other major Middle East markets is different, especially discussing the status in the Gulf Cooperation Council (GCC), Jordan and Lebanon. Despite its fragmentation, the market can generally be described as oligopolistic with a number of banks active in factoring across the region, mostly dominating the market share.

I. Factoring in Maghreb, Mainly Concentrated in Tunisia and Morocco

Factoring in Tunisia

In 1995, Tunisie Factoring was the first to offer factoring, through a specialised department of Tunisie Leasing, and from June 1999, through a dedicated subsidiary of the same company, with the support of the Société Française de Factoring (Eurofactor). Today, Tunisie Factoring and Unifactor are joint market leaders both with a global 50% market share.

In April 2000, on the initiative of three major Tunisian banks (Banque Nationale Agricole, Arab Tunisian Bank and Amen Bank) Union de Factoring was launched. Today, it manages around 30% of the market share.

Besides these two main actors, Attijari also provides factoring through its Tunisian leasing subsidiary (less than 5% market share).

The product offering is mainly a recourse product (around 90%). Most of the business is domestic, working with post-dated cheques (invoices are assigned jointly with cheques and/or drafts), and apart from a recent service provided by the Tunisian insurer, La Carte, in cooperation with Coface, the insurance credit offering is limited.

In 2016, total turnover was EUR 370 million (around 1.4% of the African factoring market) with a CAGR around 3.3% for the last decades. Most of the activity (90%) is in the domestic market. In addition to the consequences of the geopolitics of Tunisia and the Arab Spring, this low dynamism (compared with the evolution of the European or Asian market) could be explained by different factors[4]: lack of awareness of factoring solutions, which is considered to be in competition with banks, the low level of communication from factoring companies and banking authorities, exacerbated by the lack of a factoring association gathering professionals together.

In the absence of a specific law for factoring, the applicable legal texts are those of the Code of Obligations and Contracts (COC) on the transfer of obligations, most specifically the subrogation and assignment of debt. The COC dedicates an entire chapter to the transfer of debts and gives an implied definition in article 204. Modelled on French law, historical players opted for a legal mechanism as the legal basis of their operations: the *ex parte creditoris* subrogation contained in articles 224 to 228 of the COC. However, under Tunisian law, one is not entitled to use the practical argument relating to the applicability of *erga omnes* (in full right) of the subrogation which prevails under French law[5] and which made it possible to keep it as the basis of factoring. This is the case because of the express reference made by article 205 (chapter on the transfer on debt) to article 228 of the COC (chapter on subrogation). The measures of opposability of the transfer of debt can be subrogated. Tunisian jurisprudence[6], however, has never retained *ex parte creditoris* subrogation as a legal basis for factoring, neither in any published judgements, nor at any level of jurisdiction. This qualifies the transfer of debt operation, thereby encouraging factoring companies to modify their conventions and to accept equivalents for the formalities provided for in article 205 of the COC[7]: notice in writing, and correspondence with the stamp of the purchaser, or anything that proves knowledge of the debtor.

---

[4] « L'Affacturage, une industrie méconnue en Tunisie ? », interview de M. Cherif, PDG de l'Union de Factoring – Bouraoui M., PDG de Tunisie Factoring, *Finance et Vous électronique newsletter*, No. 4, février 2012.

[5] See the question, Bouraoui Fatma, *The rights of internal and international factoring*, thesis for PhD in law, faculté des sciences juridiques, politiques et sociales de Tunis 2003; Fatma Bouraoui, "Le factoring", CEJJ, 2011.

[6] Cass. 8 July 2010, RJL 2011 No. 1, Note Bouraoui Fatma.

[7] Court of referral No. 16760 of 20/6/2005 ruling as court of referral on the judgement of court of cassation, No. 1967 of 1/10/2004, RTD 2008, F. Bouraoui commentary.

Recently, a law covering banking and financial activities in Tunisia was published to support the dynamics of the Tunisian economy out of the crisis it is facing. This new law of the 11th of July 2016 defines factoring as a debt management operation, that is any commitment by which a bank or a financial establishment offers services for the management of these debts, for the benefit of the holder of a commercial debt portfolio, provided that the bank or the financial establishment is committed to giving an advance payment or to guaranteeing its recovery. This way, the banking law validates the various forms of factoring practiced in Tunisia.

Today, many elements suggest that factoring in Tunisia has a promising future: the important part (88%) of SMEs in the Tunisian economy, the emergence of a credit insurance solution, the well advanced central credit register, the need for companies to secure their receivables, and the arrival of new players: UBCI-BNP Paribas launched a factoring offering in 2017.

Factoring in Morocco

Maroc Factoring (subsidiary of BMCE Group) is one of the first factoring companies in Africa and the Arab world. It was established in 1988. In 1995, Attijari opened its own factoring subsidiary, and in 1999 BMCI (BNP Paribas) launched a factoring department.

During the 1990s, the product was primarily dedicated to international transactions. It was around the 2000s that factoring expanded on the domestic market. In a long-term payment environment with the development of retailers and large projects, factoring has been used as a lever for the domestic market. The credit insurance offering has grown with all global and Europeans key players (Axa, Cesce, Coface and Euler Hermès). The legislative recast took factoring into account, and in 2006 the new banking act provided a definition for it. The main applicable text concerns the subrogation legal technique in the COC, articles 212 and subsequent ones.[8]

This is why, while international factoring business accounted for around 90% of the total turnover in the 1990s, domestic business accounted for 70% in 2005. Nevertheless, in 2005 the total volume remained limited with a EUR 430 million turnover, i.e. about 6% of the African factoring market.

---

[8] DAHIR du 12 août 1913.

In the late 2000s and at the beginning of the 2010s, the factoring range of products started to diversify. In 2009, Société Générale launched its factoring department and in 2012, Banque Populaire did the same. Today, the entire range is covered by the market, from small and medium companies to very large corporates with international needs, while reverse factoring and confirming are also provided.

In 2016, the Moroccan market grew to reach a EUR 2,708 million turnover (around 10% of the African factoring market, second after South Africa) with a peak at EUR 4,200 million in 2014 (around 20% of the African market). This can be explained mainly by exceptional deals managed by Banque Populaire. International transactions now stand below 5% of the total turnover.

Factoring is now well established in Morocco, even if not all the players are represented in the Professional Association of Financial Institutions (APSF). With its privileged position, the Moroccan market could be a stepping stone for the development of factoring in West Africa. The recent establishment of large car factories in trade free zones, and the extension of ports and port areas, are also promising growth drivers.

II. Factoring in the Middle East, Slow Development in a Market Ripe for Expansion

Focusing on the developing factoring markets of the Middle East, the underlying economic similarities support the prospects for growth of the Industry despite the fragmented state of the business due to the lack of regulation and standardisation.

The Early Development of Factoring in the Middle East

For more than a decade, factoring has been developing and growing rapidly, supported by expanding global trade; nonetheless, it was only in early 2000 when the appeal of the Middle East market started to rise.

Banks dominate the Middle East financial sector. Aggregately, the contribution of the non-banking financial sector is considered minimal. With very few exceptions, the major deterrents for growth have been regulatory, technological and judicial.

The development globally of the Factoring Industry, however, did not prevent major market players from penetrating the Middle East market led by multinational banks that have the expertise in other markets.

The first structured rollout of factoring products dates to early 2000 by HSBC bank, a major player and supporter of the Factoring Industry in the region.

Improvement continued slowly due to a lack of clear and separate regulatory oversight for standalone factoring operations, with one clear exception in the Arab world of Egypt, where the Egyptian Financial Supervisory Authority regulates the Factoring Industry. Accordingly, the development of factoring was led by banks or through their sponsored factoring companies.

Following HSBC, expansion remained moderate with other banks rolling out factoring products. It was further supported by the evolution of the Dubai International Financial Centre. Growth however stalled in the wake of the financial crisis that highly impacted performance of the banking sector across the region.

The Factoring Market Post the Financial Crisis

In the wake of the financial crisis and the recovery of the market and the banking sector, the focus has turned more evidently towards financial system stability and economic performance, especially with emphasis on the need to provide support for SMEs that make up the majority of the Middle East economy.

The financial crisis, the unstable geopolitical landscape and volatility of oil prices have influenced the rapid change in the market over the past years. This period has highlighted key areas that have supported the growing appeal of factoring across the region:

- Reassessment of banking performance and lending practices;
- Change of market practices and payment culture with cash proving to be king;
- Government focus and support helping to expand access to finance for SMEs that are not adequately supported by the banking sector;
- Altering market dynamics with a change of governments' lending and deposits, especially GCC governments with the drop of oil prices.

As a result, attention has been drawn to the support factoring offers to SMEs as well as how it serves the banking sector in expanding their product range and growing their balance sheets efficiently. Nonetheless, despite the evident appeal and potential, the market response is not as adequate as the market viability implies. The two main reasons being first, the lack of clear regulations and restrictions on assignment, and second and most important, the lack of product knowledge in the financial sector and companies.

Current State of the Market – Oligopoly with Lack of Structure

The current status of the factoring market in the Middle East differs between jurisdictions. The GCC market enjoys similarities, while in Jordan and Lebanon the market is much smaller, and in Egypt it differs with stronger support from regulations and evident signs of continued growth.

The current state of GCC markets remain promising, however, the Jordan and Lebanon markets lack sufficient data, and the products are mainly offered through banks to select clients. To understand the state of the GCC market better, we need to take a close look at the products being offered.

The biggest support for market growth is the interest in factoring government receivables, especially for government-sponsored banks, where government deposits account for the biggest portion of the banks' balance sheets. Factoring the receivables of government and government related entities raised the need for perfecting assignments. This was the major support for growth of factoring in many GCC countries, especially the UAE, Kuwait and Qatar. However, details of the volumes are not disclosed.

As a standardised product offered to other commercial transactions involving companies, the structure is more of a discounting facility, mainly offered as an asset backed loan rather than factoring. The majority of the facilities being offered are non-disclosed recourse factoring. With the banks being selective in providing the services to SMEs, the majority of products are focusing on extending credit at the risk of the SME, and not structuring a risk-adjusted approach to factoring by the outright purchase of receivables, or by taking the risk of the ultimate obligor, as perfecting the assignment is a hurdle that banks avoid to tackle.

The nature of the offered product has essentially delayed its expansion, especially with banks not pushing forward with expanding the product range or upgrading their offering. The lack of available data in the market has stalled the growth of services, as there is no clear data from the factoring providers, whether banks or non-banking institutions. Although the market is fragmented with a number of entities providing factoring, with the available data and market intelligence, it is rather concentrated with a small number of major banks and, hence, clear oligopolistic behaviour is evident.

Growth of Sharia-compliant Finance and Alternative Products

Since 2014, we have seen new changes in the market, with a focus on Islamic finance as well as the growth of alternative lending and rise of fintech. The market for factoring in the Middle East is taking a leap forward in an attempt to follow global peers.

Despite the potential, until recently, the market lacked Sharia-compliant factoring, a product that serves SMEs and corporates with a Sharia-compliant process, to fill the gap in offered products. The main difference between Sharia-compliant factoring and traditional services is its adherence to Sharia principles, and is provided on a non-recourse basis. In essence, it embeds the importance of ethical and transparent practices based on the need to serve and support the business, leading to financial inclusion and sustainable economic growth.

There is a dearth of Sharia-compliant financial products and services, and the slow progress in their innovation has hindered the growth of many SMEs. In fact, the Sharia-compliant factoring sector has the potential to fill the widening finance gap in business financing, especially for SMEs. Islamic banks, like their conventional counterparts, offer little in the way of finance for SMEs, thanks to stringent regulations and risk aversion, which has limited SME access to finance, impeding their business scalability and potential for growth.

The ecosystem for Sharia-compliant SME financing outside the banking system is distinct and focused on dealing with a notably different assessment of risk. These methods take a more holistic approach to assessing the risk exposure of SMEs to sector specific and business risks, requiring a bottom-up approach to evaluation, irrespective of the metrics that are applied to mature corporates with clear financial standings.

Sharia-compliant factoring offers an alternative solution, focusing on working capital and off-balance sheet financing to fill the credit gap in the region. In 2015, Tawreeq Holdings was the first independent group of companies to launch Sharia-compliant comprehensive SCF solutions.

Alternative sources of finance by non-financial institutions remain limited in the region. The market for Sharia-compliant factoring and aggregate Sharia-compliant SCF solutions continue to develop but face many hurdles.

Another key trend seen over the past three years has been the growing role alternative lending providers are playing, especially fintechs. Global players have been exploring the market and, due to the lack of regulations and resistance from local banks in taking a strong interest, growth remains very promising and is expected to increase rapidly over the medium term.

III. Conclusion: Maghreb and the Middle East Offer a Promising Market for Growth

The structure of the Maghreb and Middle East markets offers potential for factoring growth. The Industry is expected to expand over the medium term with adoption of technology-enabled solutions and specialised platforms providing comprehensive answers.

In order to support expansion, the major focus is on regulation. The need to perfect the assignment to ensure its enforceability is the major restriction that is currently withholding growth. Due to the payment culture and strength of big corporates over SMEs, their ability to withhold payment is affecting market performance and preventing factoring from expanding due to the high risks associated with factors. Nonetheless, governments pressing forward with support for SMEs offer the potential to allow for factoring expansion in both regions.

23. Factoring in Africa, an Emerging Continent

Benedict Oramah

President, African Export-Import Bank (AFREXIMBANK)

It was not until the late 1990s and early 2000s that the factoring product was introduced in Africa. The global Factoring Industry has experienced tremendous growth since the 1990s with the volume of business rising from EUR 700 million in 1990 to over EUR 2.47 trillion in 2017. However, the Industry remains nascent in Africa with only five countries actively or partially engaged in factoring business. South Africa alone has accounted for an average of about 90% of Africa's volume during the last two decades nonetheless its share has trended downwards from 94% in 1998 to an estimated 80% in 2017.

Africa remains at the fringes of the factoring business despite the enormous opportunity existing across sectors and industries and the size of the SME sector on the continent. Like many other developing regions, a full level of awareness of the usefulness of factoring is, in some African countries, lacking at both the policy and/or the private sector levels. These forces, coupled with the absence of a credible credit insurance market, have combined to hamper private sector investment in the area of factoring in Africa. Nonetheless, some positive developments within the continent, aided by proactive steps being taken by a number of development financial institutions, particularly the African Export–Import Bank (hereafter Afreximbank), are combining to accelerate factoring business in Africa.

Even if the recent history only shows a nascent continent, new developments prove there is room for promising growth, initiatives for promotion and create a favourable new perspective for the Factoring Industry in the African market.

I. Factoring in Africa, a Nascent History

From the 1970s to the late 1990s, factoring businesses were considered unsuitable and less important for the African market due to a number of structural factors, including limited domestic supply chains and the dominance of commodities, including oil and other petroleum products, in Africa's trade basket. Moreover, there was (and still is) a lack of common terminology across the continent. For example, while "invoice discounting" in countries such as Kenya and Nigeria, among others, refers to a form of ABL, where the lender advances 80% or so against a revolving pool of approved accounts receivable as collateral, in other countries, like South Africa, invoice discounting refers to a purchase and sale of accounts transaction on a confidential basis, with factor financing via advances, with or without credit protection, consistent with how the term "invoice discounting" is employed in England.

The South African Model

It is no wonder then that factoring is today concentrated in only five countries – the first two, South Africa and Morocco - accounting for a combined share of over 93%. During the period 1970-1990, it was only South Africa that was able to adopt factoring in its simplest form, due partly to the relatively developed and diversified financial system, size of the economy (being the largest economy at that time), better infrastructure for information gathering, well-structured and relatively organised SME sector. Aside from the existence of a strong and large financial system, the success of factoring in South Africa has been driven by the existence of a strong manufacturing base and services industries, well integrated and interconnected industries/sectors, which creates capacity for both factoring and reverse factoring (SCF). Factoring has flourished in the following economic sectors in South Africa: manufacturing, clearing and forwarding, food, steel, clothing and textiles. Other sectors include wholesale, footwear, agriculture, chemical, transport, commodities, engineering, printing and services.

By the mid- to the late 1990s and early 2000s, the concept of factoring had been introduced in Morocco and later in Mauritius. The elements that led to the success of factoring in Morocco and Mauritius were similar, if not the same, to those which prevailed in South Africa at that time: developed financial systems, existence of domestic supply chains, growth in light manufacturing and value addition in other sectors. Additionally,

South Africa, Morocco and Mauritius all have legal frameworks in place for a factoring and credit information registry, which both protects factors and ensures efficient assessment of the credit risk of both the factoring clients, selling their O/As, evidenced by invoices to a factor, if purchased accounts have to be charged-back due to, for example, a quality dispute raised by the account debtor, and the credit risk of the client's customers/debtors obligated thereon, in the case of domestic factoring. Moreover, the judiciary and the business communities there seem to be relatively more familiar with factors and factoring law. Other North African countries, namely Tunisia and Egypt, embraced factoring as an SME financing instrument in the late 1990s to early 2000s, and are in the process of reforming their laws to put in place the fundamental structures required to create a leap in factoring volume, including a strong legal framework, back office capacities, and an information registry, among other things. In these countries, domestic factoring accounts for no less than 90% of their respective total volumes. Egypt has, in recent years, created a regulatory authority called the Egyptian Financial Supervisory Authority, which also regulates factoring business there. Due to the activities of that body, factoring volumes soared, rising from EUR 1 million in 2004 to EUR 418 million in 2017. A Factoring Association was also formed which is currently actively promoting the product in the country.

Africa's factoring activity is dominated by bank-affiliated factors, with a few independent companies, most of which are in one way or the other backed by commercial banks. Affiliation with commercial banks enables African factors to benefit from factoring lines of credit, working capital and other back office support functions. This kind of arrangement between factoring companies and commercial banks can be found in Egypt, Tunisia, Morocco and South Africa.[1]

Why Has Factoring Not Flourished in Africa?

Many authors and industry experts have suggested that weak or under-developed financial systems and the lack of credit bureaus have discouraged investments in factoring in Africa. Additionally, limited knowledge among the business community, financial industry regulators, policy makers and SMEs about the product and its various permutations, and its potential benefits, coupled with under-developed or non-existent

---

[1] Oramah Benedict O., "From the periphery to the centre - Africa as the growth market for factoring", in Bickers Michael (Ed.), *World Factoring Yearbook 2013*, 2013, p. 6-9. Kent, United Kingdom, BCR Publishing Ltd.

credit insurance and reinsurance markets, and limited or non-existent domestic supply chains, have all combined to limit the growth of factoring in the continent.

While the above-mentioned elements were and still are, important constraints, a further major hindrance remains the absence of clear legal frameworks for factoring in most African countries, coupled with the general lack of data on payment performance, potential clients' creditworthiness, such as the kind of information that is collected by public or private credit bureaus or by factors, judges and lawyers not fully familiar with the product and local courts which can sometimes be relatively slow.

Factoring usually performs well in markets that have developed supply chains, diversified export markets, where courts and the business community are familiar with the product, and there are strong manufacturing and services across inter-related industries. In Africa, however, over-concentration in commodity exports, coupled with limited linkages to industrial and services sectors and failed attempts at value addition or production of export manufactures have contributed to depressing factoring volumes in the continent. Last but not least, factoring can be viewed as a bundle of activities.

In addition to the financing component, factors typically provide three other complementary services to their clients: credit cover, in non recourse facilities, on purchased invoices arising from factor-approved sales, sales ledger management and collection services. The factor's credit services involve assessing the creditworthiness of the seller's buyers (aka debtors, or account debtors) whose accounts arising from factor-approved sales the factor will purchase from its client at factor credit-risk, in non recourse facilities, and the factor's provision of advice to its client in this area, but not credit cover, in recourse factoring facilities. Factors typically base this credit assessment on a combination of their own proprietary data along with publicly available data on the financial strength and payment performance of their factoring client's various customers and, of course, review of the particular terms of sale. The factor's collection services involve collecting both current and delinquent accounts and minimizing the associated credit losses associated therewith. This includes the factor timely notifying the account debtor obligated on a delinquent purchased account, not collected by its maturity, that its obligation to the factor on the purchased invoice is in default, coupled with the factor pursuing collection thereof through the judicial system, as may be appropriate. Factoring also allows SMEs to effectively outsource their credit and collection services to the factor. Execution of these various functions, of course, requires that factoring companies acquire back office technologies and a supportive legal environment, both of which are lacking in some African markets.

Since the early 2000s, we have seen a steady growth in the volume of factoring business in the African continent with volumes rising more than five-fold, from about EUR 4 billion in 1998 to over EUR 22 billion in 2017. Nevertheless, the African share of global factoring volumes remains disappointingly low compared to other developing regions, including Asia and Latin America. The continent currently accounts for only 0.9% of worldwide factoring volume.

During the last one and a half decades, rapid economic growth in Africa aided by the commodity boom of the 2000s, a rising middle class, a fast pace of urbanisation and increased share of manufacturing and services in GDP have established credible domestic supply chains in and diversified certain economies, thereby creating an environment in which factoring can better flourish. Indeed, recent socio-economic developments in Africa have led many people to suggest that the continent is gradually becoming the next emerging frontier for factoring. Indications, in this regard, are that strong and credible factors are now emerging in Kenya, Nigeria, Ghana, Côte d'Ivoire, Zimbabwe, Zambia and Senegal, largely assisted by the emergence of domestic supply chains and significant uptick in intra-regional trade.

Additionally, the rise of factoring in new markets in Africa is being driven by the emergence of: the middle class, which continues to drive retail trade; the growth of the telecommunications industry; discoveries of new oil and mining fields in Ghana, Kenya, Côte d'Ivoire, Mozambique and elsewhere, which is fostering the emergence of a vibrant service industry; rapid development of non-traditional export products including horticulture and specialised services; growing trade and economic relations between Africa and new markets in Asia, Latin America and Eastern Europe; and the emergence of credible supply chains across the continent. Factoring has also received a very important boost from the activities of the Afreximbank, a multilateral pan-African trade finance bank. Since 2006, when Afreximbank began actively promoting factoring in the continent, it has: introduced factoring in Nigeria, Côte d'Ivoire, Zimbabwe and Senegal; facilitated the active engagement of IFG and later FCI in Africa, enabling strong awareness campaigns. The bank has also introduced a model law on factoring and facilitated the growth of back office support functions and financing, such as rediscounting lines of credit to factors.

II. A Promising Growth in Recent Developments

Although global factoring volume has nearly doubled over the last decade (2008-2017), the volume of business has grown at a snail's pace since 2013 in response to the general slowdown of developing economies in Asia and Latin America and the debt-induced slowdown of the European economies. However, in 2017, strong growth in South America (+9%) and Africa (+9%), coupled with sound growth in Europe (7%) contributed to maintaining an appreciable volume of factoring business globally.

Africa remains an insignificant player in the global factoring market. The continent's share has averaged 1% since 1998 with only five countries accounting for this share, namely Egypt, Mauritius, Morocco, South Africa and Tunisia. Despite its relatively low share of global factoring volumes, Africa is witnessing a quickening in the rate of expansion of the business over the last few years. Total factoring volume grew by more than one third, reaching EUR 22.3 billion in 2017, compared to volume of EUR 16.8 billion in 2010. On average, 80% of the factoring business in Africa is domestic.[2] The Factoring Industry in Africa is considered highly concentrated with South Africa accounting for about 80% of factoring volume in 2017, followed by Morocco (15.1%), Egypt (1.8%), Tunisia (1.5%), Mauritius (1.0%) and Kenya (1.0%). Seven companies in Egypt, six in South Africa, four in Tunisia, two in Morocco and one in Mauritius, account for the entire volume. Given the high concentrations[3], the market in various countries is to some extent oligopolistic and therefore inefficient, does not encourage innovation and new entry is also difficult.

Domestic factoring with recourse is dominant in South Africa especially in the steel and information, communication and technology (ICT) sectors, accounting for over 93% of total turnover. Similarly, in Tunisia factoring with recourse represented about 95% of total volumes. The product is mostly available in the telecom, agribusiness, and food and beverage industries. In Egypt, factoring is mostly domestic with

---

[2] Oramah (2013) see note 1 above, Oramah, Benedict & Dzene Richman, "Evolution of Factoring" in Egypt and Implications for Factoring in Africa. *Contemporary Issues in African Trade and Trade Finance* (CIAT), African Export-Import Bank, Cairo, Egypt, 2015. See also FCI Annual Report (2014).

[3] Tomusange Robert L., *Factoring as a Financing Alternative for African Small and Medium-Sized Enterprises*, Walden University Scholar Works, 2015.

concentration in growth sectors including retail, textiles, chemicals, processed food, ICT and packaging industries. Factoring services are distributed by local factoring companies and commercial banks. These ones offer more attractive terms to SME exporters with foreign currency export proceeds outcompeting local non-bank factors.

Activity is beginning to pick up in non-traditional factoring markets in Africa. In Kenya, international factoring grew despite the bulk of business remaining in domestic factoring (retail).[4] The opportunities in export factoring were tied to agriculture/agri-business (flowers/fruits) driven by demand for O/A payment systems to support exports to Europe and the Middle East. For Zimbabwe, domestic factoring with recourse inevitably showed better growth prospects due to the introduction of legislative directives by the government that sought to improve the country's balance of trade by restricting imports of non-essential goods. Notably though, the outlook is positive for export orientated factoring, largely due to the introduction of export incentive schemes by the government. In Cameroon in particular, market information suggests factoring volumes were in excess of EUR 40 million in 2016, largely shared among six market players and mainly in services. Gabon also reported growth in both with recourse and non recourse domestic factoring, in distribution, retail, construction and services sectors. In Nigeria, Factoring and Supply Chain Limited obtained its finance company license from the central bank and started factoring business.

III. Ongoing Factoring Initiatives in the African Market

African Chapter of FCI

In 2007-2008, Afreximbank pioneered the formation of the African Chapter of IFG, prior to the merger with FCI. Until then, the only formalised groups were the Chapters in Asia and Pacific, Europe and Americas. The African Chapter, which is the association of the African members of FCI: facilitates sharing of experiences among African members of FCI; advances the interests of African members and partners; lobbies legislators, ministers, government officials and others whose decisions or advice may influence the success or otherwise of members and partners' businesses; engages in public relations activities designed to raise local awareness of the benefits of international factoring; develops

---

[4] Ibid.

awareness of FCI members' on factoring in Africa; attracts new members, partners and sponsors; and offers networking opportunities through seminars, meetings and other functions. Since the pioneering work, aggressive awareness campaigns and capacity building programmes by Afreximbank have supported growth in the membership of the African Chapter from around ten in 2008 to over 35 as of December 2017. Following the merger of IFG and FCI in 2016, the African Chapter activities were authorised by the FCI executive committee, providing additional training, awareness and networking support to the Chapter.

Creating a Legal Framework for Factoring

Lack of a regulatory framework to govern factoring has been a major impediment to the growth of factoring in Africa.[5] Evidence points to the fact that factoring (as a percentage of GDP) is higher in countries with factoring Acts.[6] Legislation of this nature serves to clarify the nature of the transaction itself, and a factoring law clearly dictates not only how judgements should be made towards factors in the event of default of sellers or buyers, but when customers can and cannot enforce set-off and other rights against factored invoices. Factoring legislation can also provide guidance on how security interests and assignments can be created, perfected and enforced in factoring transactions. The success of factoring in South Africa and Morocco could therefore be attributed, in part, to the existence of some form of legislative statutes and regulations which govern factoring activities in those countries.

In 2014, Afreximbank launched a project to assist African countries to create and adopt a legal framework to support the growth of factoring on the continent. In 2016, working with the Organisation pour l'Harmonisation en Afrique du Droit des Affaires (OHADA), and some international lawyers, the bank successfully created a model law, followed by several awareness campaigns about the model law across Africa. This effort will ensure the unification of factoring laws across the continent. The campaign is beginning to yield some positive results. In Egypt, the government has adopted new regulations to promote the growth of the Factoring Industry by enacting some laws regulating factoring activities such as licensing, registration procedures, financial adequacy and financial

---

[5] Kameni Enga, "Recent legal reforms in relation to factoring" in *Africa Contemporary Issues in African Trade and Trade Finance* (CIAT), African Export-Import Bank, Cairo, Egypt, 2015.

[6] Bakker Marie-Renée, Klapper Leora, & Udell Gregory, *World Bank*, 2004.

Factoring in Africa, an Emerging Continent 299

statements requirements along with other amendments, and the removal of stamp duties on factoring companies to enhance the development of the product. In Cameroon, the national assembly, the lower chamber of the Cameroonian parliament, adopted the first piece of legislation governing factoring activity in the country to help diversify corporate finance mechanisms.

There were also significant developments in advancing the adoption of Afreximbank's model law by the Nigerian Export Import Bank (NEXIM) working with FSS 2020 and a new Nigerian Factoring Working Group, created under the auspices of the Central Bank of Nigeria. In more specific terms, following the presentation of the draft factoring bill to the Nigerian Financial System Strategy (FSS 2020) directorate of the Central Bank of Nigeria in October 2016, the directorate has further presented the bill to the Financial Sector Regulation Coordinating Committee (FSRCC), the statutory body set up to oversee all financial institutions in Nigeria, which has endorsed the bill and has agreed to issue its approval towards its enactment process. The bill will, in the process, be reconciled with the recent Secured Transactions legislation enacted in Nigeria in late May 2017, insofar as, at present, invoice-discounting (as that term is used commercially in Nigeria), but not, as yet, factoring in the sense of a purchase and sale of invoices, is covered by the Secured Transactions law in Nigeria.

In addition, the OHADA which regulates business laws in over seventeen African countries has signalled an interest in using Afreximbank's model law as a guide in developing an OHADA uniform law on factoring.

Capacity Building Programmes

One of the key constraints to growth of factoring in Africa has been inadequate knowledge and skills, in certain countries, among the business, legal, accounting, regulatory and judicial communities regarding the use and benefits of factoring. In this regard, since 2009, Afreximbank in collaboration with the then IFG and subsequently FCI (following their merger), has been involved in organising seminars/workshops on key aspects of factoring for participants drawn from African trade finance institutions and commercial banks, factoring companies, regulators, etc. For instance, in collaboration with IFG, Tunisie Factoring and Tunis International bank, Afreximbank organised a forum on factoring in 2009; and in November 2011, the same organised a one-day workshop on factoring in Accra (Ghana). Since then, it has successively held one-day seminars on factoring as part of its annual structured trade finance program. Capacity building workshops have also been held in a number of countries, including Nigeria, Ghana, Kenya, Cameroon, Egypt and Zambia, attracting 400 participants including legislators and regulators.

In 2015-2016, Afreximbank worked with FCI/IFG and the University of Malta to introduce a capacity building programme called the COFIT for the benefit of African factors, industry practitioners, and regulators. The program aims to introduce the participants to the world of international trade, supply chain management and trade finance. The course is run over a four week period by FCI and the University of Malta and is delivered by university academics and industry experts. The course material covers a wide range of topics that run from basic theory to highly practical applications. Subjects include financial instruments, interpretation of accounting statements and economic statistics, international trade overview, trade politics and economics, trade based money laundering and financial crime, structured commodity finance, risks and challenges of international trade, international business financing, international marketing, developing countries, growth, crises and reform, Islamic finance and emerging markets, introduction to factoring and commercial finance, legal aspects, marketing, sales, account management, fraud and risk management.

Promotional/Awareness Campaign

Undoubtedly, as noted above, a major constraint to the growth of factoring in Africa is the lack of knowledge about the existence and usefulness of the product among regulators, policy makers, SMEs and the private sector across Africa. Efforts to promote factoring should therefore include continued investment in awareness creation and information dissemination. In this regard, Afreximbank, working with the then IFG and other institutions, launched a number of awareness programmes across Africa with a view to boosting interest and knowledge of the product and its benefits, particularly for SME growth. In 2015, for instance, Afreximbank, in collaboration with the then IFG, carried out a factoring promotion campaign in Senegal and Kenya. These campaigns yielded positive results and more than four members were mobilised and joined the then IFG. Also in 2015, the then IFG, in collaboration with the Egyptian Financial Services Institute (FSI), the Egyptian Factoring Association (EFA) and Afreximbank, organised the first symposium and academy on factoring in Africa in Cairo. This symposium attracted more than 70 participants from Egypt, Botswana, Kenya, Zambia, Zimbabwe, Nigeria, Morocco, and Mauritius. Since the merger of FCI and IFG, Afreximbank and FCI have organised training and awareness seminars in Tanzania, Mauritius, Cape Verde, Cameroon and Senegal.

IV. Prospective for Factoring in Africa

Factoring is witnessing a steady growth all across the African continent backed by Afreximbank's aggressive awareness campaigns and capacity building initiatives that started in 2006. Forecasts suggest that factoring volumes in the continent will rise from EUR 27 billion in 2016 to about EUR 50 billion by 2020.[7] The forecasted growth is supported by a number of positive developments that are changing the business environment in the continent. Notably, intra-regional trade has grown rapidly in recent years, amounting to more than USD 180 billion in 2015 and averaging over 17% of total African trade in that year. Intra-African trade is set to become increasingly important, expecting to reach USD 220 billion in 2018 and to USD 260 billion by 2021, contributing about 20% of Africa's total merchandise trade by 2021. This offers the best opportunity for scale economies and creates the necessary conditions for the growth of cross-border and domestic supply chains, particularly at the sub-regional levels, given that most of this trade is conducted at sub-regional levels. The emergence of large African corporates and multinational corporations in Africa that have accompanied the recent surge in intra-African trade itself provides opportunities for expansion of domestic and continental supply chains and an opportunity for the growth of factoring.

Further, African governments are beginning to adopt the right industrialisation policies and programmes. Many, including Côte d'Ivoire and Ethiopia, have designed the right industrial policies and are creating the infrastructure required for industrial growth. In addition, efforts are also underway to harmonise trade and industrial policies by Regional Economic Communities and at the continental level with the support of regional and continental policy and development institutions, including the African Union Commission, United Nations Economic Commission for Africa, Afreximbank and African Development Bank. These policy choices at national and regional levels are beginning to yield positive results for a number of countries. Supply chains are beginning to emerge

---

[7] Estimates by the African Export-Import Bank.

in a number of countries and cross-border activities are expanding as a result creating opportunities for factoring and SCF.

In addition, positive developments in a number of countries and sectors are expected to drive the growth of factoring in Africa, including:
- Oil and mining services in countries heavy in extractive industries, such as Nigeria, Ghana and Zambia. This will be policy driven through local content promotion and also by the outsourcing policies now embraced by major oil/mining companies. Annual spend on oil services currently exceeds USD 10 billion in Nigeria alone. A thriving invoice discounting business is presently being operated by local banks in support of this business, and factoring, in the sense of a purchase and sale of accounts transaction, can also take greater root there;
- Telecommunication services as a result of a rapid growth in this sector – evident in the rapid growth in the mobile cellular subscription rate – and the tendency of telecom companies to outsource key services, for example cell sites, etc.;
- Retail sector as a result of the rapid growth of the middle class in the continent. Figures show that Africa has the fastest growing middle class in the world with household consumption rising by 9.1% on average during 2006-2015, compared to 5.2% and 7.4% for East Asia-Pacific and Latin America respectively. This rapid growth has spurred outlets, and domestic supply chains are emerging;
- Non-traditional export sector, driven by a growing trade flows between Africa and other developing regions (also known as the South), with the trade estimated at 45% of Africa's total trade in 2012, compared to 27% in 2000. Africa rises as a major centre for contract farming and contract manufacturing. Evidently, manufacturing and agricultural value added have trended upwards over the last decade;
- The products traded have largely been light manufacturing, horticulture and semi-manufacturing in addition to commodities. Most of the trade is conducted on an O/A basis and trade credit is granted to buyers. The resulting accounts receivable, most often evidenced by an invoice, are, therefore, "factorable".

There are several emerging markets for factoring in Africa, especially 'new' entrant countries such as Kenya, Nigeria, Ghana, Côte d'Ivoire, Zimbabwe, Zambia, Mozambique and Senegal. The emerging companies specialised in factoring are Ghana Factoring, Palacial Invoices (Ghana),

Mauritania Leasing now Banque Populaire de Mauritanie, BPM (Mauritania), Commercial Factoring Limited (Mauritius), Oseg Capital (Botswana), Mareco Limited, Umati Capital (Kenya), Fidelis Finance (Burkina Faso), Locafrique (Senegal), Microfinance (Zambia), Bibby Apex (South Africa), without mentioning the factoring departments of Société Générale or BNP Paribas in some of those countries (Côte d'Ivoire, Sénégal, Ghana). There are also new initiatives around the factoring business such as new trading platforms in Africa, one being the Harare Receivables Exchange (HRE) in Zimbabwe. A number of these initiatives have been nurtured by Afreximbank and developed through the platforms and opportunities presented by IFG/FCI to which it is affiliated and serves as chair of the African Chapter.

V. Conclusion

In the 1970s and 1990s, factoring emerged in many developing regions, including Africa. Whereas the product grew remarkably in many countries in Asia and South America, it remained low and concentrated in a few countries in Africa. The limited growth was the result of limited supply chains, poor legal and regulatory environments to formalise and govern the industry, a weak financial services industry, and the various other forces mentioned above. Nevertheless, factoring has grown appreciably in recent years reaching an estimated EUR 27 billion in 2016, five times higher than the level in 2000. New markets are also emerging across the continent, including Kenya, Ghana, Nigeria and Ethiopia, among others.

More efforts are required to maintain the current growth momentum of factoring in Africa. Afreximbank, working with its partners has, over the last few years, embarked on a number of initiatives, including aggressive awareness campaigns, sponsoring the creation of model laws, capacity building programmes for factors and industry regulators and financial institutions. These efforts are yielding positive and noticeable results. Cameroon, Egypt and Nigeria are currently developing national factoring acts which will formalise the Industry and regulate the conduct of the business in those countries. The awareness level across the continent has grown remarkably. Despite this success, relentless effort is required to ensure the realisation of the full benefit of the product and the various interventions put in place across the continent. Funding will be required to sustain the capacity building programmes and awareness creation regarding the factoring product. Further, active participation of established factors in Europe, the Americas and Asia in Africa's Factoring Industry will foster the investment and innovation required to realise the substantial business opportunities which factoring offers in Africa. FCI, as an acknowledged leading Factoring Industry association, has an important role to play in attracting the investments and interest needed to exploit opportunities. Afreximbank is committed to fully implement its strategy for promoting factoring in Africa.

Epilogue: Disruption and New Environments in a Dangerous World

Patrick DE VILLEPIN

Global Head of Factoring, BNP Paribas

In the face of negative interest rates in the Eurozone and symbolic rates for most other currencies, factors in Europe and on other continents stand up to each other in a context of pitiless competition. In this game of extremes, the large corporates frequently dictate their price. They use their credit lines as they will, frequently with parsimony, at the end of the quarter for the sole purposes of deconsolidation. They also benefit from very low terms: derisory margins and symbolic commissions. For the factors, the return on notional equity demands of their parent bank companies represent insurmountable obstacles to improved results, in a crucial period that calls on them to invest for their future.

The period is also one of disruptive technologies in product innovation and digitisation:

- Creativity is constantly increasing in terms of the product range. Long gone is the time when factoring could pass as a single-product activity. It is now part of the ever larger and more complex family of working capital solutions: on the one hand, there is factoring vs. invoice discounting for the large corporates (see chapter 24), on the other there is reverse factoring or confirming for major accounts (see chapter 25), and finally, ABL for mid-caps (see chapter 26);
- The rise of the fintechs (see chapter 27) is putting pressure on the decidedly closed world of receivables finance. Should they be authorised to play in their sandboxes or should they compete on a level playing field, such as traditional players do? Their increasing number and the diversity of their strategies and positioning constitute a short-term threat (and maybe a mid-term opportunity) for the most established of factors. Although only a minority of them will achieve breakeven and carve out a real place in the market, their breakthrough over the long-term is all but inevitable in niche areas or market segments that factors do not always manage to penetrate. To counteract such developments, the traditional players will have to review their practices: redefine the client journey, digitise their processes and reduce their operating costs in order to become tech companies themselves. The other solution is to acquire a fintech without merging it with its own personnel in order to retain the energy, dynamism and the lifeblood of innovation.

Such disruptive approaches are all the more complicated to successfully implement due to the new environment taking shape that sits badly with creativity and improvisation:
- The new regulatory framework (see chapter 28) is increasingly imposing alignment with strict liquidity and solvency standards, with equally burdensome regular reporting requirements;
- Similarly, compliance rules (see chapter 29) are anything but vague and must be applied with rigour and discipline;
- Finally, risk awareness (see chapter 30) is a basic condition for long-term survival. To the classic credit risk must be added the factor's traditional risks, namely dilution, commingling and recovery management capacity, not to mention the major risk for the profession: operational risk management to curb the multiple forms of fraud. Faced with such risks, mitigation in the form of credit insurance is not a widespread phenomenon.

In such an environment, it is important to ensure that the various players enjoy equivalent competitive conditions. Yet this is manifestly not the case. The example of the EU demonstrates the extent to which the differences can be considerable depending on the size or location of the business:

- Location: depending on the country of origin, a factoring firm may be either an unregulated commercial company (UK or Belgium, apart from bank subsidiaries), a financial firm (Germany) or a specialist credit institution (in France, in the case of an institution holding a European passport);
- Size: according to the "sandbox" theory or the progressive increase in regulations, a fintech may be subject to a greater or lesser degree of regulatory and compliance rules, whereas more established factors are permanently subject to numerous controls and requirements by regulatory bodies.

Faced with such constraints, the defensive and self-centred attitude of Europeans does not constitute an adequate response. Legal, technical and financial unification of the conditions underpinning the exercise of the profession within the EU would only suffice if it were to become a global phenomenon. The somersaults in the Chinese market in recent years, increasing levels of default and, notably, instances of fraud, are all testament to this fact. Although the decline of the old continent might seem inevitable in the long-term, it is important that the same rules apply everywhere (single status associated with the practice of factoring) and that competitive conditions are harmonised and uniform. To this end, collaboration between regulators must be intensified and translated into reality.

A – Disruption

24. Factoring vs. Invoice Discounting

Adrian Rigby

Chief Commercial Officer and Deputy Head of Trade and Receivables Finance, HSBC

Factoring and invoice discounting are major sources of working capital and risk mitigation globally. In the past 50 years, they have progressed from niche to mainstream. In the UK, one of the largest markets, that growth has been principally through invoice discounting; a product which powerfully combines those fundamental benefits with particularly low cost, but continued high control compared to working capital loan products that makes it safe for the client and provider. Clients can choose between factoring or invoice discounting based on their needs, the balance of cost and benefits and differences of availability.

I. Understand the Client's Wants and Needs Before Presenting Product Solutions

Before we offer any product solutions, the financial institution needs to take time to understand the client's business. Only when we have that understanding can we decide whether to present a product at all. We can also establish which of a range of product solutions might best combine to address the underlying need, as well as offering the client a choice.

This approach leads to longer lasting and mutually rewarding relationships. It also helps prevent miss-selling or any misunderstanding, especially when combined with a level of sales discipline. That sales discipline includes presenting the choices, ensuring clients have time to consider offers and to take independent advice on what is a major financial decision. Financial institutions can offer comprehensive solutions as well as individual products.

This approach is also vital in the fight against financial crime, for if we truly know our clients we will keep the "bad actors" out and stop them from accessing the financial system to launder the proceeds of crime, breach sanctions, finance terrorism or steal from our business and clients.

Understanding the client's needs starts with a conversation to get to know their product including all the steps from initial order to payment. This gives insight into the working capital cycle and, from that, the underlying needs that require product solutions. For example:

Imagine a consumer goods company sourcing in Asia and supplying major European retailers. The ultimate buyers pay on O/A credit and Asian suppliers must be paid before the goods are dispatched by sea to Europe.

Table 12: Trade line analysis: A structured conversation; talk with a seller through their steps from order to payment

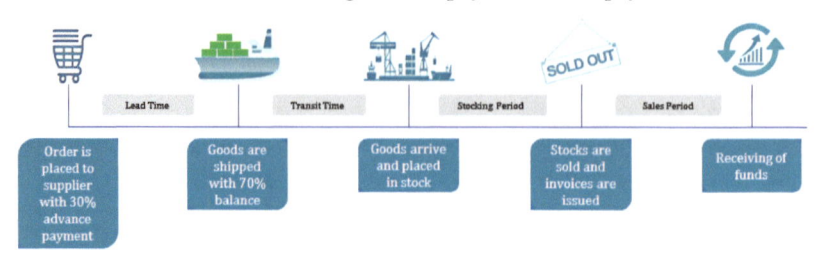

Lead Time	Transit Time	Stocking Period	Sales Period	
Order is placed to supplier with 30% advance payment	Goods are shipped with 70% balance	Goods arrive and placed in stock	Stocks are sold and invoices are issued	Receiving of funds

Record the key steps and the cash flows: money out to suppliers, money in from buyers

The detailed conversation will identify opportunities to help the business. For example:

a) O/A credit terms might be paid 40-60 days after invoice date depending upon the country:
   – Is the client performing credit control effectively? If not, then a product to help speed up buyer payment might be more appropriate than providing finance alone;
   – What degree of credit risk is the seller taking on the buyers? If the exposure is concentrated or high in relation to the capital of the business, then credit risk mitigation is a potential need;
   – If the client is publicly quoted, it might need to demonstrate the efficiency of its asset management and thus need to maximise free cash flow and avoid high gearing.

b) When do creditors need to be paid compared to incoming payments? With overseas manufacture, sea transport and a stocking period, this company has a significant cash flow gap:
- Should they consider issuing an LC instead of paying in advance? An LC could justify their suppliers providing a credit period rather than paying cash on dispatch. This will give the suppliers access to competitive local funding and narrow the cash flow gap for the client;
- Can the goods-in-transit period and any European stocking period be structured to attract self-supporting loan facilities which are repaid when the company can invoice the end buyer?
- Receivables finance can be raised once the goods are in transit to the buyers. The facilities can be structured to ensure repayment of any trade loans or LCs. Their size will increase as sales to credit worthy buyers increases, and thus increases in line with the need to pay creditors. If sales decline, and thus the need to pay creditors declines, the facility adjusts down in line. This reduces risk for the bank and client.

In summary, we need a clear picture of how cash moves out and comes into the business as trading activity is conducted. With the client, we can explore whether sales and profits can be maximised by negotiating changes in terms with suppliers and buyers (for example asking for more credit from suppliers or faster payment from buyers) and whether the client and the bank's products can be structured to drive the best results. For example, sometimes the best solution is to offer suppliers faster payment and give buyers more time to pay; with the right risk mitigation and financing in place that may optimise sales and profits for the client.

It is important to emphasise that whilst financing is the most common need it is not the only one. Accelerating cash flow through effective credit management can make a strong contribution to business success. Receivables are frequently the largest single asset a business owns and getting independent insight into the credit standing of buyers is wise and then backing that up with protection against insolvency is prudent. Buyer insolvency is not frequent, but it is potentially devastating. Cash flow can also be strengthened through a factor's mitigation of the risk of payment delay. The example above also pointed to this as a need felt by even the largest publicly quoted companies. That is to provide generous credit terms to buyers but to do so without adverse impact on key financial ratios, which are the focus of investors. Those needs, like the need for finance and services felt by unquoted or younger fast-growing businesses, can be addressed through these products.

II. Factoring Compared to Invoice Discounting

Factoring and invoice discounting are both receivables finance products with added service elements. The most common difference between them is that invoice discounting is typically undisclosed to the buyers. In the ICC "Standard Definitions for Techniques of Supply Chain Finance", invoice discounting is a variation of factoring.

In factoring, the client will deliver the goods or service and raise the invoice to the buyer. The invoice will be assigned to the factor with a notice to buyer to pay the factor when the invoice is due. The factor will pay the client 80-90% immediately and the balance when the buyer pays.

The factor can take the risk that the buyer is financially unable to pay, thus protecting the client from buyer insolvency. This is called "limited recourse" or "non-recourse" factoring and if the client does not take up that option then it is with full "recourse".

Factoring is a good choice if the client would benefit from the factor's involvement in collecting the invoices. Factors have well trained staff and good systems to do that; they can undertake the work in their own country and, through FCI, globally where selling on O/A credit is appropriate. In the example above, if the client is not collecting receivables effectively, payments will come in late and will not be properly reconciled, adding to cash flow pressure. An efficient sales ledger operation could improve cash flow materially and sometimes significantly reduce the financing requirement. Cross-border sales bring in the additional challenges of different languages, practices and time zones, while factors through FCI cooperate to bring appropriate expertise to best serve exporters.

Asking the factor to undertake collections has often been a choice for young and fast-growing companies, so they can focus on growing sales and avoid having to put in credit management teams that become fixed overheads for the business. That need is not confined to SMEs. In fact, some of the largest manufacturers use this service in supporting their distributors.

To maximise sales, the distributors need generous credit terms, as they are frequently operating on relatively small capital bases that requires very careful credit management from their supplier, something which can be delegated to the factors.

Factoring is also a good choice when the legal environment in the client's country provides a sound basis for disclosed assignments but leaves the position of undisclosed assignments ambiguous or weak. Factoring is almost universally recognised as a business tool which gives the financial community a direct security interest in the receivables and thus it is an alternative to taking charges over property or personal guarantees. Invoice discounting is recognised in some jurisdictions but is not as universal as factoring and must frequently be supplemented by additional security.

The factor's ability to contact the buyer directly also provides a high degree of reassurance that the invoice is valid and collectable, and this underpins the high level of finance that is provided to the client. This is especially important to fast growing and younger businesses who have a limited capital base: if they have a good product and good clients, ready access to working capital finance removes a significant barrier to achieving higher sales and profits.

Invoice discounting also provides post-sale finance and the option of buyer credit risk mitigation. The difference with (full) factoring is that the buyers are not normally told of the assignment of the invoices and continue to pay the seller. The seller collects the buyer payments on behalf of the discounter. This will be a good choice for clients who have an established infrastructure to collect the receivables and a strong enough capital base such that the discounter does not need the immediate reassurance of direct contact with the buyers.

When providing invoice discounting, the benefits to the financier of regular direct contact with buyers must be replaced by other risk mitigants. That is typically through audits of collections activity, supporting evidence for the invoices, plus specific security such as registration of the security interest where a local registration system exits, such as in the USA and UK.

Both products benefit from specially designed systems and highly trained staff. These ensure that the close understanding of the client's needs established at the start of a relationship continue throughout. Clients' needs change and so it is important to adjust the size and structure of any facility. Most businesses survive and thrive but rarely without challenges during the journey and of course some get into difficulty. The systems and people need to be able to recognise those challenges and direct appropriate support. It helps of course when the client is open about their issues.

The factoring and invoice discounting industry has a strong commitment to training and professional standards. Industry bodies such as FCI take a leading role, providing professional training and examinations in all the specialist areas and they deliver that globally.

Thus, in summary, factoring and invoice discounting are both products that enable a business to offer credit terms to buyers in support of sales whilst accessing immediate liquidity to pay their suppliers. They do that by providing a high level of advance against the invoice values anticipating settlement from the buyers. The financier has the security of being entitled to the sales proceeds and is able to check that validity of the receivables through buyer contact, audit visits and careful monitoring.

The clients benefit from access to liquidity, so they can pay suppliers on time and they avoid the "over-trading" risk when growing sales, as access to liquidity grows with sales.

Both services offer the option of buyer credit risk mitigation. This is an alternative to trade credit insurance. Factoring also relieves the client of much of the policy compliance burden.

A factor will be in direct contact with the buyers usually undertaking the credit control activity. This relieves the client of a task and validates the receivables to justify a high level of advance to even young and fast-growing businesses.

A discounter leaves the credit control activity with the client. For clients with the infra-structure to do this well this means the service charges of invoice discounting can be lower than factoring. Some will prefer that their financing arrangements are not disclosed to their buyers and thus they prefer "confidential "invoice discounting.

The key point is that any decision between the products is made after a thorough evaluation of the underlying needs and then the client can be presented with the most appropriate solution and potentially with choices from the range of alternatives.

III. Factoring and Invoice Discounting Products Within the Trade Finance Product "Family"

As in the example illustrated, factoring and invoice discounting are typically complementary to traditional trade finance products such as LCs. When reviewing the working capital needs of a business, each has its place, and the client and financer both benefit when they can be structured together in an integrated solution.

Factoring vs. Invoice Discounting 315

The products can also be alternatives with a different balance of prior commitment and risk mitigation. A "risk ladder" may be used to bring out the risks and opportunities that arise when competing for clients. The products can be chosen based on the appetite for risk and the acceptability of the terms from buyers.

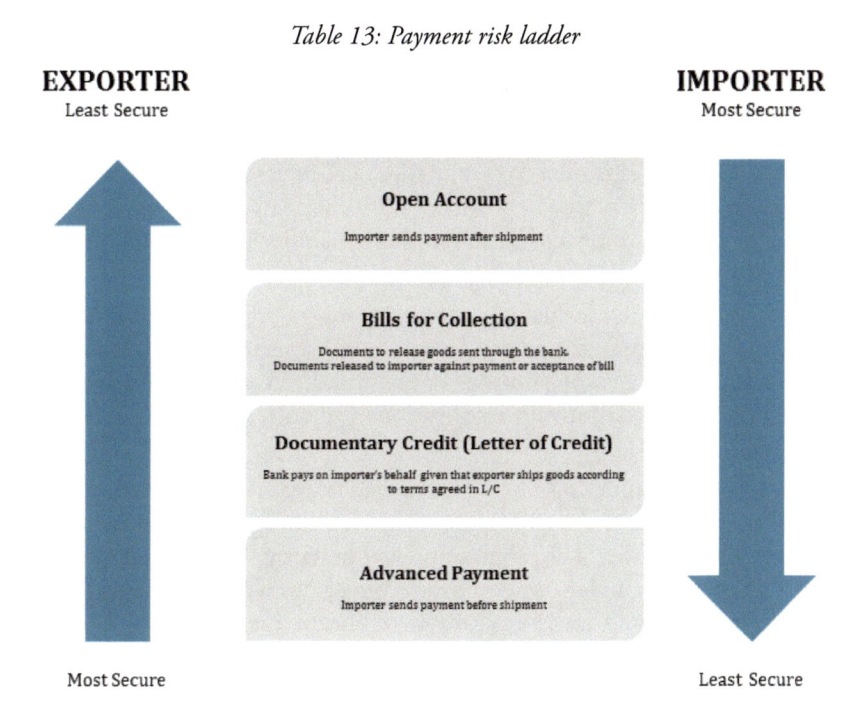

Table 13: Payment risk ladder

EXPORTER — Least Secure (Most Secure at bottom)

IMPORTER — Most Secure (Least Secure at bottom)

- **Open Account**: Importer sends payment after shipment
- **Bills for Collection**: Documents to release goods sent through the bank. Documents released to importer against payment or acceptance of bill
- **Documentary Credit (Letter of Credit)**: Bank pays on importer's behalf given that exporter ships goods according to terms agreed in L/C
- **Advanced Payment**: Importer sends payment before shipment

Thus, if a supplier asks clients to pay in advance, there is very little risk to the supplier but lots of risk to the buyer. A buyer would either be desperate for a unique product or ordering in very small quantities. Next in the ladder is an LC: it allows the buyer a period of credit and ensures there are strict standards for proof of shipment, for example, and in exchange the buyer gives a strong payment commitment. O/A credit gives the buyer maximum flexibility. The buyer does not have to provide a bank guarantee but may choose the exact timing of payment. The seller faces the risk of buyer default but is offering the maximum credit support to encourage sales. Factoring and invoice discounting can provide finance and risk mitigation to O/A sales, whilst traditional trade products provide the LC and related finance products to the buyer that depend on the LC.

IV. Factoring and Invoice Discounting Compared to SCF

SCF is typically "buyer" initiated whereas factoring and invoice discounting are "seller" initiated. It is another source of working capital finance that can complement factoring and invoice discounting; it can also be an alternative.

SCF is initiated from the buyer. The motivation is to enable the buyer to take the maximum amount of supplier credit so that his own free cash flow is strong. It ensures the supplier has access to finance from the point at which the buyer accepts the goods or services until payment is due. The buyer can also use its own, typically high, credit standing to ensure that financing costs are as low as possible. With their supplier having assured access to finance at low cost, the supplier reliability is strengthened, and costs of supplies are kept as low as possible for the buyer.

SCF is normally available only from buyers who are highly credit worthy and strongly supported by their relationship banks. These are not facilities that can be completely uncommitted, and withdrawal can have important relationship implications for both the buyer and SCF Supplier.

A supplier considering whether to use factoring or invoice discounting, or take advantage of their buyer's supply chain programme, is fortunate to have choices. The SCF programme will be fairly simple to set up and gives assess to financing as soon as the buyer has approved the invoice. The legal structure that is typically used means the supplier no longer faces any credit risk on the buyer, because the invoice has been paid. Of course, the supplier remains fully accountable for the product quality.

A supplier might prefer factoring or invoice discounting depending on how many other buyers there are and whether, by entering a factoring programme, they can more readily finance, and risk manage, all their sales.

In addition, the timing of access to finance can be important differences. Factoring is normally accessed once goods have been dispatched rather than when goods have been delivered, checked by the buyer and the invoice approved for payment. For some companies, that process will take one week, for others it can be a month or more. If the time is extended before a buyer approves invoices under an SCF programme, then the financing need may be better addressed through factoring or invoice discounting.

One unsung benefit of setting up an SCF programme is that it motivates the buyer and supplier to reduce the time it takes to approve invoices. That will typically require an in-depth review of the process and reveals scope to improve, for example, the accuracy of orders, dispatched quantity and quality, and invoice details; all issues which will have slowed approval in the past. All this reduces waste and speeds the flow of cash.

Factoring and invoice discounting can provide support to a client across all their buyers. This gives a comprehensive solution and offers the factor/discounter sufficient spread of risk and size of facilities to justify their most competitive terms. The client who has the option of a SCF programme for one or some of their buyers can usually agree to exclude them from the factoring/discounting programme if the overall terms will be most favourable.

25. Reverse Factoring and Confirming

Josep Sellés

Manager for Factoring and SCF, Gedesco Services Spain
Vice Chairman FCI, Chairman of the SCF Committee

ONCE UPON A TIME, in a respectable European kingdom called Spain, the factoring subsidiary of an important bank was worried because they were not able to get sufficient lines on debtors and they were not able to build factoring contracts. The economic situation of the country (1990) was not good, the health of the companies was not the best and risk was an issue.

The management of this company, Banco Santander (it is not a secret), started thinking about how they could manage to use the good risk of existing, financially solid companies to develop factoring. But the problem is that they knew the solvency of these companies, these potential debtors, but they did not have sellers asking for lines on them.

What could they do?

Finally, they decided to create a product based on the risk of the debtor, with risk under their control, starting the process of reverse factoring. Up to then (and even many years after), reverse factoring was a product involving a buyer and a seller, but normally, after contacting the seller, it ended with the signature of a factoring contract with the financial company, with only one debtor, on which it put the weight of the risk. In the new product, at that time still without a name, the arrangement was not between one seller and one debtor, but among one debtor and many sellers. This was a very important difference that converted the product into a new one.

At the beginning, it was not easy to convince people, companies, about the relevance of the product, including their own internal organisation of the Bank that was doubtful about the possibilities of the product. The team had to work hard to convince people internally first and the potential clients later on. The clients were apparently interested in the product but at the same time they had some fears. For instance, one of the doubts was if the bank should pay the suppliers on time. The buyer is externalising all the payments to its suppliers to the bank. If the bank fails to do it, the suppliers will blame the buyer, not the bank, as it is the buyer's responsibility for payment management, not the banks.

Another important issue was that the product obliged the buyer, in many cases, to change the organisation of the company. The time spent by the purchasing department to approve an invoice was not important at that time, as the payment terms in Spain were long ones (90/120 days).

Now, using this product, this time lapse became very important as the supplier was waiting for the financial proposal and it could not wait one month. So, the buyer had to adapt its internal circuits to the product demands and it took time.

But on the other side, the product offered the big buyers the possibility of helping their suppliers that, in times of crisis, had problems in obtaining facilities to finance their sales to them. Using the quality of the risk of the buyer, the supplier had the possibility of easily financing the invoice.

And another attractive point was that the buyer was able to unify the different payment tools existing in the market, bills of exchange and promissory notes, while the supplier could avoid paying the obligatory "stamp duty" tax on these tools.

With this panorama, the bank started to commercialise the product but the result at the very beginning was discouraging. Most of the companies looked interested but no one signed a contract. Many were reluctant to be the first using the product. If something failed, the commercial consequences could be important, since what was at risk was the buyer's relationship with his suppliers. Doubts about the future of the product were on the table and at times the possibility of throwing in the towel was present as well.

But the bank had the sufficient cold blood and patience and, why not to say, the confidence in the product to maintain the original plan and keep on trying to sell it. And the reward arrived, one year after the starting day, the very first client!

And it was the starting signal. After this client, others arrived, and, with progressive development, the product started being known by the suppliers (another barrier at the beginning was the lack of awareness of the suppliers) and the percentage of acceptance of advanced payments started to grow.

I. Why Confirming?

Sometimes it has been said that the name was inspired by the confirming houses, basically located in London, companies that have gradually almost disappeared.

The answer is simpler. At that time, all the departments ending with "ing" were together in the structure of the bank: leasing, renting, factoring, forfaiting, and – as the product was based on confirmed invoices – Santander decided to call it *confirming*. It registered the name, a situation that created tension with other competitors but also confusion, as clients were visited by different banks trying to sell the same product under different names. And probably, this is my opinion, this is one of the reasons why, internationally, the product has been called under different names too.

SCF was the first name identifying the product at an international level. We have many examples of advertisements of financial institutions offering SCF when in reality they are offering confirming. And this confusion has gone far till today in which, according to some, confirming is "something that we do in Spain". On the contrary, confirming is the same product offered to clients around the world, also referred to as SCF, reverse factoring, payables finance, including other names as well. But it is the same. I have always seen a resistance to accept that the product was born in, and expanded from, Spain.

When tackling new markets, Spanish banks always start by offering "confirming" as the driver to have those markets on boarded. Then, competitors react accordingly, as is the rule, and the product expands in those new countries. And it is still happening today, 27 years later. That is how the product was born. It is interesting to know it, as this product, that we have seen come to life, has been offered today in many markets to clients.

After all this time, the experience accumulated in Spain is monumental! The product has evolved always with three focuses:
- To offer an excellent service to the buyer and the suppliers;
- To reach a percentage of acceptance of advance payment as high as possible, as this is where the profitability of the product lies;
- To improve the automation of the process to make the product easy to handle, reducing operating costs at the same time.

II. Volumes

We have problems in getting the exact figures of the product around the world. Some countries do not collect the figures because, in certain cases, the product is offered by the bank, not the factoring subsidiary: in other cases, because it is aggregated with factoring volumes, unfortunately. Therefore, we cannot count on reliable figures.

That said, FCI's Annual Global Industry Activity Report estimates SCF/reverse factoring/confirming to be around 8% of the reported 2016 world industry turnover of EUR 2,375.9 billion, that is approaching EUR 200 billion.

Equally, each year, BCR publishes an interesting book on SCF, trying to collect information from countries that do declare the volumes. In the 2016 figures, the total amount exceeded EUR 447 billion. If we consider that Spain alone accounts for more than EUR 50 billion, the BCR total may be somewhat high.

Talking with American banks, they calculate (they do not have official figures either) that the volume in the USA is about EUR 25 billion. And like the USA, some other countries are not in the BCR collection of figures. Therefore, this suggests the total volume worldwide may reach close to EUR 200 billion, lower than BCR's figures but more in line with FCI data. This indicates the increasing importance of the product. And it is going to expand, first, because awareness of the product keeps growing, and second, because it is complementary to the activity of a factoring institution.

Probably the most important change is regarding the credit assessment. Up until now, traditional factoring companies were working on clients whose risk was spread, partially, relying on the risk of multiple debtors. With reverse factoring/confirming, it is the contrary: all the risk is focused on one buyer. As a consequence, it means concentration, a word that does not provoke enthusiasm among the Factoring Industry.

III. Future Development

Two years ago, FCI decided to start a project that can foster the development of the product.

Reverse/confirming is, at the end of the day, a factoring deal. The supplier, when accepting the advanced payment proposal is at the same time assigning the invoice to the financial institution, transforming the operation into a factoring one.

The product has been developing without any sort of association or other kind of institution waving its flag. FCI decided that it could take this role, but it needed to build something that could help the Industry and attract new members to the organisation.

One of the main assets of FCI is the network of correspondents, quite impressive after the union with IFG: 400 members in 90 countries. How could this network be beneficial, how could it be used in the SCF industry?

SCF was born to cover domestic business. But, over the years and with the acceleration of globalisation, companies buy more and more outside their own country. Sometimes, it creates difficulties in on-boarding suppliers due to legal and tax regulations, or simply due to the lack of knowledge that the supplier has about the product. The supplier receives a proposal of being paid in advance from a distant country, from a bank that he probably does not know. We cannot blame him for doubting what he has in his hands and its reliability. Here is where FCI's network can play a role and be useful to its members.

The financial institution of the buyer can ask for help from a correspondent in the country of the supplier for different reasons such as:

- To perform KYC/AML procedures;
- To explain to the supplier the benefits of the product to on board it;
- To organise a traditional cross-border factoring arrangement involving seller and buyer, export and import factoring.

This is a reality. FCI is already in the launching phase. FCI is now defining, through the GRIF, the responsibilities of the import and export factor, commissions to be paid, etc., opening the Chain to this new activity and adding another service to the current list of products that the Chain already provides today.

For the anchor buyer's Financial Institution, to find a performing IT platform that allows to develop reverse factoring with their clients and to avoid the significant initial investment normally required by the IT vendor has been a challenge. With FCI's solution, it introduces a big step forward for this business.

FCI has called this product FCIreverse.

To make reverse profitable you need to have an effective platform to avoid operational costs. And buying this platform implies an investment that, depending on how mature the market is, for instance, may not always yield a sufficient return. This was a barrier for many to start doing this business.

What FCI is offering is to eliminate this initial investment, this initial barrier. The platform will also offer the possibility of doing not only cross-border but also domestic business. This is new in FCI, always immersed in the world of cross-border business, cross-border factoring.

Now FCI, with FCIreverse, offers a complete service for both domestic and cross-border business.

The potential of this initiative lies in opening the possibility to many members of FCI to start offering this business, and normally the beneficiaries will be more of the medium and small members rather than the big ones, which normally have their own platforms already.

Another aspect that FCI will cover is education. Today it is difficult to find a course about SCF in the market. Some are for the internal use of the banks; others are more focused in convincing potential buyers. FCI will offer its members a complete range of courses with the objective of providing them with an SCF education.

This is why I am convinced and optimistic regarding the future of this business. It not only has to do with the natural growth as experienced up to now: there is now an accelerator for having more and more companies convinced that reverse/confirming is an interesting product to offer to clients.

Everything started 27 years ago, with a lot of difficulties. But finally, the product has reached a considerable success. Everybody, in conferences and articles around the world, talks about SCF as a product for the future. But today, it is already a reality.

In this case, FCI is not inventing a product. SCF is already in the market and what FCI will do is to facilitate access to it. In fact, 50 years ago, FCI did not invent factoring. What FCI did was to establish the necessary rules, create the necessary network to foster cross-border factoring that up to that moment was very difficult to offer to clients due to the lack of correspondents and legal uncertainty.

IV. Conclusion

This is what it was, this is what it is, and this is what I think the future of this product will be, curiously known under different names, but being the same at the end of the day.

A product that can be a driver of development for factoring in emerging markets in which the suppliers can benefit from the solvency of a big debtor, maybe a multinational company located in the country, helping them at the same time to finance the invoices that, due to the low development of the financial system in the country, they cannot easily get from banks.

I am not going to write in the 100 years' commemoration book, if books still exist by then. But I am sure that the book will have a chapter talking about this product and its strong development along the years.

26. Asset Based Lending (ABL)

John Brehcist

Roundwindow Consultancy Services

ABL is an evolving funding solution which owes much of its thinking, as well as many of its techniques and approaches, to traditional factoring practice and yet, in many ways, operates with a significantly different philosophy to its precursor. Its strengths facilitate greater secure leverage against a borrower's assets; its limitations mean that it is not viable in all circumstances or jurisdictions.

It takes advantage of the borrower's wider range of assets and therefore, in principle, its attraction is more broadly based; yet its providers will be more selective in their target demographics. In structure, it is often generally closer to a bank lending product than a traditional factoring purchase product, but it uses similar methodology. Whilst traditional receivables finance usually involves some form transfer of ownership, ABL is a secured lending solution. And although it is now a mainstream funding product in the USA, it has a much lower penetration in other markets. Its positioning is therefore unusually enigmatic for a finance solution; this chapter will consider the development of the product, explore this Janus character and consider the possibilities for its wider adoption.

I. The Start of ABL in the USA

ABL began to supplant factoring in the USA for several reasons.[1] The Factoring Industry had developed and was focused within a relatively limited number of industries: clothing, footwear, furniture and textiles dominated. Starting in the early 1970s, in pursuit of lower labour costs, manufacturing within these sectors was increasingly outsourced away

---

[1] In this brief history of the development of ABL in the USA, I am indebted to Charles Johnson of the CFA for his insights.

from the USA to lower cost countries. With these users moving offshore, demand for factoring reduced and providers watched as their portfolios began to shrink. Accordingly, the Industry started rapidly to consolidate down to a much smaller number of competitive suppliers.

At the same time, receivables ledgering, which had been one of the key full factoring offering elements, was becoming less attractive to users as low cost and increasingly sophisticated computerised accounting packages became easily available. Everyone could afford a PC and the software to keep track of debt; the thinking was why would one want to pay a factor to do this for them?

In such a changing market, providers needed to evolve. ABL became a way of exploiting the existing skill sets but operating in larger scale environments, funding growth, merger and acquisition and recovery situations. Banks that had greater financial resources than traditional factors began to see the benefit of the solution in the corporate market. The focus inexorably changed.

Today, ABL is used in a broad spectrum of US domestic and cross-border finance. Large and medium sized transactions of many types including buyouts, recapitalisations, Chapter 11 financing and corporate restructuring are actively supported across a range of sectors. Working capital finance for profitable, positive cash flow, smaller businesses using ABL techniques is now offered by the community banking system. For those that are unable to demonstrate such positive trends, specialist independent and entrepreneurial factoring companies offer traditional factoring solutions (and these finance providers are also now developing their own generally smaller scale markets successfully).

Key to the success of ABL's expansion in the USA has been the development of a common Bankruptcy Code and the implementation of the Universal Commercial Code which, between them, have created a consistent and reliable legal and regulatory environment. This consistency, combined with the introduction of common standardised documentation, has also allowed the development of syndicated deals where multiple providers cooperate to offer funding to deals that would ordinarily be beyond either the scale or the credit appetite of a single provider.

By the end of 2015, according to the CFA of America, the level of ABL credit commitment lines had reached approximately USD 218 billion, with actual loans advanced around USD 87 billion. The funding solution is now a significant element in the funding of corporate America and it is currently estimated to directly employ around 2,900 people.

II. The Development of ABL Outside the USA

With its common-law approach, relatively low levels of regulation and similar language, it is perhaps not a great surprise that the export and development of ABL took root in the United Kingdom via the channels of its USA bank relationships.[2]

Early pioneer Ted Ettershank developed the product through connections with the CFA of the USA and originally the approach taken was through assignment rather than being lending based, making delivery in the UK more closely aligned with a traditional factoring and discounting methodology. This operational difference was also reinforced by the legislative environment, where in the early 1990s, case law disallowed fixed charges on loan books, which made all but specialist providers tending to avoid the solution.

However, by the end of the 1990s, there was an emergence of providers with a mandate for developing cross-border funding. Structured deals over different classes on an international basis started to become more mainstream.

In the early 2000s, further providers started appearing and entered the market with ever increasing risk appetites and deals that were becoming more ambitious; there was talk of the first billion-pound syndication (although in reality it is unlikely that the market went much more than half this figure) and funding deals became very much more competitive and flexible. There was considerable concern that some of the deals at the fringe were becoming unsustainable, and the global financial crisis in 2008 brought this to the fore.

In the wake of the crisis, demand effectively collapsed; there was no countercyclicality. The next few years led to a series of sweeping up operations and from 2013 until the present there has been a radical consolidation in the number of ABL players, with significant changes of ownership.

That said, over recent years, much of the growth seen in the UK commercial finance industry has been at the medium and large corporate

---

[2] In this assessment of the development of ABL in the UK, I am indebted to Andrew Knight of Squire Patton Boggs for his insights.

end of the user spectrum, and ABL has been a significant part of that mix.

Data from UK Finance, the association for Asset Based Financing in the UK, suggests that its members' ABL grew to USD 5 billion of advances as at the third quarter of 2016. By that measure the sector currently represents around 6% of the scale of that of the USA; it is the longest established country outside the USA but is now being joined by other European countries where the legal environment is amenable to this type of solution.

According to FCI's Global Industry Activity Report of 2016, ABL is also reported in Belgium, Poland and the Czech Republic with end 2015 advance figures of EUR 5.1 billion, EUR 3.7 billion and EUR 0.6 billion respectively.

On this basis, at the end of 2015, ABL was globally advancing around EUR 92 billion versus the EUR 367 billion estimated for the traditional receivables finance industry.

III. The Mechanics of ABL

In ABL, the total funding availability is calculated by considering the ongoing values and liquidities of the individual asset classes that are suitable to be included within the facility.

The amount that will be offered against each class will depend on the ABL provider's relative ability to turn the particular asset type into cash (both in live and in distressed or gone situations); quite simply, the greater the level of confidence in eventual liquidity, the higher the relative level of funding that will be made available.

Accordingly, trade receivables will generally attract the same or a similar level of funding as a traditional invoice finance arrangement and an advance rate will be set contingent on debtor creditworthiness, ageing and concentration. Typical rates are therefore found in the range of 80-90%.

With stock or inventory the position is more complex and requires more careful consideration. This class may have subdivisions, for example raw material, work-in-progress, finished goods etc. In general terms, the less processed the asset, the more likely it will be easy to liquidate; the more finalised and specialised, the more challenging. Typical advance rates are in the order of 50% of the net realisable value of eligible assets.

Whilst some deals are inventory based or led, in general, on a global basis, the great majority of lending and activity is focused on receivables as the first line asset.

Although the ABL provider may typically have expert in house receivables valuation skills, it is also frequently the case that it may use third party specialist agents for inventory valuations. Such a decision to outsource is, of course dictated by issues such as the provider's internal scale and its risk management capability and policy.

Both plant, machinery and property classes will generally attract lower advance rates because of their greater complexity, challenge and risk in liquidation. With these asset types, external agents are more generally used by the lender as valuation can be a highly specialist and industry specific task. Rates reflect the increased risk in liquidation and may be in the 25-30% range.

Although (now) infrequently done, it is possible to consider intangible assets (such as brand value) as a basis for lending, providing they can be shown to have an independent market value; however, this is currently an unusual exception for most lenders.

Finally, the lender may offer an additional "cash flow" related element which will be based upon the projected cash generation of the borrower being sufficient to provide interest cover and capital repayment; to consider this option, the lender will accordingly need a high level of confidence in the realism of the projections, forward planning and management capacity.

The deal will be assessed and structured to ensure that it generates adequate liquidity and headroom for the anticipated needs of the client user.

This assessment of the ability of the user to generate cash to repay loan elements differentiates ABL credit risk from that of traditional receivables finance, where the credit risk is focused on the debtors only. That said, in general terms, such ABL deals are likely to be relatively covenant light compared to traditional lending structures as the assets are being monitored on an active and real-time basis by the lender.

Receivables and inventory lines are usually structured on a revolving basis, whilst other assets are generally treated on a term loan basis.

Of course, using the valuation approach above gives the lender an answer at a particular moment in time; the art and skill of the provider is to undertake this measurement and monitor continuously to maximise funding to the client whilst maintaining security in the collateral.

This constant monitoring and control is probably the key differentiator from a traditional balance sheet lending approach. Given its continuous nature, it is likely to be relatively more labour intensive and therefore potentially costlier both to provide and to pay for, although recent developments in software extraction for client enterprise resource planning (often known as ERP) systems are driving this cost down. However, for the lender this increased cost is offset by the greater security that monitoring provides, and the opportunity to lend securely to a higher level in any given situation, so generating an improved return on assets. For the borrower, there is very likely more leverage to be gained from the assets than from any other comparable source.

IV. The Applications of ABL

In recent years, both traditional finance providers and specialist financiers have been looking for new product markets. The result has been a shift in focus in mature markets from supporting mostly SMEs to finding ways of serving the corporate scale sectors as the providers, users and their advisors have learned to understand better the potential opportunities.

For the provider, ABL can create a new route to market, risk diversification, attractive return on assets, together with (in Basel terms) low Loss Given Default (LGD), secure lending (and therefore a lower cost of capital).

For existing invoice finance providers, ABL is an extension of their existing skills base, which already has a focus on asset dynamics and represents a logical progression through asset liquidity.

The lending nature of the product, and the now widespread use of consistent compatible loan documentation, also means that joining forces with other providers to offer facilities that otherwise would be beyond individual credit appetite has become readily feasible.

For the informed user, there is access to a finance vehicle that provides it with proportionately higher levels (compared with traditional bank lending products) of competitively priced funding, with potential headroom to support (for example) M&A activity, where for users increasing the level of debt funding and reducing the level of equity that must be released in a deal can be a very attractive option.

A rare win-win scenario is therefore available to both provider and user. So why is it that the market is not effectively limitless?

ABL is no panacea; it can only work effectively when, for example, receivables are for simple, discrete, identifiable goods and services, when inventory has intrinsic and sustainable value, where plant and machinery is not so specialised that it cannot be easily used in any other environment. It also requires an amenable and supportive legal environment; the asset class must be one where effective security can be perfected and maintained. Whilst most countries allow for this in their treatment of receivables, this is not always so, for inventory in particular.

At the lower end of the scale spectrum, ABL tends to compete with traditional invoice finance products; at the higher end, with securitisation and traditional lending products.

There is always a tension between the relatively high cost of labour intensive delivery and the user's willingness to pay for the service; the cost: utility ratio is not always compelling.

However, with this acknowledged, ABL can potentially make a significant contribution to the funding mix available for real economy businesses through extending the choices and solutions available to users. Not only is it viable in domestic situations, it can also be a highly effective tool in cross-border funding of international business, particularly where providers work in partnership to share their respective local market expertise.

27. Fintech, Between Innovation and Regulation

John BREHCIST

Roundwindow Consultancy Services

When the term was first coined, fintech (a portmanteau word derived from FINancial TECHnology) narrowly described the technology which supported and drove the back end of the established financial institutions, both consumer and trade. In recent years, its meaning has evolved into something which more describes both the technological innovations and also the organisations themselves that exist to provide financial services by making use of novel software and modern technology.

Fintech companies cover a comprehensive range of financial sub-industries, from crowdfunding and peer-to-peer lending, to algorithmic and themed asset management and investment. They also operate in payments, e-invoicing, financial data collection, credit scoring, digital currencies, asset and invoice exchanges, as well as working capital management. Their influence is even broader in impact if one considers operations like Amazon, Uber and AirBnB which rely on using disintermediating fintech payment solutions.

Providing innovatory on-line approaches, fintechs are starting to compete directly with traditional banks in many areas of the financial services and solutions sector. In general, banks tend to be less fleet footed in innovation than these new arrivals; their structures often tend to be more effective at maintenance than creativity. As a result, they often struggle to keep up with fintech start-ups in driving systemic change. On the other hand, they have the financial clout to market, monitor, acquire and absorb the winners among such generally small and investment hungry fledglings.

However, unlike the case of traditional providers, regulation and control have in general not yet caught up with the opportunities and challenges presented by these new models; indeed, in certain quarters, there is a clear political will to differentially promote these new solutions in light of a perceived lack of support for SMEs from traditional lenders, and a welcome for the disruption they provide. There is still a non-level playing field, a discrepancy in control which is especially apparent in the more highly regulated markets.

I. Boosting Innovation

For some, the arrival of fintech has created a potential "big bang" in terms of disruption; the technologies can, in principle, create the capacity to facilitate an integrated end to end online experience, something which the so-called millennial user now sees as an imperative.

Automation of traditionally time consuming financial checks such as risk analysis and credit assessment, the ability to reduce radically the time and workload of client on-boarding, and ability to meet money laundering driven requirements of KYC mean that the user experience of the process can be lighter, simpler and faster than existing methodologies allow.

It is also a worldwide phenomenon which conceptually has rapidly spread in both developed and emerging markets, providing an impetus which is bringing new approaches to online invoicing and collection services, online factoring, outsourced accounting and the arrival of a new breed of virtual neobank.

The effect and role of fintech in the receivables finance industry is accordingly developing rapidly and exponentially. The landscape of its application is changing and evolving continuously. On one hand, its impact represents a rising tide that is becoming more widespread, more influential and more an everyday phenomenon. And as such, it ranges from technologies and concepts that are now around ten years old, for example invoice trading platforms, to technological developments with as yet nascent applications such as blockchain payment methodologies, which are cutting edge within the established factoring and commercial finance business. On the other hand, direct market penetration is as yet trivial – and it is to be seen whether the eventual role of these alternative players will match the undoubted hype that is greeting their arrival.

That said, the changes are rapid and sometimes unexpected both in nature and in direction. The pace of innovation means that the sector is generally ahead of regulation and traditional practice, a fact that is creating considerable disquiet in terms of seeking a level playing field for all actors. It also means the arena is a hotbed of challenge and operational risk which may provide traps for both the innocent and the unwary.

II. Challenging Traditional Factoring Players

From a receivables finance industry perspective, we need to consider whether the fintech entrants are creating a completely new experience, or whether the approaches are simply a logical extension of current practices, facilitated by new technology and utilising third party partners more effectively, to create a so called "factoring 2.0". Such an argument is not simply theoretical but central to considering the future direction and extent of these developments. So where do things stand?

Until now, probably the best known and most widespread form of fintech with a direct impact on the factoring and commercial finance business has been the invoice trading platform. In the broadest sense, these are technology driven channels to connect sellers of invoices with buyers of invoices. To this extent, although there are many variations on a theme, they do not represent a fundamental shift in the nature of the factoring transaction; an invoice is offered for sale and is purchased at a discount. What the platforms do, however, is to facilitate the trading, generally on a spot single invoice (or parcel of invoices) basis, and offer these to a range of competing buyers who may often bid on a reverse auction basis to finance the particular assets. The winning bidder is usually the funder who offers to provide the lowest rate/extended period combination.

The interparty relationship models vary. Often, between the seller and the platform, it is one simply of agent, where the platform introduces the seller to potential buyers without taking ownership or any financial responsibility, merely charging what is effectively an introduction fee, which may be a set price or a proportion of the invoice value. But at another extreme the process may involve acquisition (using the platform's own capital) and then collection from the debtor by the platform on behalf of the buyer.

The range of operational approaches is also very broad, with some providers looking simply like an "e-bay" auction house for invoices and having minimal involvement with the transaction, others looking remarkably like a traditional factoring company with a web based front end operating full services on a spot invoice funding basis.

Such platforms often have Applicaton Programming Interface (API) links into other fintech providers who offer (usually cloud based) interactions in terms of e-invoicing, payment and accounting solutions, KYC and on-boarding support.

This integration of often disparate individual financial applications offers both a challenge and an emulation opportunity for the traditional factors.

The breadth and range of provider models, of course, reflect the legal and regulatory environments where the platforms operate, but also the entrepreneurial mindset of their founders, and these often evolve as their exposure to risk and practical experience develops.

The fact that in many environments, the regulatory regimes have yet fully to appreciate, understand and certainly to encompass these rapidly developing associations and frontiers means however that at least some of the advantages currently available to the new entrants may be transient.

III. Trading Platforms' Development and Practice

The first major (USA based) invoice trading platform was The Receivables Exchange, set up by entrepreneurs who used their experience in competitive electronic asset trading to bring the platform together. The plan was to offer SMEs' invoices to potential investors via their proprietary trading platform which would offer the invoices in an auction and sell to the lowest discount bidder. In the early years, the first stage operation attracted high profile investments as a technology business e.g. from blue chip name Bain.

When, in 2011, NYSE Euronext acquired a minority stake the business was then split in two, with one stream focusing on what was described as "Corporate Receivables Program" which moved the model from SME levels to match corporate sellers in the Fortune 1000 with institutional and high net worth purchasers. The other stream continued to support the original SME business finance model. This element also created a venture with another business, Ariba, to seek to generate growth, but it appears that the anticipated volumes did not materialise, and it is understood that the stream closed down in 2012.

At the beginning of 2016, The Receivables Exchange business was rebranded as LiquidX and recapitalised, no longer having the involvement of the former NYSE as an equity partner. As at the beginning of 2017, LiquidX claims to be trading USD 400 million per month.

Whatever the specific final reasons for the disappearance of the first major name in the invoice trading platform space, more generally there appear to be two frequently experienced issues for trading platforms to face; first, their structural challenge in building profitable scale when working with transactional rather than relationship-based business, and second, an associated potential vulnerability to fraud related activity.

Public domain reports on the internet record that, over time, The Receivables Exchange undertook a number of high-profile, high-value recovery actions where alleged fraudulent invoicing had been involved. Fundamentally, invoices were being traded as though they were negotiable instruments with intrinsic value; this of course was not the case.

The reputational vulnerability of any on-line invoice finance provider to being associated with non-viable debt is something which, as platforms evolve, becomes more of a concern.

Outside the United States, it is in Western Europe that there has been the greatest proliferation of fintech entrants. The United Kingdom has the most established – albeit still somewhat limited – invoice trading platform experience.

Market Invoice, launched in 2011, was the UK's first online marketplace allowing companies to selectively sell outstanding invoices to raise working capital. The platform allows incorporated SMEs, who have unpaid sales invoices, to trade these with institutional investors online. The platform facilitates funding but does not collect the debt on behalf of the seller. In 2013, the UK government invested GBP 5 million lending funds through the British Business Bank, which it later increased to GBP 10 million in 2015; the PR effect of this high-profile support of fintech was considerable. In an evolving approach, it announced a tie up with an accounting software provider Xero to facilitate connection and upload of invoices offered for finance, and also launched a stream Market Invoice Pro aimed at larger turnover SMEs looking for a more continuous relationship. As at mid-2017, Market Invoice's website stated it has funded GBP 1.4 billion of invoices in the years since its inception.

Platform Black launched soon after, in 2012, and after initially operating with a simple trading platform structure and vociferous PR, it later developed a back-office function run by an experienced factoring professional, which replicated many elements of a traditional factoring company. In early 2017, its operations were rebranded by its owner as Sancus Finance, in which invoice finance would be co-presented with asset backed loans, vendor finance, SCF and education finance.

So divergent, evolving strategies have already been in evidence in this nascent market. To put it in context, the current combined trading volume of all UK invoice finance platforms is estimated by the author to represent around 0.2% of the total UK traditional invoice finance annual market.

And whilst overall volumes are increasing, this level of market penetration (achieved after more than four years' trading) compares in scale with that achieved by some individual smaller independent traditional providers. Substantial market disruption or substitution has not yet been evident.

At the same time, Aztec, an Irish based pioneer platform offering cross-border invoice discounting finance appears to have ceased to trade, only months after being included in Forbes' top 50 fintechs list.

At this relatively early stage in market development of invoice platform trading, the author is open to correction that it is hard, if not impossible, to find in any country a platform lender that can be valued as a commercial operation rather than a technological start up.

IV. Other Competitors to Traditional Receivables Finance

Whilst the direct competitive impact of invoice trading platforms on the Factoring Industry has been to date insubstantial, the rise of the Peer to Peer (P2P) lending market for providing short-term working capital and loans to SME businesses has perhaps been attracting greater awareness and interest. At this stage of market development, it has had marginally more overall impact than direct invoice finance as a potential competitor, offering a source of short-term working capital. Such P2P platforms provide the borrower with a very simple, quick and easy route to raising funds that are generally much less onerous and administration heavy than traditional routes. Whilst pricing may be marginally (or considerably) more expensive than traditional sources, the ease and speed of access can be a real differentiator.

These platforms have effectively disintermediated the lending market by matching potential lenders with potential borrowers with little on-line administration. As with invoice trading platforms, identity/KYC and underwriting checks are usually facilitated through proprietary or third-party applications, and the decision making is often highly automated.

Lender risk mitigation is an often-offered feature (and which again tends to differentiate from the invoice trading models where risk often remains with the seller). Lending may be made on a one-to-many basis, which reduces an individual investor's LGD, or, where lending is organised on a one-to-one basis, some providers have default protection funds which will pay the lender in case of debtor default. Whilst these are generally not regulated or supervised, and indeed can provide no absolute guarantees of payment, they do provide some comfort to participants (although this protection has not yet been tested in a downturn).

As with invoice trading platforms, the scale is still relatively small and does not match the hype. For example, in the UK, altfi.com data indicates *all time* total P2P Business lending to February 2017 is GBP 4.35 billion and platform invoice finance GBP 1.27 billion. Contrast this with traditional invoice finance turnover which, according to the trade association ABFA, is in the order of GBP 300 billion *per year*.

In Europe, the corresponding figures show the markets are even less penetrated. The same source of data indicates *all time* total P2P Business lending to February 2017 is EUR 388 million and platform invoice finance EUR 97 million. Again, this contrasts with traditional invoice finance turnover of EUR 1.5 trillion in the EU28 as reported by the EUF for 2016.

A more established and widespread fintech service is exemplified by the provision and management of supplier payment services on behalf of large scale buyers. The potential benefits of such a service have been significant; outsourcing non-core activity, standardising interaction with suppliers, standardising (and imposing) payment terms. Many banks and third-party providers offer these services and they are used by many of the largest global retail and manufacturing organisations. Arguably, this is a clear case of where a fintech approach has matured to mainstream.

A further step in the supplier payment program logic is to introduce supplier finance (in this narrow case sometimes called reverse factoring or confirming) which can be offered additionally to this otherwise administrative service, offering the sellers access to early payment at a discount.

The extension can be taken further by making the system entirely electronically based and operating the service exclusively on an e-invoice basis.

One of the key movers in this development was Tungsten Corporation which, in order to facilitate the financing element, signalled its commitment by acquiring a bank to deliver the treasury function of providing such funding, which it would deliver using its OB10 e-invoice payments management system. The argument was vociferous and the PR compelling and the initial public offering stock price reacted accordingly. However, the reality has been that the organisation has not yet achieved the anticipated benefits; despite the acquisition of some global scale, very well-known household name clients. There has been a high-profile departure of the founder, a restructuring which divested the bank, and a seriously reduced share price. The business now states that it expects to be profitable in 2017.

Of the fintech developments that are coming on stream, it is blockchain supported applications that might potentially have a widespread impact on existing financial transaction models. Originally based on the development of the cryptocurrency Bitcoin (allowing for all the "dark web" negative connotations that may still go with that), a blockchain is a type of distributed ledger, comprising unchangeable data packages. Transactions are referenced by multiple records outside the chain (a distributed ledger) and this ensures all data in the overall chain is effectively tamper proof, cannot be changed retrospectively and remains constant – an apparently "perfect" audit trail.

It is this ability to securely track groups and trains of related transactions in a clear time-based and verifiable manner that has significant implications for financial process management. However, until now, this has been rather uncharted territory with many different, inconsistent and non-interchangeable approaches. Rationalisation of the plethora of initial applications will be inevitable.

At the date of writing, some observers have therefore been reserving judgement about the potential for change that blockchain can deliver, believing it has been over promoted by its proponents. In any case, many businesses will be reluctant to use nascent "bleeding-edge" technologies at the heart of their operations until they see it risk-proven elsewhere.

At this stage, there have also been relatively few operational products which have matured from the pilot/concept stage. In Belgium, KBC with IT specialist Cegeka has recently launched a Digital Trade Chain (DTC) service, a blockchain solution that facilitates secure international trade between SMEs without the need for traditional documentary credits. The network is being expanded, with big name partners now including ING, RABO, ABN, Natixis, Unicredit, SocGen, Deutsche Bank and HSBC.

That said, there are two caveats the author would add regarding the development of blockchain; the first is a structural issue – the new technology relies on distributed ledgers. This is an issue which could potentially be countercultural to many organisations seeking to contain and centralise their operations and data control in order to optimise their compliance capability. The second is more fundamental – that the blockchain only describes the transaction, it is not the actual transaction. As with invoices, it is the credibility of the underlying trade that is critical, not the trail that records it. Whilst blockchain has the potential to increase security significantly and reduce the opportunity for tampering, it cannot intrinsically guarantee veracity of a transaction. A panacea it is not.

V. The Regulatory Environment

There is a continuing uncontrolled rush of new starters into the fintech environment, and, in general, regulatory bodies are neither yet fully cognisant of the potential impact, nor appropriately addressing the issues associated with the digital market,

That said, regulatory interest is starting to catch up. For example, in the case of the UK, any platform that has obtained Financial Conduct Authority permissions suddenly now has a financial value, whether or not it has any commercial business.

In an evolution that mirrors the developing awareness of the implications for the cross-border taxation status of auction/selling sites, and the need for consistency in operational regulation of gig economy applications like Uber and Airbnb, the financial and prudential regulatory authorities are becoming increasingly engaged with the challenges that fintech creates.

And in this context, the level of enthusiasm and support for fintech varies; the EU's DG FISMA has been very positively disposed to the nascent industry, for example in its "Advisory Support for SME Access to Finance", citing it as a potential source of capital for the SME population (that the EU sees as having been) under-served by traditional funders. On the other hand, the EBA and Basel Committee recognise the risks of quasi-banking to investors who have limited awareness of the risk and little in the way of protection or redress. Are fintech funding applications therefore something that should be considered in the context of shadow banking?

Their speed can certainly bring the fintechs some particular heightened risks; for example, their typically low touch, distributed risk analysis and credit evaluation can lead to increased fraud vulnerability, their fast turn-around can create time pressure to deal with AML, sanctions and anti-terrorism funding, leading to compliance risk. Accordingly, should they be regulated in the same way as traditional financiers? Or, recognising the need for flexibility in enabling a new approach to develop, should they be allowed to operate in a sandbox environment with a more fluid regime to allow experience and learning? Should they be left to their own entrepreneurial risk control?

There is not yet a consistent answer to these questions, and relative enthusiasm for imposing controls tends to mirror the level of regulation prevalent in the local country markets. But the author would suggest that as the market consolidates and as/should pioneer players fail, there will almost inevitably be investor and buyer fall-out, which will lead to increased pressure for greater regulatory control.

VI. Conclusion: the future Trajectory of Fintech

Fintech innovation can bring disruptive, challenging pioneers onto the scene, with their efforts rapidly engendering "me too" followers and proliferation. As the examples given show, there will always be winners and losers in this typical developmental scenario; the markets will eventually rationalise and concentrate; many of these alternative offerings will fall at the wayside. Where the technology proves itself, acquirers will look for the fittest and most able providers and target them for takeover, and these lucky few will become the norm of operation. As mentioned, at this early stage of the market, acquisitions are taking place on the basis of technology valuations, not because of the commercial value of the targets and this looks likely to be the position for some time to come.

The issue remains that, although fintech, in principle, can deliver a disruptive set of technologies which has the potential to fundamentally alter business models to make them more efficient and cost effective, they can also often be seen more prosaically as simply creating a technology-supported, alternative communication mechanism between provider and user.

The example of the invoice trading platforms demonstrates how the pioneers have struggled to gain traction and market penetration in direct competition with traditional providers. This may principally be because of a lack of (cost effective) differentiation that would prove ultimately to be either critical or sustainably valuable for users. Routes forward can include continued niche competition, sell-out, or partnerships. Traditional factoring companies (especially the smaller independents) may well also have capital or concentration issues that could make them open to operating income risk sharing arrangements with platforms.

Similarly, partnerships and referrals have become evident in the P2P loan environment, where tie-ups with banks and other lenders, who will refer potential borrowers that do not necessarily fully meet the institutions' lending requirements, but which nonetheless could represent legitimate realistic lending propositions.

It seems to the author the reality of the situation is that the arrival of fintech can be seen in two distinct lights. On one hand, it is yet another sequential development in the financial services sector (that started with the invention of coinage in Aegina, Ephesus and India around 700 BC) and as one which simply facilitates communication and trade between user and provider. On the other hand, it is a phenomenon delivering an industrial revolution that will cause disruption and reinvention in the delivery of existing financial services, with potentially earth-moving implications for the existing monolithic structures.

But it seems to me that scale disruption is likely to require scale players to deliver. As yet, there appears only to be a low level of interest and impact coming from the tech giants Apple, Google, Amazon and PayPal, who are for now (in the financial sphere) more focused on getting online C2B payments facilitated; only PayPal has had any meaningful involvement in the business credit market with online merchanting. They remain, however, to be heavyweight actors who could, without doubt, bring significant and potentially game changing influence should they become motivated to do so. In terms of fintech impact, it is they who present the greatest potential for global disruption; their trajectory for now remains the greatest unknown.

Notwithstanding these issues about who will drive the change, in the longer term, virtualisation of trade, end-to-end supply chain solutions, e-invoices, the progressive removal of cash from day to day transactions, and the imminent "Internet of Everything" all point to the reality of fintech evolving to become the essential driver of tomorrow's actual financial services industry.

Successful providers that are flexible and agile will adopt, deliver and profit from the strategies created and pioneered by the fintechs. A regulatory regime which adapts with an appropriate level of touch will follow to ensure these fintech facilitated services are both safer and more reliable. And, with this in place, the ultimate winner will be the end user who will have access to better, cheaper and faster services.

B – New Environment

28. From National Laws to European Supervision, Factors in a Varied and Changing Regulatory Landscape

Diego Tavecchia
Head of Technical Committees, International Affairs, ASSIFACT

Magdalena Wessel
Legal Department, Deutscher Factoring-Verband e.V., Chairperson Legal Committee, EUF

It is a common feeling with factoring professionals that the Industry is too regulated with respect to its short-term, low credit risk nature and to the lack of potential to generate and spread systemic risk. Although the answers vary from country to country, the feeling is quite diffused across the borders. From a lawyer's point of view, it is always a challenge to compare, and hence somehow evaluate, different jurisdictions and their laws – each jurisdiction has evolved separately for historical reasons, taking into account not only political and cultural specificities, but also economic developments and interests which are likely to have developed over decades or even centuries. The differences in the legal frameworks also involve different rules about licensing and application of prudential supervision, the level of which may also vary from country to country, as well as differing approaches to the measurement of capital requirements in the case of factoring. In the following, without in any way claiming to be exhaustive, we will provide the reader with a brief and simplified "map" to orientate him in the varied, challenging and changing regulatory landscape in which European factors operate, while also trying to answer the aforementioned question as to whether factoring is too regulated.

I. National Factoring Laws, a Various and Unequal Landscape

Legal Status: Regulated and Non-regulated Factoring Companies, Financial Institutions and Bank Assimilated Companies

First of all, it is necessary to highlight that there is no clear trend towards or against licensing and other supervisory requirements for factoring companies. Instead, the existence, as well as the absence, of such legal prerequisites is nearly evenly distributed throughout the EU.[1]

In some countries, factoring companies do not have to fulfil any supervisory requirements unless they are part of a banking group, which in itself entails meeting certain requirements. In other jurisdictions, factoring companies are required to obtain a license and be supervised as financial or even credit institutions, which generally entails a number of regulatory requirements such as capital or risk management requirements. However, the scope of these requirements varies from having to comply with only certain, more basic rules, for example regarding the corporate governance of the factoring company, to having to comply with nearly all the rules which apply to traditional banks, including requirements on, for example, regulatory capital and liquidity. Poland, Germany and Austria are good examples of these three levels of licensing and supervisory requirements.

Over recent years, however, a general trend has evolved of introducing regulation which is more detailed and extensive. Supposedly, this will make the financial sector more aware of certain risks and hence more stable and resistant in case of recession and crisis. This general trend increasingly affects the Factoring Industry, and up until a few years ago, such regulation was mainly a matter for the member states. However, with different European institutions such as the European Supervisory Authorities (ESAs) and the European Central Bank (ECB) taking on more and more supervisory, regulatory and even legislative tasks in the field of financial supervision, this part of the wide topic "compliance" is becoming more and more European.

---

[1] To help in getting a picture of the whole landscape, one can make good use of the *EUF Legal Study (Factoring, Receivables Finance & ABL – A Study of Legal Environments Across Europe*, 2013, updated in 2018.

Moreover, strong endeavours to regulate the so called shadow banking sector have been made over the past few years, partly as one of the lessons learned from the banking crisis and following the credit crunch of 2007 onwards.[2] In this context, the term "shadow banking" has been defined with a very wide scope: according to the Financial Stability Board's (FSB's) definition, which is mainly based on classification by economic functions, otherwise unregulated (i.e. generally non-bank) entities or companies offering factoring are also part of the shadow banking sector as they offer "loan provision that is dependent on short-term funding".[3] Although it may well be questioned whether factoring companies and, for example money market funds, should both be classified as part of the shadow banking sector in order to receive similar treatment from a regulatory and supervisory perspective, the wide scope of this definition is another reason for the increasing amount of regulation and supervision in the financial sector.

Factoring Laws and Legal Instruments: Differences and Similarities

If such supervisory environments in which factors operate vary among European countries, it is still worth noting that factoring and similar forms of receivables financing are practised in all EU member states, as well as in all five important non-EU jurisdictions contained in the EUF Legal Study 2013, which was updated recently. Unfortunately, this is where the unanimity ends and the differences start, beginning at such basic features such as the names given to these forms of receivables financing.

Something like a majority consensus can, however, be found regarding the question of how factoring is generally effected. In roughly four fifths of the jurisdictions, written contracts are concluded, be it because the law requires this written form (for example in Portugal for assignments) or because adequate evidence may be required in subsequent arguments (for example in Sweden and Poland). Hence, oral factoring agreements are very rare animals.

---

[2] Cf. e.g. the FSB's report "Strengthening Oversight and Regulation of Shadow Banking – An Overview of Policy Recommendations", 29 August 2013, http://www.fsb.org/wp-content/uploads/r_130829a.pdf.

[3] FSB's Global Shadow Banking Monitoring Report 2016, p. 47, http://www.fsb.org/wp-content/uploads/global-shadow-banking-monitoring-report-2016.pdf.

In some cases, requiring a written form goes hand in hand with requiring that the debtor be notified of the assignment of the receivable to the factoring company (this is the case in the Czech Republic), either directly or through registration in a public register. However, these requirements are apparently not acceptable to a wide majority of jurisdictions – they are one of many national legal specificities regarding factoring, with very different consequences if they are not fulfilled.

Another matter which may be considered more of a legal formality, but on which a large consensus exists, is that factoring is mostly carried out by the assignment of receivables from the factoring client as assignor to the factoring company as assignee. However, also in this case the saying of "there is no rule without an exception" seems to apply: The Netherlands handle things differently by using a pledge as the common legal instrument in factoring transactions, entailing further requirements such as written deeds and registration of the pledge.

These variations with regard to some basic traits of factoring and receivables financing already show that the legal framework in which factoring companies operate and offer their financial services is by no means uniform or harmonised. Notwithstanding this, there are also widespread similarities which can be detected.

In some, though not many countries, such as Germany and Latvia, a legal definition of factoring exists. Even though the number of such countries is quite small, it is interesting to note that more or less detailed and specified laws, acts and statutes on factoring and on the assignment of receivables exist in nearly all jurisdictions. Some of these laws are specific laws on factoring or the transfer of trade receivables such as in Turkey and Italy, while other laws deal with the transfer of receivables in a more general context, such as in the Austrian Civil Code. Germany is a good example for the combination of the two aforementioned approaches: for matters of civil or contract law, the more general Civil Code also covers factoring, whereas in the case of financial supervisory law, the Banking Act defines and regulates factoring.

In the EU as a whole, the European Court of Justice (ECJ) tried to define factoring with and without recourse in a VAT context in its 2003 judgment in the case of Finanzamt Groß Gerau and MKG Kraftfahrzeuge-Factoring GmbH (C-305/01), thereby providing some basic insights into what factoring is or is not, if only for VAT purposes in a case based in Germany.[4]

As for the definitions themselves, widespread similarities can be found. In Germany, factoring is the continuous purchase of receivables on the basis of a framework agreement, with or without recourse, while in Latvia it is the assignment of pecuniary debts in B2B-relations in return for the payment of a purchase price. In Malta, the definition is narrower in scope. There, factoring is seen as the assignment of one or more debts arising out of, or in connection with, the business of a trader as the assignor to a person licensed to carry out the business of banking or the business of factoring as the assignee.

Another legal question which is at the centre of each factoring transaction is whether the debtor needs to be notified of the transfer of receivables. In more than four fifths of all the jurisdictions included in the EUF's Legal Study, such a notification is required by law – another similarity revealed. Yet the reasons for this notification requirement differ. In some countries, such as Slovakia, this is a requirement for the assignment to be generally valid, while in Portugal and Poland, such a notification is only necessary for the factor to be able to collect the debt in his own name, or to ensure that the debtor can only pay with discharging effect if he pays the factoring company and not the assignor. In yet other countries such as England, Wales, Northern Ireland and Italy, the debtor's notification is also used to determine who has priority in the case of competing assignments of the same receivable.

Another similarity between the European jurisdictions with regard to factoring is that a large majority not only know of, but also allow for, assignments of future receivables, and even though the prerequisites for the validity of assignments in advance are rather cumbersome in certain jurisdictions, such as in France, most jurisdictions only require that the receivable and/or the debtor can be specified clearly enough in order for an advance assignment to be valid.

Factoring companies throughout Europe often have to tackle the question of third party rights affecting either the assignment as such or the transferred receivable. Such third-party rights can result from the factoring client's suppliers and their extended retentions of title or

---

[4] ECJ judgment of 26 June 2003 in Case C-305/01 Finanzamt Groß Gerau v. MKG-Kraftfahrzeuge-Factoring GmbH, http://curia.europa.eu/juris/document/document.jsf;jsessionid=9ea7d2dc30d6826761bd6f95461db4bbc53e910f8b3e.e34KaxiLc3qMb40Rch0SaxyMa3b0?text=&docid=48453&pageIndex=0&doclang=EN&mode=lst&dir=&occ=first&part=1&cid=162737.

other sureties and collateral. In roughly two thirds of the jurisdictions contained in the EUF's Legal Study, such third-party rights have some kind of effect on the factoring transaction, although the extent of the effect on the factoring transaction, and ultimately the factoring company as assignee, varies, often depending on what kind of factoring (with or without recourse) has been agreed upon.

Similarly, contractual prohibitions of assignments are either just tolerated, theoretically possible, or even straight-out legally valid in nearly two thirds of European jurisdictions, even though the effect again varies, from having no effect whatsoever on the factoring transaction (for example in Hungary) or having only an effect limited to the validity of the assignment against the debtor (for example in Poland). Once more, this simultaneously shows similarities and differences between jurisdictions all over Europe with regard to factoring, as well as differences regarding the question of how much regulation may be considered "necessary" or "too much".

All in all, this short overview and summary of some of the results of the EUF's Legal Study shows that the national legal frameworks for factoring in the EU contain certain similarities, especially concerning basic concepts and questions, but that there are also a number of differences and national specificities which need to be taken into account when considering the European factoring market's development. The diffuse feeling of factoring being too regulated may be true in some cases, while not in others.

II. Recent Attempts at Harmonisation in Europe

Over the past few years, there have been many legal developments on the EU-level which have had more or less direct effects on factoring. Three recent and/or current developments that may serve as examples are:

- The EU General Data Protection Regulation (GDPR) which will apply in all EU member states as from mid-2018;[5]
- The proposal for a new insolvency directive focusing mainly on the restructuring of companies, issued in November 2016; and
- The EU Commission's public consultation on the conflict of laws

---

[5] Regulation (EU) 2016/679 of the European Parliament and of the Council of 27 April 2016 on the protection of natural persons with regard to the processing of personal data and on the free movement of such data, and repealing Directive 95/46/EC (General Data Protection Regulation).

for third party effects of transactions in securities and claims, which may finally pave the way for a regulatory gap in the so-called Rome I-regulation[6] to be filled.

In January 2012, the EU Commission proposed a comprehensive reform of EU data protection rules and it was agreed that a (general) regulation should replace the old directive, thus enhancing legal harmonisation. Ultimately, it took more than three years to agree on the GDPR which will be applicable as from the 25th of May 2018. Even though the GDPR concerns personal data of natural persons and factoring transactions mainly take place between businesses (B2B), factoring is expected to be affected by the new rules contained in the GDPR, both directly and indirectly: B2C-factoring is practised in many EU member states, and it also has to be noted that B2B-factoring includes factoring transactions with owner-managed micro businesses where the line between personal data of a natural person and data regarding the legal person is very thin. Hence, even though factoring will continue to be possible, the numerous new requirements on transparent information to be provided to the data subject by the controller may well increase the administrative burden on both factoring clients and factoring companies. Credit agencies and others, on whose information factoring companies often rely, may have to comply with these increasingly strict data protection rules, which may also have indirect effects on factoring.

In November 2016, the EU Commission published its proposal for a directive "on preventive restructuring frameworks, second chance and measures to increase the efficiency of restructuring, insolvency and discharge procedures and amending Directive 32012/30/EU".[7] The background to this directive proposal for an EU insolvency framework lies in the general idea that insolvencies (and hence the liquidation) of companies should be avoided – rather, companies should be encouraged and assisted to survive a crisis through restructuring measures which are supported at least by a majority of creditors. This is a view which is apparently shared by many national legislators within the EU, so much so that it could perhaps even be called something of a legislative trend. The implementation of the proposed directive could have various negative effects on factoring, depending on the directive's final wording and its

---

[6] Regulation (EC) No. 593/2008 of the European Parliament and of the Council of 17 June 2008 on the law applicable to contractual obligations (Rome I).

[7] Cf. document 2016/0359(COD) of 22 November 2016, http://ec.europa.eu/information_society/newsroom/image/document/2016-48/proposal_40046.pdf.

national implementation, ranging from the risk of factoring companies being forced through a court decision to continue a factoring relationship during a restructuring process, to so called cross-class cramdowns causing negative consequences for factoring companies who, as creditors, may unsuccessfully vote against a restructuring plan.

Lastly, the EU Commission is considering introducing conflict of laws rules for third party effects of transactions in receivables. The background to these deliberations lies in a regulatory gap in the Rome I-regulation which, since it came into force, lacks provisions on the law applicable to the priority of several assignments of the same receivable and to the effectiveness of assignments against third parties, such as insolvency practitioners or suppliers of the factoring client with a (prolonged) retention of title. This regulatory gap is of particular relevance for cross-border factoring transactions where the question of which assignment takes priority can be essential for factoring companies. For years, the EUF has advocated for the law of the place where the assignor has its centre of main interest (law of the assignor) to be applicable as this offers a well-balanced solution, predictable not only for the assignment parties but also for third parties. It remains to be seen whether the EU legislative institutions share this view.

These are three current examples which show that more regulation can have both up and down sides – it is not black and white.

III. The Necessity to Adapt Prudential Regulation to Factoring, a Secured Short-term Business

Capital Requirements for Receivables Based Finance and Purchased Receivables

If comparing legal environments for factoring across EU Countries can be challenging, trying to provide a picture of the prudential regulation for factoring companies is even trickier. As stated above, a big source of confusion stems from the variety of regulatory environments across Europe in which non-banking intermediaries operate, ranging from totally non-regulated markets to markets subject to full bank-like regulation, with many "shades of grey" in between. European regulators themselves appear to be sometimes puzzled by this variety. Moreover, factoring happens to be offered by banks, too. Just understanding what applies to whom results in a very difficult exercise, also because the

Capital Requirement Regulation (CRR)[8] provides for some waivers for companies held by a supervised banking group.[9] The exercise of listing the differences would require an entire book on its own, so we will focus on the treatment of factoring as a product within the prudential regulation, and specifically on the issues that mostly impact the calculation of capital requirements for credit or default risk, namely the accounting standards, the applicable risk weight for financial transactions collateralised by trade receivables and purchased trade receivables, and the definition of default.

The peculiarities of factoring require paying attention to the client, the assigned debtors and the supply relationship between them. In factoring, default risk, i.e. the risk of a loss due to the insolvency of the client, is just a part of the whole picture. When assessing a factoring agreement, one also needs to take into account other important elements, namely the debtor risk (or asset risk, looking to the whole portfolio) and the factorability of the receivables (defined as the features of the receivables that assure the self-liquidating nature of the financial facility).

The CRR provides, both for standardised and internal rating-based approaches, that the value of the exposure is based upon the "accounting value".[10] In this regard, inhomogeneous accounting rules applying around Europe bring about inhomogeneous balance sheet reporting among factoring companies, adding to practical difficulties when speaking of capital requirements.

The differences in particular relate to the treatment of factoring operations with recourse. Traditional standards focus on the legal basis of the transaction (a purchase of an asset) and make no difference between with and without recourse (at least for on-balance sheet items). Such standards still apply in many countries, like France and Belgium, and were applied, before the IAS were introduced, for example in Italy until 2006. The IAS/IFRS-like framework (usually applied at a consolidated level but also to individual financial companies in, for example, Italy and Spain), focuses on "substance over form", so that the balance sheets of the factors express the risk on the client (just as if it was a loan) or the risk

---

[8] Regulation (EU) No. 575/2013 of the European Parliament and of the Council of 26 June 2013 on prudential requirements for credit institutions and investment firms and amending Regulation (EU) No. 648/2012.
[9] See art. 7 of the CRR.
[10] It is worth noting that according to the text of art. 111 and 166, the actual value of the exposure is not necessarily the same under the two approaches. However, what is relevant, for our purposes, is that both are based on the accounting value.

on the debtors (represented by the invoices purchased where risks and rewards are fully transferred to the factor).[11]

The Basel agreement and the CRR allow adjusting the calculation of the Risk Weighted Asset (RWA) for receivables-based transactions, also differentiating between the Standardised Approach (SA) and the Internal Rating Based Approach (IRB).

Under the SA, institutions are required to calculate capital requirements applying a risk weight on the accounting value of the exposures that is based on the external credit assessment made by an authorised External Credit Assessment Institution (ECAI) (100% in case of unrated counterparties).

Exposure to purchased receivables are weighted according to the risk of the client or the assigned debtor depending on the accounting of exposure. There is no special treatment for asset based receivables finance transactions, so "traditional accounting" companies may rely on the general approach to credit risk mitigation in order to consider the guarantee provided by the recourse to the client.[12] This approach can therefore be considered as simpler, but less adaptive.

In contrast, the IRB approach is more flexible and allows for different treatments that, in principle, should reflect the actual company policies regarding the management of receivables-based transactions. Under the IRB approach, the institution is allowed to use its own estimates of Probability of Default (PD), LGD, exposure at default and maturity.

For financial transactions collateralised by trade receivables, under certain conditions, institutions may then apply a lower regulatory LGD[13] in acknowledgment of the lower risk of receivables-based finance.

With regard to exposures to purchased trade receivables, the Basel Committee on Banking Supervision (BCBS) proposes two approaches to calculate RWA for purchased receivables, namely bottom-up and top-down[14], both recognised by the CRR.[15] While the bottom-up approach requires the calculation of risk parameters for each single

---

[11] The so-called "derecognition test".
[12] See CRR, art. 201 & following. That means that not all the factoring clients may be eligible as providers of "unfunded credit protection" as this depends on e.g. a credit assessment by an ECAI and some further requirements.
[13] See CRR, art. 209 & art. 230.
[14] See BCBS, *International Convergence of Capital Measurement and Capital Standards A Revised Framework*, 2004, § 362-373.
[15] See CRR, art. 184.

debtor, the top-down approach refers in principle to pools of purchased receivables, which are highly diversified and fractioned, and allows institutions to estimate the one-year expected credit loss on the pool of receivables.[16]

Under the IRB approach(es), the factor must also assess whether dilution risk is irrelevant or not, and, in the latter case, calculate the appropriate capital requirement. Prudential treatments try to consider the actual business model and give value to the low risk nature of factoring, in particular when the factor adopts its own internal rating model. Hence, an increase in adaptivity often also entails increased complexity.

The Definition of Default

Independently from the adopted approach to capital requirement calculation, the CRR in art. 178 defines the term "default". In order to determine a default, the rule requires a persistency of delay for over 90 days and materiality of past due exposures. Before the introduction of the CRR, the concept of "materiality" of the past due exposure was defined by each single national supervisory authority, thereby creating a fascinating variety of national methods and thresholds. For example, in the UK, the whole single credit obligation was deemed as defaulted if any part of it is past due more than 90 days. In Italy, a default was detected when the past due obligation of a client exceeded 5% of the whole exposure, provided there was at least one exposure due by more than 90 days. In France, a case-by-case approach was applied. Since the introduction of the CRR, the regulation now provides that "EBA shall develop draft regulatory technical standards to specify the conditions according to which a competent authority shall set the threshold". At the moment of writing this contribution, the EBA has already published its draft regulatory standards and guidelines to harmonise the definition of default. The way to detect past due over 90 day exposures will fundamentally change when these enter into force (currently, this is foreseen for the 1st of January 2021). In particular, the EBA suggests that a client should be deemed as "defaulted" when the past due amount exceeds an absolute threshold of EUR 500, and a relative threshold of 1% of the total outstanding amount for a consecutive 90 days.

The EBA has also introduced peculiar treatments for factoring, proposing an IFRS-like conception of exposure in factoring, where the

---

[16] See CRR, art. 154.

counting starts at the moment the advances paid on the outstanding receivables exceeds the agreed percentage for exposures to clients, or at the moment a single receivable becomes due for exposures to debtors.

The application of such a rule to factoring will be tricky. A past due trade receivable is not the same as, for example, a past due mortgage or leasing instalment. While (at least in some countries) 90 day due invoices are not at all a sign of deterioration in the creditworthiness of the account debtor, 90 days could be even too late to detect default in other cases. Moreover, there are many other reasons, linked to the seller-buyer relationship and unrelated to credit risk, why a receivable may be overdue. However, the EBA provides for a number of waivers and clarifications about the application of the harmonised definition of default to factoring, including the exclusion of disputed and diluted invoices from the calculation. Nevertheless, it looks like the introduction of the new thresholds will generate major (and unnecessary) issues for the Factoring Industry, thereby showing that harmonisation and/or simplification are not always the best option from all perspectives, nor do they necessarily go hand in hand.

Towards an Overall Reform of Capital Requirements for Credit Risk

The BCBS has recently issued consultation papers on an overall reform of the Basel framework for credit risk. As most of the changes are still under (fierce) discussion and radical changes to the proposed approaches are still likely, it is best to focus on what the Factoring Industry would like to see in such a reform: a recognition of the low LGD of receivables based finance both in SA and IRB, either through a lower risk weight for exposures to purchased receivables or through an even lower LGD; a recognition of the role of credit insurance or exemption as an effective risk mitigation technique; and a relief to the 90 day past due rule to take into account the specificities of trade receivables in order to implement better performing internal models.

The Introduction of Liquidity Requirements in Factoring

The recent update of the Basel agreements (so-called "Basel III") introduces new requirements for credit institutions, namely the Liquidity Coverage Ratio (LCR) and the Net Stable Funding Ratio (NSFR). Supervised factoring institutions will also be required to fulfil them, but with some adaptations. With regard to the LCR, the new requirement asks supervised institutions to keep a liquidity buffer made of high quality liquid assets in excess of the net liquidity outflows over a 30 days calendar stress period. In order to take into account the nature of factoring inflows and outflows, as well as the absence of high quality liquid assets in the usual business model of factoring companies, the European Commission provided a waiver for specialised factoring companies from the general rule that put a cap on the liquidity inflows.[17] Most recently, the introduction of the NSFR is still being discussed, as are certain adjustments for factoring, as requiring a very large amount of medium- or long-term funding would be extremely detrimental to factoring if not corrected to take into account the (very) short-term nature of factoring activities and the very low (if any) systemic risk.

IV. Conclusion

Factoring is different from traditional bank lending and the requirements and the ways to offer and secure factoring transactions are not homogeneous across Europe, following the development of each legal and economic environment during the centuries. The Industry, made up of banks, financial companies held by banking groups and stand-alone factors, shows a very varied environment with regard to licensing and the application of prudential supervision standards. The whole picture is difficult to get and, therefore, significant practical difficulties may arise when it comes to applying harmonised rules, especially relating to supervision and capital adequacy. Even though factoring has proven to be a stable and low risk form of financing, and despite the fact that the main focus of most new supervisory and regulatory requirements does not lie in factoring, the Factoring Industry is more often than not affected by such new requirements, making factoring specific adaptations necessary. However, all these examples show that there is no clear answer to the question of whether factoring is too regulated or not. Rather, it seems the real issue is not "how much" factoring is regulated but "how", and if the applicable regulation actually fits the peculiarities, as well as providing a correct representation of the risk borne by factoring companies. The keyword for regulators, when approaching factoring, should be "proportionality". Factoring companies continuously strive to ensure

---

[17] Commission Delegated Regulation (EU) 2015/61 of 10 October 2014 to supplement Regulation (EU) No. 575/2013 of the European Parliament and the Council with regard to liquidity coverage requirement for Credit Institutions Text with EEA relevance, art. 33.

that the level of regulation and supervision is, or remains, adequate and appropriate, mainly by taking into account the specificities of factoring – after all, factoring differs greatly in many aspects from "conventional" forms of financing such as loans, thereby making many financial supervisory rules which apply to credit institutions inappropriate and even practically inapplicable for factoring companies.

29. Compliance, a Necessary Constraint

Peter Ball

*Global Head of Regulatory Compliance,
Global Trade and Receivables Finance, HSBC*

The Factoring Industry acts in a very varied environment with regards to supervisory and regulatory requirements. There are related reasons for this. In some markets, it is conducted by factors that are Non-Bank Financial Institutions (NBFIs). Consequently, the automatic regulatory requirements that are needed of banks are not present. Of course, that does not stop legislators and the regulators they create, from writing laws and regulations for NBFIs or any product, service or activity. Legislators' motivation has tended to be the protection of the interests of consumers, maintaining the stability of the financial system, or the integrity of the wholesale financial markets. Factoring's place on the periphery means it generally is not a focus for resultant laws and rules.

This position of relatively light regulation is not unique and, to an extent, much of the commercial business banking sector is similar, at least in some countries. For example, in the United Kingdom the regulation of lending by banks to small-medium sized businesses has been subject to self-regulation in the SME segment through the Lending Standards Board's Lending Code and latterly the Standards of Lending Practice for business clients. At the level of factoring, the UK's ABFA has its own standards framework including a code and complaints process. With the merger of the ABFA and the British Bankers Association with other Industry bodies (2017), some convergence of standards is likely. This does not sit in a regulatory vacuum:

- Firstly, regulators are allowing this;
- Secondly, ineffective voluntary regulation could be a precursor for imposed rules;
- Thirdly, principles-based regulation (more on this later) places behaviour as a regulatory requirement.

Financial institutions, especially factoring ones, have an interest in developing their own standards and ensuring they are complied with by the members of their industry. This brings self-regulation into the sphere of regulatory compliance as well.

In contrast to this, some countries' regulations place factoring as a licensed activity and can impose important parts of their banking regulation on factoring companies. There are examples of this in several European countries such as Germany and Italy. Whether required or not, the inclusion of factoring companies and departments as part of banking groups causes them to be impacted by internal policies too, quite often a company translation of local and international banking regulation.

Inevitably regulation is jurisdictional, meaning that it belongs to the geographic place where the activity occurs. In some countries this might simply be that a central bank regulates everything in the financial services sector, but in many places there are multiple regulators. The United States, for example has the Federal Reserve Board (and its twelve regional Federal Reserve Banks), the Office of the Comptroller of the Currency, the Federal Deposit Insurance Corporation, and the Office of Foreign Assets Control – Department of the Treasury (OFAC – dealing with sanctions) as well as state banking regulators. In the United Kingdom, the two main banking regulators are the Financial Conduct Authority and the Prudential Regulatory Authority. NBFIs conducting factoring are not generally in their scope, albeit banks conducting factoring are, even if there is not much specific regulation for factoring. In the EU, country level regulators such as Germany's BaFin share banking regulation with the EBA.

This feature of cross-jurisdictional regulation is a rising trend both as activities globalise and also where individual states want to use the banking system as a tool of foreign policy. This is most obvious in the area of economic embargo and sanctions where, for example, United States sanctions can apply not only to sanctioned designated nationals and states, but also to any institution facilitating a breach of sanctions. This means that a bank or NBFI involved in financing a transaction that breaches such sanctions, which are administered by OFAC, could become sanction listed themselves, and consequently be excluded from the USD clearing system. This means that OFAC's impact can extend into other jurisdictions.

Thomson Reuters collects data on regulations and reports a rapid increase in the volume of regulation globally post 2012. As an example, the volume rose from 17,763 per annum then to 52,563 in 2015, so that in 2015-16 an average of 200 international regulatory publications, changes and announcements were captured daily.[1] Regulation comes in many forms with variety in its direction and nuances. Its scope includes subjects that are not exclusive to financial services, such as taxation, occupational health and safety, and financial reporting (for example Sarbanes-Oxley Act 2002 – SOX), through to very specific banks' capital requirements i.e. prudential regulations. We deal with the capital requirements in another chapter and in this one the focus is on three things:

- Anti-money laundering regulation and sanctions;
- Regulatory direction on conduct and behaviour in financial services;
- Compliance risk management in organisations.

In summary, whilst we can say that in some countries factoring is generally not specifically regulated, this does not mean that it is entirely exempt from regulation. Regulation itself comes in many forms and increased volume. It can lie with multiple regulators but could also lie with industry bodies' standards. Compliance with regulation and applying standards of compliance and conduct is therefore an increasing part of the business of banking and financial services, of which factoring is a part.

I. Money Laundering and Sanctions

Nowhere is the rising tide of regulation more obvious than in the world of AML, combatting terrorist financing and sanctions. With this, come regulatory requirements for controls to mitigate the risk. This is sometimes called financial crime compliance as distinct to regulatory compliance.

AML is characterised by a high degree of international coordination that is translated into regulation. The G-7 countries established the Financial Action Task Force (FATF) at the July 1989 summit in Paris and it later extended its brief to combatting Terrorist Financing (TF). The FATF's stated objectives are: "to set standards and promote effective implementation of legal, regulatory and operational measures

---

[1] Cost of Compliance 2016, Stacey English & Susannah Hammond, Thomson Reuters.

for combating money laundering, terrorist financing and other related threats to the integrity of the international financial system. The FATF is therefore a "policy-making body" which works to generate the necessary political will to bring about national legislative and regulatory reforms in these areas.[2] This translates into legislation and regulation. In the EU, for example the fourth EU Money Laundering directive 2015/849 (fourth ML directive) follows FATF's recommendations and, in turn, individual states incorporate this into national law and regulation.

For factoring, both the FATF and the fourth ML directive are of interest. The latter has credit and financial institutions in its scope and in EU law the definition of a credit institution specifies factoring. The FATF publishes reports on many aspects of AML and TF and factoring has featured in two reports on trade based money laundering.

Trade Based Money Laundering (TBML)

The FATF defines TBML and provides typologies for money laundering techniques, "TBML is the process of disguising the proceeds of crime and moving value through the use of trade transactions in an attempt to legitimise their illicit origins. Criminal organisations and terrorist financiers move money for the purpose of disguising its origins and integrating it into the formal economy."

TBML involves the abuse of both the financial system and the physical movement of goods through the trade system. The basic techniques of trade-based money laundering include:

- Over- and under-invoicing of goods and services;
- Multiple invoicing of goods and services;
- Over- and under-shipments of goods and services; and
- Falsely described goods and services.

Factoring professionals will recognise that these techniques are not unique to money laundering but also apply to fraud. For example, the under shipment of goods at its extreme is *phantom shipments* or *fresh air invoicing*, used to fraudulently create finance through factoring or invoice discounting. Similarly, *multiple invoicing* is recognisable as *double*

---

[2] International Standards on Combating Money Laundering and the Financing of Terrorism & Proliferation, The FATF Recommendations, Updated June 2017.

factoring where the same transaction is used to create additional financing. The critical differences between fraud and TBML are:
- For fraud, the target is to illegitimately obtain finance from the factor, and potentially cause them a loss of money;
- For money laundering, the target is to use the financial system to make the source of money and value seem legitimate.

For example, a seller invoices for goods at a price far in excess of their market value creating an audit trail of a receivable and shipment. The seller factors the invoice, the factor verifies the transaction using the proof of shipment or contacts the buyer. The buyer is connected to an illegitimate source of funds and is cooperative in verifying the transaction and finally paying the inflated invoice with those funds. The net effect is that illegitimate funds and value pass through physical trade in goods and several financial transactions, so that in the end they appear to be legitimate proceeds of normal business and can be integrated in the legitimate economy. This illustrates the use of over-invoicing.

Factoring could also be used to disguise illegitimate funds coming from the seller instead. For example, a seller could procure goods from the proceeds of selling narcotics, ship the goods, under-invoice compared to their market value, factor the invoice, the buyer could then resell the goods at the larger, true value. The buyer would then use only a small part of the proceeds to settle the factored invoice leaving the rest available as seemingly legitimate funds, perhaps in the country or control of narcotics production. Such a technique would be effective in legitimising the movement of value across borders where the risk of money laundering is perceived to be higher. This example illustrates the use of under-invoicing.

II. Compliance with AML Regulation

The fourth EU ML Directive, which stems from the FATF, places extensive responsibilities on financial and other institutions to undertake new client due diligence checks. It also includes obligations to report suspicious transactions and maintain records of payments. The obligation for reporting suspicious activity is to the country's financial intelligence unit and the institution and individuals must not knowingly disclose their suspicion to the client or any other party. This is known as *tipping off* and it can be a criminal offence.

Article eight of the fourth EU ML Directive is specifically interesting for factors since it clearly demonstrates that the controls required extend beyond client due diligence and into the products and transactions. Senior managers are responsible for developing proportional "internal policies, controls and procedures, including model risk management practices, client due diligence, reporting, record-keeping, internal control [and], compliance management... to identify and assess the risks of money laundering and terrorist financing, taking into account risk factors including those relating to their clients, countries or geographic areas, products, services, transactions or delivery channels."[3]

The directive does not define requirements for products and transactional monitoring perhaps as specifically as they do for client due diligence and, from FATF through to the EU directive, there is a requirement to take a *risk-based approach*. Such an approach needs to use evidence-based decision-making, meaning that a factor cannot simply permit low levels of control. The assessment and identification of ML/TF risk in factoring is therefore a requirement.

III. Controls and Sanctions

AML Controls

There are few sources to rely upon but the UK Joint Money Laundering Steering Group (JMLSG)[4] identified that many of the credit controls used in factoring would mitigate ML risks, a position that reflects the fact that the techniques of the money launderer and the fraudster are the same or similar, even if the target is different. The Wolfsberg Principles on Trade Finance, revised and republished in 2017 with the ICC and the BAFT[5], do not yet have factoring in their scope but provide some hints, especially in respect of correspondent factoring. The Monetary Authority of Singapore has a small reference in its paper on Trade Finance and AML/TF[6] where it identifies factoring between related parties as being an inconsistent form of finance and a potential red flag for ML.

---

[3] Directive (EU) 2015/849 of the European Parliament and of the Council, 20 May 2015.
[4] The Joint Money Laundering Steering Group, Section 21, Prevention of money laundering/ combating terrorist financing, 2017 Revised Version.
[5] The Wolfsberg Group, ICC and BAFT Trade Finance Principles 2017.
[6] Monetary Authority of Singapore Guidance on Anti-Money Laundering and Countering Terrorism Controls in Trade Finance and Correspondent Banking, MAS Information Paper, October 2015.

This concept of red flags is used extensively in documentary trade finance. They are risk indicators of ML/TF arising mainly from the inflight manual transactional monitoring of trade documents (for example LCs, commercial invoices and bills of lading). The risk of TBML in trade finance and factoring may be very similar but the factor does not have the integral involvement in the trade transaction, whilst the trade financier does. For example, the control of a bill of lading in a LC transaction is fundamentally part of trade finance, whilst a factor might sometimes ask for sight of a shipping document to evidence the validity of an invoice where it is factoring the underlying receivable. Conversely, the factor is likely to have strong controls around understanding the underlying business and sales contract from which a receivable results, the seller and buyer counterparties and the flow of funds from the buyers. In designing its risk-based approach to transactional monitoring it is more likely to use these areas for AML controls as well as its credit and fraud risks.

Sanctions

The potential impact of breaching sanctions was highlighted in the earlier paragraphs on the regulatory environment, including their cross jurisdictional impact. For the factor, especially one providing import or export services, there is a need for controls notably around the countries and entities it is dealing with on both the buyer and seller side of transactions. This is likely to be in the form of name screening the inward payment transactions from the buyers in the factored transaction (unlike outward payments that are from the factor to the suppliers who are their customers, so presumably already screened). To minimise the risk of facilitating a sanctioned transaction by factoring it, screening might occur earlier in the process when the supplier and their buyers are accepted and when invoices for their transactions are factored.

In summary, financial crime regulation does impact factoring. The demand for compliance to have specific rules exists for many factors, including non-banks, but the demand is wider, extending to managing financial crime as another form of risk.

IV. Conduct Agenda and Compliance

Conduct Agenda

Since the 2007-2008 financial crisis until the end of 2016, regulatory enforcement has resulted in fines of USD 321 billion.[7] The cause of these fines is varied, including financial market conduct, misselling and insufficient controls for mitigating financial crime. However, there are two clear conclusions to draw: firstly, the cost of non-compliance has been huge and secondly, the underlying behaviours of banks have not met regulatory expectations.

In the same period, regulators have been developing a different approach to regulation based not only on rules, but on principles and conduct. The United Kingdom's financial conduct authority applies eleven principles to the institutions it regulates, ensuring proper standards of market conduct, due regard to the interests of clients, and treating them fairly. This impetus to change banking behaviour is sometimes described as the conduct agenda. This approach appears in other jurisdictions as illustrated below:

> Promote a sound corporate culture that supports prudent risk management and contributes towards incentivising proper staff behaviour leading to positive customer outcomes and high ethical standards in the banking industry – Hong Kong Monetary Authority.[8]
>
> Ultimately, trust and conduct boil down to culture more than any externally imposed rules … Financial institutions must get the culture right. This requires setting the right moral tone from the top – Monetary Authority of Singapore.[9]
>
> Prevent misconduct at all levels by requiring banks to adopt behaviours, practices and internal control and compliance mechanisms that are conducive to limiting the opportunities for misconduct. – European Systemic Risk Board.[10]

The impact on factors of regulatory principles and demands to adopt cultural change is to extend the reach of regulators beyond those specific rules that might not touch factoring. This, alongside the risk of significant evidence of enforcement, drives a growth of importance and resourcing of compliance in institutions.

---

[7] Boston Consulting Group, "Staying the Course in Banking", 2017.
[8] HKMA Circular 3 March 2017.
[9] Ravi Menon, managing director of MAS in a speech, 6 September 2016.
[10] "European Systemic Risk Board Report on misconduct risk in the banking sector", June 2015.

Compliance

The structure of compliance has evolved in response. The responsibilities of management are being redefined to ensure they have risk control frameworks in place. In the United Kingdom, for example, senior managers are accountable for failures in the organisation even if they did not know they were occurring. These risk management frameworks typically utilise the three lines of defence model:
- The first line is the business management who own risks and have primary control of them. This includes the risk of not complying with regulation or regulatory expectation;
- The second line is risk specialists such as credit risk teams or compliance departments, who are there to have oversight and provide advice;
- The third line is an independent audit function, which provides assurance.

Whilst the three lines should provide a risk management framework, 'whistle blowing' allows individuals to report a suspected wrongdoing anonymously as an alternative to going through their management.

Inside each line of defence, there are specialists such as regulatory, financial crime, conduct compliance and product experts, such as factoring professionals. One of the challenges faced is to ensure each line understands the other's position. It is hoped that in some small way, this chapter assists!

V. Conclusion

Compliance is an evolving environment. For multiple reasons, the reach of regulation into factors, whether they be banks or NBFIs, is increasing in most jurisdictions bringing with it a need to ensure and understand compliance risk. The volume of factoring specific rules and regulations may be low; however, it would be quite wrong to consider this as an unregulated environment. There is significant focus on financial crime generally and a specific need to assess the product as a potential target of TBML. The Conduct agenda is being promoted by multiple regulators, bringing with it a heavy demand for compliance and behavioural change that factors need to be cognisant of, in terms of how they behave, how they manage the factoring products, and how they apply regulation or even self-regulation.

30. Risk Awareness to Tackle Fraud

Patrick DE VILLEPIN
Global Head of Factoring, BNP Paribas

Peter MULROY
Secretary General, FCI

At the heart of the trade receivables operating cycle, factors demonstrate the ability to effectively manage their own risks day in and day out, compared to traditional bank lending. They will underwrite and manage the client's request from a credit and operational risk standpoint in their own name, including:

- On-boarding the client relationship: managing credit, dilution and commingling risk and the ability to manage the collection of receivables for companies in difficulty;
- Transactional risk: managing the operational and, most notably, fraud risk. These two aspects of risk awareness are fundamental. When factoring firms pay particular attention to managing such risks, they continually experience a very low PD and excellent operational profitability, which ultimately leads to a successful track record. Conversely, in cases where the product and the range of processes within the 'factoring wheel' (from on-boarding selection criteria to the quality of client management, the automation of invoice processing in the IT system and the day-to-day monitoring of atypical transactions) do not receive adequate attention, control can be lost very quickly and dramatically. And the potential risk to the factor could result in disastrous consequences in terms of provisions, internal disruption (delayed payments) and even external disruption (clients choked off via the boomerang effect). In recent years, a certain number of massive external frauds have hit the headlines, threatening well established companies and even entire countries crippled by impenetrable procedures and the failure to comply with the most elementary rules of administration.

The issue of security permeates the day-to-day activity of professionals in the sector. It is a prerequisite to success throughout the duration of a receivables purchase procedure and contract.

I. Securing the Client Relationship

The risk mitigation tool used against the risk of insolvency and non-payment vis-à-vis the buyer is at the heart of the process of factoring. It constitutes one of the fundamental responsibilities of the factor even if, in most cases, the debtors under non-recourse contracts are backed by credit insurance.

Credit Risk

- In addition to specific risks related to 'factorability' or operations management, the funds provided by the factor effectively depends on the creditworthiness of the buyers, i.e. the ability to pay the receivables assigned by the due date. In this area, the solution depends as much on the selection and pooling of the risk as on the nature of the guarantee;
- Selecting the buyer risk: before or after signing the factoring contract, the purchase or the assignment of receivables, the factor takes a position by assessing the short-term creditworthiness of each buyer and monitors its development. Alerts enable the factor to update the information held in real time and to constantly adjust each buyer's level of authorisation or the credit line which it is guaranteeing on behalf of the client. Of course, reinsurance of the risk at a level of 90% (most frequently) with a credit insurance company offers real-time security, modelled on and adjusted to that of the insurer;
- Pooling buyer risk: apart from exceptional circumstances, the client submits all of the receivables of their own client, at least from a single category or a single business sector. If this is not the case, the risk is not properly managed, and the factor is exposed. For the factor, buyer risk must therefore be spread and pooled. Concentrating activities on a single client remains an exceptional event. The simultaneous cascade of insolvencies more often than not exists solely as an educational hypothesis which only really occurs in the event of large-scale fraud.
- Nature of the guarantee: provided it has been assessed *ex ante*, buyer risk can be insured. The factor decides to insure the client

against non-payment and, where applicable, to reinsure themselves via a credit insurance policy or to benefit from the insurance policy taken out by the client by way of delegation.

By accepting a wide scope of responsibility at all stages, and for all components of its products (financing, guarantee and administration), the factor optimises its clients' risks in order to obtain maximum security. Depending on the laws of the country in question, it will be protected from the risks inherent to the banking profession to a greater of lesser degree: improper support, wrongful termination and interference in management. In Italy, the *Revocatoria* does not protect it from such risks, whereas in many other countries the factor in fact finds itself to be immune. Yet it does bear specific and operational risks: dilution, commingling and the ability to take over management of invoices if the company is experiencing financial difficulty.

Dilution Risk

So-called 'dilution' risk is the difference between the nominal value of the receivable and the amount actually paid by the buyer, due to any reason other than the insolvency of the buyer. A receivable of which the rights have been assigned retains its status prior to the assignment: the beneficiary creditor becomes the holder of all related rights. But the assignment does not purge the receivable of any possible defects, which may relate to the receivable itself or to the rights of the original creditor, in relation to the buyer or a third party. Contrary to credit risk, dilution risk is concentrated (it is solely incurred by the remitter, the client), and is difficult to assess *ex ante* (how can you measure the quality of the receivables that will be assigned in x years?). It is therefore virtually uninsurable. There are multiple causes of dilution, namely the reasons why an assigned receivable may not be paid:

- Non-conforming performance of the service at the root of the receivable. This may be related to a technical problem, partial or faulty delivery, or a price or lead time variation set out in advance. Payment will only be made once the defects have been corrected, if this is still possible;
- A legal obstacle likely to prevent proper settlement of the receivable assigned, causing non-payment or non-remuneration of the said receivable;
- A clawback clause proportional to the turnover achieved in favour of the buyer, as can exist in the mass retailing sector.

- A priority clause in favour of a subcontractor (notably transport or the agency work sector) or of a preferred creditor (in tax matters) may also be set out in law in the event of the insolvency of the principal;
- Finally, fraud by a client under pressure can constitute uncertain receivables being assigned to the factor accompanied by forged documents. This destroys the basis of any factoring contract: trust.

Commingling Risk

Of a completely different nature to dilution risk, commingling risk concerns a solvent buyer: a duly compliant service is provided, without any third party in competition with the factor to receive settlement of the receivable. In such a situation, the only risk that exists is of not receiving the funds, and commingling (meaning to mix up or combine funds or assets) is a risk of variable scale depending on the nature of the products, the type of buyers or their means of payment. In order to manage this risk, the factor conducts audits at the prospect phase which are generally repeated on a quarterly basis (UK) or annual basis (notably France) in order to verify the quality of the client's management, especially regarding delegated or non-managed contracts. Such audits cover the pertinence and effectiveness of the procedures implemented for collection and the receipt of means of payment. On a day-to-day basis, analysis of account inflows and outflows is able to detect the amount and scale of any late payment by buyers.

Ability to Take over Management of Receivables, Collections and Payments

In delegated management contracts where the buyers are unaware of the factor's relationship with their suppliers, the factor authorises the client to collect the assigned receivables: The factoring contract is confidential, and its administration is delegated to the client. The factor therefore lacks a whole block of data and a significant degree of awareness about its client's risks.

Such an authorisation may be revoked. In the event of the client falling into difficulties or failing to adequately comply with the contract, it may be in the factor's interests to take over management itself, i.e. to administer collection and payment directly vis-à-vis the receivables it has been assigned.

It must therefore assess its own administrative capacity: notification of buyers that the receivable has been assigned in its favour, payment reminders to buyers and administration of payments. Such a process largely depends on the "factoring factory" of the factor, but also on the number and type of buyers, the product in question and the assignment technique, the scope of intervention and the formal requirements in order to meet deadlines.

To ensure such an ongoing capacity to take over management, not only are the factor's own resources required but also those from other sources to cover essential services, audited and validated by the factor and using its own IT systems. Service Level Agreements (SLAs) with collection companies enable the factor to increase its activity in this area and enhance its effectiveness.

II. Securing Transactions

Where the mobilisation of the receivables held by a client from its own clients is backed by ownership of invoices, the operation becomes self-liquidating as soon as the factor receives reimbursement for the finance provided.

Operational Risk

Operational risk is defined as "the risk of loss resulting from the inadequacy or failure of internal processes or external events, whether deliberate, accidental or natural". At first sight, in factoring it is mainly related to external frauds. This is not illogical as fake invoices are the most important and striking risk within the factoring world. Nevertheless, other than fraud, different types of operational risks either happen rather frequently or are rare but can have a significant impact:
- Frequent execution errors: generally unintentional, they are made by employees because the core factoring system is not efficient or reliable enough, or because clients negotiated tailor-made products that do not fit the standard system leading to the need for manual entries;
- Rare: claims from clients who consider they have not been well treated by the factoring company. Cyberattacks may also disturb daily operations or lead to data leakages.

Even if the gross amount may be high, the amount at stake generally does not generate provisions as in most cases the amount can be fully recovered leading to a net loss amount close to zero.

In the case of external frauds, the risk can also be considered to be limited. Even if the client is on the verge of bankruptcy, the quality of the portfolio of invoices assigned is able to offer comfort. In reality, self-liquidation is based on both the solvency of the buyers, the quality of the receivables assigned and the cashing-in of payments. Execution is a complicated art and, as we have seen, there are many non-reimbursement risks: insolvency of the buyer, contested receivables, non-performance or poor performance of the service in question, deficiency related to the receivables themselves, legal obstacles, direct payments to the seller, early invoicing, internal and external fraud, etc.

In order to handle such risks, the solution could consist of only offering full notification factoring. But control over the collection circuit is not always enough, even in this *a priori* secure configuration. Notification and administration do not constitute a defence against all forms of fraud, notably in the case of collusion between the client and their buyer(s). The industrial factory of payment processing and reminders is not always adequate, nor is the operational arsenal of prevention and control: strict client eligibility criteria, appropriate delegation and authorisation levels, and even the centralisation, interconnection and automation of databases. File verification is also a vital process: inclusion of the latest balance sheet, verification that the insurance premium has been paid by delegation clients, compliance with authorisation limits, controls on degraded files, abnormal levels of non-valuation, etc.

Fraud and Its Many Forms worldwide

No human organisation is immune from operational failings or risks, given the limitless inventiveness of the fraudsters. To avoid any industrial-scale risk, in statistical terms, constant vigilance is required.

Factoring Frauds in Europe, Central America and South Africa

It is a rare country indeed that is able to escape large-scale fraud, frequently amounting to tens and even hundreds of millions of euros:
- In France in the early 2000s, the profession was shaken by two incidents of several tens of millions of euros each in the agri-food sector: Poulets Bourgoin (2000) and Champagne Bricout (2003). In both cases, the inadequacy of verification and sampling

procedures at the time of invoice purchase anaesthetised the factor's ability to react;
- In Italy, the Parmalat case (2003), once again in the same sector (dairy products), is the story of an unprecedented bankruptcy (EUR 14 billion) at the root of a cascade of insolvencies, for both the client and its buyers and suppliers;
- In Spain, Pescanova, a giant in the frozen fish sector, experienced a similar misadventure in 2013, following an affair of accounts falsification and insider trading. The case provoked a number of bad debts and provisions, affecting both banks and factors. Three of them were even obliged to seek arbitration from FCI. The litigation was settled in 2017 by a hefty provision for one of the parties involved;
- In Germany, the fifth largest factor in the market, a subsidiary of a *Landesbank*, was the victim of a succession of frauds (2010-2014). In total, the losses, estimated at a hundred million euros, seem to have necessitated a full recapitalisation of the company;
- In Mexico, the Banamex scandal (2014-2015), a Mexican subsidiary of the US bank Citigroup, highlighted a vast network of frauds, both internal and external, as well as a breach of the obligation to conduct anti-money laundering controls. Apart from the millions of dollars of losses, Citigroup was ordered by the US courts to pay nearly USD 100 million and to inject over one billion dollars in its subsidiary, renamed Citibanamex;
- In South Africa (2014-2015), the factoring market suffered a nearly USD 300 million fraud from a well-established and well-known textile company that adversely impacted the entire factoring market;
- And in UK, the recent collapse of Carillion (2017) has shown that a third of its debt (EUR 1.7 billion) was made up of reverse factoring with early payment facility programme which happened to be unsecured trade credit risk.

Factoring Frauds in China

However, the biggest story of the early 21st century took place in China, which initially escaped the aftershocks of the great recession, felt mostly by the developed world during the 2008-2012 period. Shortly thereafter, China's economy began to slow, after a significant stimulus intervention by the government. Although the initial impact proved positive, long-term the market could not escape the lasting effect of the global recession, which resulted in a significant drop in exports to developed markets, a significant decline in commodity prices, and an overall drop in factoring volumes. In fact, between 2015 and 2016, the market saw a nearly 30% reduction from the industry's peak in 2014. The decline led to a significant rise in defaults stemming from fraudulent activity and criminal misconduct, almost all driven by domestic factoring transactions. One finding is that the market experienced over USD 15 billion in losses stemming from fraudulent activity during this period. Domestic factoring in China has more inherent risks due to the limited transparency compared to cross-border trade, as there is neither official third party verification such as customs checks, nor any kind of shipment investigation in the domestic market. Therefore, it can be more challenging to prove the authenticity of underlying transactions in the domestic market. It was reported that there were, at one time, over 400 domestic fraud cases sitting in the lower courts in China, a sign that the legal system could not grapple with this onslaught of factoring cases.

The problem is that there is neither centralised codified law on factoring by the People's Congress, nor any policy that has been handed down by the People's Supreme Court. Instead, nearly every provincial court in China has, over time, had to create their own policies based on their own lessons learned from past judgements, and not always in harmony with each other. Several High Courts like the People's High Court of Tianjing, Beijing, Shanghai or Jiangsu Province are believed to have developed their own best practices and have published guidance for their respective courts to follow. The problem is that these guidelines may contradict each other from region to region. So, in principal, the problems in the factoring market in China will need both operational and legislative fixes. And with FCI's support, the Industry will have to advocate for greater legal reforms.

The growth of factoring in China is expected to come back to a steady level by 2018 or 2019. The growth in the next few years is not expected to be as fast as it was in the past, nor like the dramatic drop witnessed in the past two years, but will stabilise as the recovery continues. As business begins to pick up, in part from the ever expanding impact from the OBOR initiative, the banks and commercial actors in China will continue to be challenged, but we expect to witness the rebound of a healthy factoring sector in China, and at the same time support the evolution of a more robust legal and regulatory framework to instill confidence in the development of factoring in China into the future.

In summary, the increase in frauds and insolvencies declared in this period in China must be laid at the door of inadequate overall regulation, lack of product clarity, a lack of investment in proper technologies that raise red flags and minimise fraudulent activity, a lack of effective controls and a loosening of standards, and also non-compliance with rules covering procedures and vigilance. Excessive staff turnover and inadequate training were also prevalent, realising the necessity and irreplaceability of effective human management in such a sensitive profession.

Fraud Prevention and Operational Risk Management

By their very nature, the causes of fraud are very varied and may involve either a client, a buyer or a third party. Different types of fraud come in many guises: false invoicing (services not ordered, cancelled or diverted, over-invoicing in terms of quantity or rate, or falsification of documents, etc.) early invoicing (services not performed or disputed, undelivered goods, etc.), dual mobilisation or invoicing (multiple submission of the same invoice to obtain additional financing, or multiple factors for a given service), non-reimbursement of direct payments or, quite simply, swindling (client/buyer collusion, cross-compensation, cheque kiting, transactions between parent company and subsidiaries, usurpation and changing of bank details, doctoring of accounts, usurpation of the identity of the client, buyer or factor).

With the rise of new modes of communication, the 2000s saw a surge in the number of cases of fraud (false e-mail addresses and websites, use of mobile phone numbers rather than landlines, shell companies without any real or legal existence, letterbox companies, CEO fraud by phone, etc.).

Similarly, cross-border transactions have been affected by attempts at destabilisation (absence of legal and economic existence of certain buyers, foreign client/buyer collusion, false notifications of changed bank details of the factor and/or client), which are all the more difficult to counteract where the nationality of the competent jurisdiction is difficult to identify, leaving room for impunity of the perpetrators who are frequently related to organised crime and the various international Mafia.

Automation and the speed of escalating operational incidents, the preconditions for optimum responsiveness, but also prevention and ongoing training at all levels, therefore constitute the vital complements in the ability to control operational risk and, ultimately, to be able to secure the development of international trade. Internal control is the responsibility of everyone, regardless of their level or responsibility. In other words, to put in place a robust internal control framework and a real embedment of permanent control within the culture of the factoring organisations is essential to bring, in the long run, added value in the form of avoidable operational losses (claims, fraud cases, fines, etc.). In global terms, the quality of the organisation in place and the permanent and periodic control mechanisms also underpin the system over the medium term.

III. Conclusion

In conclusion, transfer of the client risk to a mutualised portfolio of debtors and use of credit insurance coverage are the best ways to mitigate credit risks. Risk awareness is applied in all steps of decision making, preferably upstream (new product validation via new activity committees, regular business continuity planning, both IT and operational, fight against cyber-crime, etc.), rather than downstream (lessons learned from experience, post-mortem analysis of incidents), in order to prevent rather than to deal with and resolve operational incidents and serious failings as and when they occur, unfortunately when it is too late. A sound credit and operational risk framework, including incident, fraud, third-party risk and cyber-security management is, and will remain, at the very heart of a factor, defining its professionalism and excellence.

Be that as it may, the recent white paper by the EUF (2016) highlighted the extent to which the real risks to which factors are exposed were being managed and controlled. The amounts of financial losses with clients of the profession (provisions net of credit insurance coverage) remain very low: one-quarter of the provisions necessary compared to a classic unsecured bank loan, which proves that factoring is a low-risk product for the financial system, provided that the actors stick to the rules of the game, implementing control procedures and applying best practice regarding risk management.

Conclusion

Ten Proposals to Promote Factoring

Patrick DE VILLEPIN

Global Head of Factoring, BNP Paribas

Factoring is a profession of general interest that merits recognition by public authorities, regulators and the entire world of finance, which should promote it throughout the world. The best ally of risk departments and regulators, the Industry is promised a bright future if it manages to unite all O/A products (from ABL to SCF, reverse factoring and all other forms of receivables finance) under its banner to avoid future economic bubbles and certain speculative derivatives of international trade.

Using a factor provides a company with the cash flow it so desperately require in order to grow or even survive. As a cash accelerator, it brings funds in quickly. It is therefore an operational and secure solution to the demands of the real economy:

- Operational, to the extent that early financing of invoices and the quality of services enables clients to benefit from necessary funds virtually in real time and also to reduce inter-company payment delays;
- Secure, against insolvency as companies benefit from a guarantee protecting them against non-payment of invoices. Most frequently, factors only finance invoices that are established, certain and due. For the regulator, this activity should not constitute a threat of a virtual financial bubble as long as it is exercised by informed and experienced professionals.

Faced with such a situation, promotion of secured credit is a precondition for the sustainable development of responsible finance increasingly determined to serve its clients rather than serving itself. Today, factoring is undoubtedly the most reasonable solution for managing operational risk and for complying with security rules, financial sanctions and embargoes in an increasingly hazardous world. Backed by an invoice, factoring is the anti-speculation weapon of a finance that is both sound and conscious of its obligations on which governments, regulators and banks must be able to rely.

To this end, factors around the globe are all united in the defence of their profession via three projects for the future:

- To increase *awareness* about the benefits of the factoring product for financing the real economy at low risk for the financial system;
- To improve *acceptance* of factoring throughout the world at all levels of stakeholders: corporates, banks and policy makers;
- To create an *appropriate legal and regulatory environment* for the Industry in order to facilitate the emergence of factoring in new countries and to create a level playing field for competition.

Conclusion

Based on these three work streams, the Industry makes the following ten proposals:

1. Recognise the virtues of factoring, this unique, secured short-term method of financing trade, based on qualified and eligible intangible receivables on the client's balance sheet, the cash flow accelerator and lifeblood of so many companies of all shapes, sizes, sectors and stages of development of a company's life;

2. Harmonise the conditions of creditworthiness (consumption of RWAs) and liquidity (favourable weightings for calculating LCR and NSFR ratios, on both an individual company and consolidated basis) between the operators and ensure that this secure and very short-term self-liquidating profession benefits from favourable conditions vis-à-vis the banks and other specialist professions;

3. Promote credit insurance as a risk mitigation vehicle and a means to fairly and adequately measure the requirements for regulatory capital, in order to avoid the dual penalty of double accounting, which is currently a real obstacle to the growth in global trade;

4. Develop a blockchain solution strategy to increase the lead time of the transaction and the efficiency of communication between the whole parties, import/export factors and their buyers/suppliers;

5. Push the use of full notification factoring, an all-too-unrecognised financing, guarantee and secure management solution to all SMEs, from the very small businesses to the Midcaps, in order to ensure quantitative growth and open access to a much wider spectrum of companies;

6. Establish a fair, light regulatory environment for the factoring community, both within the EU (with a common status) and worldwide, in order to create fair and equal competitive conditions and a level playing field which is neither over-regulated nor excessively deregulated;

7. Improve the coordination of working capital products and adapt them better to the corresponding segments in accordance with specific needs: vis-à-vis the public authorities (remove legislative and regulatory obstacles) and parent-company banks (harmonisation of distribution conditions and elitism of the solutions preferentially offered to large corporates). In particular, explore the possibilities of increasing the coupling of securitisation and factoring and show creative engineering in the propagation of receivables solutions;

8. As is currently the case in Belgium, Czech Republic or Poland, study the regulatory conditions for extending ABL to countries outside the already established markets of the UK-US base (notably continental Europe, except perhaps France and Italy where a law would be needed) and assess the possibilities of optimising its coexistence with factoring and other existing solutions;
9. Contribute to the emergence of fintechs and other digital platforms alongside, and even within factoring firms, in order to support the birth of a next generation, innovative factoring 2.0 environment that continuously seeks perfection;
10. Promote education as the key differentiator and rosetta stone for understanding the benefits and mechanics of this essential service, in terms of both initial (university) and vocational training (MOOC, FCI seminars, e-learning courses, etc.).

To conclude, these series of techniques – somewhat complex and esoteric yesterday but ever simpler and more legible tomorrow – currently constitute a powerful driver of growth and value creation. The lifeblood of companies at all stages of the life cycle, modern factoring is just at the very early stages of its development. After 50 years, it is yet to reach maturity. Without a doubt, it is promised a very bright future as the potential standard bearer for renewal in the world of finance. Factoring can be considered the last frontier of finance for some, an unexplored country for many, and certainly a new way of financing trade for most, a service that combines the excellence of the past with the new key technology developments of the future.

Hand in hand, FACTORS AND ACTORS strides boldly ahead to the centenary!

Appendices

Factoring History at a Glance

- 1750 BC: Hammurabi code, first factoring roots
- 1430 AD: Jacques Coeur's *facteurs*
- 1450: Blackwell Hall Factors (London)
- 1650: Plymouth Rock Factors (Massachusetts)
- 1898: Morton H. Meinhard & Co., ancestor of CIT
- 1958: Mittelrheinische Kreditbank Dr Horbach & C° KG, Mainz, signs the first factoring agreement in Germany
- 1961: FNBB launches International Factors Ltd
- 1963: International Factors Group (IFG)
- 1963: IF-Italy (IFITALIA)
- 1964: IF-France (Société Française de Factoring)
- 1968: Factors Chain International (FCI)
- 1980s: Start of factoring in Asia (Japan and Korea)
- 1987: Bank of China signs Master Factoring Agreement with Disko Factoring, Germany and launches factoring in China
- 1988: Unidroit Ottawa convention on international factoring
- 1988: First factoring transaction in Turkey (bank division)
- 1990: First factoring company established in Turkey
- 1992: Bank of China launches international factoring activities
- 1994: Launch of factoring activities in Russia
- 2009: EU Federation for Factoring and Commercial Finance (EUF)
- 2016: Merger between FCI and IFG, birth of a new FCI
- 2018: FCI 50th anniversary

FCI at a Glance

1. FCI Annual Meetings

1968: Stockholm (Sweden)
1970: Cannes (France)
1971: Marbella (Spain)
1972: Baden by Vienna (Austria)
1973: Lausanne (Switzerland)
1974: Edinburgh (Scotland)
1975: Mallorca (Spain)
1976: Bermuda (Caribbean)
1977: Florence (Italy)
1978: Helsinki (Finland)
1979: Algarve (Portugal)
1980: Monte Carlo (Monaco)
1981: San Francisco (USA)
1982: Corfu (Greece)
1983: Stockholm (Sweden)
1984: Hong Kong
1985: Munich (Germany)
1986: Marbella (Spain)
1987: New Orleans (USA)
1988: Madeira
1989: Singapore
1990: Istanbul (Turkey)
1991: Cancun (Mexico)
1992: Budapest (Hungary)
1993: Hong Kong
1994: Venice (Italy)
1995: Vancouver (Canada)
1996: Bali (Indonesia)
1997: Prague (The Czech Republic)
1998: San Diego (USA)
1999: Bangkok (Thailand)
2000: Paris (France)
2001: Buenos Aires (Argentina)
2002: Sidney (Australia)
2003: Berlin (Germany)
2004: Montreal (Canada)
2005: Shanghai (China)
2006: Antwerp (Belgium)
2007: Santiago (Chili)
2008: Kyoto (Japan)
2009: Istanbul (Turkey)
2010: Vienna (Austria)
2011: San Francisco (USA)
2012: Beijing (China)
2013: Athens (Greece)
2014: Vancouver (Canada)
2015: Singapore
2016: Cape Town (South Africa)
2017: Lima (Peru)
2018: Amsterdam (The Netherlands)

2. FCI Chairpersons

1969-1970: Ruve Bennun
1971-1972: Claes-Olof Livijn
1973: Öivind Gunnerud
1974-1975: Hermann Vertessen
1976-1977: Heinrich Sommer
1978-1979: Leif Bjoernstad
1980: Ben Hosh
1981-1982: Wilhelm Pruckner
1983: Hermann Vertessen
1984-1985: Hermann Ehrenberger
1986-1987: Philip Black
1988-1989: Andrea Luquer

1990-1991: Ronald Kissling
1992-1993: Nils Otto Nielsen

1994-1995: Friedrich Wilhelm Höche
1996-1997: Clive Isenberg
1998-1999: Michel Aussavy
2000: Mo-Na Chien
2001-2002: Friedrich Wilhelm Höche
2003-2004: Dirk Driessens
2005-2006: Karl-Joachim Lubitz
2007-2008: Alberto Wyderka
2009-2010: Peter Mulroy
2011-2012: Cagatay Baydar

2013-2014: Daniela Bonzanini
2015-2016 (December): Michel Leblanc
2017 (January): Cagatay Baydar

3. FCI Secretary General

1969: Rolf Svirsky
1972: Bertil Friberg
1972 (October): Jeroen Kohnstamm
2013 (July): Peter Mulroy

Glossary

Source: EU Federation for Factoring and Commercial Finance (EUF)

Accounts payable (A/P)	A legally enforceable liability to a creditor recorded in the balance sheet, usually arising from purchases of goods and services and evidenced by a received invoice due to be paid within an agreed timeframe.
Accounts receivable (A/R)	A legally enforceable claim for payment held by a business entity against its client for goods supplied or services rendered in execution of the client's order, and recorded on the balance sheet. Such claim generally takes the form of an invoice raised by a seller and delivered to the buyer for payment within an agreed timeframe. Also called "Receivables".
Advance	Utilisation or drawing by the assignor of funds made available by a factor or a lender against an asset.
Advance payment	A payment made in advance of a prescribed event such as a due date or a contract commencement.
Advance ratio	The maximum percentage of the value of an asset or assets by reference to which factor is prepared to make funds available.
Advances on debtors outstanding	Funds advanced by a factor or a receivables financier (prepayments) to an assignor against debtor balances. Sometimes referred to as current account, utilisation or drawing, this is the actual currency advance at a certain moment in time. See also "Prepayment".
Agency factoring	Sometimes called bulk factoring, a service which enables the client to retain the collection function, but which is disclosed to the debtor.

Anti-Money Laundering policy (AML)	A policy put in place to help detect and report suspicious activity including the predicate offenses to money laundering and terrorist financing, such as securities fraud and market manipulation.
Asset Based Lending (ABL)	An agreement between a business (client) and a financial company in which the latter provides the client with a structured facility combining secured loans and revolving credits. The client may pledge/assign as collateral any combination of assets used in the conduct of its business (e.g. receivables, stocks, plant and machinery, property, brands, etc.).
Assignable	Receivables which can be assigned without any legal constraints.
Assignee	The entity to which a receivable is assigned.
Assignment	The transfer of all rights to the receivables from the assignor to the assignee.
Assignment clause	Written notification to the debtor/buyer that the A/R has been assigned and is payable to the designed factoring company. This usually appears on the invoice.
Assignor	The entity disposing of an asset by an assignment. See also "Client".
Availability	The amount of money that is available for drawing to the assignor. This would be the value of all approved receivables multiplied by the pre-agreed prepayment percentage less any amounts already paid to the assignor.
Back-to-back factoring	The provision of factoring services to a debtor in order to provide security for the approval of the debtor's indebtedness arising from the sales of another client (Salinger 1995).
Bad debt	A debt that is unlikely to be paid because of the inability of the debtor to pay the debt when it falls due.

Ban on Assignment	Clause in a contract between the seller and the buyer which prevents the supplier from assigning the related receivables. It can render ineffective any assignment of the receivables arising out of the contract, although in some legal environments the factoring agreement may overrule the ban of assignment.
Bank Payment Order (BPO)	An inter-bank instrument to secure payments against the successful matching of trade data. The BPO offers the benefits of a letter of credit in an electronic environment, without the drawbacks of manual processing associated with traditional trade finance. Using SWIFT's Trade Services Utility (TSU) or an equivalent transaction matching program, a BPO is an irrevocable undertaking given by one bank to another bank that payment will be made on a specified date after a specified event has taken place.
Basel III/IV	"Basel III/IV" is a comprehensive set of reform measures, developed by the Basel Committee on Banking Supervision, to strengthen the regulation, supervision and risk management of the banking sector. These measures aim to: • improve the banking sector's ability to absorb shocks arising from financial and economic stress, whatever the source; • improve risk management and governance; • strengthen banks' transparency and disclosures.
Borrower	The party to whom a lender makes a loan.
Bulk Factoring	See "Agency factoring".
Buyer	See "Debtor".
Client (Seller)	A supplier business which has a contractual relationship with a factor or an asset based lender. See also "Assignor".

Collection only	An arrangement in which the factor is required to pay the purchase price on the collection date only (i.e. with no prepayments). Often goes with non-recourse facility.
Commercial Finance	Commercial finance is a generic term for a range of asset based finance services which include factoring, invoice discounting, international factoring, reverse factoring and ABL facilities.
	There are many variations on each of these product sets (and the precise nomenclature varies from market to market) but all exist to provide working capital funding solutions to businesses.
Commission charge	Charge made by the factor for services rendered including receivables management and collection and/or credit protection services. The commission is usually calculated as a percentage of the total assigned turnover. Also known as "factoring fee".
Concentration	Usually expressed as a % and says to which percentage one buyer represents the seller's total A/R.
Confidential Factoring	See "Non notification factoring".
Confirming	See "Reverse factoring".
Correspondent Factor	A factor that acts as an import factor or export factor under the two-factor system.
Country risk	The risk associated with investing in or creating exposure to a particular country.
Credit Approval	Is given when the factor accepts the credit risk assumed by taking a debt from a client without recourse to that client in the event of a payment default.
Credit limit	The maximum amount of outstanding debts which a factor is prepared to approve with regard to a specific debtor.

Glossary

Credit Note	Accounting documents which reduce the value of an outstanding invoice or debtor account. See also "dilution".
Credit protection	A service offered by a factor or a receivable purchaser where the factor accepts the risk of non-payment in the event of the inability of the debtor to repay the debt. See also "Non recourse factoring".
Credit risk	The risk for the factor that a credit covered buyer is unable to pay for receivables assigned to the factor.
Days Payable Outstanding (DPO)	The average number of days a business takes to pay its suppliers.
Days Sale Outstanding (DSO)	The average number of days a business takes to collect the proceeds of invoices due from its buyers.
Debtor (Buyer)	A business that has been supplied with goods or services by the client and is obliged to make payment for them. Also referred to as the purchaser of goods or services supplied by a client whose debts have been assigned/sold to a factor.
Debt collection	A service offered by a factor (or a receivables purchaser) where the factor collects the receivable on behalf of the assignor. It may also include all actions aimed at collecting due amounts from insolvent debtors.
Dilution	Every situation that legally allows a buyer to reduce the value of an outstanding invoice, except the default of the debtor.
Direct export factoring	Export factoring without the use of a correspondent factor. Export factor covers the risk of counterparty in another country (usually backed up by an insurance policy). Similar to domestic factoring, except buyers are abroad.
Direct import factoring	Similar to domestic factoring, except seller is abroad.

Discount Charge	Charge made by the factor (or the receivables purchaser) for advanced funds. Usually calculated by applying a discount rate (which in practice works like an interest rate) to the amounts advanced over the outstanding period.
Dispute notice	Written notification to the client from the factor informing the client of a dispute.
Domestic Factoring	Form of factoring in which both assignor and debtor are based in the country of the factor.
Due date	The date on which a payment is due to be made.
Due diligence	A business term for conducting an investigation into the 'facts'. Usually in respect of the client or prospective client. Part of the KYC process. In existing agreements, usually applied to the portfolio of debtors to check the outstanding invoices.
EBRD	European Bank for Reconstruction and Development. See: www.ebrd.com.
Electronic Invoice (e-invoice)	An invoice electronically issued and received in any electronic format. Electronic invoice, exactly the same as an invoice in paper form, must contain the elements required by the VAT Act. In addition, the issuer has to ensure the authenticity of origin, integrity of content and legibility of the invoice.
European Committee for Standardisation (CEN)	CEN-French: Comité Européen de Normalisation, is a public standards organisation whose mission is to foster the economy of the EU in global trade, the welfare of European citizens and the environment by providing an efficient infrastructure to interested parties for the development, maintenance and distribution of coherent sets of standards and specifications.

Glossary

European Federation for Factoring and Commercial Finance Industry (EUF)	The representative body for the factoring and commercial finance industry in the EU. It comprises national and international industry associations that are active in the EU. See: www.euf.eu.com.
Export Factor	The factor, usually located in the seller's (or exporter's) country, with whom the seller has a factoring agreement or contract.
Export Factoring	Form of factoring in which the assignor, usually based in the country of the factor, assigns/sells receivables due by debtors based in another country. See also "international factoring".
Face Value	The principal or redemption value of a financial instrument or claim.
Factor	A financial entity providing factoring facilities.
Factorable Receivables	Receivables that are free from lien and are assignable and collectible.
Factoring	An agreement between a business (assignor) and a financial entity (factor) in which the assignor assigns/sells its receivables to the factor and the factor provides the assignor with a combination of one or more of the following services with regard to the receivables assigned: advance of a percentage of the amount of receivables assigned, receivables management, collection and credit protection. Usually, the factor administers the assignor's sales ledger and collects the receivables in its own name. The assignment can be disclosed to the debtor.
Factors Chain International (FCI)	A global association that facilitates two factor cross-border international factoring in a structured environment under the General Rules for International Factoring (GRIF).
Fintech	Non-banking, innovative company creating products or services offered so far by the financial industry.

Forfaiting	Form of receivables purchase, consisting of the without recourse purchase of future payment obligations represented by financial instruments or payment obligations, at a discount or at face value in return for a financing charge.
Full Service Factoring	Form of factoring in which the factor provides the assignor with all the following services with regard to the receivables assigned: advance of a percentage of the amount of receivables assigned, receivables management, collections and credit protection. See also "Non recourse factoring".
Funding limit	The maximum value available to a client against his assigned receivables.
Funds in use	The total amount of funds advanced to the client prior to collection by the factor.
General Rules for International Factoring (GRIF)	The rules which the members of FCI agree to adopt when transacting two factor cross-border factoring.
Import Factor	A correspondent factor, usually located in the country of the debtor, who is responsible for the collection and/or credit risk by sub-assignment of the debts.
Import Factoring	Form of Factoring in which an export receivable is managed and collected by an import factor usually based in the same country as the debtor. See also "International factoring".
Indirect payment	A payment made to the client by a debtor.
Insolvency	Situation when an entity can no longer meet its financial obligations with its creditors as debts become due.
Interfactor agreement	An agreement between correspondent factors whereby they mutually agree to act as import and export factors in accordance with a code of practice.

Glossary

International Chamber of Commerce (ICC)	ICC provides a forum for businesses and other organisations to examine and better comprehend the nature and significance of the major shifts taking place in the world economy. It also offers an influential and respected channel for supplying business leadership to help governments manage those shifts in a collaborative manner for the benefit of the world economy as a whole. See: www.iccwbo.org.
International Commercial Terms (INCOTERMS)	Internationally recognised standard trade terms used in sales contracts. They're used to make sure buyer and seller know: who is responsible for the cost of transporting the goods, where the goods should be picked up from and transported to and who is responsible for each step of the transportation process.
International Factoring	Includes import and export factoring. It is usually performed through the two factor system.
International Factors Group (IFG)	A global association for factoring providers. The activities of IFG were integrated into FCI as from the 1st of January 2016.
International Finance Corporation (IFC) International Organisations of Factoring	A member of the World Bank Group, is the largest global development institution focused exclusively on the private sector in developing countries. See www.ifc.org. Network of businesses acting as factors whose common aim is to facilitate international trade through factoring and to act as trade organisations representing the Industry.
Introductory letter	A letter sent by the seller to each of its debtors to advise them that the client has entered into factoring agreement.
Invoice	A post contractual document or electronic version of document issued by a seller to a debtor stating among other information the amount of the receivable and the terms of payment.

Invoice Discounter	A financial entity providing invoice discounting facilities.
Invoice Discounting	An agreement between a business (assignor) and a financial entity (an invoice discounter) in which the assignor assigns its receivables and the discounter provides the assignor with an advance of a percentage of the amount of receivables assigned, normally without notification of the discounter's interest to the debtor. The assignor retains full control of its sales ledger function.
Invoice Trading Platform	An alternative to factoring, the on-line platform allows sellers to place individual invoices for auction. Investors or buyers can then bid for the invoice resulting in an advance payment to the seller. An example of "fintech".
Know your client/ customer (KYC)	A customer/client identification process which involves making certain efforts to verify the true identity of key individuals in a business, their standing and the character of the business or transaction they generate. Part of the AML/ due diligence process.
Lender	The party, usually a bank or a financial entity, who lends money to a borrower.
Liquidity Coverage Ratio (LCR)	Ratio of current assets to current liabilities. An essential component of Basel III regulation. LCR shows if a bank has an adequate stock of unencumbered high-quality liquid assets (HQLA) that can be converted into cash easily and immediately in private markets to meet its liquidity needs for a 30 calendar day liquidity stress scenario.
Margin	The percentage margin added to the cost of funds or a base rate to establish the interest rate or discount charge.
Maturity date	The date on which a receivable becomes due and payable.

Maturity Factoring	Form of factoring in which the assignor receives the payment of the receivables on the due date or on a certain and fixed date, usually pre-agreed on the basis of the average payment period taken by the debtor.
Net Stable Fund Ratio (NSFR)	The NSFR is a significant component of the Basel III reforms. It requires banks to maintain a stable funding profile in relation to their on- and off-balance sheet activities, thus reducing the likelihood of losing a bank's liquidity position in a way that could increase the risk of its failure and potentially lead to broader systemic stress.
Non-Notification Factoring	Form of factoring in which the assignment has not been notified to the debtor. The seller performs the sales administration and collects the receivables as an agent for the factor. Also referred to as "confidential factoring".
Non-Recourse Factoring	Form of factoring in which the factor offers a credit protection service and therefore the credit risk of debtor failure remains with the factor.
Notification of Assignment	A notice which can be issued by the factor (or the invoice discounter) or by the assignor to a debtor and which informs the debtor that its related debts payable have been assigned to the factor.
Outstanding	A receivable which has not yet been paid.

Open Account (O/A)	An open account transaction is one where goods are shipped and delivered (or services are provided) to the buyer before the respective payment is due. A credit period is offered by the seller to the buyer, and this is usually in the range of 30 to 90 days. This type of sale is the best option for the buyer in terms of both cash flow and cost, although it may equally be the highest risk option for a seller, who will have fulfilled its side of the contract but has to wait for payment.
Payment terms	The specific terms which determine when payment of an invoice is due. Usually stated on each invoice.
Peer-to-peer lending	The practice of lending money to unrelated individuals, or "peers", without going through a traditional financial intermediary such as a bank or other traditional financial institution. See also invoice trading platform. An example of "fintech".
Prepayment	Payment in advance (prior to maturity) of all or part of the purchase price of the receivables assigned (the balance being paid when the debt is paid by the buyer). See also "advance".
Pre-shipment credit cover	Covers the cost of production for goods and services in a supply contract up to the maximum of the contract value.
Pre-shipment finance	Pre-shipment finance is issued by a financial institution when the seller requires payment of the goods before shipment. The main objective behind pre-shipment finance or pre export finance is to enable the exporter to: procure raw materials, carry out the manufacturing procedure, warehousing of goods and raw material, shipping costs and other financial costs, pre-shipment.
Purchase Order Management (POM)	An FCI product developed to finance cross-border pre-shipment business.

Purchase price	The amount payable by a factor or a receivables purchaser to an assignor for an assigned receivable.
Reassignment	The transfer of an assigned receivable from the original assignee back to the original assignor.
Receivable	A monetary obligation owed by one person to another in payment for the supply of goods or services.
Recourse Factoring	Form of factoring in which the credit risk on the debtor remains with the assignor.
Reserve/Retention	The part of the receivable retained by the factor to cover specific risks such as dilution.
Retention of title	Sometimes called a Romalpa clause in some jurisdictions. It is a provision in a contract for the sale of goods that the title to the goods remains vested in the seller until certain obligations (usually payment of the purchase price) are fulfilled by the buyer. Especially prevalent in Germany.
Reverse factoring	Form of factoring in which the agreement is set up between the factor and a (usually strong) debtor and the factor offers each supplier the possibility to assign/sell (usually without recourse) those receivables approved for payment by the debtor (also known as supplier finance).
Romalpa Clause	see: "Retention of title".
Sales Ledger	A report of outstanding receivables, usually analysed by debtor balance and debt ageing.
Securitisation of receivables	A financing process by which the receivables are structured into debt securities that can be sold to investors on the capital market for cash capital.
Seller	See "assignor" and "client".

Society for Worldwide Interbank Financial Telecommunications (SWIFT)	A network that enables financial institutions worldwide to send and receive information about financial transactions in a secure, standardised and reliable environment.
Subrogation	The acquisition of the rights of a creditor by a third party who pays the original creditor.
Supplier Finance	See "Reverse factoring".
Supply Chain Finance	Portfolio of financing and risk mitigating practices and techniques to optimise the management of the working capital and liquidity invested in the supply chain processes and transactions. Supports the trade and financial flows along the end-to-end business supply and distribution chains, domestically and internationally.
Trade Finance	The financing of international trade (also domestic trade) can include: letters of credit, guarantees, bills of exchange, factoring, forfaiting or export credit.
Turnover	Total value of all receivables assigned/sold to the factor by assignors during the reporting period.
Two-Factor system	System whereby a factor uses, by sub-assignment, a factor in another country (correspondent factor) to collect the receivables of an assignor exporting to a buyer in that country with or without credit protection. The relationship between the correspondent factors is usually governed by an interfactor agreement.
Undisclosed factoring	Another term for "confidential Factoring".
Verification	A service offered by the factor/financier to establish the validity of a debt/receivable before its due payment date.

Bibliography

Blackwell Hall Factors

A Hint to the Blackwell-Hall Factors, being the True State of the Case between Mr Samuel Wetherhead, Blackwell-Hall Factor, and Mr John Hellier, London, *Merchant*, 1705, 22 p.

Defoe Daniel, *The Complete English Tradesman*, London, Charles Rivington, 1727, p. 337.

Gill Conrad, *Blackwell Hall Factors. The Economic History Review*, Vol. 6, Issue 3, Wiley, 1954, p. 268-281.

Hatton Edward, *Gent, Merchant's Magazine*, London, 1726, p. 211-213.

Hillyer William, Hurd, *Four Centuries of Factoring. The Quarterly Journal of Economics*, Vol. 53, No. 2 (February 1939), Oxford University Press, p. 305-311.

Maitland W., *History and Survey of London*, London, T. Osborne and J. Shipton 1739, p. 464.

Tatge David, *Legal Aspects of Factoring,* Washington (presentation), 2014, Epstein Becker Green.

Toshio Kusamitsu, *Markets and Manufacture in Early Industrial Europe*, London, 1991, Routledge, p. 125-126.

Westerfield Ray Bert, *Middlemen in English Business, Particularly Between 1660 and 1760*, 1915, Yale University Press, New Haven, p. 296-304.

Factoring in America

Billboard, January 30 1965 (article concerning sale by Automatic Canteen Company of Hubshman Factor Corporation to First National City Bank).

Biscoe Peter M. Biscoe, *Credit Factoring*, Butterworth's, London, 1975.

Chapin, *Credit and collection principles and practice*, 6th ed., New York, McGraw-Hill, 1953.

Chicago Tribune, June 25 1967 (article concerning expansion by banks into factoring and ABL).

Daily News Record, April 23 1979 (various articles concerning Sterling Bancorp, Rosenthal & Rosenthal, and Citicorp Industrial Credit).

Factoring atypical arrangements, Commercial Finance Association, 1978, bound speech minutes.

Foulke Roy A., *The Story of the Factor*, Dun & Bradstreet, Inc., 1953.

Kuhns William R., Ed., *Present day banking 1952*, American Bankers Association, 1952.

Lazere Monroe, Ed., *Commercial financing*, The Ronald Press Company, 1968.

Moskowitz Louis A., *Dun & Bradstreet's handbook of modern financing and commercial finance*, New York, Thos. Y. Crowell Co., 1977.

New York Times, August 30 1983 (article concerning the frauds perpetrated by Irwin Margolies and Irwin Feiner).

New York Times, June 22 1984 (article concerning the fraud and murders perpetrated by and convictions of Irwin Margolies).

New York Times, October 25 1985, (article concerning the fraud perpetrated by and plea deal of Irwin Feiner).

New York Times, December 27 1989 (obituary of Thomas A. Savage).

New York Times, September 27 1997 (article concerning Dai Ichi Kangyo's sale of 20% stake CIT).

Saulnier & Jacoby, *Accounts receivable financing*, Bureau of Economic Research, Inc., 1943.

Seidman Walter S., *Accounts receivable and inventory financing*, Masterco Press, 1957.

Tatge, Flaxman, Tatge & Franklin, *American Factoring law*, BNA/Bloomberg (AFL), 2009, with 2017 Cum. Supp.

Tatge David and Jeremy, *A Brief Look at Factors Under Early English Commercial Law*, 18 Commercial Factor, No. 2, March/April 2016, p. 18-24.

Tatge Jeremy B., *Pilgrim's Pride: America's Very First Factoring Agreement*, 19 Commercial Factor, No. 2, April 2017, p. 30-39.

The Bridgeport (CT) Telegram, January 16 1965 (article concerning sale of Hushman Factors to the First National City Bank).

UPI Archives, February 23 1993 (article concerning loan fraud perpetrated by Irwin Feiner using sham yatchts and overvalued aircraft).

Wright Robert E., Sylla Richard, *Genealogy of America Finance*, Columbia Business School Publishing, New York, 2015.

Factoring in the UK

Bickers Michael, *Factoring in the UK*, 12th edition, London, BCR Publishing, 2008.

Bickers Michael, (Ed.), various contributors, *World Factoring Yearbook* 2017, London, BCR, 2017.

Biscoe Peter, *Law and Practice of Credit Factoring*, London, Butterworths, 1974.

Bolton John, *Report of the Committee of Inquiry on Small Firms*, Cmnd 4811, London, HMSO, 1971.

Clarke Robin, Wilde Edward, *Cashflow Finance*, Factors & Discounters Association, 2005.

Crichton Susan, Ferrier Charles, *Understanding Factoring and Trade Credit*, London, Waterlow, 1986.

Davidson Nigel, Mills Simon, Salinger Freddie R., *Salinger on Factoring*, 5th edition, London, Sweet and Maxwell, December 2016.

Department for Business Enterprise & Regulatory Reform (Berr), *Small and Medium Enterprise Statistics*, London, National Statistics publication, 1994-2007.

Figgis Patrick, *The Credit Factor*, London, The Institute of Chartered Accountants in England and Wales, 1988.

Goddard S. & Jay S., *A Survey of Credit Control and Debt Collection Policies and Practices*, Management Survey Report No. 52.

Goode Roy M., 'Conclusion of the Leasing and Factoring Conventions – II', Journal of Business Law, November 1988.

Goode Roy M., Foreword to *Factoring Law and Practice*, London, Sweet and Maxwell, 1991.

Growth through Asset Based Finance – Best-Practice Guideline 65, Institute of Chartered Accountants of England and Wales (ICAEW) Corporate Finance Faculty, ABFA.

Hawkins D., *The Business of Factoring*, London, McGraw-Hill, 1993.

Hawkins Richard, Wilde Edward, Peers Robin, *Asset Based Working Capital Finance*, Canterbury, Financial World Publishing, 2001.

Hillyer William Hurd, "Four Centuries of Factoring", *The Quarterly Journal of Economics* 53, No. 2, 1939, p. 305-311.

Kirkman Patrick, *Modern Credit Management*, London, George Allen and Unwin (Publishers) Ltd, 1977.

Macmillan Committee, *Report on Finance and Industry*, London, Cmnd 3897, HMSO, 1931.

Oditah Fidelis, *Legal Aspects of Receivables Financing*, London, Sweet and Maxwell, 1991.

Radcliffe Committee, *Report on the Working of the Monetary System*, Cmnd 827, London, HMSO, 1959.

Salinger Freddie R., *Factoring Law and Practice*, London, Third Edition, Sweet and Maxwell, 1999.

Wilson Committee, *Report to Review the Functioning of Financial Institutions*, London, Cmnd 7937, HMSO, 1979.

Factoring in France

Alexopoulos Dimitri, « Affacturage : comment trouver la solution optimale ? », *Les Échos*, supplément *Les Échos Business*, 15 septembre 2014, p. 3.

Alexopoulos Dimitri, « Vers un affacturage 2.0 ? », *Business Les Échos*, 7 octobre 2014.

Allard Laurence, « L'affacturage mise sur les nouvelles technologies », *Le Figaro Économie*, 2 novembre 1998.

Aussavy Michel, Berthelier Philippe, *Manager ses comptes clients avec l'affacturage*, Paris, Foucher, 1993, 96 p.

Aussavy Michel, Rachline Michel, *Tout savoir sur l'affacturage*, Paris, éditions Atlas, 1996, 95 p.

Béguin Jacques, « La convention d'Ottawa du 28 mai 1988 sur l'affacturage international : une étape vers l'adoption de règles uniformes sur les cessions de créances dans le commerce international », *Aspects actuels du droit des affaires. Mélanges en l'honneur de Yves Guyon*, Paris, Dalloz, 2003, p. 59-82.

Beuscart Fanny, « L'affacturage prospère dans la crise », *Le Monde-Économie*, 11 janvier 1994, p. VII.

Bey El Mokhtar, « L'affacturage international », *Revue de jurisprudence et de droit des affaires*, éditions Francis Lefebvre, avril 1996, p. 326.

Biaggi Joseph, *Les Joies de la création ou un quart de siècle au Crédit universel*, Paris, Albin Michel, 1980, 172 p.

Bodescot Anne, « De nouveaux outils pour gérer votre poste clients », *Le Figaro*, 22 octobre 2001.

Bogaert Raymond, Kurgan-Van Hentenryk Ginette, Van Der Wee Herman, *La Banque en Occident*, Anvers, Albin Michel, Fonds Mercator, 1991, 400 p.

Bonhomme Régine, « Affacturage », *Répertoire commercial Dalloz*, 2006.

Bonin Hubert, « Aux origines de l'assurance-crédit en France (1927-1939) : la création de la SFAC et le repli de ses concurrentes », *Histoire, Économie et Société*, 3e trimestre 2002, p. 341-356.

Bonin Hubert, *Histoire et Histoires de notre métier, 50 ans de l'affacturage en France*, (ed.) Crédit agricole, Leasing & Factoring, novembre 2014, 26 p.

Bonin Hubert, *50 ans d'affacturage en France : des pionniers et leaders aux groupes bancaires (1964-2016)*, Genève, Droz, 2016, 224 p.

Bourland Yves, « L'affacturage », Revue *Banque*, 1977, p. 1078.

Cassandro-Sulpasso Bianca, « Affacturage à l'exportation : une réglementation uniforme est-elle possible ? », *RTC Com.*, 1984, p. 639.

Chalmin Philippe, *De la SFAC à Euler 1927-1997*, Paris, Public Histoire, 1997, 131 p.

De P.A., « Affacturage, un mode de financement qui se généralise », *Option Finance*, No. 1196, 12 novembre 2012, p. 22-24.

Deschanel Jean-Pierre, Lemoine Laurent, *L'Affacturage*, Paris, Presses universitaires de France, collection « Que sais-je ? », 1993, 128 p.

Deschanel Jean-Pierre, Lemoine Laurent, « Droit et pratique de l'affacturage », *éditions techniques*, Jurisclasseurs, fascicule 580, collection « Banque et crédit », 1994/8, p. 1-20.

Desjardins Cécile, « Les sociétés d'affacturage SFF et Slifac se fondent dans Eurofactor », *Les Échos*, 15 mars 2000.

Desjardins Cécile, « Dominique Charpentier : La fusion de SFF et de Slifac est aujourd'hui achevée », *Les Échos*, 24 juillet 2001.

Desjardins Cécile, « Factofrance Heller, le numéro un français de l'affacturage, tombe dans l'escarcelle de GE Capital », *Les Échos*, 1er août 2001.

Desjardins Cécile, « Affacturage. Les banquiers reprennent la main avec leurs filiales spécialisées », *Les Échos*, 14 novembre 2001.

Desjardins Cécile, « Le jeune groupe Eurofactor se lance à l'assaut du marché européen », *Les Échos*, 14 novembre 2001.

Effosse Sabine, « Les débuts de l'affacturage en France », journée d'études « Prêter ce que l'on vend, emprunter ce que l'on achète, le crédit inter-entreprises en France en perspective historique (XVIII-XIXe siècles) », université de Paris Ouest Nanterre-La Défense, 24 octobre 2012.

Effosse Sabine, « Les débuts de l'affacturage, 1961-1973 », diaporama, université de Paris Ouest Nanterre, 2014.

Effosse Sabine, « Les débuts de l'affacturage en France, 1961-1973 : un secteur marginal en quête de reconnaissance », *Entreprises et Histoire*, No. 77, décembre 2014.

H. Ch., « Les banques se lancent en force dans l'affacturage », *L'Express*, 9 septembre 1993.

Galzy Gérard, Hemmelé Jacques, Vangasse Ollivier, *Les Cessions de créances professionnelles (loi Dailly)*, Villennes-sur-Seine, Castelange Diffusion, 1984, 142 p.

Gavalda Christian, Stoufflet Jean, « Le Contrat dit de Factoring », *JCP*, 1966, I, 1044.

Gavalda Charles, Stoufflet Jean, *Droit de la banque*, collection « Thémis », Paris, PUF, 1974.

Gavalda Charles, Stoufflet Jean, *Droit bancaire. Institutions, Comptes, Opérations, Services*, Paris, Litec, 1994 et 1999 (4e édition).

Gerbier Jean, *Le Factoring*, Paris, Dunod, collection « L'économie d'entreprise », université de droit et sciences économiques de Paris, 1970, 293 p.

Guingand Michel, « Affacturage et loi Dailly », revue *Banque et droit*, 1988, p. 15.

Halpern Nathalie, « L'affacturage séduit les grands groupes », *L'AGEFI Hebdo*, 18 décembre 2014.

Hemmelé Jacques, Galzy Gérard, Chopard Lionel, *La Loi Dailly*, Villennes-sur-Seine, Castelange Diffusion, 1988, 208 p.

Institut D'études Bancaires et Financières, *Les Exportations françaises et leur financement. Problèmes, institutions et techniques*, Paris, PUF, 1982, 274 p.

Jacquin Jean-Baptiste, « La guerre de l'affacturage », *L'Expansion*, 26 juin 1995, No. 504, p. 72-74.

Jasor Muriel, « Les sociétés d'affacturage ont doublé en quatre ans leur nombre de clients en France », *Les Échos*, 16 février 1999.

Jasor Muriel « Le Crédit lyonnais et Allianz veulent créer le premier factor européen », *Les Échos*, 27 juillet 1999.

Jasor Muriel, « Le marché de l'affacturage se restructure sur fond de consolidation bancaire », *Les Échos*, 27 juillet 1999.

Jude Pierre, *Technique et pratique du Factoring*, Paris, Clet, éditions Banque, 1984, 208 p.

Launois Hélène, « Les banques et l'affacturage », *La synthèse financière*, 10 juin 1991.

Lemasson François, « Restructurations bancaires : la place des établissements spécialisés », *Revue d'économie financière*, No. 78, 2005, p. 221-237 (voir notamment p. 231-232 sur l'affacturage).

Le Brun François, « Du bon usage de l'affacturage », *Les Échos*, 30 juin 2011.

Le Toux Janine, *Le Contrat de Factoring*, thèse, université de Rennes, 1977, 425 p.

Maillat Jacqueline, « Les affactureurs s'adaptent à la crise », *L'Agefi*, 12 mars 2009.

Maillat Jacqueline, « Crédit Agricole Leasing & Factoring pose des jalons à l'international », *L'Agefi Hebdo*, 22 avril 2010.

Maître Jean-Louis, « Des financements mieux adaptés : crédit-bail et factoring », *La Vie française*, dossier La banque de demain, supplément au No. 1431, 10 novembre 1972, p. 51-53.

Marazzato Pierre, « L'Affacturage international et la Convention d'Ottawa », mémoire de droit DESS « Banques et finances », université René-Descartes Paris V, 101 p.

Martin Pierre, « Hubert Bonin, 50 ans d'affacturage en France. Des pionniers et leaders aux groupes bancaires (1964-2016) » in *Risques, Les cahiers de l'assurance*, No. 111, septembre 2017, p. 146.

Mathias Frédéric, *Un Nouveau Mode de financement en France : le Factoring*, thèse de troisième cycle, université Paris I, 1970, 428 p.

Mordoh Jean-Luc, *Affacturage version 3ᵉ mi-temps*, Paris, Books on Demand, 2009, 221 p.

Noly Roger, *Le Factoring : modalités nouvelles du financement des entreprises, ses effets sur la rentabilité de l'exploitation, son rôle dans le financement de l'entreprise*, Paris, Éditions d'organisation, 1969, 127 p.

Pisar Samuel, « Aspects juridiques du Factoring international », revue *Banque*, 1970, p. 251.

Philippon Rodolphe, « Affacturage, un outil d'optimisation pour les entreprises », *Option Finance*, 27 mars 2000, p. 6-7.

Plihon Dominique, « Les banques : nouveaux enjeux, nouvelles stratégies », *Notes et études documentaires*, No. 5078, Paris, La Documentation française, 1998.

Precepta, *L'Affacturage et l'assurance-crédit, Reprendre l'initiative pour tirer parti des gisements de croissance*, Paris, 2015, 170 p.

Raulin Nathalie, « Deux valeurs à la loupe. La Sofirec fait de la résistance », *Libération*, 28 juillet 1995.

Revers-Cadoret Madeleine, *Le Factoring : une nouvelle méthode de crédit ?*, Paris, Dunod, 1969, 114 p.

Rolin Serge, *Le Factoring, une prise en charge des créances*, Verviers, Marabout, 1972, 172 p.

Rousseau Hervé, « L'affacturage fait peau neuve », *Le Figaro*, 22 octobre 2001.

S.L., « Fissures dans la Grande Muraille », *Les Enjeux Les Échos*, No. 317, février 2015.

S.n., « Affacturage : la percée des filiales bancaires », *Les Échos*, 4 novembre 1993.

Stoullig Antoine, « 25 ans d'affacturage en France », revue *Banque*, No. 506, 1990, p. 593-598.

Sussfeld Louis-Edmond, *Le Factoring*, Paris, Presses universitaires de France, 1968, 133 p.

Teston Jean-Claude, « Le Factoring et ses implications pour l'entreprise », mémoire d'expertise comptable, 1965, 197 p.

Thomas Romain, « Affacturage, une solution d'amorçage », *Le Nouvel économiste*, 13 novembre 2014.

Tovi Laurence, « Les factors sur le bon chemin », *Les Échos*, 29 octobre 1996.

Villepin Patrick de, *Notre Histoire a de l'avenir, BNP Paribas Factor 20 ans après*, Paris, BNP Paribas Factor, 2015, 318 p.

Villepin Patrick de, *La Success story du Factoring*, Paris, Association for Promotion & History of Factoring, 2015, 192 p.

Villepin Patrick de, « Le factoring, une innovation européenne » *in* Descamps (Florence), Nougaret (Roger), Quennouëlle-Corre (Laure), *Banque et société XIXe-XXIe siècle, identités croisées, Hommage à Pierre de Longuemar*, P.I.E. Peter Lang, 2016, p. 131-146.

Vissière Hélène, « Les banques colonisent l'affacturage », *L'Agefi*, 28 mai 1991.

Willot Didier, « Factors à succès », *Le Nouvel Économiste*, 18 avril 2014, p. 1-7.

Willot Didier, « Affacturage(s), l'envol du marché », *Le Nouvel Économiste*, 6 juillet 2014.

Zenner Alain, *Le Cadre juridique du Factoring*, Bruxelles, Centre d'études bancaires et financières, 1972, 67 p.

Factoring in Germany

Deogun Nikhil, Murray Matt, *The Wall Street Journal Online*, 30.07.2001; http://www.wsj.com/articles/SB996441111697437428.

Hagenmueller K.F., Sommer Heinrich Johannes, Brink Ulrich, "Factoring Handbuch" Frankfurt/Main, Fritz Knapp Verlag, 1997.

Kelm, Michael, "Anforderungen an die Kreditinstitute und Möglichkeiten der Mandantenunterstützung durch die Steuerberater zur Optimierung des Ratings", Hamburg, Diplomica Verlag, 2007.

Knopig G., "Factoring – Neue Wege der Absatzfinanzierung", *Zeitschrift für das gesamte Kreditwesen*, 1957.

Mueller Gerhard, Loeffelholz Josef, *Bank-Lexikon: Handwörterbuch für Das Bank- und Sparkassenwesen*, Heidelberg, Springer-Verlag, 2013.

Nett, Cornelia, *Die Einbindung von Factoring in andere Finanzierungsformen*, Publikation/Verlag, Date unknown/submitted by Serviceplan PR.

Secker Joachim, Weimer Hermann, "Factoring und ergänzende Finanzdienstleistungen", Heller Bank AG, Universitätsdruckerei H. Schmidt, Mainz, 2006.

Secker Joachim, Diewald Jörg, "Mittelstandsfinanzierung", Frankfurt, Börsen-Zeitung Spezial, 19.05.2016, p. 15.

http://www.spiegel.de/spiegel/print/d-46273040.html.

http://www.spiegel.de/spiegel/print/d-9134366.html.

https://www.bundesbank.de/Navigation/DE/Aufgaben/Bankenaufsicht/Basel2/basel2.html.

https://www.svea.com/de/deu/News-Archiv/Factoring-Geschichte-Eine-4000-Jahre-lange-Tradition/.

http://www.spiegel.de/spiegel/print/d-13686447.html.

http://www.factoring.de/factoring-branchenzahlen-1-halbjahr-2016-wachstum-trotz-niedrigzinsumfeld.http://www.factoring.de/factoring-branchenzahlen-1-halbjahr-2016-wachstum-trotz-niedrigzinsumfeld.

Factoring in Italy

Fossati Giorgio, Porro Alberto, "Il Factoring", *Il Factoring in Italia*, Milano, Giuffré, 1985, 103 p.

Fossati Giorgio, Porro Alberto, "Il Factoring", Milano, Giuffré, 1985, *Il Disegno di legge italiano*, 164, 249 p.

Gazzetta, "Valutaria e del Commercio Internazionale", No. 2/1985, *Natura e modalità di impego del Factoring e del Finanziamento sull'incasso dei crediti nella vendita dei beni di consumo all'estero.*

Quatraro Bartolomeo, *Factoring e Procedure Concorsuali che condivide la struttura del Factoring come una cessione dei crediti futuri*, 984 p.

Musacchia Maria Luisa, *Disciplina dei crediti d'impresa e il Factoring*, 2008.

Bianchi Renzo, *Il Factoring*, 215 p.

Terzani Sergio, *Aspetti Economici e finanziari dell'attività del Factoring*, p. 147-148.

Abruzzese Italo, *Assicurazione e Finanziamento dei Crediti all'Esportazione di Merci e di Servizi*, in la Legislazione valutaria Italiana M. Brocardo, Roma, Editrice Commercio Estero, 1979, p. 819-900.

Espansione, "Il Tocco Magico del Factoring", Settembre 1984, No. 172, 61 p.

Il Sole 24 ore, "L'Italia è leader nel Factoring", Giuseppe Chiellino, 26 Aprile 2012.

Azienda Banca Italia, *Paese Leader nel Factoring*, Rony Hamaui, Assifact Chairman, Marzo 2016, 56 p.

Azienda Bancaria, Marzo 2016, 17 p.

Fact&News (Assifact) *La valutazione della performance degli operatori specializzati nel factoring*, anno 17, No. 2, Maggio-Giugno 2015.

Parabancaria, *Il Factoring nell'informatica*, Alberto Mazzuca, Roma, Editoriale Lavoro, Ott.-Dic 1993.

Troia Marco, "Il factoring in Italia: evoluzione operativa e regolamentare", *Atti convegno Assifact*, Milano, 18 settembre 2008.

Anfossi C., Berlanda P., Clariza R., Mella P., Velo D., " Il Factoring", *Aspetti Giuridici, economici, finanziari e contabili*, Milano Pirola Editore, 1992.

Factoring in Russia

Letter of the State Bank of the USSR of 12.12.1989, No. 252 "On the procedure for conducting transactions on assignment by suppliers to the bank of the right to receive payment on claims for goods delivered, work performed and services provided".

The Civil Code of the Russian federation (part two) of 26.01.1996, No. 14-FZ (adopted by the State Duma of the Russian Federation, 22 December 1995, as amended 17 July 2009).

Beklaryan Levon A., Treyvish Mikhail I., "Factoring operations: methods of analysis of efficiency and reliability", Preprint # WP / 96/003, Moscow, CEMI RAS, 1996.

Beklaryan Levon A., Treyvish Mikhail I., "Model of factoring operations functioning", *Economics and Mathematical Methods*, Moscow, 1997, t.ZZ, Vol. 4.

Treyvish Mikhail I., "Methods for analyzing the efficiency and reliability of factor operations". Author's abstract. Diss. Cand. Econ. Sciences, Moscow, 1997.

Pushtorskiy Stanislav, "Factoring – a modern solution for marketing policy", *Banking in Moscow*, 2000, No. 6.

Pyatanova Victoria I., "Modern aspects of international factoring", *Finance and credit*, 2000, No. 5.

Novoselova Ludmila A., "Financing for the assignment of a monetary claim". *Bulletin of the Supreme Arbitration Court of the Russian Federation*, 2000, No. I-12; 2001, No. 1.3-6, 8.10, I; 2002, No. 1.

Treyvish Mikhail I., "Expansion of factoring operations helps solve the problem of non-payments", *Financial news*, 2002, No. 6.

Novoselova Ludmila A., "Financing for the assignment of a monetary claim", *Bulletin of the Supreme Arbitration Court of the Russian Federation*, 2000, No. I-12; 2001, No. 1.3-6, 8.10, I; 2002, No. 1.

Novoselova Ludmila A., "Transactions of assignment of rights (claims) in commercial practice. Factoring", Moscow, *Statute*, 2003.

Pokamestov Iliya E., "Factoring – tangible support for business", *Financial Technologies*. 2004, No. 4.

Aleksanova Yliya A., "Legal regulation of financing under the assignment of monetary claims", Moscow, 2004.

Pokamestov Iliya E., "Factoring", Moscow State University of Economics, Statistics and Informatics, Moscow, *MESI*, 2004.

Yudanov Andrei, "Geniuses of national business", *EXPERT.ru*, 23 April 2007, No. 16.

Pokamestov Iliya E., "Mechanisms of organisation of factoring business", *Bank crediting*, 2007, No. 4.

Pokamestov Iliya E., Patrin D.A., Rodionov M.M., Steshina M.O., "Factoring: sales, technology, risk management. Practical manual", Moscow, *Regulations*, 2008.

Gritsay Olga E., "State Regulation of Factoring Activity", *Regulation of Banking Operations. Documents and comments*. 2008, No. 1.

Pokamestov Iliya E, Podlesnova A.Y.U., "Budgeting and business planning of factoring activity", *Factoring and trade financing*, 2008, No. 1.

Gyulgyulyan Karen G., "The software of successful factoring", *Factoring and trade financing*, 2008, No. 2.

Karyakin Mikhail, "Non-recourse factoring – the insurer's view", *Factoring and trade financing*, 2008, No. 2.

Treyvish Mikhail, "Fantastic prospects open for factoring", *FACTORINGPRO.ru*, 13 January 2010.

"Results of the survey of the top managers of the Factors at the XIIIth Annual Conference 'Factoring in Russia – 2017: in anticipation of state orders'", *RAEXPERT.ru/researches/ Factoring*, 5 May 2017.

"The Russian factoring market in 2016: in anticipation of state orders", *RAEXPERT.ru/researches/ Factoring*, 26 April 2017.

"Factoring market in Kazakhstan and Belarus: we hold on to profitability", *RAEXPERT.ru/researches/ Factoring*, 31 October 2016.

"The Russian factoring market in the first half of 2016: recovery growth", *RAEXPERT.ru/researches/ Factoring*, 17 October 2016.

"Results of a survey of top managers of Factors at the XII Annual Conference 'Factoring in Russia – 2016: Sectoral Shift'", *RAEXPERT.ru/researches/ Factoring*, 5 May 2016.

"Russian factoring market in 2015: Sectoral shift", *RAEXPERT.ru/researches/ Factoring*, 18 May 2016.

"The Russian factoring market in the first half of 2015: there will be no growth", *RAEXPERT.ru/researches/ Factoring*, 6 October 2015.

"Results of the survey of the top managers of the Factors at the XIth Annual Conference 'Factoring in Russia – 2015: development by decreasing'", *RAEXPERT.ru/researches/ Factoring*, 4 April 2015.

"The Russian factoring market in 2014: stumbled, but did not fall", *RAEXPERT.ru/researches/ Factoring*, 8 April 2015.

"The factoring market in the 1st quarter of 2015 declined by 22%", *RAEXPERT.ru/researches/ Factoring*, 6 April 2015.

"The factoring market – the results of 9 months of 2014: slow growth", *RAEXPERT.ru/researches/ Factoring*, 17 October 2014.

"The Russian factoring market in the first half of 2014: the hunt for liquidity", *RAEXPERT.ru/researches/ Factoring*, 14 November 2014.

"Results of a survey of top managers of Factors at the 10th Annual Conference: 'Factoring in Russia – 2014: cooling is expected'", *RAEXPERT.ru/researches/ Factoring*, 9 June 2014.

"The Russian factoring market in 2013: cooling is expected", *RAEXPERT.ru/ researches/ Factoring*, 6 May 2014.

"Overview of the factoring market for the 1st quarter of 2014", *RAEXPERT. ru/researches/ Factoring*, 18 April 2014.

"The Russian factoring market in the first half of 2013: state order as an incentive", *RAEXPERT.ru/researches/ Factoring*, 2 October 2013.

"Results of the survey of top managers of Factors at the XIXth Annual conference 'Factoring in Russia – 2013: dispersed in niches'", *RAEXPERT. ru/researches/ Factoring*, 10 June 2013.

"The Russian factoring market in 2012: dispersed in niches", *RAEXPERT.ru/ researches/ Factoring*, 21 May 2013.

"Results of the review of the factoring market for the first quarter of 2013: going the same course", *RAEXPERT.ru/researches/ Factoring*, 15 April 2013.

"The Russian factoring market for the first half of 2012", *RAEXPERT.ru/ researches/ Factoring*, 22 October 2012.

"Results of the survey of the top managers of Factors at the VIIIth Annual Conference 'Factoring in Russia – 2012: Pass the Turbulence Zone'", *RAEXPERT.ru/researches/ Factoring*, 31 May 2012.

"The Russian factoring market in 2011: while taking off", *RAEXPERT.ru/ researches/ Factoring*, 15 May 2012.

"The Russian factoring market in the first half of 2011: Played with liquidity", *RAEXPERT.ru/researches/ Factoring*, 11 February 2011.

"Results of the survey of top managers of Factors at the 7th Annual Conference 'Factoring in Russia – 2011': Looking to the Future", *RAEXPERT.ru/ researches/ Factoring*, 31 May 2011.

"The Russian factoring market in 2010: at idle", *RAEXPERT.ru/researches/ Factoring*, 19 May 2011.

"The Russian factoring market in the first half of 2010: The biggest come and win", *RAEXPERT.ru/researches/ Factoring*, 3 November 2010.

"The Russian factoring market in 2009", *RAEXPERT.ru/researches/ Factoring*, 15 April 2010.

"The Russian factoring market in the first half of 2009: Interrupted flight", *RAEXPERT.ru/researches/ Factoring*, 12 October 2009.

"The ranking of factoring companies, 2006-2008", *RAEXPERT.ru/researches/ Factoring.*

Authors' Biographies

Agut (Damien)
PhD in historical and philological sciences (Ecole Pratique des Hautes Etudes, Paris, 2005), temporary research assistant at the Collège de France (2009-2012), permanent researcher at the French Centre National de la Recherche Scientifique (CNRS) since 2012; manager of the CNRS-HAROC (Histoire et archéologie de l'Orient cunéiforme) research-team in Nanterre; lecturer at the École des Hautes Études en sciences sociales (EHESS, Paris), has published around 50 papers on the social and economic history of Egypt during the First Millennium BC, focusing more closely on the Persian period (526-332 BC). As specialist of the Demotic script, an ancient Egyptian cursive script, Damien Agut is involved in several archaeological missions in Egypt, in the Western Desert (Kharga Oasis) and, more recently, in the eastern part of the Nile delta. With his CNRS's colleague, Juan Carlos Moreno Garcia, he published in 2016 a handbook concerning the Pharaonic history of Egypt, *Pharaon. Histoire politique des monarchies pharaoniques (3150 av.-340 ap. J.-C.)*, éditions Belin, Paris, 2016.

Al Refaie (Haitham)
Group CEO of Tawreeq Holdings, his career spans over two decades in financial services, corporate governance, and commercial and SME banking, much of it in the UAE and the GCC in general. Prior to co-founding Tawreeq Holdings (parent company of Tawreeq SCF Investments), Haitham Al Refaie led the Business Banking Group at the National Bank of Abu Dhabi (NBAD), a role he held since 2010. While at NBAD, he was responsible for crafting the business banking group's vision and strategy and oversaw implementation of best practice and corporate governance standards. Haitham Al Refaie served previously as Executive Manager at Invest Bank for over ten years, where he was heavily involved in restructuring risk and credit policies, as well as playing a key role as a member of the senior management team in charge of developing the corporate and commercial banking business. Al Refaie has also held senior positions at other leading banks, including Abu Dhabi Commercial Bank (ADCB), Citibank and HSBC.

Ball (Peter)

Member of FCI's compliance committee, he has extensive experience of factoring, initially in the UK's Griffin Factors Ltd, subsequently rebranded as HSBC Invoice Finance, where he undertook several customers facing, risk management and business roles. After a short period initiating a new supply chain product, he moved to Dubai to manage HSBC's factoring operations for the Middle East through extraordinary growth then the 2009 financial crisis. After his return to London, Peter Ball became the global product management head for receivables finance operating within HSBC's combined trade finance business covering around 50 countries. In 2014, perhaps uniquely to a new global role in compliance for trade finance, initially building an AML program for receivables finance and then specialising in regulatory compliance. He is responsible for oversight of regulatory compliance and conduct across HSBC's trade finance business, including receivables finance, and supporting a network of compliance officers across the world.

Baydar (Çağatay)

Has 30 years of professional experience in financial institutions, such as banking, factoring, leasing, real estate development and auditing. He has been working for the Factoring Industry for over 27 years, being one of the pioneers who introduced factoring to Turkey. Presently, he is leading TEB Faktoring, one of the largest export factors in Turkey and a joint venture of a worldwide financial group, BNP Paribas. TEB Faktoring has been chosen six times as "The Best Export Factor" of the year by the members of FCI. Çağatay Baydar is presently the FCI chairman of the executive committee and the vice chairman of the AFI in Turkey.

Bickers (Michael)

Michael Bickers is managing director of BCR Publishing Ltd, a specialist publishing company dedicated to the provision of market information on areas of receivables finance, particularly factoring and SCF, through books, the Internet (trfnews.com) and receivables finance conferences. He is author of twelve editions of *Factoring in the UK* (published by Her Majesty's Stationery Office, and BCR Publishing); editor of thirteen editions of *World Factoring Yearbook* (BCR in association with FCI); publisher and editor of the *World Supply Chain Finance Yearbook 2010-16* (BCR in association with the International Finance Corporation – part of the World Bank); series editor of the International Business Intelligence Reports series (published by The Stationery Office Ltd, 1997). Michael

Bickers' views, opinions and findings have been printed in leading newspapers and journals including *The Financial Times*, *The Sunday Times*, *The Times*, *The Daily Mail*, *Daily Telegraph*, *Director Magazine*, *Accountancy Age*, *Business Age*, *Chartered Banker*, *Investors Chronicle* and *Export Today*.

Bonzanini (Daniela)
Has a long career background in international trade and factoring and more than 30 years' experience in international factoring. In 2002, she joined Banca IFIS to start the international activity. She is head of international, responsible for the development of business and international networks. She is also directly involved in the management of the bank's foreign activities as CEO of IFIS Finance Sp. z.o.o, the daughter company of Banca IFIS in Poland, and director of India Factoring and Finance Solutions Pvt. Ltd, the JV established in India in 2009. From 2006 till 2015, Daniela Bonzanini has been a member of the board of Associazione Italiana Commercio Estero (AICE) in Milan. She is a speaker at international conferences and a lecturer at universities. After serving FCI as chairperson of the education committee, member of the executive committee and, over the last few years, vice chairperson, she was appointed as chairperson of FCI in June 2013. At the end of her mandate, she has returned to chair the education committee and has remained as member of the executive committee.

Bouraoui (Fatma)
Associate professor at the faculty of law of Tunis Carthage (Tunisia), she is a lawyer at the bar of Tunis and senior legal advisor. She has a PhD in business and private international law. She was an independent researcher at UNIDROIT, and is a specialist in financial and banking contracts and factoring. She also published several articles and notes in Tunisian and international Revues and Journal, such as the oxford Journal or the *Revue Tunisienne de Droit*. She is an international speaker and has collaborated with UNIDROIT, the UNCTAD and John Hopkins University, The Human Project, particularly in fields such as commercial law, contracts law, business law and international commercial law.

Brehcist (John)
Has 30 years experience in the Industry and is well known as a writer and conference speaker. His "roundwindow" consultancy specialises in strategic management, helping businesses develop their strategy, structure,

process and people. Now in its ninth year, the business has a portfolio of clients in the UK, mainland Europe, Turkey, Russia and South Africa. Retained as a consultant to FCI, he also acts as the coordinator of the EU Federation for the Factoring and Commercial Finance Industry. He has also been a non-executive director of two commercial finance companies. Previously the head of strategy and research for Lloyds TSB Commercial Finance, one of the largest invoice finance companies in the UK, he also has senior level Factoring Industry operational experience. John has an MA from Oxford University and a distinction level MBA from Warwick Business School.

Brister (Stuart)

He is the head of Wells Fargo's factoring groups and is based in Atlanta, Georgia. He joined Wells Fargo in 2005, was named the Trade Capital division president in 2007, and head of all of Wells Fargo's factoring groups in 2013. Prior to joining Wells Fargo, he was president of GMAC Commercial Services, managing director of strategic investment at Bank of America, and president of Bank of America Commercial Corporation. He has served on multiple advisory and corporate boards and is a member of the Commercial Finance Association, Turnaround Management Association, and Association for Corporate Growth. He holds a finance degree from the University of Georgia.

Chankowski (Véronique)

Professor of Aegean history and antique economy at Lyon II University, director of the laboratory HiSoMA (UMR 5189)-Maison de l'Orient et de la Méditerranée. Ancient member of the Institut Universitaire de France (IUF), she has been studies director of the French Scholl of Athens (École française d'Athènes). She is correspondent of the Deutsches Archäologisches Institut, Kommission für Alte Geschichte und Epigraphik and vice-president for ancient history of the Association française d'Histoire économique. Alone or in collaboration, Véronique Chankowski is the author of a few books related to economy of classic and hellenistic Greece through epigraphic, numismatic and archaeological sources, among others *Athènes et Délos classique. Recherches sur l'administration du sanctuaire d'Apollon délien* (2008). She is also responsible for research programs in antique history and archaeology of Mediterranean worlds (markets in Antique world, closed in 2012; warehouses and storage areas in ancient Greece and Rome).

Fournoux (Alexandre de)
BNP Paribas factoring manager for Africa, he graduated from Paris X University with a Master in economics and has spent over ten years working in the factoring business. Since 2012, Alexandre de Fournoux has been developing BNP Paribas factoring franchises in West Africa and Maghreb countries. He is also involved in BNP Paribas factoring activities in Poland and Turkey.

Gielen (John)
Graduated from Solvay Business School (Brussels Free University), he has 35 years experience as a banker. He was general manager of Bank Brussels Lambert and ING Bank since 1987 in Luxemburg, Brussels and Paris. From 1995 to 2003, he was chosen to chair the Cercle des Banques étrangères in France. His experience in factoring started in 1975 when he entered and then chaired (1990-2007) the board of International Factor Belgium. Also, board member of IFG (2002-2009), John Gielen chaired the Group in 2007-2008. He was elected independent chairman of the EUF when it was founded in May 2009 and stayed in the position till April 2016.

Graslin-Thomé (Laetitia)
After studying economy and ancient history in Paris (École Normale Supérieure), Chicago (Oriental Institute of the University of Chicago) and Tours (France) University, Laetitia Graslin-Thomé is now assistant professor at the University of Lorraine in Nancy, France, where she teaches ancient Greek and oriental history. In 2009, she published *Les échanges à longue distance en Mésopotamie au premier millénaire av. J.-C.*, an investigation on how economic models may be helpful to better understand ancient economics through the example of long distance exchange in first millennium Mesopotamia. Developing trans-disciplinary methods to confront historical evidence to some economic theories, she wrote several articles on Mesopotamian economy. Member of research programs focusing on political, social and economic history of Hellenistic Babylonia, Laetitia Graslin-Thomé has co-edited three books on Hellenistic world, *Communautés locales et pouvoir central dans l'Orient hellénistique et romain*, Nancy, 2012, *Le projet politique d'Antiochos III*, Nancy, 2014 and *Antiochos III et l'Orient*, 2017.

Innocenti (Liliana)

Graduated from Istituto Tecnico Pacinotti (Pisa, Italy), has attended the economics faculty of the Pisa University and Cattolica in Milan. From May 1970 to January 2008, she has been employed by Ifitalia, factoring subsidiary of BNL, appointed as: international operational manager; international commercial manager; senior international manager; member of EDP committee, legal committee of IFG. From February 2008 to 2015, Liliana Innocenti joined BNP Paribas Factor France as consultant international manager.

Jamme (Armand)

PhD in medieval history of Sorbonne University, member of the École française de Rome, is research director at the French CNRS since 2012. In continuity with Professor Philippe Contamine's works, he has been studying war during the Middle Ages, especially in Italy and south of France. But he is also undertaking research on interactions between institutions, subjects and papal authority in the church state between the 11th and 15th century. Armand Jamme has directed a program financed by the Agence Nationale de la Recherche on accounting practices between 13th and the 15th century, the results of which will soon be published.

Khan (Ilyas Ahmed)

With a management degree from K.J Somaiya (Mumbai), he is presently the head of receivables finance for the Standard Chartered Group in Singapore. Being one of the eminent industry speaker and an authority in O/A trade space, Ilyas Khan has been working in trade and SCF industry for more than a decade. Having vast field experience in launching receivables finance across various countries, he has been instrumental in the growth of receivables finance with SCB and many industries first initiatives in multiple geographies. Currently responsible for the growth of trade and SCF business for the Bank, he is also part of the marketing committee of FCI since 2015.

Longhurst (Jeff)

Former CEO of the Asset Based Finance Association (ABFA), Chair of the Invoice Finance and Asset Based Lending board, and now Managing Director, Membership Events and Training of UK Finance – the trade body for invoice finance and ABL in the UK which is the market leader worldwide – he has over 35 years experience in invoice finance and ABL, managing businesses both small and large, bank subsidiary and independent, with responsibility for a range of shareholders in the UK, USA, South Africa and France. His career has included roles as managing director of Crédit Agricole Commercial Finance UK (Eurofactor), chief executive and founder of Independent Growth Finance (IGF) and several positions within the Lloyds Banking Group. Jeff Longhurst has a MA in Law from Cambridge (Trinity Hall) and is a fellow of the Chartered Institute of Credit Management.

Lütschg-Emmenegger (Margrith)

Has worked in trade finance with a special focus on forfaiting and factoring for most of her professional life, first with Barclays Bank, and then with Midland Bank Aval in London, before joining West Merchant Bank (now WestLB AG) where she had global responsibility for forfaiting and factoring within WestLB AG. Margrith Lütschg-Emmenegger joined FIMBank in April 2003 as executive vice-president, responsible for business development and was appointed to president on September 2004. She retired as president on December 2014, after more than a decade as president to become an advisor to the FIMBank group and other industry members. In October 2013, she was elected chairman of IFG where she served as a board member since 2011. Retiring as chairman of IFG in 2014 after she had led IFG to the merger with FCI to create the One Voice for the Industry, she had played a leading role in supporting the training and education efforts/projects of IFG, especially the certificate of finance in international trade (COFIT) in cooperation/ certified by the University of Malta.

Martin (Brian)

He is Southeast Regional Manager for Wells Fargo's factoring unit and is based in Atlanta, Georgia. He joined Wells Fargo in May 2005 and assisted in establishing Wells Fargo's first factoring office in the southeast. With over 30 years of factoring sector experience, he previously held senior management, relationship management, and business development positions with Action Capital Corporation, Wachovia Bank of Georgia, SouthTrust Bank of Atlanta and Citizens & Southern Bank. He holds a BA degree in history from The University of the South and an MBA with a concentration in finance from the University of Georgia.

Minaud (Gérard)

PhD in History (EHESS), PhD in Law (Aix-Marseille University) and diploma of Institut supérieur de gestion (ISG, Paris), he has been managing construction companies for twenty years. Since 2003, as an independent researcher, Gérard Minaud is fully dedicated to the history of management in Ancient Rome. In addition, he is associate researcher at the Centre Camille Jullian (CNRS/Aix-Marseille University).

Mulroy (Peter)

As secretary general of FCI, based in Amsterdam (The Netherlands), he assists entrepreneurs, bankers, regulators and governments in educating the benefits and introducing the concept of factoring, a facilitator of liquidity and mitigator of risk for SMEs and large corporates in the O/A, receivables finance space. Prior to joining FCI, Peter Mulroy was managing director with CIT in the US, a Fortune 500 financial services company and one of FCI's original founding members. Peter Mulroy also served on the management committee of CIT, supporting their global growth strategy. He came to CIT through the acquisition of the factoring division of SunTrust Bank, where he developed their international business. Past chairman of FCI (2009-2010), he has served on the FCI executive committee for over a decade. He received his bachelor's degree from Rutgers University and MBA from Thunderbird, School of Global Management in the US.

Oramah (Benedict Okey)

President and chairman of the board of directors of the African Export-Import Bank (Afreximbank) since September 2015, after being the executive vice president responsible for business development and corporate banking (October 2008-September 2015). He had joined Afreximbank as chief analyst (1994) and was promoted to the position of senior director, planning and business development (2007). Benedict Oramah holds an advanced management certificate from the Colombia University (2015), an MSc (1987) and a PhD (1991) in agricultural economics from Obafemi Awolowo University (Ile-Ife, Nigeria). He obtained a BSc degree in agricultural economics from the University of Ibadan (Nigeria) in 1983. He recently published *Foundations of Structured Trade Finance* and has written over 35 professional/scholarly articles. Benedict Oramah is a member of the emerging markets advisory council of the Institute of International Finance (IIF), an executive committee member of FCI, and a fellow of the Institute of Credit Administration (ICA). He also serves on the editorial boards of *Trade and Forfaiting Review* (TFR) and the *Journal of African Trade* (JAT).

Petroni (Mario)
Currently senior advisor at Lazard-Milan and Investitori SGR (Allianz group), he started his career in 1960 at BNL where he was appointed as senior executive and commercial manager. In 1981, he moved to IFITALIA, where he occupied the position of deputy general manager, general manager and managing director until 1987 with the aim of promoting and implementing factoring business. During his mandate, he cooperated with BNL Holding managers' staff to set up many captive factoring companies. Later on, he was appointed senior bank manager at Banco di Santo Spirito and Banca di Roma. He has also been in the position of general manager at Banca Agricola Mantovana (1995-2001) and deputy general manager and sales senior manager (2002-2010) at Banca Esperia (private bank of Mediobanca and Mediolanum).

Rigby (Adrian)
Chief commercial officer and deputy head of trade and receivables finance for HSBC, he has been with HSBC over 28 years working in Asia and Europe, specializing in commercial banking and trade and receivables financing. Previous roles have included head of product for trade and receivables finance, head of commercial products for the UK Commercial and Corporate Bank, chief operating officer for the Commercial Bank in Asia and senior manager within strategy and planning.

Russo (Enza)
Doctor of València University with a thesis (2016) on "The General Treasury in the Corona of Aragon and the Budget of Naples Kingdom during the reign of Alphonse the Magnanimous (1416-1458)", Enza Russo is professor of literature disciplines at the Higher Institute of Turin, cultrice of medevial history at the Naples University Federico II and pursues investigations on medieval finances and states.

Secker (Joachim)
Currently CEO of TARGO Commercial Finance, created after the acquisition of GE Capital's German factoring and leasing business, led by Joachim Secker as CEO since 2008, by the French banking group Crédit Mutuel. Trained in industrial business management and a graduate of the Frankfurt School of Finance and Management, Joachim Secker has been immersed in the factoring business for over 35 years. His career began in 1980 when he moved from a medium-sized electronics business to GE Capital Bank AG, then Heller Factoring Bank AG, in Mainz. From there,

he rose from junior salesperson to director with power of attorney. In 1992, the supervisory board of GE Capital Bank AG appointed Joachim Secker deputy chief executive of GE Capital Bank AG. Three years later, he became a full member of the board. In October 1999, he became CEO of GE Capital Bank AG which has traded under the name of TARGO Commercial Finance AG since August 2016. In addition, he represents the German Factoring Association as spokesman, holds supervisory board positions and is a board member of the Rheinland-Pfalz Banking Association.

Sellés (Josep)

In the Factoring Industry since 1993, he started managing the factoring and confirming department in Banco Sabadell, moving to Eurofactor in 2005. Today, he is managing the factoring and SCF Area at Gedesco Services Spain, an independent company. Vice chairman of FCI, he has served in the executive committee of this association for more than ten years. Josep Sellés is also chairman of the SCF committee of FCI, aiming to open a second business line in the association. Vice chairman of the Spanish Factoring Association and representative of this association in the board of the EU Federation since its creation, he was involved in the setting up of a factoring department in Banks of Uruguay and Mexico. He lectures in different Spanish business schools and is a frequent speaker at conferences around the world. He has also written many articles for different publications.

Tananbaum (Andrew H.)

Executive Chairman of White Oak Commercial Finance, LLC, he was previously the executive chairman of Capital Business Credit, the company he owned and operated with Perry Capital, an investment management firm, from 2005 until its acquisition by White Oak Global Advisors in December 2016. Previously, Andrew Tananbaum was president and CEO of Century Business Credit Corporation, before selling it to Wells Fargo in 1998. Previously, he worked for The Merban Corporation and as an associate for Weil, Gotshal & Manges. Mr Tananbaum also served as a law clerk to a United States District Judge for the Southern District of New York. He is an active member of the CFA, previously sitting on the executive committee of the Board of Directors. He received a JD from Fordham University School of Law and a BA from the University of Michigan.

Tatge (David B.)

Member of the Virginia and District of Columbia bars, he is a shareholder in the Washington DC office of the 225-attorney law firm Epstein Becker & Green, PC. He represents clients in commercial finance, business litigation and creditors' rights matters, coast-to-coast. An inactive Certified Public Accountant (Maryland, 1979), he is lead author of two books: Tatge, Flaxman, Tatge & Flaxman, *American Factoring Law* (Bloomberg/BNA 2009, with a 2017 cumulative supplement) and the *Chapter 7 Bankruptcy Trustee's Manual* (John Wiley & Sons, 1993, with 1995 supplement). David Tatge has written and co-authored fifteen articles on commercial finance, litigation and tax matters. He holds a bachelor's of administration degree from the College of William & Mary (1978), a master's of science (taxation) from American University (1982) and received his juris doctorate, cum laude, from the George Washington University Law (1986).

Tatge (Jeremy B.)

Is the sole manager and member of Capitol National Factors Company, LLC in Oak Hill, Virginia, US. A graduate of the University of Virginia, in both economics and commerce, he holds a MBA degree from Georgetown University.

Tavecchia (Diego)

Graduated in International Finance and Economics from Università degli Studi in Milan, he holds a PhD in management from the same University, with a dissertation on the effects of factoring on Italian firms. Since 2007, he has been working at Assifact, the Italian Factoring Association, where he is currently head of technical committees and international affairs. Since 2016, Diego Tavecchia has been chairing the prudential risk committee of the EU Federation. Previously, he chaired, for six years, the economics and statistics committee of the Federation. He is author of several papers and lecturer in several education courses about the Factoring Industry.

Timmermans (Erik)

Managing Director of the Belgian Consulting & Management Company BZIX BVBA, he has been deputy secretary general of FCI until December 2017. Before the integration of activities into FCI, Erik was secretary general of IFG, focusing on the development of IFG's trade association activities in education, Industry information, lobbying and networking.

Erik Timmermans worked for 19 years at International Factors Belgium (now KBC Commercial Finance) in various sales, marketing and general management positions. Belgian, he holds a university degree in economics (specialisation in marketing) and followed a wide range of additional executive education programs in Belgium and in France (INSEAD). He has been also chairman of the EUF (2016-2018).

Treyvish (Mikhail)
Internationally recognised as the founder of the Russian factoring market, he started in 1995 with Rossiyskiy Credit Bank as head of the factoring department and then served as the CEO of National Factoring Company (2004-2009). Member of the board of directors (2004-2015) of IFG, Mikhail Treyvish was elected chairman of IFG (2008-2009) and of the Asian Chapter since 2009. As from 2014, he has been a consultant on factoring for the European Bank for Reconstruction and Development (EBRD). Participating in consulting projects on factoring in Kazakhstan, Armenia, Indonesia and Vietnam, he is the founder of a universal crowdsourcing agency, OmniGrade (www.omnigrade.com).

Villepin (Patrick de)
Factoring global head within BNP Paribas Group since 2003, Patrick de Villepin has been fully invested in the Factoring Industry during the last fifteen years. Leader in Europe, BNP Paribas Factoring is the umbrella name for the whole business line: a competence centre (located in Brussels) and its fifteen factoring entities (twelve in Europe, three out of Europe), all full or associate members of FCI. BNP Paribas Factor France has been voted best export-import factor, FCI grand prize, in 2014, 2015 and 2017. Patrick de Villepin holds a PhD in history (Sorbonne University), a diploma of Institut d'Etudes Politiques (Sciences Po. Paris) and of the École Nationale d'Administration (ENA). Auditor at the French Accounting Court (Cour des comptes), afterwards he joined BNP Paribas, almost 30 years ago. Chairman of the French Factoring Commission (within l'Association française des Sociétés Financières, ASF) since 2014, he has published in French *La Success Story du Factoring* (2015).

Wessel (Magdalena)
Fully qualified German lawyer, she has an MA in European studies from the KU Leuven in Belgium. Since 2008, she has been working in the legal department of the German Factoring Association, Deutscher

Factoring-Verband e.V. (DFV), which she also represents at the level of the EU Federation for Factoring and Commercial Finance (EUF) by being a member of the EUF executive committee and by chairing the EUF legal committee. Before joining DFV, Magdalena Wessel worked in the legal department of an internationally active bank in northern Germany.

Wyderka (Alberto)

Latin American Chapter Director of FCI, he is responsible for strengthening and expanding the network in the Region. For eighteen years, he has been a member of the FCI executive committee and vice chairman five times. In 2007, he was elected chairman, the first Latin American appointed in that position. Alberto Wyderka was international business advisor and representative in Argentina of Tanner Servicios Financieros, the largest non-bank owned factoring company in Chile, reporting to its president. Previously he was senior vice president, head of trade finance of Banco Galicia and CEO of Galicia Factoring, the first company to introduce international factoring in Argentina. Alberto Wyderka was resident vice president of Citibank, Argentina, head of foreign trade operations and senior product manager of international products. Alberto Wyderka was secretary of the Foreign Trade Commission at ADEBA, the Argentine Bank Association and held various positions in organisations related to international trade. He is a certified public accountant with a degree obtained in the University of Buenos Aires.

Xu (Jiang)

Deputy general manager of Global Trade Services Department of Bank of China, Head Office, he was, prior to this, head of SCF and head of factoring of Global Trade Services Department at the Bank of China, HO. Jiang Xu is an expert in factoring and SCF and was responsible for setting up Bank of China's factoring and SCF infrastructure. Member of the executive committee of FCI from 2006 to 2015, he was vice chairman of FCI in 2008 and from 2010 to 2013. He holds a BA and MA degrees from Peking University of China.

Photo Credits

1- Introduction: Blackwell Hall. © Private collection
2- Prologue: first Annual Meeting, FCI Stockholm (Sweden), 1968. © FCI
3- First part: Hammurabi code. Hammurabi facing the god Shamash, detail of the stone bas-relief. © Photo RMN - Franck Raux
4- Second part: Pegasus, FCI Grand Prize, Export-Import Factor of the year award, 2017. © Dominique Rault
5- Conclusion: Jacques Coeur's galley, stained glass, Jacques Coeur's palace, Bourges, XVth century. © Hervé Champollion

Acknowledgments

The author wants to thank and congratulate especially the persons below for their strong support, global or specific, throughout the project:

- John Brehcist, for chapter 4 (Factoring trends);
- Doruk Bahceci, Head of Marketing and Communication, Factoring BNP Paribas, for tables and graphs;
- Michèle Cardoens, assistant FCI, for a formal review of the whole book;
- Fausto Galmarini, chairman of ASSIFACT, for reviewing chapter 14 (Italy);
- Laetitia Graslin-Thomé, for coordinating chapters 5, 6 and 7 (Factoring roots);
- Philippe Gresta, BNP Paribas Factor's Business Line Manager, Large Corporate and International Client Relationships, for reading and correcting the first manuscript;
- Peter Mulroy, for global coordination of the project, constant support and tireless review of the book;
- Françoise Palle-Guillabert, ASF General Delegate, for chapter 12 (France);
- David Tatge, for his expertise and value-added on many legal and historical references;
- Erik Timmermans, permanent FCI representative on the project, for his strong, proactive support and help, at each step of the two-year implementation since the launch;
- Joost Vastenavondt, Head of Compliance, Factoring BNP Paribas, for chapter 29 (Compliance);
- Gwendoline de Viron, Head of Marketing and Communication, FCI, for internal and external coordination;
- Mine Volle, Global Chief Risk Officer, Factoring BNP Paribas, for chapter 30 (Risk awareness);
- Jacqueline Wolde Yohannes, FCI director of administration, for her support with the organisation of the 50th FCI annual meeting and the distribution of the book;

– Last but not least, Maria Dunne, Commerical Team Division Manager at HPD, who has entirely reviewed the manuscript, harmonising and optimising the English language.

Without you all, it would not have been possible. You made it real. Now, we are ready for the centenary!

www.peterlang.com